| *exploring* |

InDesign CS3

| *exploring* |

InDesign CS3

Terry Rydberg

THOMSON
™
DELMAR LEARNING
Exploring InDesign CS3
Terry Rydberg

Vice President,
Technology and Trades ABU:
David Garza

Director of Learning Solutions:
Sandy Clark

Managing Editor:
Larry Main

Senior Acquisitions Editor:
James Gish

Product Manager:
Nicole Bruno

Editorial Assistant:
Sarah Timm

Marketing Director:
Deborah Yarnell

Marekting Manager:
Kevin Rivenburg

Marketing Specialist:
Victoria Ortiz

Director of Production:
Patty Stephan

Production Manager:
Andrew Crouth

Content Project Manager:
Andrea Majot

Technology Project Manager:
Kevin Smith

Cover Image:
Front Porch Geometry, oil on canvas, © David Arsenault

Library of Congress Cataloging-in-Publication Data:

Rydberg, Terry.
 Exploring InDesign CS3
 / Terry Rydberg.
    p. cm.
 Includes index.
 ISBN-13: 978-1-4180-5263-8
 ISBN-10: 1-4180-5263-9
 1. Adobe InDesign. 2. Desktop
  publishing. I. Title.
 Z253.532.A34R943 2007
 686.2'2544536--dc22
 2007014949

NOTICE TO THE READER

contents

CONTENTS

contents

CONTENTS

vii

contents

11 Designing with Type 252

12 Production Essentials 274

13 Basic Graphic Elements 306

Index 324

| *preface* |

INTENDED AUDIENCE

This book is intended for designers who are serious about their craft. It is ideal for students who desire an approach to instruction that focuses on software proficiency. It is an excellent choice for instructors and industry trainers who have been looking for a comprehensive textbook that includes handouts, syllabi, and resources. *Exploring InDesign CS3* was not written to be an InDesign reference book. Instead, the focus of the content was narrowed to concentrate on those InDesign operations that you will use 90% of the time, with the goal of total mastery. *Exploring InDesign CS3* was written for those who have keyboarding skills and already know computer basics such as launching programs, using a mouse, saving, and printing. Ideally, users will have access to a computer with Adobe InDesign CS3 in order to complete the practice exercises.

Just knowing software does not guarantee success. Some designers can use software, but their typesetting looks crude and unprofessional. Other designers produce pieces that look great, but later become problematic when technical errors are discovered during prepress operations. Successful designers are able to use type effectively, and produce pages that are printable. Those are the issues this book addresses.

BACKGROUND

Typesetting is an art, and typography is emphasized throughout *Exploring InDesign CS3*. Teaching software without teaching typography creates technicians, not designers. The power of Adobe InDesign, when combined with the knowledge of typography, will give you the ability to create documents with visual impact.

A textbook must go beyond the step-by-step approach and provide opportunities for independent problem solving and application. *Exploring InDesign CS3's* in-chapter exercises are supplemented with an array of projects at the end of the each chapter. These supplemental projects will require a higher degree of independent problem solving skills.

Chapters should be read in order, from the beginning to the end. Earlier skills create the foundation necessary for moving to the next level. Techniques are introduced and then applied in the context of industry-level projects. This project-based approach uses critical thinking, review, and practice to move you toward mastery.

TEXTBOOK ORGANIZATION

The textbook is organized sequentially and skills are added layer by layer.

Chapter 1: **The InDesign Workspace** Introduces the basic tools and functions of the program. If you are already familiar with Photoshop and Illustrator, this chapter will be a great review.

Chapter 2: **Type, Tools, and Terms** Creates a knowledge base essential for setting type. You will use the Character and Paragraph formatting options in the Control panel, modify attributes of type and text frames, and learn to distinguish between serif and sans serif typefaces.

Chapter 3: **The Fine Art of Setting Type** Teaches how to identify the anatomical parts of letters, read markup, format paragraphs, and use hyphens and dashes correctly.

Chapter 4: **Combining Type and Images** Shows how to create linked and multi-column text frames; place, scale and crop images; use optical and manual kerning; and apply the coordinates and measurement system for precise sizing and placement.

Chapter 5: **Tabs and Tables** You will learn to set tabs and create tables from "scratch" and from text.

Chapter 6: **Grids, Guides, and Aligning Objects** Increases your productivity by creating publication grids, aligning and distributing objects, and managing stacked objects.

Chapter 7: **Text Wrap and Layers** Brings order to your documents through the power of layers and text wrap. Object effects, including feathering and transparency, will be introduced.

Chapter 8: **Type Continuity: Applying Styles** Focuses on speed and efficiency in preparing text-heavy documents. You will learn how to use the Pages panel and an object library, and to create character and paragraph styles in the construction of an actual newsletter.

Chapter 9: **Page Continuity: Master Pages** Introduces Object Styles and covers page continuity through the use of master pages. You will learn how to setup automatic page numbering and create continuation and jump lines. You'll create an object library and also use the Pages panel to add and delete pages.

Chapter 10: **Business Forms** Shows you how to create a corporate identity for a new business. You will focus on design, typographic, and production considerations as you put together business forms and collateral material.

Chapter 11: **Designing With Type** Introduces special type techniques including text on a path, creating outlines and gradient blends, using the Pathfinder tool, and creating inline graphics.

Chapter 12: **Production Essentials** Discusses how to define and create color, as well as preflighting and packaging your document upon completion.

Chapter 13: **Basic Graphic Elements** Explores InDesign's drawing functions. You will learn how to create basic shapes, use the Pen tool, and integrate drawn elements with text. A great introduction to Adobe Illustrator, another member of the *Creative Suite*.

FEATURES

The following list describes some of the salient features of the text:

▶ Learning goals are clearly stated at the beginning of each chapter.

▶ Meets the needs of students and professionals who desire a visually-oriented introduction to basic design principles and the functions and tools of *InDesign CS3*.

▶ Exercises and projects utilize tools and techniques that a designer might encounter on the job.

▶ *In Review* sections are provided at the end of each chapter to quiz the learner's understanding and retention of the material covered.

▶ The accompanying CD-ROM contains directions and all the necessary components for completing additional projects that correspond to each chapter's learning goals.

▶ Podcasts provide an introduction to the chapter and projects. To access these podcasts, please visit *www.designexploration.com/podcasts*.

INSTRUCTOR'S GUIDE ON CD ROM

This electronic manual was developed to assist instructors in planning and implementing their instructional programs. It includes a detailed lesson plan for each chapter. The lesson plan summarizes the concepts, keyboard shortcuts, and projects covered in classroom demonstrations. Lesson plans are designed to be printed and saved in a three-ring binder. It also includes a sample syllabus, a midterm, and a final written and lab exam. The complete Instructor's Guide enhances consistency in instruction among faculty members with diverse backgrounds and skill levels.

ISBN: 1-4180-5264-7

HOW TO USE THIS TEXT

The following features can be found throughout the book.

▶ Chapter Objectives

Chapter objectives describe the competencies that the reader should achieve.

▶ Chapter Review and Projects

Review questions and supplemental projects assess learning and provide skills application.

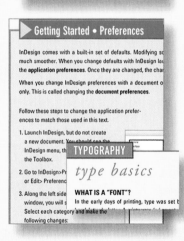

▶ Keyboard Shortcut Cues

Keyboard shortcuts are prominently displayed for ease of use.

▶ Getting Started

Located at the end of Chapter 1, this section provides the steps for customizing the application defaults that will be used throughout the book.

▶ Typography

Principles of typography are presented with corresponding chapter content. These basics will help the reader use type in a manner that is technically correct.

▶ Moving Toward Mastery

Key concepts are grouped together for easy reference and review.

ABOUT THE AUTHOR

Terry Rydberg is an instructor at the Harry V. Quadracci Printing and Graphics Center at Waukesha County Technical College. Terry has extensive experience working in the graphics industry as a page layout professional and a corporate trainer. *Exploring InDesign CS3* is her third book published with Thomson Delmar.

Her educational background includes undergraduate degrees in graphic design, printing and publishing, and adult education; and a masters in education. Her career parallels the industry's evolution from phototypesetting and paste-up, to digital production methods. Rydberg teaches advertising design, graphic design, typography, portfolio development, digital page layout, advanced digital page layout, and color theory. She is a regional InDesign trainer at colleges and conferences.

A committed educator, Rydberg has served as school board chair, graphics advisory board member, new instructor mentor, curriculum writer, and student advisor. In 2007, she received an award for excellence in teaching from the National Institute for Staff & Organizational Development.

ACKNOWLEDGMENTS

Others whose contributions to this book should be acknowledged are James Gish, Acquisitions Editor; Nicole Bruno, Product Manager, Media Arts and Design; Andi Majot, Content Project Manager; and Sarah Timm, Editorial Assistant. Their expertise, combined with Thomson's great marketing team, made this third edition a reality.

Deepest thanks to my colleagues and students who have shared a vision for this book. John Shanley, from Phoenix Creative Graphics, poured his heart and soul into this project as he performed his copy and technical editing "miracles." Karen Ferrell and David Bate spent evenings and weekends proofing final pages. Illustrator David Espurvoa and prepress expert James Wamser enthusiastically shared their expertise. Finally, my gratitude to the students who generously allowed their artwork and photography to be included in this book.

Many thanks to the instructors who are using this publication at the Harry V. Quadracci Printing and Graphics Center and at various colleges throughout the United States. Your suggestions and comments have been so helpful, and have been incorporated in this third edition of *Exploring InDesign CS3*.

Finally, heartfelt thanks to my parents, Paul and Shirley Tollefson and my husband, Mark, who are the most valuable resources in my life.

QUESTIONS AND FEEDBACK

Thomson Delmar Learning and the author welcome your questions and feedback. If you have suggestions that would be of benefit to others, please let us know and we will try to include them in the next edition.

To send your questions and/or feedback, contact the publisher at:

Thomson Delmar Learning
Executive Woods
5 Maxwell Drive
Clifton Park, NY 12065
Attn: Media Arts and Design Team
800-998-7498

Or the author at:

Harry V. Quadracci Printing and Graphics Center
Waukesha County Technical College
800 Main Street
Pewaukee, Wisconsin 53072
trydberg@mac.com

Creativity can solve
almost every problem.
The creative act,
the defeat of habit by originality,
overcomes everything.

☞ George Lois

| the InDesign workspace |

1

objectives

- **Become familiar with the Adobe InDesign CS3 environment**
- **Identify and use basic panels and tools**
- **Learn to use keyboard shortcuts**
- **Learn the concepts of frames, stroke, and fill**
- **Customize your workspace**
- **Save and print documents**

introduction

You are about to explore new horizons in digital page layout. This book will introduce you to Adobe® InDesign® CS3, the emerging new standard in page layout software. Those of you who are already familiar with a page layout program will be delighted and impressed with InDesign's extraordinary capabilities and innovation.

I must admit I was a bit skeptical when I began working with InDesign—after teaching and working with other major page layout programs for 15 years. But in just a few weeks I was convinced that Adobe InDesign is the most creative, comprehensive, complete page layout program on the market today. By the time you finish this book, I hope you will think so, too. No other program in the graphics industry can compete with the bold imagination and astounding new features of InDesign. Welcome to the wide world of Adobe InDesign CS3!

THE INDESIGN WORKSPACE

WELCOME TO INDESIGN CS3!

Before you begin this book, you should be familiar with a computer keyboard and have a basic understanding of how to operate a mouse. You should know how to launch applications, make choices from menus, click with a mouse to select objects, and drag to highlight text. If you are already familiar with Adobe Photoshop or Adobe Illustrator, this chapter will be a quick review.

The InDesign workspace consists of the following items:

1. Document window
2. Menu bar
3. Toolbox
4. Control panel
5. Panels
6. Command bar

Each will be described in sequence as you proceed through Chapter 1. Following the overview of the InDesign workspace, we will cover the basics of using tools, saving, and printing. Finally, a *Getting Started* section at the end of the chapter will guide you through customizing InDesign's default preference settings. Modifying your InDesign default preferences will assist you as you complete the exercises in this book. As you work through this text, you will notice that in addition to the exercises included in the narrative of the text, more projects are presented at the end of chapters. Completing these projects will strengthen your skills and help move you toward mastery. To work on these projects, you will need to access text and images files from the *Exploring InDesign CS3* compact disc accompanying this book. A folder that corresponds to each chapter (*01 Artwork & Resources, 02 Artwork & Resources, 03 Artwork & Resources*, etc.) can be found in *Student Packets*, a folder on the *Exploring InDesign* CD. Each chapter folder contains text and image files, and a .pdf document with instructions for the end-of-chapter projects. It would be a good idea to place a copy of the *Student Packets* folder on your hard drive.

Throughout the book, you will be encouraged to use keyboard shortcuts whenever possible. Activating a keyboard shortcut instead of selecting menus or opening panels is a more efficient method of working. Keyboard shortcuts usually consist of a combination of modifier keys and letters or symbols. For Mac users, the modifier keys include Shift, Control, Option, and Command. Windows users use Shift, Control and Alt. Both platforms utilize function keys (F1–F12) found above the numbers on the keyboard. When a keyboard shortcut is listed as *Command+S*, this means: "Hold the Command key, press the **S** key, and release." *F5* means: "Press Function Key 5, and release." Throughout the text, important keyboard shortcuts will be displayed in color for easy reference (Visual 1–1). Try to memorize these shortcuts!

visual | 1–1 |

These colored tables will provide quick reference to the keyboard shortcuts used throughout this book.

Keyboard Shortcut	
Cmd + S (Mac)	**Save**
Ctrl + S (Win)	

The Document Window

Launch InDesign by clicking the icon on the dock shown in Visual 1–2, or by double-clicking the icon in the Applications folder (Mac), or by selecting Adobe InDesign CS3 from the Start menu (Windows). When the program launches, you will be welcomed to InDesign by a screen that contains a host of options, including an overview of new features in CS3, tutorials, and learning resources (Visual 1–3). You can create new documents and open recent documents from this screen. You may want to place a check in the box in the lower left corner so that this screen will not appear when launching the program, but do this only after you have gone through the tutorial and overview opportunities.

visual | 1–2 |

Look for this icon to launch Adobe® InDesign® CS3

visual | 1–3 |

This screen welcomes you to Adobe InDesign CS3.

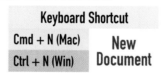

Keyboard Shortcut

Cmd + N (Mac)
Ctrl + N (Win)

New Document

We'll get started immediately by creating a sample document to introduce us to the document window and navigating through InDesign dialog boxes.

1. Press Command+N (Mac) or Control+N (Windows) to create a new document.

2. Press the Tab key to jump to the next field in the New Document dialog box (or any dialog box in InDesign). Press Shift+Tab to move backwards through the fields. Practice moving through each field in the New Document dialog box using these methods.

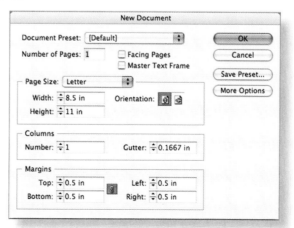

visual | 1–4 |

The New Document dialog box.

Pressing the Tab key is an excellent method of selecting any field. Another excellent method is to select the field by clicking on the field name to the left of the field (Visual 1–5). Once you grow accustomed to selecting fields by clicking on the name to the left of the field, you'll wish all the software you use had that feature! (The most inefficient method of selecting a field is to place the cursor in the field and double-click or drag to highlight the area.) Once a field is highlighted, type your new information over the old information in the field. Don't re-select a field that is already highlighted!

visual | 1–5 |

Select a field by clicking on the name to the left of the field.

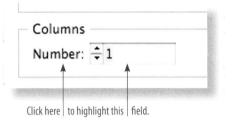

Click here | to highlight this | field.

3. Enter these values in the New Document dialog box: Number of Pages: **1**. Page Size: **Letter** (8.5" × 11"). Be sure that the Facing Pages and Master Text Frame options are not selected. Columns: **3**. Margins: **0.75"**. Orientation: **Portrait** (first icon). *Portrait* orientation means that the height of your document is greater than the width. *Landscape* orientation means that your document is wider than it is high (Visual 1–6).

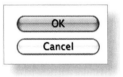

Portrait Orientation   Landscape Orientation

visual | 1–6 |

Portrait orientation means the height of your document is greater than the width.

NOTE: In the middle of the Margins section is a link icon. This button appears on numerous InDesign panels. When the link is closed, the value you enter in one field is automatically transferred to the rest of the fields. If the link was closed when you entered the margin value, 0.75" automatically appeared in the other three margin fields.

Apply the same value in all the fields.

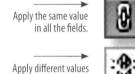

Apply different values in fields

visual | 1–7 |

Press Return (Mac) or Enter (Windows) instead of clicking OK. Press Command + period (Mac) or the Esc key (Windows) to activate the Cancel button.

OK

Cancel

4. To accept changes and exit the dialog box, press Return (Mac) or Enter (Windows). It is not necessary to use your mouse to select OK. Similarly, you can press Command + period (Mac) or Esc (Windows) to exit the dialog box without accepting changes. We will continue working on our document, so keep it open.

visual | 1–8 |

Preview modes can be selected from the bottom of the Toolbox.

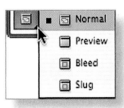

Normal
Preview
Bleed
Slug

Four view modes can be found at the bottom of the Toolbox (Visual 1–8). You are viewing your document in *Normal* mode, the default viewing mode. When Normal is selected, you will see the document outlined in black, with magenta guides designating the 0.75" margin on all sides. Violet lines designate the column guides. Press **W** to switch to *Preview* mode. In this mode, all guides are hidden, and the *pasteboard* is changed to gray, the default preview background color. (The pasteboard is

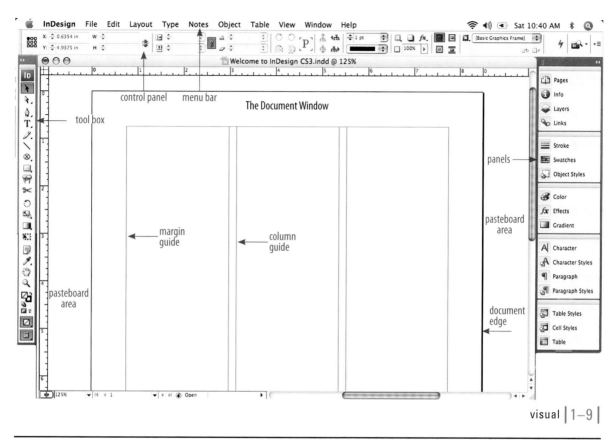

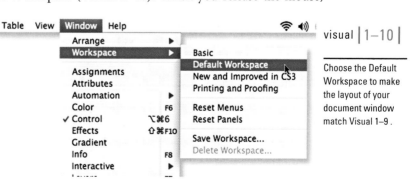

visual |1–9|

The document window shown in the InDesign Default Workspace setting.

the area surrounding the document, as shown in Visual 1–9.) Press **W** again, and you return to Normal mode. Bleed and Slug view modes show areas created outside the document size. Bleeds and slugs will be introduced in Chapter 6.

You may see some differences as you compare your document window to the example shown in Visual 1–9. Let's make sure we're all looking at the same document window setup. From Menu bar, go to Window>Workspace. Notice that InDesign has several selections from which to choose. Choose Default Workspace (Visual 1–10). When you release the mouse, your document window should look like Visual 1–9. The Save Workspace menu option allows you to save any customization you've made to the InDesign workspace. We'll cover that at the end of the chapter.

visual |1–10|

Choose the Default Workspace to make the layout of your document window match Visual 1–9 .

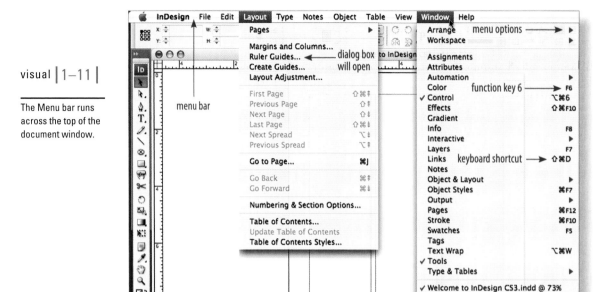

The Menu bar runs across the top of the document window.

The Menu Bar

The Menu bar stretches across the top of the document window (Visual 1–11). As you press and move your pointer across the Menu bar, you will see that underneath each category are menu items, most of which can be accessed by using keyboard shortcuts. Keyboard shortcuts are listed to the right of the menu items. Visual 1–12 shows how to interpret the symbols listed with Mac keyboard shortcuts:

These symbols are used throughout the Mac version of InDesign for activating keyboard shortcuts.

Symbol	Mac Keyboard
⌘	Command
⇧	Shift
⌥	Option

Some menu items are followed by a triangle or ellipsis. When a triangle follows a menu item, it means that a submenu will open and more menu options will be displayed. An ellipsis means that a dialog box will open when the menu item is selected.

The Toolbox

By default, the Toolbox appears in two vertical columns on the left side of the document window. You can move the Toolbox to different areas of the document window by dragging it by its title bar (Visual 1–13A). Although you can't reposition the location of the tools inside the Toolbox, you can customize the overall layout of the Toolbox. If you click on the arrows in the upper left corner, above the title bar, you can toggle the display of the Toolbox between a single or double vertical column (Visual 1–13A and D). When you hover your pointer over a tool, you will see the tool name, and keyboard shortcut (Visual 1–13C). Select a tool by

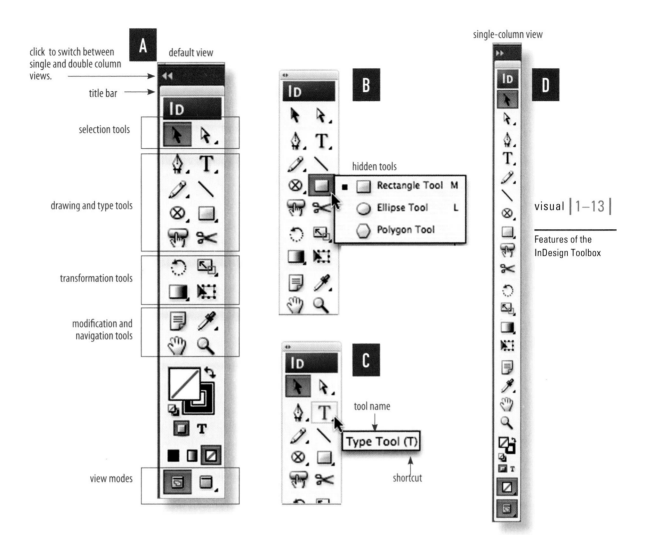

click to switch between single and double column views.

default view

title bar

single-column view

selection tools

drawing and type tools

transformation tools

modification and navigation tools

view modes

hidden tools

Rectangle Tool M

Ellipse Tool L

Polygon Tool

tool name

Type Tool (T)

shortcut

visual | 1–13 |

Features of the InDesign Toolbox

clicking on it. When a tool is selected, its icon becomes highlighted. Notice that some tools have an arrow in the lower right corner. When you click on these tools and hold the mouse down for a second, you will see more choices "hidden" underneath (Visual 1–13B). These hidden tools are related to the main tool displayed in the Toolbox. Tools are grouped according to function: selection tools, drawing and type tools, transformation tools, and modification and navigation tools.

Pressing the Tab key alternately hides and shows the Toolbox and panels. Pressing Shift+Tab displays the Toolbox, but hides the panels. If the Toolbox becomes hidden on your document, go to the Menu bar, select Window>Workspace and choose your desired workspace arrangement. The Toolbox will return to its default location.

The Control Panel

The Control panel offers quick and convenient ways to accomplish much of what you need to do in your documents. By default, the Control panel is located at the top of the document window. You can move it to the bottom of the window, or change it to a floating panel, by choosing either of these options from the panel menu located at the far right end of the Control panel. (Visual 1–14). Like the Toolbox, tool tips will be displayed when you hover over an item with the pointer. The fields and options in the Control panel are like a chameleon, changing from Character formatting mode to Paragraph formatting mode, or to any number of other modes, depending on what type of object you have selected. At times, the Control panel will duplicate the options and settings of other InDesign panels that are displayed on your screen. The Control panel will display additional options, depending on your monitor size and resolution. If the Control panel does not appear on your desktop, press Option+Command+6 (Mac) or Alt+Control+6 (Windows) to toggle the Control panel on and off. You can also display the Control panel by selecting Window>Control from the Menu bar. You will be using the Control panel continuously, and each of its options will be introduced as you progress through the chapters.

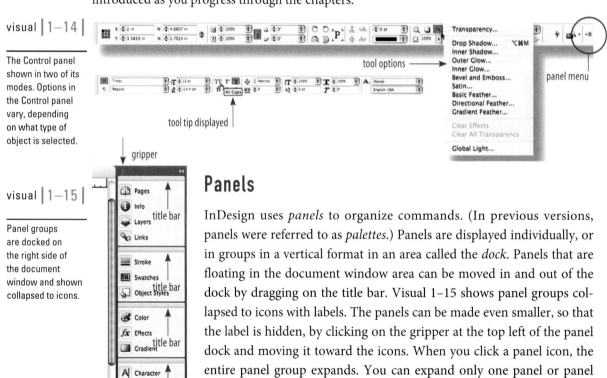

visual | 1–14 |

The Control panel shown in two of its modes. Options in the Control panel vary, depending on what type of object is selected.

tool options

tool tip displayed

panel menu

visual | 1–15 |

Panel groups are docked on the right side of the document window and shown collapsed to icons.

gripper

Panels

InDesign uses *panels* to organize commands. (In previous versions, panels were referred to as *palettes*.) Panels are displayed individually, or in groups in a vertical format in an area called the *dock*. Panels that are floating in the document window area can be moved in and out of the dock by dragging on the title bar. Visual 1–15 shows panel groups collapsed to icons with labels. The panels can be made even smaller, so that the label is hidden, by clicking on the gripper at the top left of the panel dock and moving it toward the icons. When you click a panel icon, the entire panel group expands. You can expand only one panel or panel group at a time. Select the title bar of the panel group that includes Stroke, Swatches and Object Styles and pull the title bar to the left. This process undocks the panel group. If you remove all panels from a dock, the dock disappears. A new dock will be created when you move a panel to edge of the workspace.

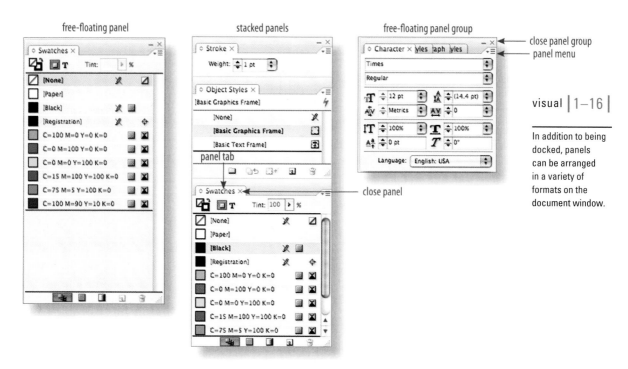

free-floating panel   stacked panels   free-floating panel group

close panel group
panel menu

visual | 1–16 |

In addition to being docked, panels can be arranged in a variety of formats on the document window.

panel tab

close panel

Once a panel or panel group is undocked, it can be dragged into another panel group, or made to be free-floating (Visual 1–16). InDesign allows you to customize the combination of panels to fit your preferences and the jobs you do. You can work in a panel while it is still grouped with other panels in vertical formation, or you can drag it out on the desktop area, whichever is more convenient for you. If you want, you can even dock the panels to the left edge of your screen. Click the close button in the upper-right corner of the tab to remove a panel. To add a panel, first select it from the Window menu and then choose a place to dock it.

Panels can be stacked vertically on the document window. To stack panels, drag a panel by its tab to the narrow drop zone at the bottom of another panel. Most panels have menus which are opened by clicking on the menu icon in the upper right corner of the panel (Visual 1–16).

The Command Bar

The Command bar, a feature familiar to PageMaker users, can be displayed from Window>Object & Layout>Command Bar. This bar contains features frequently used in document construction and editing operations (Visual 1–17). The Command bar won't be referred to in the directions for any of the projects in this book, but go ahead and use it if you find it a help.

visual | 1–17 |

The Command bar is found under Window>Object & Layout> Command Bar.

Using Tools

Set your Toolbox so that it is displayed in a single column down the left side of your document window. The top tool (black arrow) is the Selection tool. Use it when you want to select, re-size, or move an entire item (frame, line, text path, etc.). The second tool down, (white arrow) is the Direct Selection tool. Use it when you want to select just part of an item, the points on an item's path, the content inside the item, or to modify its shape. (If you are familiar with QuarkXPress, the Selection tool is sim-ilar to the Item tool and the Direct Selection tool is similar to the Content tool.)

Jump over the Pen tool and you will come to the Type tool. You will spend much of your time using the Type tool—typing, ed-iting, or working with tables. Because you'll be using it so much, you'll learn to use keyboard shortcuts to switch from the Type tool to other tools without going over to the Toolbox. This will make you very efficient. Below the Pencil tool is the Line tool. Use this tool for drawing straight or diagonal lines.

Below the Line tool is the Rectangle Frame tool. Notice the little arrow in the lower right corner. This means that other tools are "hidden" underneath the tool that is showing. We will use several of these tools as we continue working on the document created earlier.

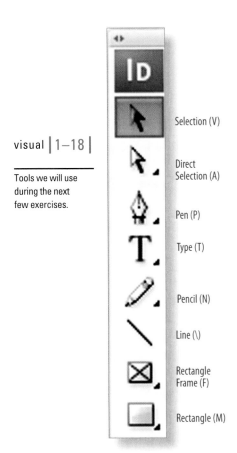

Selection (V)

Direct Selection (A)

Pen (P)

Type (T)

Pencil (N)

Line (\)

Rectangle Frame (F)

Rectangle (M)

1. In the Toolbox, click on the Rectangle tool. Your cursor will turn into little crosshairs with a dot in the middle. Go back to your document, click your mouse button somewhere on the left side of your document, and make a rectangle by dragging your mouse down and to the right. Release the mouse.

2. Let's take a look at the rectangle you have just drawn (Visual 1–19). The eight small hollow boxes at the corners and at each side of the rectangle are called *selection handle*s. When

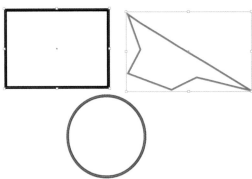

the selection handles are visible, the item is considered *active*. Click somewhere else on your document. The selection handles disappear, meaning the item is not active. An item must be selected in order to work with it. In addition to selection handles, shapes have *bounding boxes*. Bounding boxes indicate the outermost points of a shape. The bounding box for the rectangle you have just drawn is the same dimension as the rectangle. Look at the odd-looking shape in Visual 1–19. The rectangle that delineates its outer edges is the bounding box. A bounding box always has four straight sides, no matter what shape you have drawn. If the circle shown in the Visual 1–19 was activated with the Selection tool, the bounding box would be displayed as a square.

3. Go back to the Toolbox and click on the Selection tool. Your cursor should now look like a black arrow (Visual 1–20). Slowly move the Selection tool toward the edge of the rectangle (do not click the mouse button). When the arrow touches the edge, a small square appears next to the tail of the arrow. This means you can now select the rectangle again. Click when the small box appears by the tail of the arrow and you will see your selection handles again. Your rectangle is now selected. Notice that when your rectangle is selected and you move your cursor over the edge of the rectangle (without clicking the button), the arrow icon loses its "tail."

visual | 1–20 |

A. Default Selection tool cursor.

B. A small square indicates that an object is ready to be selected.

Recognize these selection icons:
A. The Selection tool is over the document.
B. The Selection tool is ready to select an object.
C. The Selection tool is ready to move an item.

4. With your rectangle selected, you can move the rectangle to a different place or change its size. To move it, click on the edge of the rectangle and drag it. Release the mouse button to "drop" the rectangle in the new location. To resize the rectangle, move the cursor over one of the selection handles. The icon turns into small opposing arrows, with a line in between (Visual 1–21). Drag the selection handles in, out, or diagonally to change the dimension of the rectangle.

C. A "tail-less" cursor means that you can click and drag the selected object.

In the following exercise you will use shortcuts to make a new document and to create and modify a rectangle.

1. Close, but don't save, the document you just made by pressing Command +W (Mac) or Control + W (Windows). Use keyboard shortcuts to make a new document: Command+N (Mac) or Control+N (Windows). When the New Document dialog box opens, accept the document defaults, including Letter for page size, and 0.5" for all margins. Choose the Basic workspace.

visual | 1–21 |

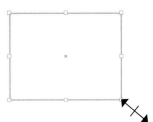

When the Selection arrow is over a frame handle, it changes shape. The double-ended arrow means that you can drag the handle to change the dimenstions of the object.

2. Next, you will draw a rectangle, but instead of going over to the Toolbox, press the letter **M**. This will instantly select the Rectangle tool. Draw a rectangle and then press the letter **A**. You have now selected the Direct Selection tool. The Direct Selection tool differs from the Selection tool because you can modify just part of an object—one side, or one or more *anchor points*—instead of the whole item.

The Direct Selection tool uses many of the same visual cues as the Selection tool, shown earlier. Notice that the solid tiny square means that the whole frame can be moved.

A. Default Direct Selection tool cursor.

B. The Direct Selection tool is ready to select the side of the frame.

C. The Direct Selection tool is ready to select an anchor point on a frame.

D. The Direct Selection tool is ready to move the whole object.

3. Modify the shape of your rectangle using the Direct Selection tool by selecting and dragging the sides and anchor points. Your rectangle will quickly lose its rigid, 90-degree angles.

4. With your shape selected, bring the Direct Selection arrow slowly to the tiny box in the center of the object. Notice that the white arrow becomes a black arrow. Click and move the object around.

NOTE: To avoid unpleasant surprises, always deselect an object when you are finished working on it. You can deselect an object by clicking off it, or by using the keyboard shortcut: Shift+Command+A (Mac) or Shift+Control+A (Windows).

Keyboard Shortcut	
Shift + Cmd + A (Mac)	**Deselect**
Shift + Ctrl + A (Win)	**All**

Placing Text into a Frame

You will appreciate good typing and keyboard skills as you begin to spend more time working with text. In the next exercise, you will learn how to enter text and draw some basic shapes.

1. Close your document without saving it by pressing Command+W (Mac) or Control+W (Windows). Use the keyboard shortcut to make a new, 1 page document that is 7 inches wide and **6** inches high (use the 0.5" default margins). Set your Toolbox so that it is displayed in a double column, down the left side of your document window.

The appearance of the Type tool cursor changes, depending on how it is being used.

A. The Type cursor positioned over a selected frame.

Enis nulla corero consed duis at erosto odo dolorperosto et aute dip enibh er aliquisi er adigna aliquat, volestrud etumsan dignit ipis duisci exero odolor sumsandre feu facinis elesto odoloreet er sis accummy nis alissi bla consequ

B. The Type cursor positioned over a frame already containing text.

2. Notice that your document is landscape format, because it is wider than it is high. Press **M** to select the Rectangle tool and draw a rectangle. Now press **T**. Your cursor changes into a vertical bar with a small crosshair near the bottom and dotted lines around it (Visual 1–23A). Click inside the rectangle. Your cursor now becomes a blinking cursor in the upper left corner of the rectangle, your rectangle has become a text frame, and you are ready to type in it.

NOTE: You can also create a text frame by dragging with the Type tool cursor. When the cursor is blinking inside the frame, you are ready to type.

visual | 1–24 |

The Type cursor is ready to create a text frame by clicking and dragging.

You can create a text frame by dragging the Type tool cursor.

3. Type a sentence or two about yourself, your dog, or your weekend—anything you want. Highlight all the text with Command+A (Mac) or Control+A (Windows). There are other methods of selecting your text. For instance, you can drag and highlight text with your mouse, or choose Select All from the Edit menu, but those methods are slower. Keyboard shortcuts are always the way to go!

Keyboard Shortcut

Cmd + A (Mac)

Ctrl + A (Win)

Select All

4. With the text highlighted, you can use Shift+Command+> (Mac) or Shift+Control+> (Windows) to increase the size of the selected type. Try it. Hold down Shift+Command or Shift+Control and press the *greater than* key (>), six or seven times, and watch the size of your type get larger. You could use the Control panel to increase the size of the type, but using keyboard shortcuts is essential for efficiency. You can substitute the *less than* symbol (<) in combination with the same modifier keys to reduce the type size. Keep your document open.

Keyboard Shortcut

Shift + Cmd + > (Mac)

Shift + Ctrl + > (Win)

Increase Type Size

Keyboard Shortcut

Shift + Cmd + < (Mac)

Shift + Ctrl + < (Win)

Decrease Type Size

Stroke and Fill

A *stroke* is a line that goes around the edges of a shape, like a border; or around type, like an outline. A *fill* is a color that is placed inside a shape or type. Near the bottom of the Toolbox are two squares—one square overlaps the other (see Visual 1–25). The square on the right is the Stroke box; to the left is the Fill box. Click back and forth on these squares a few times. Whichever icon you click overlaps the other, to indicate that it is active. If you want to add a border, you must have Stroke active. If you want to fill something with a color, you need to activate Fill. You cannot have both Stroke and Fill modes selected at the same time.

Now let's go back to the document we were working on in the last series of steps and see what we can do with stroke and fill.

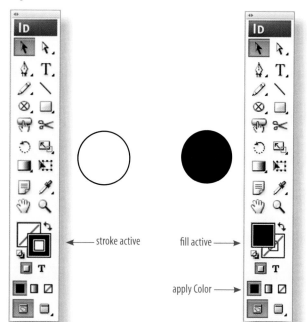

stroke active   fill active

apply Color

visual | 1–25 |

The square on top indicates whether the Stroke or Fill mode is active.

1. Set the Toolbox to display in 2-column mode. With the type cursor inside the frame, select all of the type and click the Fill box. There is a black "T" in the box indicating that the Fill will be applied to your type (see Visual 1–26). Near the bottom of the Toolbox is a row of three icons. Click on the small square with the red diagonal line. A diagonal red line replaces the "T" in the Fill box and it looks like your text has disappeared! It hasn't. All you have done is removed the fill of your text by using the Apply None button. Now, select all the invisible text again using Command+A (Mac) or Control+A (Windows).

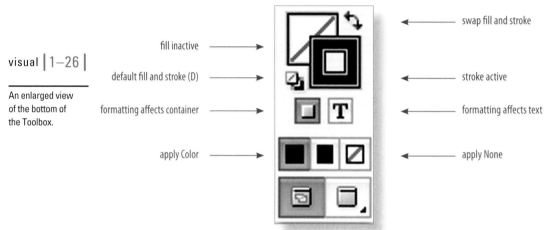

fill inactive

default fill and stroke (D)

formatting affects container

apply Color

swap fill and stroke

stroke active

formatting affects text

apply None

2. Select the Stroke icon. An outlined "T" will appear, indicating the outline will be placed on type. Click on the Apply Color button, the small black square on the left side of the row containing the Apply None button (Visual 1– 26). You have just used the Apply Color button to outline your text with a stroke. Press the Swap Fill and Stroke icon and the text will alternate between having an outline and a fill.

3. Press **M** to activate the Rectangle tool. Draw a perfect square by holding down the Shift key as you drag the frame. By default, the Rectangle tool has a stroke and no fill. Press the Swap Fill and Stroke icon to change the square from outlined to solid. The square is now filled with black. Press Shift+X to swap the fill and stroke. Press **D** to restore the default fill and stroke.

Keyboard Shortcut	
Shift+ X (Mac)	**Swap**
Shift+ X (Win)	**Stroke & Fill**

NOTE: Press lowercase **X** to toggle between the Stroke and Fill icons. Press Shift+X to swap the stroke and fill color. Press **D** to activate the default stroke and fill.

4. Select the Line tool (the keyboard shortcut is a backslash, \). Click and drag to draw several diagonal lines on your document. Switch to the Selection tool and select any line. Notice the shape of the bounding box. Now, select the Line tool again, hold down the Shift key, and draw perfectly horizontal and vertical lines (Visual 1–27). By default, the line has a .5 pt. stroke. Lines do not have fills.

5. Hold down the Shift key and draw one more line, but do not release the mouse button. Instead, move the mouse to rotate the free end of the line in a circle, like hands on a clock. Notice how the line snaps to 45-degree increments. The Shift key constrains lines to horizontal, vertical, or 45-degree increments. Close this document without saving it.

NOTE: Holding down the Shift key constrains rectangles to perfect squares, ellipses to perfect circles, and lines to horizontal, vertical, or 45-degree increments.

Text can also have a stroke and fill. The fill colors the letters, the stroke outlines the letters. Whenever you apply a stroke to text, make sure the width of the stroke doesn't distort the shape of the letters (Visual 1–28). You'll learn to adjust the width of a stroke in Chapter 2.

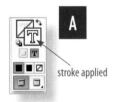
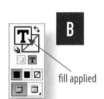
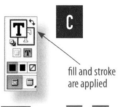

stroke applied

fill applied

fill and stroke are applied

visual | 1–28 |

A. Text with a stroke.
B. Text with a fill.
C. Stroke is too thick for the size of the text .

About Frames

InDesign includes two tools for making rectangular boxes called *frames*. One frame has an X in it, one doesn't. Both frames can hold either pictures or text—there's really no difference between a "picture" frame and a "text" frame. When you click inside any frame with the Type tool, a blinking cursor will appear, which means the frame is ready for you to begin typing.

1. Make a new document using the default settings. Use the Rectangle tool to draw a rectangle in the left half your document.

2. Now choose the Rectangle Frame tool (the box with the X inside it) to the left of the Rectangle tool. You may also select this tool by pressing **F**. Draw a second rectangle on the right half of your document. There will be an X inside the new rectangle (Visual 1–29).

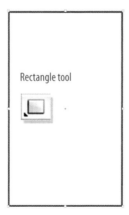
Rectangle tool

Rectangle Frame tool

visual | 1–29 |

On the left is a frame made with the Rectangle tool. The frame on the right was made with the Rectangle Frame tool. Either frame can hold text or graphics.

So, why are there two frame tools? For convenience. If you were laying out a 16-page news-letter you could use frames made with the Rectangle tool to indicate where the type should be placed and frames made with the Rectangle Frame tool, with the X, to indicate where photos should be placed. This would be particularly helpful if another person was going to work with you on part of your project.

Navigating

Let's do a little navigating around your document with the two frames. Your document sits in the middle of an area called the pasteboard. At the right and bottom of the pasteboard are

visual | 1–30 |

Scroll bars and arrows
help you position
your document.

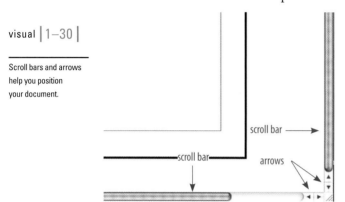

scroll bar

scroll bar

arrows

scroll bars (Visual 1–30). You slide the scroll bars up and down or right and left to reposition your document inside the InDesign window. You can also click on the triangles to move your document around. If you are working in Windows, these triangles will be at either end of the scroll bars. If you are working on a Mac, the triangles will be in the lower right corner.

Another way to move your document around is to use the Hand tool. Whenever the Type tool is not active, you can hold down the spacebar to switch temporarily to the Hand tool (Visual 1–31). You will see a little fist appear on the screen. Press and drag with your mouse and the fist will grab on to your document and move it wherever you like.

visual | 1–31 |

Hold down the Spacebar
and click to make the
Hand tool turn into the
grabber hand. If you
are using the Type tool,
access the grabber
hand by pressing the
Option (Mac) or Alt
(Windows) key.

Henit, quisi elis ad tat utatie feum zzrilit, quat praestrud ming et nulputp atuerci tat, commolut ad tis doluptat, con henim alisitMet incin euipsum veniamet aliqui bla feu facidunt lumsan eugiat velestrud euguer sustrud et at niam, si tat.

Henit, quisi elis ad tat utatie feum zzrilit, quat praestrud ming et nulputp atuerci tat, commolut ad tis doluptat, con henim alisitMet incin euipsum veniamet aliqui bla feu facidunt lumsan eugiat velestrud euguer sustrud et at niam, si tat.

To access the Hand tool while you are using the Type tool in an active frame, you press the Option (Mac) or Alt (Windows) key. (If you press the spacebar to access the grabber hand while using the Type tool, you will simply add spaces to the text you are working on.) You can also select the Hand tool in the Toolbox or by using the **H** shortcut key, but using the Spacebar (or Option/ Alt) and mouse is probably faster and more convenient.

NOTE: If the Type tool is active but you are not typing in an active frame, you must use Option+Spacebar (Mac) or Alt+Spacebar (Windows) to access the Hand tool.

Changing Your View

In the lower left corner of your document window is the Status bar. This bar displays the page number you are working on and the status of a file. You can also move from page to page by clicking the Next Page, Previous Page, or Go To Page arrows on each side of the current page number. The Status bar also shows the size at which your document is being displayed on the screen, the document *zoom percentage*. When you are viewing your document at its actual size, the zoom percentage is 100%. You can access the zoom percentage preset list by clicking on the downward-pointing triangle to the right of the zoom percentage field. Notice that you can view your document from 5% all the way to 4000%! If none of those view percentages is just right, you can type any percentage in the zoom percentage field and press Return or Enter, and your document view will immediately change.

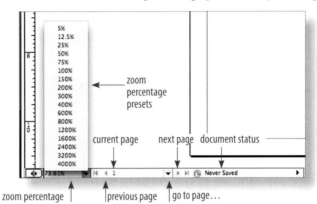

visual | 1–32 |

The Status bar in the lower left corner of the document window.

Another way to change your view is to use keyboard shortcuts. For a quick view of the document at actual size, press Command+1 (Mac) or Control+1 (Windows). This method is quick and efficient, and after using it awhile, it becomes automatic. Other keyboard shortcuts for viewing options are shown in Visual 1–33. Practice using each of the keyboard shortcuts until its use becomes automatic.

Function	Mac	Windows
View at 100%	Cmd+1	Ctrl+1
View at 200%	Cmd+2	Ctrl+2
View at 400%	Cmd+4	Ctrl+4
View at 50%	Cmd+5	Ctrl+5
Fit page in window	Cmd+0 (zero)	Ctrl+0 (zero)

visual | 1–33 |

Keyboard shortcuts for changing zoom percentage.

Access the Zoom tool in the Toolbox by pressing **Z**. Hold the Zoom tool directly over the place in your document you want magnified, and click. That area will come to the center of your screen. Hold down the Option (Mac) or Alt (Windows) key and click to reduce the zoom percentage. Get in the habit of zooming in and zooming out, quickly and frequently. Too many beginning designers work with very small text at 100% view—or less! Give your eyes a break. Zoom into your document so you can comfortably see punctuation marks, where your cursor is, how many characters you have highlighted—all the small details of your document. After you have finished working up close, zoom out, using the appropriate keyboard shortcut.

Customizing Your Workspace

Arrange the panels on your desktop where you want them to be. Place the Toolbox where it is most convenient for you. Even if you don't yet have a preference for panel configurations, pull a couple panels out onto the desktop just for fun and note their names and placement. Choose Window>Workspace>Save Workspace. In the Save Workspace dialog, type **Workspace 1** and press Return or Enter.

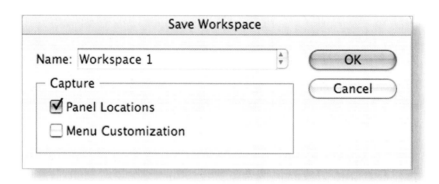

Now rearrange your desktop with a different dock for the Control panel, different panels, and Tools placement. Choose Window>Workspace>Save Workspace and name it **Workspace 2**. Toggle between the two workspaces by selecting their names from the Windows>Workspace menu. You can customize your desktop to just about any configuration you want. Very neat. Very organized.

Saving Your Work

Your old typewriter had one—and only one—advantage over word processing: Once you typed a word on your typewriter, it was there to stay! Not so with electronic page layout programs. You need to save your work and save it often.

To save your document, press Command+S (Mac) or Control+S (Windows) or select File>Save. The dialog box will ask you first of all what you want to name your document. The Save As (Mac) or File Name (Windows) field will be highlighted when the dialog box is displayed, so just begin typing the name you want for the document. Next, tell your computer where you want it saved: on the desktop? on your hard drive? on a server? in a folder? which folder? Be sure to remember where you save your document because you will need to find it later.

Keyboard Shortcut	
Cmd + S (Mac)	**Save**
Ctrl + S (Win)	

NOTE: If you lose a document but know you saved it somewhere, you can do a Find or Search (if you remember the name of the file) and your computer will locate it for you.

Save and Save As

After you have saved a project the first time, pressing Command+S (Mac) or Control+S (Windows) automatically saves your document, with the edits you have made, in the same location and with the same name as your previous Save. Save As also saves your work, but the Save As dialog is displayed to allow you to rename and relocate your document (Visual 1–35).

Keyboard Shortcut

Shift + Cmd + S (Mac)
Shift + Ctrl + S (Win)

Save As

For instance, you have been working on a Valentine's Day ad for South Side Grocery. You complete the ad, save and print the document, and get the customer's approval. The customer loves your layout and decides you should make a version for three other stores in the city. And all the other versions need to be done by 5:00 p.m. today!

This is a great time to use Save As. Open the original file, named *South Side Grocery*. Immediately use Save As, and name the new file *North Side Grocery*. The *South Side Grocery* file remains unchanged, but you are now working on a different file—the *North Side Grocery* ad. When this ad is done you save it, print it, and again use Save As to name the next file *West Side Grocery*. The previous file, *North Side Grocery*, stays just as you left it while you complete the *West Side Grocery* ad, and so on. You can also use Save As to rename your document, such as *North Side Grocery_Backup* and then save the backup version to a CD, flash drive, or a file server.

visual | 1–35 |

The Save As window in the Mac operating system.

Save a Copy

The keyboard shortcut for Save a Copy is Command+Option+S (Mac) or Control+Alt+S (Windows). Save a Copy is a little different than Save As. Suppose you want to keep a visual record of each production step in a project. You begin the project and perform the first step.

Use Save a Copy and name the file *Step 1*. Your original file is still on the screen and you continue on to the next step. When you finish this step, use Save a Copy and name this file *Step 2*. You will continue building your document, saving and naming incremental versions.

Keyboard Shortcut

Cmd + Option +S (Mac)
Ctrl + Alt + S (Win)

Save a Copy

Unlike Save As, the Save a Copy option allows you to continue working on the original file while the copy goes wherever you tell it to go.

How can Save a Copy come in handy? Let's say it's 10:15 a.m. and you are busy getting the Zaza Toys layout ready for a client meeting at 10:30 a.m. All of a sudden you get a huge brainstorm that will radically change the look of the layout. The client has already approved the layout you are just finishing and, since it's due in 15 minutes, you don't want to take the chance of messing it up. So you use the Save a Copy option and name the copy *Client_ Approved*. This file, completed at 10:15 a.m., is now saved somewhere on your desktop, but the original Zaza Toys file is still open. You make all kinds of changes. You go wild.

Your creative director walks by to see if you are ready for the meeting that will begin in just a few minutes. She looks at your screen and gently but firmly suggests you change the document back to the way it was about 10 minutes ago. In a few clicks you have *Client_Approved* opened and printed. You arrive at the client meeting on time and unruffled.

Printing Your Document

When you are ready to print your document, press Command+P (Mac) or Control+P (Windows) or choose File>Print. There are many options displayed in the Print dialog box (Visual 1–36), but the first thing you need to do is select the printer you want to use on the General options page of the dialog. Now, select the Setup options page (in the list on the left side of the dialog box), set Paper Size to **Letter**, and make sure Orientation is **Portrait**. If your document is smaller than 8.5 × 11, your finished piece will look better if you set Page Position to **Centered**.

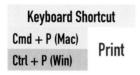

Keyboard Shortcut

Cmd + P (Mac)
Ctrl + P (Win)   **Print**

visual | 1–36 |

The Print dialog box lists option pages down the left side of the dialog box.

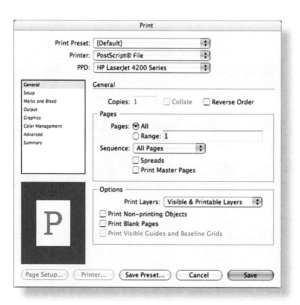

In the lower left corner is a shaded box with a white rectangle and the letter "P." This is a preview of how the printer is set to print your document. The white area is the size of your paper. The "P" is the size of your document and is represented with a light shade of blue. If you change Paper Size to something other than letter, this preview will give you an idea of how your document will print in relation to the size of the paper it will be printed on (Visual 1–37).

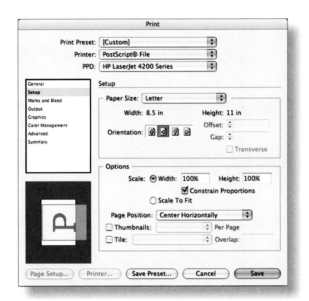

Check the page position preview before printing to make sure document size and orientation work with the paper it will be printed on.

SUMMARY

If you are already familiar with Adobe Photoshop or Adobe Illustrator, this chapter was an easy review. If learning Adobe InDesign is your first adventure into the world of digital page layout, this chapter covered a lot of new territory. Finding your way around the InDesign workspace was the focus of this chapter. The next chapter will build on these concepts. Like practicing the piano, using InDesign for at least 30 minutes each day will help solidify these basics and help pave the way for a continual increase in your skill level.

The following section, *Getting Started*, walks you through changing InDesign default preferences. When you are finished modifying your InDesign application defaults, you will be ready to begin some enjoyable and challenging projects.

▶ Getting Started • Preferences

InDesign comes with a built-in set of defaults. Modifying some of these defaults will make your production much smoother. When you change defaults with InDesign launched, but no document open, you are changing the **application preferences**. Once they are changed, the changes will apply to all future documents.

When you change InDesign preferences with a document open, the changes apply to the current document only. This is called changing the **document preferences**.

Follow these steps to change the application preferences to match those used in this text.

1. Launch InDesign, but do not create a new document. You should see the InDesign menu, the Control panel, and the Toolbox.

2. Press **Command+K** (Mac) or **Control+K** (Windows) to open the Preferences dialog.

3. Along the left side of the Preferences window, you will see a list of categories. Select each category and make the following changes:

   • Type: select **Apply Leading to Entire Paragraphs**

   • Units & Increments>Ruler Units: Origin: **Page,** Horizontal: **Inches,** Vertical: **Inches**

   • Units & Increments>Keyboard Increments: Size/Leading: **1 pt** Baseline Shift: **1 pt**

4. Accept changes and exit the dialog box.

5. Go to File>Document Setup. Deselect **Facing Pages.** Make sure the Page Size is set to **Letter**.

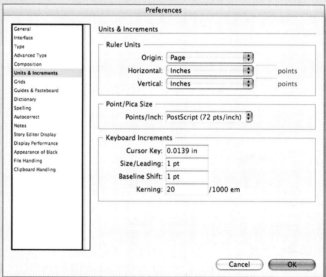

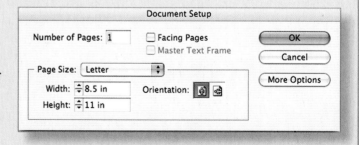

Getting Started • Best Practices

1. Open documents from a local hard drive.
When you store a document on a portable drive or a server, it is important to move the document to your local hard drive before opening it. Opening documents from storage media can cause damage.

2. Do a *Save As* when your project is completed.
Each time you Save a document, InDesign adds more data to the document, but doesn't remove outdated data. When you choose Save As, InDesign completely rewrites the document, using only current information. This keeps your file size smaller and decreases the time required for printing or redrawing the image on the screen.

3. Use the least number of text frames possible. This keeps your document smaller and easier to maintain.

4. Use context-sensitive menus. These are activated by holding the Control key (Mac) or the right mouse button (Windows) when you have an object selected. This is a quick method of choosing commonly used commands.

5. Use keyboard shortcuts whenever possible.
Over the course of your professional career, the time you save using shortcuts will be significant.

6. Use shortcut keys in dialog boxes. Press Return (Mac) or Enter (Windows) instead of choosing OK. Press Command + period (Mac) or Esc (Windows) to exit a dialog box. In some dialog boxes, holding Option (Mac) or Alt (Windows) changes the Cancel button to a Reset button, allowing you to make changes without exiting the dialog box.

7. Never remove the .indd file extension from any of your files.

8. Use quality fonts. InDesign works best with OpenType, Type 1 (PostScript), and TrueType fonts. Corrupt fonts can damage your document and crash your computer!

9. Create folders to organize your projects. Keep images used in the document organized inside the folder. Use the Package operation (introduced in Chapter 12).

Document Recovery

InDesign has a built-in document recovery system that protects your files against unexpected power failures or computer crashes. Automatic recovery data exists in a temporary file that is separate from your InDesign document. When you see a file that contains your document's name and a padlock icon, you are seeing the recovery file.

If you crash, here are the steps to recover your file.
• Start your computer.
• Launch InDesign.
• InDesign will display any recovered documents. The word [Recovered] will appear after the file name in the title bar of the document.
• Choose File>Save As and specify a new location and name for the file.
• If you had saved the document before crashing, and the recovered document is an older version that you don't want to keep, close the file without saving it.
• If InDesign can't open your document, it means it was permanently damaged during the crash.

This feature is designed for emergencies only. You should still save your documents often, and **make backups!**

in review

1. How can a floating panel be placed back on the panel dock?

2. What is the difference between the Selection tool and the Direct Selection tool?

3. What are the keyboard shortcuts for accessing (a) the Selection tool, and (b) the Direct Selection tool?

4. The rectangle that shows the outermost dimensions of any shape is called the _____ _____.

5. How are the Rectangle Frame and Rectangle tools different?

6. What are two methods of deselecting an object?

7. What is a stroke? What is a fill?

8. What is the difference between Save and Save a Copy?

9. What is the keyboard shortcut for increasing the size of type?

10. Describe the features of the Status bar.

11. What is the keyboard shortcut for New Document?

12. What is the keyboard shortcut for View at 100%?

13. What is the keyboard shortcut for toggling between Stroke and Fill?

14. What is the keyboard shortcut for the Rectangle tool?

15. Where can you preview how your document will print on the paper you have selected?

projects

Red text
with a black stroke.
Always use with
caution!

Chapter Project Although it looks amazingly simple, this project will review most of the skills you learned in this chapter. And don't worry—the projects get much more interesting and difficult as the chapters progress.

Find the *01 Artwork & Resources* folder on the accompanying CD. Inside that folder is a file called *01 Student Packet.pdf* that contains instructions for this project. You can print it out and refer to it when creating the Chapter 1 project. As you are working on chapter projects, concentrate on using keyboard shortcuts to adjust your view so that you are not straining to see your work. Remember to practice using InDesign for 30 minutes each day!

Every **great ability**
    develops and reveals itself
increasingly
      with every new assignment.

℞ Baltasar Gracian

| type, tools, and terms |

objectives

- Distinguish between serif and sans serif typefaces
- Read and interpret project markup
- Define type family, typeface, font, point size, and leading
- Define picas and points
- Use Character Formatting Controls in the Control panel
- Use Paragraph Formatting Controls in the Control panel
- Modify the attributes of text frames
- Apply fills and strokes
- Insert glyphs

introduction

You are dreaming a designer's worst nightmare. A weary vacationer has just come home and his mailbox is overflowing. He plops the stack of mail onto the kitchen counter and begins the sorting process. "Keep, throw, keep, keep, throw, throw…oh, this one looks interesting, maybe I'll look at it later…" until the whole stack of mail has been separated. He picks up the stack of rejects and moves slowly to a designer's nemesis—the circular file. You helplessly call out in your sleep, "Hey, don't throw that stuff! I spent days designing those direct response mailers!" You watch your pieces fall into the dark abyss of the garbage can and you shudder as the lid closes, sealing the fate of all your hard work.

This "nightmare" is actually reality for many designers who do not know how to set type. It doesn't take the average reader more than a glance to decide whether or not to read a printed piece. If a design doesn't pass the "once-over" test, out it goes. That's the bad news. The good news is that by picking up this book, you have taken the first step in learning how to use type as a powerful communication tool. And by the time you complete Exploring InDesign you will know how to correctly set type. In the first chapter you learned how to find your way around the InDesign workspace. This chapter will introduce you to basic typographic terms and concepts. Knowing both InDesign and typography will give you a competitive edge in the marketplace—and save your printed pieces from the garbage can!

AN EYE-Q TEST...

The ability to use type as a powerful design component is a distinguishing characteristic of an experienced designer. Visual 2–1 shows some examples of typical newspaper display ads. The difference between each pair is how the type is used. Each row shows two versions of the same ad. Which example in each pair would you most likely read? Which examples successfully communicate the message?

visual | 2–1 |

Use of type is the main variable in each pair of designs.

A

B

If you selected "B" for each pair, you have just proven the power of good typesetting. Typesetting should enhance readability and strengthen the message. The type on a page should attract the reader's attention and create a visual path for the eye to follow. How you use type can make or break a layout!

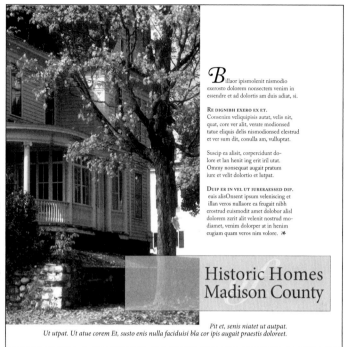

Headline   Historic Homes
of Madison County

Copy   Billaor ipismolenit nismodio exerosto dolorem nonsectem venim
in essendre et ad dolortis am duis
adiat, si.

Re dignibh exero ex et, consenim
veliquipisis autat, velis nit, quat,
core ver alit, verate modionsed
tatue eliquis delis nismodionsed
elestrud et ver sum dit, conulla
am, vulluptat, suscip ea alisit, cor-
percidunt dolore et lan henit ing
erit iril utat.

Caption   Pit et, senis niatet ut autpat. Ut
utpat. Ut atue corem Et, susto
enis nulla faciduisi bla cor ipis
augait praestis doloreet.

visual |2–2|

The upper left
example is a rough
layout. Client-
provided copy
(lower left) indicates
headline and text.
The final piece
is on the right.

FIRST THINGS FIRST

When a client gives you a rough layout, how exactly do you get started? First, you must read the text and understand the purpose of the piece you are going to design. Determine which information is most important. Second, never assume that the copy provided to you is totally accurate. Take responsibility for ensuring the document's accuracy and ultimate success, by making it a habit to check the following items:

- Proofread phone numbers and zip codes.
- Go online and test web addresses.
- Ask if product names require a ™ or ® symbol.
- Check that names are spelled correctly throughout the document.
- Consult a calendar to verify days and dates. Check that day, date, and time information is consistent throughout the document.
- Proofread headings and subheads (they are often overlooked in the proofing process).

If the client gives you actual samples of the printed pieces to re-create, look for ways the pieces could be improved and discuss those changes with the client. Often project samples are filled with typesetting mistakes in form and type use. Do not duplicate poor typesetting! You are the professional—the client is coming to you for your insight and expertise.

Finally, ask how the job will be printed and finished. Will it be drilled (three-hole punched)? Will it be stitched (spine stapled)? Will it be mailed? Will there be photos and colors? These specifics will determine how you build the InDesign document.

Select an Appropriate Typeface

Once you understand the purpose and the specifications of the project, you must put some thought into the personality you want the piece to express. The blend of typeface, image, layout, and color will create a distinct personality in each piece you design. Personalities can range from formal and powerful, to wacky and whimsical. The typeface you select will play a big part in communicating that personality.

Let's say you just inherited a huge amount of money and can now have the cosmetic surgery you always dreamed of. You look in the yellow pages to choose a cosmetic surgeon. Which surgeon will you choose from the list shown in Visual 2–3?

visual | 2–3 |

The selection of appropriate typefaces is one of the most critical steps in any design job.

1 John Davis, M.D.
2 JOHN DAVIS, M.D.
3 John Davis, M.D.
4 JOHN DAVIS, M.D.
5 John Davis, M.D.

6 John Davis, M.D.
7 John Davis, M.D.
8 JOHN DAVIS, M.D.
9 John Davis, M.D.
10 JOHN DAVIS, M.D.

Selecting Typeface and Point Size

The following exercise will focus on the basics of text handling in InDesign. Launch InDesign. Follow these steps to create a sample document.

1. Press Command+N (Mac) or Control+N (Windows) to create a new document.
   The New Document dialog box will open. Your settings should be:
   Document Preset: **[Default]**
   Number of Pages: **1**
   Facing Pages: **Off** (Facing pages is another way of saying two-page spreads, similar to the left- and right-hand pages of a book. If you changed your InDesign defaults in the *Getting Started* section in Chapter 1, this should already be turned off.)
   Master Text Frame: **Off**
   Page Size: **Letter**
   Width: **8.5 in.**, Height: **11 in.**
   Orientation: **Portrait**
   Number of columns: **1** (ignore the Gutter field for now)
   Margins: **0.5 in.** (top, bottom, left, right).

Keyboard Shortcut	
Cmd + N (Mac)	**New**
Ctrl + N (Win)	**Document**

2. Press the Return or Enter key. Remember, it's easier and faster to press the Return key rather than to click OK with your mouse.

3. Your document will appear in a window with two rulers—one at the top and the other along the left side of your window. The upper left corner of your document should be at zero on the horizontal ruler, and the upper right corner should be at 8.5. Along the vertical ruler, the upper left corner of your document should be at zero and the lower left corner should be at 11. Your document should look like Visual 2–4. You will also notice a colored line around the inside of your document. This is the half-inch margin you set in the New Document dialog box. (If you did not change your InDesign defaults in the *Getting Started* section in Chapter 1, your measurements will be displayed in picas. This measurement system will be discussed later, and we will cover changing the ruler units of measure in the next chapter, so don't worry about them for now.)

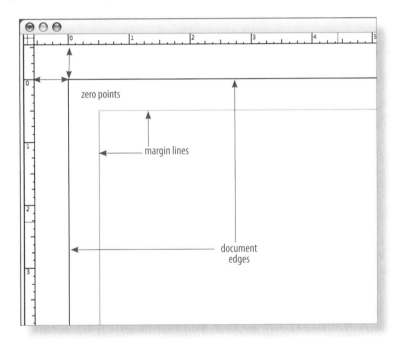

visual | 2–4 |

The upper left half of your newly created document. Note the upper left corner positioned at 0,0.

Adding Text

4. Use the keyboard shortcut **T** to select the Type tool from the Toolbox. Put your cursor inside the upper left margin of your document, and then click and drag a text frame down and across the page. Wherever you stop will determine the size of your frame. If your frame is too small or you don't like the shape of it, hold down Command (Mac) or Control (Windows) and press the letter **Z**. This is one of the best shortcuts to know—Undo. (InDesign allows you unlimited undos. Don't you wish your life had unlimited undos?) Repeat drawing frames and "undoing" them until your frame stretches nicely from the left to right margins.

Keyboard Shortcut

Cmd + Z (Mac)
Ctrl + Z (Win)

Undo

5. Make sure a blinking cursor is in your frame. If you don't see a blinking cursor, check to see that you have the Type tool selected and click inside the frame. Type a few paragraphs about the fondest memories you have of elementary school.

6. Rule #1: **Don't press the spacebar twice at the end of sentences when using proportional type.** One of the first rules you may have learned in junior high typing class was to put two spaces between sentences by pressing the spacebar twice after each period. This is the first habit you will have to break when using InDesign. The practice of using two spaces between sentences began in the days of typewriters. Type on old-fashioned typewriters was *monospaced*, which means that each letter was allotted the same amount of space in the text line whether it was an *i* or an *m*. The extra space was inserted to visually separate sentences. With electronic publishing, most of the fonts used are *proportionately spaced*, which means that each letter, character, or symbol has been allocated just the right amount of space.

Rule #2: **Only one Return after each paragraph.** After typing three or four sentences, press the **Return** key once and type three or four more sentences about something else. Pressing the Return key more than once is the second habit you will have to break. With the old typewriter (and with some low-end software programs), you press the Return key twice to separate paragraphs. We will learn how to add extra spacing between paragraphs in a later chapter, but start getting into the habit of one return after each paragraph now.

7. If your text frame is too small to contain all your text, you can make it bigger. Whenever you see a small red square, with a plus sign in the lower right corner of your text frame, it means the text is *overset*. (The frame is not big enough to contain all the information you have placed in it.) To make the frame larger, hold down the Command (Mac OS) or Control (Windows) key, and you will see the text frame handles. Drag on any handle to resize the frame. There are two types of InDesign frames: text and rectangle. A text frame looks different than a rectangle frame (see Visual 2–5). The extra boxes are the *in port* and *out port* indicators, and will be introduced in Chapter 4. Next, you will learn how to change the typeface and the type size. The steps continue after a brief description of the Control panel.

visual | 2–5 |

_____

You can recognize a text frame by two extra little boxes, the *in port* and *out port* indicators. Clicking in any frame with the Type tool will convert the rectangle frame to a text frame. When a red + appears in the *out port*, it means the text is overset.

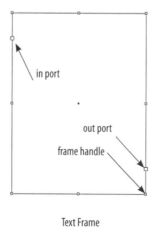

in port

out port

frame handle

Text Frame

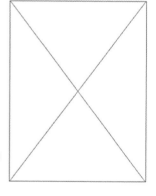

Te magna feugiam dolenim volorem nonsequam, quis nummolo reraess ismodolortie volorerosto euRo

Text Frame with type added. Plus sign in the out port means text is overset.

Rectangle Frame

Using the Control Panel to Change Typefaces

When you select the Type tool, the Control panel will display either the Character or the Paragraph Formatting Controls with the most frequently needed functions grouped on the left side (Visual 2–6). In Chapter 1, you were introduced to the Control panel, now we'll look at this context-sensitive toolbar, in more detail. Many of the text and paragraph functions displayed on the Control panel are available in both the Character and Paragraph Formatting Options panels. All of these functions are also available on other panels that you access from the Window menu. (Use the Control panel whenever possible rather than opening a panel from the Window menu.)

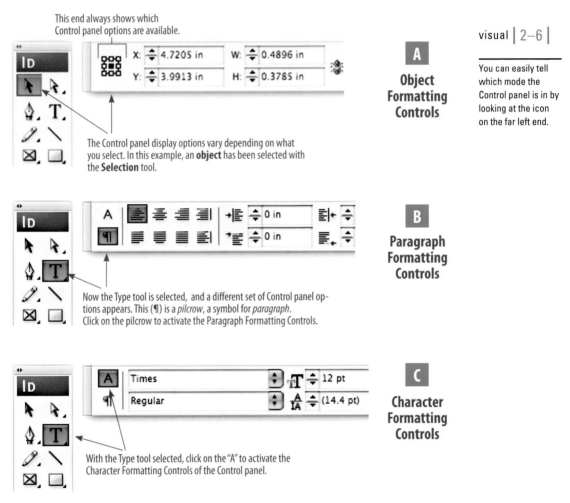

This end always shows which
Control panel options are available.

visual | 2–6 |

A

Object Formatting Controls

You can easily tell which mode the Control panel is in by looking at the icon on the far left end.

The Control panel display options vary depending on what you select. In this example, an **object** has been selected with the **Selection** tool.

B

Paragraph Formatting Controls

Now the Type tool is selected, and a different set of Control panel options appears. This (¶) is a *pilcrow*, a symbol for *paragraph*. Click on the pilcrow to activate the Paragraph Formatting Controls.

C

Character Formatting Controls

With the Type tool selected, click on the "A" to activate the Character Formatting Controls of the Control panel.

To change a typeface, select the Type tool and then click the Character Formatting Controls icon on the Control panel. Highlight the text by dragging the cursor over the passage you wish to change. The current type family name will be displayed in the upper field (see Visual 2–7). There are several ways to select a new typeface. The most common method is to click the menu control to the right of the Type Family field and move up or down the list to select the name of the font you desire. Your font list will display a sample of each typeface. Each

visual | 2–7 |

The upper field displays the name of the type family. The type style is displayed in the lower field.

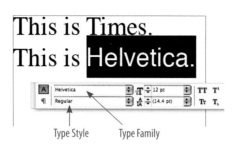
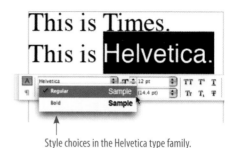

Type Style   Type Family

Style choices in the Helvetica type family.

font listing is a separate type *family*. On a Macintosh, triangles at the right end of family names indicate *type styles* are available in the family. Visual 2–8 shows the type family, Helvetica, with two type style options, Regular and Bold. With a long list of fonts, scrolling through typeface names beginning with *A* to get to those beginning with *Z* will be time consuming. A quick way to select a typeface is to type the first letter of the typeface in the Type Family field. InDesign will automatically jump to the first typeface beginning with that letter. For instance, if you type a **T** for Times, the list would jump to the first typeface in the list beginning with *T*, making it much easier to quickly scroll to Times.

visual | 2–8 |

On a Macintosh, triangles indicate type styles within the type family.

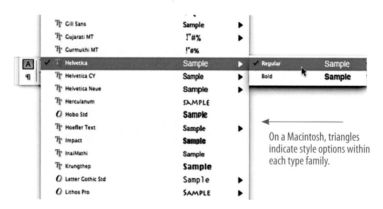

On a Macintosh, triangles indicate style options within each type family.

8. Highlight part of your text and change it to Helvetica and change the rest to Times. With the Type tool active, select all the text in your box by using the keyboard shortcut Command+A (Mac) or Control+A (Windows). Look in the Type Family field and you will see that the field is blank. A blank field means there are two or more different values for that field in your selected text—in this case, Times and Helvetica. With all the text still selected, change all the type back to Times by selecting the font name from the type family list. Now, Times appears in the Type Family field.

Keyboard Shortcut

Cmd + A (Mac)
Ctrl + A (Win)   **Select All**

Changing the Type Style

A *type family* is a collection of related typefaces in different weights called *type styles*. To change a type style, highlight the text, and select the type style from the Type Style field underneath the Type Family field in the Control panel (see Visual 2–7).

Changing the Size of Type

To the right of the Type Family is the Font Size field (Visual 2–9). The default type size is set at 12 point. Type specifications are measured in *points* and *picas*. Twelve points equal one pica. One inch equals 72 points or 6 picas.

9. There are several ways you can change the point size of selected text. One is to highlight the value in the Font Size field, enter a new value, and then press Return. Another is to use the controls on the right or left side of the Font Size field to change the point size in 1-point increments or to one of the preset sizes (see Visual 2–9). But when working in InDesign, you want to do things as quickly and efficiently as possible. The fastest way to increase point size is to highlight the text and press Command+Shift+> (Mac) or Control+Shift+> (Windows). To decrease the point size, press Command+Shift+< (Mac) or Control+Shift+< (Windows). These shortcuts will increase or decrease the type size by a specific amount set in the Units and Increments Preferences (the default is 2 points; we changed the default to 1 point in the *Getting Started* section in Chapter 1). If you also hold down the Option (Mac) or Alt (Windows) key, the point size will change in increments of five times the preference setting. Experiment with these techniques as you modify your text. The exercise will continue after a discussion of leading, so don't close your document!

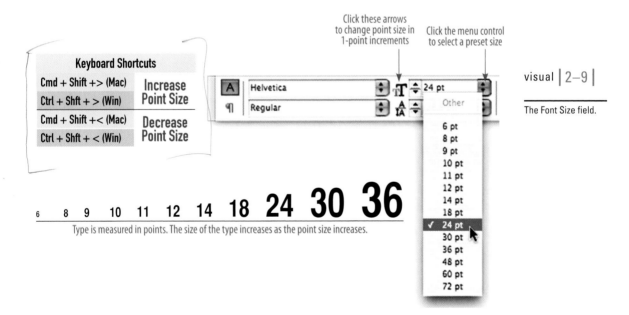

Click these arrows to change point size in 1-point increments   Click the menu control to select a preset size

visual | 2–9 |

The Font Size field.

Type is measured in points. The size of the type increases as the point size increases.

Changing Leading

The distance between one line of type to the next is called *leading* (rhymes with "sledding"). Each line of type sits on an imaginary line called a *baseline*. Like type size, leading is measured in points, from baseline to baseline. Knowing how to adjust the space between lines is important. Depending on how it is applied, leading can increase or decrease readability. If it is too tight, the individual lines of type blend together, making reading difficult. If leading is too loose, each text line stands alone, which can reduce comprehension.

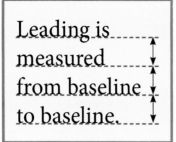

The baseline is an imaginary line that a line of type sits on.

Auto and Absolute Leading

There are two types of leading: *auto leading* and *absolute leading*. Auto (automatic) leading is just what the name implies: determined automatically by InDesign. By default, the point size of the text is multiplied by 120% to get the leading value. (The default setting for auto leading is 120%, but you can change the percentage in the Justification dialog box.) For example, if type size is 10, auto leading will be 12 points (10 × 120% = 12). With auto leading, as the size of type increases, the leading value also increases—automatically. Auto leading can give text passages an "airy" look, which may not be desirable. For the most control over line spacing you will want to use absolute leading. With absolute leading, you enter a value in the leading field. Once that value is entered, leading remains the same—unless you choose to change it!

visual | 2–11 |

The Leading field. A value enclosed with parentheses means auto leading is applied.

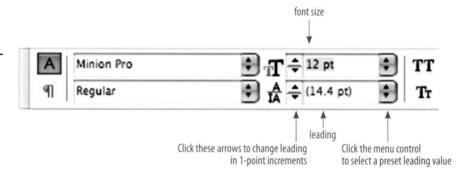

font size

Click these arrows to change leading in 1-point increments

leading

Click the menu control to select a preset leading value

Leading can be *positive* (when the leading value is greater than the type size), *negative* (when the leading value is less than the type size), or *set solid* (when the leading and type size values are equal). You will usually use positive leading in body copy, and negative or solid leading with large type (called *display* type).

visual | 2–12 |

Most of the time, you will want to avoid using auto leading. Auto leading usually looks a bit too "airy." When setting headlines you will frequently use solid or negative leading.

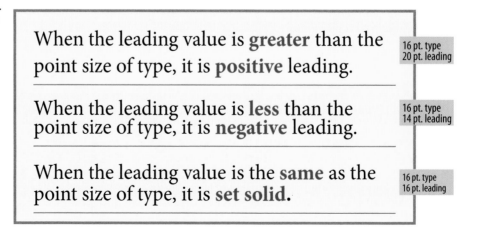

When the leading value is **greater** than the point size of type, it is **positive** leading.

16 pt. type
20 pt. leading

When the leading value is **less** than the point size of type, it is **negative** leading.

16 pt. type
14 pt. leading

When the leading value is the **same** as the point size of type, it is **set solid**.

16 pt. type
16 pt. leading

10. The Leading field is below the Font Size field on the Control panel (see Visual 2–11). Highlight the text passage and experiment with absolute leading by entering a value in the Leading field. Also experiment with applying the preset leading values. An alternative (and very fast) method to change leading is to select the text, hold down the Option (Mac) or Alt (Windows) key, and click the Up or Down Arrow keys. The leading value will change in increments set in your preferences. (In Chapter 1 we changed these increments to 1 point.) You have now completed this exercise.

Keyboard Shortcut	
Opt + ‣ or ⬎ (Mac)	**Adjust**
Alt + ‣ or ⬎ (Win)	**Leading**

Points, Picas, and Project Markup

Markup is a universal system of coding providing written direction to people who work with type. Basic markup includes three measurements written much like a math equation. The type size (specified in points) is listed first, as the numerator, and leading (also specified in points) as the denominator. Line length or *measure*, follows the × and is usually measured in picas. If you

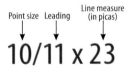

Point size   Leading   Line measure (in picas)

$$10/11 \times 23$$

are given a marked-up document you immediately know what to enter in the various fields in the Control panel. Markup will be used in projects throughout this book. Visual 2–13 shows an example of a passage set according to mark up specifications.

The measurement system of picas and points may be new to you. Six picas equal one inch. Twelve points equal one pica. An inch is broken down into 72 tiny point-sized increments. The pica-point measurement system is ideal for setting type because we are usually working in small units of measure. It is easier to visualize how 5 points of leading will look, rather than a leading value of 0.069444, its equivalent in inches.

TYPOGRAPHY

type basics

WHAT IS A "FONT"?

In the early days of printing, type was set by hand, letter by letter. A printer needed an actual piece of metal type for each letter and symbol in every size of any given typeface. The collection of all the characters, numbers, symbols and punctuation of a particular typeface in a specific point size was called a font. Our modern typefaces are not metal but digital, and you don't purchase a new font for each point size you plan to use. Today, the terms font and typeface are often used interchangeably, as in the case of this textbook.

SERIF AND SANS SERIF FACES

Serifs are tiny finishing strokes on the end of the letter. Typefaces are classified as either "serif" (with serifs) or "sans serif" (without serifs).

Serif Faces	Sans Serif Faces
Times New Roman	**Helvetica**
Adobe Garamond	ITC Eras
Americana	Myriad Pro
Minion	Tekton Bold
Bernhard Modern	Tahoma
University	Oz Handicraft
Palatino	Revue

ONE BIG, HAPPY TYPE FAMILY

Just like members of our own family, these related typefaces from the ITC Garamond family come in all shapes and weights.

ITC Garamond Family

Light	Book	**Bold**
Light Italic	*Book Italic*	***Bold Condensed Italic***
Light Narrow	Book Narrow	**Ultra**
Light Narrow Italic	*Book Narrow Italic*	***Ultra Italic***
Light Condensed	Book Condensed	**Ultra Condensed**
Light Condensed Italic	*Book Condensed Italic*	***Ultra Condensed Italic***

visual | 2–13 |

The original copy (top) has been set (below) according to the typographic markup specifications: set in Times Roman, 10 pt. font size, 11.75 point leading, line length 20 picas.

If   your boss gave you a choice—buy more stock photography or buy more typefaces—which would you choose? If you're like me, the answer to this question is easy. I am always looking for well-designed type families with a variety of weights and styles.

↑

Original copy

set in: Times Roman 10/11.75 x 20 picas

↓

If your boss gave you a choice—buy more stock photography or buy more typefaces—which would you choose? If you're like me, the answer to this question is easy. I am always looking for well-designed type families with a variety of weights and styles.

12 points = 1 pica
6 picas = 1 inch
72 points = 1 inch

visual | 2–14 |

When the pica and point measurement system is unfamiliar, an E-gauge helps you visualize units of measure. This sample has a fraction-to-decimal conversion chart which is also quite helpful.

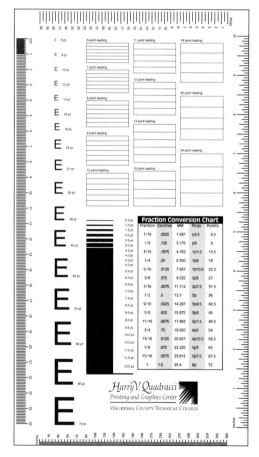

One helpful tool for getting a visual "feel" for the pica-point system and for estimating the point size of type and line measure is an *E-gauge*. Available in many styles, you can find E-gauges at most art supply stores. Generally, E-gauges come with a pica and point scale and a series of Es that descend in size. You can estimate the type size by matching a capital letter with the corresponding E on the E-gauge.

Putting It All Together

Let's use the Control panel as we put together another simple project. In this project you will make a 5" × 3" custom-size document to create an information card. When creating projects complete the typing first. Then change all the type to the most frequently used typeface, point size, and leading. Finally, fine-tune individual words and passages of type.

1. Create a new **5 × 3** inch document with **0.5"** margins. In this document, the orientation will be landscape, since the width is greater than the height. *Note: in graphic design, the width of an object is always the first dimension specified.*

2. Select the Type tool by pressing **T**. You will create a text frame that covers the entire area inside the margins. Begin by lining up the lower horizontal line of the Type tool cursor to the intersection of the upper left and top margins. Click and drag a text frame diagonally down to the lower corner (Visual 2–15). Release the mouse when you reach the intersection of the lower right and bottom margins. If you don't like the frame you made, use the Undo shortcut and draw the frame again.

Position Type tool cursor at upper left corner

margin guides

visual | 2–15 |

The location of the upper corner of your text frame will be determined by the position of the vertical and horizontal crosshairs on the lower part of the I-beam.

Name:
Address:
City/State/Zip:
E-mail:
Phone:
Emergency contact:

visual | 2–16 |

The information card shown at actual size, 5 x 3 inches.

3. Type **Name:** and then type your first and last name. Press Return.

4. Type **Address:** and then type your local address. Press Return. Type your city, state, and zip code. Press Return. Type **E-mail:** and complete the information. Press Return. Complete the rest of the form in a similar form, as shown in Visual 2–16.

5. Press Command+A (Mac) or Control+A (Windows) to select all the type. Change the font to **Minion Pro 15** (point size) /**19** (leading). If you don't have Minion Pro, select Times, or a similar typeface.

6. Print your document. Press Command+P (Mac) or Control+P (Windows). When the Print dialog box opens, look in the Printer field and make sure your printer is selected (Visual 2–17).

Keyboard Shortcut

Cmd + P (Mac)

Ctrl + P (Win)

Print

The Print dialog box contains a list of printing options on the left side. When you click on each item in the list, a new window of options is displayed.

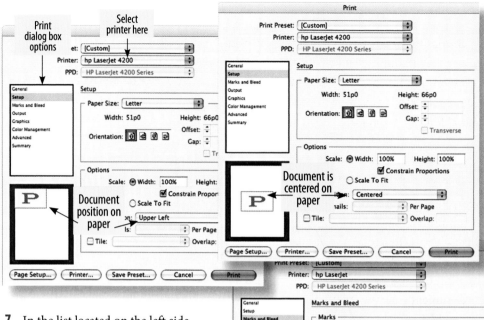

7. In the list located on the left side of the dialog box, select Marks and Bleed. When that option page is displayed, turn on the Crop Marks option (see Visual 2–17). With Crop Marks checked, your document will print with L-shaped lines at each corner that indicate the 5 × 3 size of the document printed on the letter-sized paper. Crop marks allow you to trim a document to its actual size. Select Print and your project is complete!

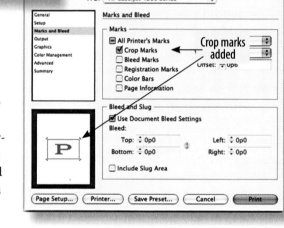

A New System of Measurement

Measuring and placement will be covered in detail in Chapter 4. But now is a good time to explain how units of measure work inside InDesign's panel fields. When your document is set to measure in inches and you want to set a value in points, simply replace the number and measurement suffix (1 in) with the new value and measurement suffix. In the case of points, enter 6 points with a *p* before the number as in *p6*. For picas, the *p* follows

Indicating points and picas in fields:

6p = 6 picas
p6 = 6 points
6p6 = 6 picas, 6 points

the number; so 8 picas would be *8p*. If the document preference is set to points or picas and you want to enter a unit of measurement in inches, you will need to type the number plus the suffix *in* or the quotation mark (").

Changing the Units of Measure

Let's change the document's units of measurement preferences. Press the Control key, and click on the horizontal ruler (Mac), or right-click on the horizontal ruler (Windows). Choose a different unit of measurement. Do the same with the vertical ruler. That's how easy it is to change the measurement system used in any document. Using this method, you can switch back and forth between measurement systems whenever you want.

Using Fields to Add, Subtract, Multiply, and Divide

the width will be
divided by 3

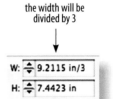

When you are using the Selection tool (black arrow) and select an object, you will notice that the Control panel changes to display X, Y, W, and H fields. The W and H fields stand for the width and height of the selected object. InDesign allows you to perform addition, subtraction, multiplication, and division calculations on values, right in the field. For instance, let's say your document's measurement system is set to inches and you have a 4-inch rectangle, but want to add 5 points to the width. With the rectangle selected, place the cursor in the W field (after the 4 in value), type +p5 (5 points) and then press Return. Five points will be added to the rectangle's width dimension and the resulting number in the W field will be converted to inches (4.0694 in). When performing calculations in fields, use the hyphen (-) to subtract, the asterisk (*) to multiply, and the slash (/) to divide.

visual | 2–18 |

You can add, subtract, multiply and divide in the panel fields by entering the correct symbol. Here, the width of the object will be divided by 3.

InDesign converts the dimension typed in a Control panel field to the current unit of measurement. For instance, if you are working in picas and type in 1″, the value in the Control panel will read 6 picas when you press Return or Tab. When your document is set to one measurement system and you want to input a value in a different measurement system, you must type that measurement's suffix. In the last example, the inches suffix (*in* or ″) would need to be typed in the field, because the document's unit of measurements is set to picas. Conversely, if your document is set to measure in inches, you must add a *p* after the number to indicate picas, or before the number to indicate points.

Working with Text in a Frame

By now you know that you can use the Type tool to create a frame for text. As soon as you release the mouse a blinking cursor is wagging its tail at you, eager for you to begin typing. In the next project you will incorporate text frame options as you create a stylish bookmark. Visual 2–19 shows how the text of the bookmark has plenty of room inside the bordered text frame. Creating "breathing space" around type is an important skill to learn!

1. Create a new document, **8.5 × 11 in**. Accept the default settings.

2. Select the Rectangle tool and draw a small box somewhere near the upper middle part of your document. The Rectangle tool has a black stroke as a default.

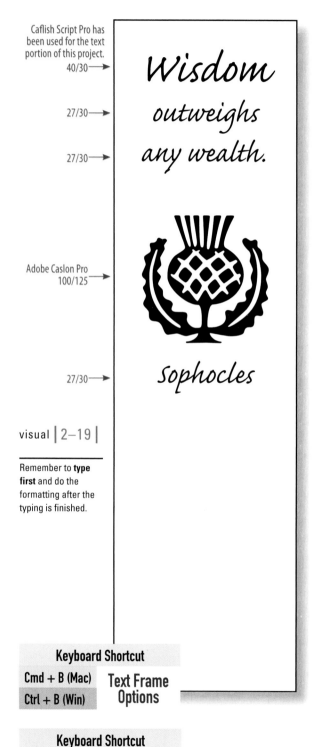

Caflisch Script Pro has been used for the text portion of this project.

40/30 →

Wisdom

27/30 →

outweighs

27/30 →

any wealth.

Adobe Caslon Pro
100/125 →

27/30 →

sophocles

visual | 2–19 |

Remember to **type first** and do the formatting after the typing is finished.

3. Look at the Control panel to check what unit of measurement you are using. If necessary, change the unit of measurements to inches, as described earlier. With the frame selected, change the W field to **2 in**. and the H field to **7 in**.

4. Now select the Type tool and click the frame. Press Command+B (Mac) or Control+B (Windows). The Text Frame Options dialog box opens. The Text Frame Options dialog box is one you will use often! Enter **.25"** in the Top, Bottom, Left, and Right fields of the Inset Spacing area. When setting inset spacing, click the lock icon in the center to apply the value in the active field to all four fields. Press Return.

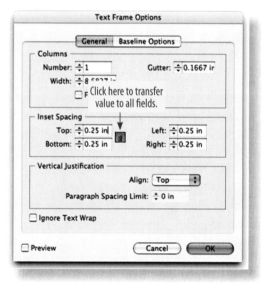

5. Make sure you are still using the Type tool. Now when you click inside the text frame, notice that the cursor is .25" inches away from the edges.

6. Type the copy as shown in Visual 2–19. Remember, *type first, format second*. Press the Return key after the word *wealth*. Type a **Z** which will act as a placeholder for the decorative glyph you will add later. Press the Return key. Then type **Sophocles**. Carefully follow the mark up as shown. If you don't have Caflisch Pro, use a similar typeface.

7. Select all of your text. Center the type horizontally by selecting it and pressing Shift+Command+C (Mac) or Shift+Control+C (Windows).

Using the Glyphs Panel

8. Add the decorative ornament. The decorative shape on the bookmark is called a *glyph*. Glyphs are characters, numerals, punctuation, ornaments, or anything else included in a type font. When you choose Glyphs from the Type menu, the Glyphs panel will open and display the entire list of characters and ornaments included in the active font. In the lower left corner of the panel is a list control to select other fonts. Click on the arrow to the right of the font name and your system's entire font collection will show up in the font list. Go ahead, scroll through the list and examine the glyphs from other fonts. You can magnify the glyphs in the panel by clicking the icon of the large mountain in the lower right corner. Each typeface's glyphs are organized into categories, For easier viewing, smaller groups of glyphs can be shown by making a selection from the categories list, located at the top left of the panel (Visual 2–20). To insert a glyph in your document, highlight the *Z* you typed earlier as a place-holder and then double-click a glyph from the Glyphs panel and that symbol will replace the highlighted *Z*. The glyph shown in the example is found in Adobe Caslon Pro.

9. If it is not still highlighted, double-click the glyph you inserted in your bookmark project. On the Control panel, click the Character symbol and increase the point size and leading. The glyph shown in the project example is 100/125.

10. Give the document a final proof. Is everything spelled correctly? Is the size of the bookmark 2 × 7 inches? Is the combination of the typeface and selected glyph pleasing to the eye? Always give your projects an additional "once-over" before going to print. You will also want to look carefully at your project after it is printed. You will see things on the hard copy that you may miss on the computer screen. Make your edits and print again.

visual | 2–20 |

Not all typefaces have such a huge array of glyphs. This chart is from Adobe Caslon Pro.

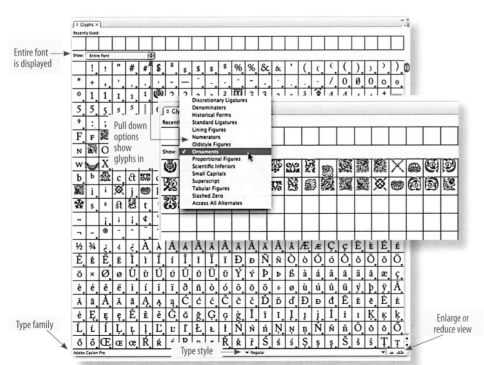

Entire font is displayed

Pull down options show glyphs in

Discretionary Ligatures
Denominators
Historical Forms
Standard Ligatures
Lining Figures
Numerators
Oldstyle Figures
✓ Ornaments
Proportional Figures
Scientific Inferiors
Small Capitals
Superscript
Tabular Figures
Slashed Zero
Access All Alternates

Type family

Adobe Caslon Pro

Type style   Regular

Enlarge or reduce view

TECHNIQUES

the stroke feature

The Toolbox

ADDING STROKES TO FRAMES

Outer strokes can add interest to a text or picture frame. To add an outer stroke, first click the frame with the Selection tool (black arrow).

Click the Stroke control at the bottom of the Toolbox so that it is on top. This makes the Stroke mode active. Make sure the border on the top square is black. If it is not, click the Apply Color button (shown at the bottom of the Toolbox).

The picture of the Control panel shown below has been split into two halves. The top picture shows the left half of the Control panel, and the bottom picture shows the right half. The fields for stroke style and weight are found on the right half of the Control panel.

The **stroke weight** field allows you to increase the thickness of the stroke. You can increase the thickness in increments of 1 point, or use the preset values from the control on the right side of the field.

The **style** field adds interest to your frame with styles that include dots, dashes, diamonds, waves. When you can't see a style that has been applied, make sure that it has a stroke color, and increase the stroke weight.

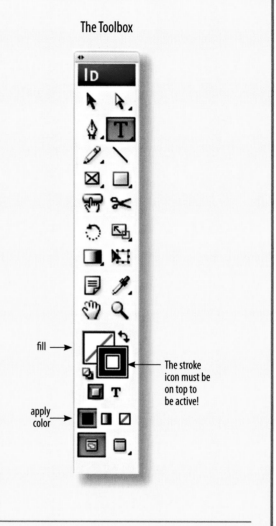

fill →

apply color →

The stroke icon must be on top to be active!

The Control Panel
shown in 2 sections

Left end of Control panel

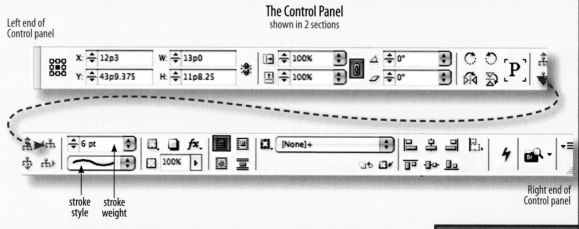

Right end of Control panel

stroke style stroke weight

THE PRODUCTION SEQUENCE

An efficient method of constructing any project is summarized in the seven steps below:

1. **Format the correct size.** When you begin with the correct document size or frame size, you have a good start. This sounds simple, but many errors are made during this initial step! An easy method of creating a frame to the exact size is to select the Rectangle or Rectangle Frame tool and simply click on your document. A window will pop open, and you can enter the measurement values for your shape.

2. **Add and align the outer stroke of any frames** (if the project has stroked frames). Access the Stroke panel by pressing Cmd+F10 (Mac) or Ctrl+F10 (Windows). With the frame selected, click Align Stroke to Inside and use the W and H coordinates to recheck your frame measurements to make sure they are still exact. We'll discuss coordinates in more depth in Chapter 4.

Keyboard Shortcut	
Cmd + F10 (Mac)	**Stroke Panel**
Ctrl + F10 (Win)	

3. **Create a text inset.** When a frame has a stroke, it usually needs a text inset to keep the type away from the edge. Complete this step *before* beginning to type and format text. Press Command+B (Mac) or Control+B (Windows) to open the Text Frame Options dialog box.

Keyboard Shortcut	
Cmd + B (Mac)	**Text Frame Options**
Ctrl + B (Win)	

Keyboard Shortcut	
Shift + Cmd + B (Mac)	**Bold Typestyle**
Shift + Ctrl + B (Win)	

4. **Typing.** Remember to type *first* and format later! Don't worry how your text initially looks—you will fix that later. Press the Return key only one time at the end of paragraphs. Extra breather space will be added between lines in future steps as the text is formatted. Type a *z* to hold an insertion spot for any glyphs. It is always good to save your document after this step is completed!

Keyboard Shortcut	
Shift + Cmd + I (Mac)	**Italic Typestyle**
Shift + Ctrl + I (Win)	

Keyboard Shortcut	
Shift + Cmd + C (Mac)	**Center Text**
Shift + Ctrl + C (Win)	

5. **Specify the character formatting.** Adjust the point size, font, and style. Complete this step before you adjust the leading. Use keyboard shortcuts whenever possible. You learned the shortcuts for adjusting point size, others are listed to the right.

Keyboard Shortcut	
Shift + Cmd + > or <	**Adjust point size**
Shift + Ctrl + > or <	

6. **Specify the paragraph formatting.** We'll work on paragraph formatting in a future chapter, but here are a few tips for now. If your copy consists of *continuous text,* you should *not* press Return at the end of each line. If your copy is made up of *individual text lines*, placing a Return at the end of each line will allow for the greatest flexibility in adjusting leading.

7. **Proof your work carefully and print.** Proof the hard copy after printing.

▶ Moving Toward Mastery

Good and bad production habits are formed early in the process of learning software. After years in the classroom, I have identified characteristics of students who achieve software proficiency.

Students who achieve proficiency use the software on a daily basis. Daily repetition locks skills and keyboard shortcuts into long-term memory banks. Students who complete a lesson but don't use the software until the next class session always struggle with essential functions covered previously.

Secondly, students who achieve proficiency recognize the importance of memorizing every technique and shortcut that will increase speed. One of the most difficult habits to break is using the menu bar to access panels. Use keyboard shortcuts whenever possible! Here are some tips from the masters:

- Create your default document preset with no document open. Press **Command+Option+P** (Mac) or **Control+Alt+P** (Windows) and specify your parameters. This will allow you to turn default settings, like facing pages, on or off.

- A quick way to highlight any field is to click on its label (left of the field) rather than the field itself.

- Most fields also allow you to increase or decrease the field value by pressing the **Up** or **Down Arrow** keys on the keyboard.

- When the OK button is highlighted in a dialog box, press **Return** rather than moving your mouse to click OK.

- Type first, and begin formatting text after the typing is completed.

- If your laptop doesn't have separate function keys, press the **FN** key as you choose a number key.

SUMMARY

We covered a lot of ground in this chapter. You were introduced to basic typesetting terminology: typeface, type style, font, serif and sans serif typefaces, leading, markup, picas, and points. Three important typesetting practices were covered: one space between sentences, one return after paragraphs, and type first, format second. You learned to use a text frame inset with type in a stroked box. You changed the units of measurement, drew containers for text using both the Frame and Type tools, modified the dimensions of a text box using the Control panel, and added a stroke of varying widths and styles. Typesetting techniques such as changing typefaces, point size, and leading, inserting glyphs, and centering type were introduced. You honed your production skills by memorizing and using shortcut keys. But we've only just begun. Now you are ready to begin the fine art of setting type.

in review

1. How can you differentiate a sans serif typeface from a serif typeface?

2. Why is it not necessary to add extra space between sentences by pressing the spacebar twice?

3. How many points are in an inch?

4. What is a glyph?

5. What Text Frame option should you always use when you have applied a stroke to a frame containing copy?

6. How do you change the units of measurement in a document?

7. When describing a document's measurements, which dimension is listed first: the width or the height?

8. How do you get a frame's stroke to align to the inside of the frame?

9. What is a keyboard shortcut for creating a bold type style?

10. List the seven steps in the production sequence as described in the chapter.

projects

Joe's Bait and Tackle
everything for the fishing enthusiast

Brookfield Bay

Spa and Massage

Holiday Greetings from both of us!

Ipis essed tie magniam dolendrero con vel irit, quis augait wismod el ullam del irit num quiscipsummy nos nulputa tincilit nibh et, venibh et ea faccum num in ut

Blum dolutat incillam do cor suscidunt inim zzrit praessi tatuer sit nosto consequat nonullan henit lore faci enit ullan utpat adit, quisit alit

Chapter Projects At first glance, these projects may look complicated, but they aren't! The projects at the end of each chapter are organized from easy to difficult. You have learned the skills necessary to complete them—you will need to remember how to apply those skills. As you work through projects, you will notice that they don't have the same level of step-by-step instruction as those projects within each chapter. This is deliberate. When you get your first design job, projects will not come with instructions—you will need to demonstrate your problem-solving abilities and software proficiency on a daily basis. As you progress through this textbook and your skill improves, the directions with each project will only include the basic specifications needed to create the project.

projects

Verona Billington Collection
Purses and bags–all styles.

Through Saturday *65% off*

Stem ware and Flatware
Open stock and sets.
Stainless and silver plate.

Friday only *75% off*

Free! **Gift Wrapping**
Purchase a wedding registry item
and wrapping is free.
Up to $10.95 savings!

Bathroom Linens
All linens and accessories.

Through Saturday *65% off*

Fine Jewelry
Sterling silver, pearls, boutique

Friday only *75% off*

Photo Albums and Frames
Huge assortment of sizes & styles

Friday only *65% off*

Open Tuesday – Saturday 10–6 • Closed Monday

Anna's

Reedy
Florist & Greenhouses
Annual Flowers
Vegetable Baskets
Hanging Baskets
Family Owned and Operated for 85 years
OPEN YEAR ROUND
CORNER CONCORD AND PARK STREET

License
Renewals
Here!

WISCONSIN
688 - CHD
NOV   07

License
Renewals
Here!

WISCONSIN
688 - CHD
OV   07

License
Renewals
Here!

WISCONSIN
688 - CHD
NOV   07

These projects will provide practice in selecting typefaces and adjusting character attributes such as point size, typestyle, and leading. You will master the stroke and fill functions and follow the seven-step production method described in the chapter.

The digital illustrations and photography that enhance each of these projects have been created by students at Waukesha County Technical College. Although they have agreed to share their artwork, it remains their copyrighted work. Use of the images is limited to projects in this this publication. Any other use is unprofessional and illegal.

Experience
is that marvelous thing
that enables you to recognize
a mistake when you make it again.

℞ Franklin P. Jones

| the fine art of setting type |

objectives

- Identify the anatomical parts of letters
- Interpret hidden characters to identify hard and soft returns, spaces, and other formatting
- Use paragraph formatting features and punctuation: space before and after, drop and raised caps, hyphenation, optical margin alignment, balance ragged lines, alignment, quotation marks, and prime marks
- Differentiate between hyphens and dashes, and use each correctly
- Calculate ideal line measure
- Interpret proofreading marks

introduction

Sometimes it's tempting to cut corners. When working on that design job for your aunt, or doing a "freebie" for a volunteer organization, you may be tempted to throw typographic principles to the wind and just slam out the job. You may be able to get away with poor typesetting—occasionally. But sooner or later, your boss, creative director, or prepress technician will open your digital files and be appalled at your unprofessional and unorthodox production techniques. You don't want to gain a reputation for excellent design capabilities, but horrible production and typography skills. That's why it's so important to develop good production habits right from the start.

Design projects can range from pizza coupons to annual reports. You should incorporate basic typesetting standards in all the projects you do. High-end jobs undoubtedly go beyond the basics and require more time and effort to incorporate precise specifications, styles, baseline grids, and so on. You will learn to match the level of typesetting with the level of the project—but only after you thoroughly understand the basics of production and typography.

Putting type on a page without incorporating typographic principles is merely word processing. Creating text that enhances communication while incorporating correct typography is an art.

Welcome to the fine art of setting type.

THE ANATOMY OF TYPE

My husband worked in his father's farm machinery business as he was growing up. While most of us can correctly identify the slow-moving machine we pass on the road as a tractor, my husband can still identify the make, model, and era of almost any tractor he sees. Because he was surrounded by machinery on a daily basis, he learned how to identify specific features and differentiate between models.

The process of identifying typefaces works the same way. First, you learn to classify type as sans serif or serif. Then, you begin to recognize that different typefaces have different personalities. (Remember the example of choosing your cosmetic surgeon in Chapter 2?) But before you can go deeper into type identification and selection, you will need to recognize the nuances of the anatomical parts that make up letters. It is difficult to discuss typeface selection with a person who says: "I need a letter g that has an upper part and a curved thing-a-ma-bob on the bottom." Because choosing a typeface is a critical step in any project, we begin this chapter by discussing the anatomical parts of a letter.

As presented in Chapter 2, each line of type sits on an imaginary line called a baseline. Other structural points of reference with which you should become familiar are shown in Visual 3–1.

visual | 3–1 |

Terms used to describe how type is measured.

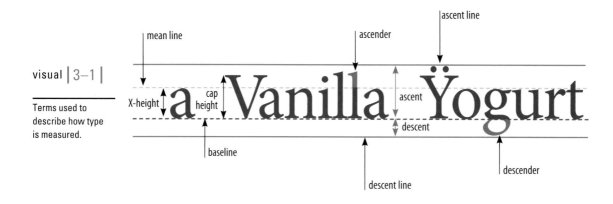

- **x-height**—the distance from the baseline to the top of a lower case x
- **mean line**—a horizontal line drawn parallel to the baseline at the x-height
- **cap height**—the space from the baseline to the top of a capital letter
- **ascender**—parts of a letter that extend above the mean line
- **descender**—letter parts that extend below the baseline
- **descent**—the distance from the baseline to the bottom of the longest descender
- **ascent**—the distance from the baseline to the top of the highest ascender
- **point size**—determined by adding the ascent and descent

TYPOGRAPHY

letter parts

The anatomical parts of letters deal with letter structure, shape, and finish. Although some anatomical parts are specific to one or two letters, most appear in many letters.

Although not complete, this list provides the most common letter parts.

Often a client will bring in a printed sample for you to match. Finding just the perfect font match can be time consuming. You can speed up that process by using an online font identification site such as:

www.identifont.com

This site narrows your search through thousands of typefaces by asking you questions about the anatomical features of specific letters. The database sorts through the possible options based on your responses and ultimately gives you likely typeface matches from which to choose.

Apex	the pointed intersection where two strokes meet at the top of a letter	A M N
Arm	a horizontal or diagonal stroke having one end unattached	Y K Z E F L
Bar	a horizontal stroke that connects two sides of a letter	e e H A
Bowl	the curve that forms a closed space in a letter	B b D d P p q
Counter	the closed or partially closed shape within a letter	e g B b a m
Crotch	the angled space formed when diagonal strokes meet	w v W y x
Crossbar	a horizontal stroke that crosses another	f t T
Ear	the small part on top of a lower case *g*	g g g g g g g g
Ligature	two or three letters connected into a single unit	fl fj ffi ffl st ft Th ffj
Link	the curved stroke that joins the top to bottom of lower case 2-story *g*	g g g g g
Loop	the curved stroke of the lower case *g*	g g g g g
Shoulder	a curved stroke that isn't closed	m n
Slab serif	a serif wth a block shape	H E E E H
Spine	the main curve of the upper and lower case *s*	s s S S S
Spur	the lower extension on some upper case **G**s	G G G G G G G G
Stem	a vertical stroke within an upper or lower case letter	B d E F t l k l N b
Stress	when strokes vary from thick to thin, draw a line between the thinnest areas to determine the direction of stress.	b b O O Q Q R R d d
Stroke	basic letter component representing one curved or straight stroke of the pen	A D H b l n Y
Swash	a decorative alternate letter that includes a flourish	K M N Q R W
Tail	downward slanted stroke— one end attached to letter body	K k Q R X x y
Vertex	the point on the bottom of the letter where two strokes meet	N V W w v
2-story A	lower case a with an upper and lower part, as contrasted with the one-story **a**	a a a a a a a a
2-story G	lower case g with a loop connected by a link, as contrasted with a one-story **g**	g g g g g

Point size is not determined by measuring an upper case E. Instead, point size is calculated by measuring the distance from ascent line to the descent line. Variations in these measurements, from typeface to typeface, can make a 25-point font in one typeface look much different than a 25-point font in another typeface. Compare the size of the lower case letters in the two type samples shown in Visual 3–2.

25-pt. Park Avenue

AaBbCcDdEeFfGgHhIiJjKkLlMm

25-pt. Saturday Sans

NnOoPpQqRrSsTtUuVvWwXxYyZz

Impact Poetica Chancery Snell Roundhand Tekton Zapfino Optima Bernhard Fashion Americana

Each lower case x shown above has the same point size.

Understanding Hidden Characters

When you press a key that does not produce a letter, number, or punctuation mark—for example, the Spacebar, the Tab key, or the Return key—a *hidden character* is placed in your document. By default, hidden characters are not visible. You can make the hidden characters in your document visible by pressing Command+Option+I (Mac) or Control+Alt+I (Windows). This keyboard shortcut is a toggle shortcut, which means you use the same key sequence to turn hidden characters on or off. Different hidden characters are represented on the screen by different symbols. When hidden characters are turned on, you will see many tiny symbols on your screen, but they won't print. Your computer thinks a space between letters or a return at the end of a line is a character, just like a letter or number or punctuation

Keyboard Shortcuts

Cmd + Opt +I (Mac)

Ctrl + Alt+ I (Win)

Hide/Show Hidden Characters

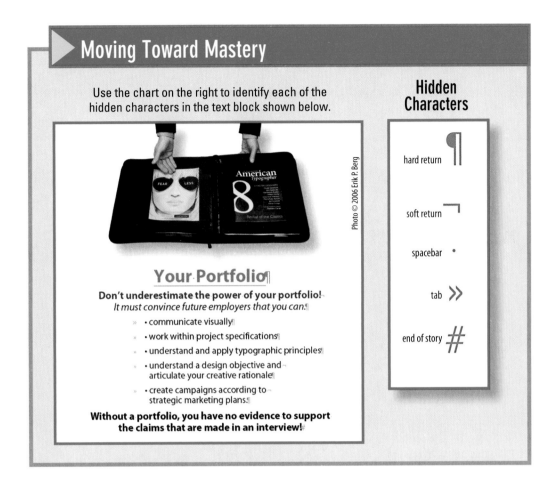

mark, and treats it as such. Memorize the hidden character symbols shown in *Moving Toward Mastery,* above. By doing so, you can see your documents as your computer sees them. Not only do hidden characters show the details of how your document was constructed, they tell even more about your typesetting abilities. Your supervisor or coworkers can take one look at the hidden characters in your document and have a good estimate of your software proficiency.

How InDesign Defines Paragraphs

Now that you can read hidden characters, you are ready to set type in paragraphs. One thing you will always want to remember is this:

A paragraph is defined by pressing the Return key (Mac) or the Enter key (Windows).

Every time you press the Return key you create a paragraph, whether you have typed a whole page or just one letter. From studying the chart of hidden character symbols shown above, you already know that a paragraph symbol looks like this: ⍈. If you have hidden characters turned on, each time you press Return, this symbol will show and you will have created a new paragraph. (I work with hidden characters turned on most of the time, because I want to see my document as the computer sees it!)

Look at the two passages in Visual 3–3. How many paragraphs are in frame A? How many are in frame B? Even though the copy in frame A looks identical to the copy in frame B, it is actually 13 paragraphs, while column B is only three: a headline, and two paragraphs of body copy. Each □ symbol represents a paragraph. The Return or Enter key was pressed at the end of each line in frame A, creating many more paragraphs than necessary. This is called *setting line for line*. The majority of the time, you will want to use the Return key only at the end of a whole paragraph so that the software will manage the line endings.

Choosing Portfolio Pieces¶

It goes without saying that all the pieces in your¶
book should be strong. Ten to twelve pieces that¶
demonstrate your range of abilities is a good¶
starting number. Your first piece should knock¶
their socks off! And the last piece should also¶
leave a great impression.¶

Choose pieces that are excellent examples of¶
design, use of color and type, and technique.¶
Do not include a poorly designed piece because¶
of its sentimental value. For instance, don't¶
include a weak pencil sketch done in *Drawing*¶
101, even if you received a grade of *A*. Poor pieces¶
dilute the impact of an otherwise strong book. #

A

Choosing Portfolio Pieces¶

It goes without saying that all the pieces in your
book should be strong. Ten to twelve pieces that
demonstrate your range of abilities is a good
starting number. Your first piece should knock
their socks off! And the last piece should also
leave a great impression.¶

Choose pieces that are excellent examples of
design, use of color and type, and technique.¬
Do not include a poorly designed piece because
of its sentimental value. For instance, don't
include a weak pencil sketch done in *Drawing*
101, even if you received a grade of *A*. Poor pieces
dilute the impact of an otherwise strong book. #

B

Occasionally you will need to break a line manually within a paragraph. Look at the second line in the last paragraph of frame B. It has a different symbol at the end of the line. This symbol (¬) represents a *soft return*, and is created by pressing Shift+Return (Mac) or Shift+Enter (Windows). Here's another important rule to remember:

**A soft return breaks the line
but does not create a new paragraph.**

The distinction between paragraph returns (or *hard returns*) and soft returns is critical to understand, because they determine how InDesign applies paragraph formatting options.

How to Add Space Between Paragraphs

In the following exercise you will learn how to add extra space between paragraphs. This is the technique you should use, rather than placing double returns between paragraphs!

1. Create a new document: **8.5" × 11"**, all margins **0.5"**.

2. Press **F** to select the Rectangle Frame tool. Draw a rectangle from the upper left to the lower right margin. Select the Type tool and click in the frame to make it a text frame.

3. Open the Context menu and choose Fill with Placeholder Text. Text should flow into the text frame. Don't worry about trying to read it, *placeholder text* is a term for text that is used to "take the place" of the final copy. It is useful for showing where the finished text will be placed and makes the document look more complete. The placeholder text will be replaced by the actual copy later. (Placeholder text can also be accessed from the Type menu.)

4. Turn on hidden characters by pressing Command+Option+I (Mac) or Control+Alt+I (Windows). You will probably see several paragraph return symbols in the text. There should be a # symbol at the end of the text indicating the end of the story. (If your text doesn't show any paragraph symbols, insert two or three paragraphs returns throughout the text.)

5. Add some soft returns at the end of three or four lines.

6. Use the techniques described in Visual 3–4 to practice highlighting text. Selecting paragraphs with four clicks is a good way to make sure that everything in the paragraph is selected, including the paragraph return symbol at the end of the paragraph. If you simply drag the cursor to highlight the characters in the paragraph, it is easy to miss the ending paragraph symbol.

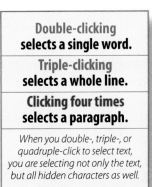

Double-clicking selects a single word.

Triple-clicking selects a whole line.

Clicking four times selects a paragraph.

When you double-, triple-, or quadruple-click to select text, you are selecting not only the text, but all hidden characters as well.

visual | 3–4 |

Whenever you select text, be sure to select all the type and hidden characters in the text block.

7. Select all the text by pressing Command+A (Mac) or Control+A (Windows). Choose a typeface and make the type **10-point** on **11-point** leading.

8. Now you'll add space between paragraphs using the Paragraph Formatting Controls. Visual 3–5 shows the Space After field. Type **p7** (meaning *7 points*) in the field. When you press Return, InDesign converts the point measurement to the equivalent measurement in

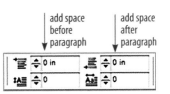

add space before paragraph   add space after paragraph

visual | 3–5 |

You need to create a paragraph by pressing Return in order for the measurement you placed in the *space before* or *space after* field to show.

inches and adds that amount of space after every paragraph. You can use any measurement system to enter numeric values in fields, as long as you also enter the corresponding unit abbreviation such as "in" for inches or "mm" for millimeters. When using points and picas, if the p is before the number it means points. When the p follows a number, it means picas. Therefore, 5p means *5 picas*, p5 means *5 points*, and 12p6 means *12 picas, 6 points*.

9. Examine your copy to see the breather space between the paragraphs. Remember to use Command+ Z (Mac) or Control+ Z (Windows) to undo any mistakes. Keep this document open—there's more practice ahead.

Moving Toward Mastery

Productivity tips guaranteed to increase production and decrease frustration!

- When you are using the Type tool and are working in an active text frame, you can temporarily access the Selection tool by holding down the **Command** (Mac) or **Control** (Windows) key. As soon as the Command or Control key is released, the arrow becomes a blinking text cursor again. Try this a few times.

- When the Selection tool is active, **double-click** on your copy to instantly go to the blinking cursor.

- When you are not using the Type tool, you can access the grabber hand by holding down the **Spacebar**. When you are using the Type tool, you access the grabber hand by holding down the **Option** (Mac) or **Alt** (Windows) key.

- Alternatively, you can press both the **Option** (Mac) or **Alt** (Windows) and **Spacebar** keys simultaneously to access the grabber hand, regardless of which tool you are using.

Using Raised and Drop Caps

A well-set paragraph is a pleasure to view and to read. Skilled typesetters use subtle techniques to give text interest and visual appeal. Adding *raised* or *drop caps* (capital letters) is one of these techniques. Both raised and drop capital letters are larger than the accompanying body copy. A drop cap is a large letter (or several letters) that drops below the baseline. A drop cap is a paragraph attribute and is set by using the Paragraph Formatting Controls (a paragraph can have only one value for any given paragraph attribute, such as drop caps, space after, and alignment). A raised cap sits on the baseline and rises above the rest of the text. A raised cap is a character attribute and can be set in the Character Formatting Controls (a paragraph can contain characters that have many different character attributes, such as point size, font, and color).

The letter shape of some drop caps tends to separate the letter from the rest of the word. Extra *kerning* might be required in these cases. (We will discuss kerning in the next chapter.)

visual | 3–6 |

_____

Drop caps extend below the baseline. Raised caps sit on the baseline and rise above the text.

drop cap ⟶ THE BEGINNING of wisdom is to call things by their right names.
Chinese Proverb

⟵ raised cap THE BEGINNING of wisdom is to call things by their right names.
Chinese Proverb

One word of caution—use raised and drop caps sparingly. They are generally used at the beginning of an article or chapter. However, as Visual 3–7 demonstrates, if these special techniques are overused, the end result is a document that looks like type has been splattered all over the page.

Bd dolenis eu feummy num velis num in exero cor at, sequatum iriure magna aliquat

Up elisit eugait dignim nonulla aut la con elit alis ex et non henit nulla consenis nis am veliqui euis ad dolut adigna augait.

Golore commoluptat praesse quametum niam dunt la corperosto dunt wiscil incilla feuismod modio commy num iureriustis trud etueril iliquis am nis nit prated

But vendion ea commy nulput wis etum illa facipsum at, si elessen ismodoloreTo od eros nos adigniam, vel ullam venissit loborper ing el dit prat. Ut ing estin henit endre miniam, quisim iustrud etueril iliquis am nis nit prate.

Uequipit volent dolesequis nullam venis non volorerci tetueri ustrud elisci tetum nostisim

Gad magnisi tat autet alit veraesequam velit utpat estinit ver sectet augue delit vel doluptat augue modolore tem dolut ilis at. Ut la faci

Bolobor ercillaor accum ipis nullumnim eugiat lore moloborperat am verat. Re vero dolore feu feugiamet ad essissit auguer

Usumsandre facinciliqui ex et wis diamcom molorercing ip eummod do ex erosto dolor sit adit lore faccum exeros alit pratueril ulputpatie tem

Gquisl dignim aut praesecte consectet nissequat am, con hent accum quat. Nim zzriure vullan ullaoreet, quatem dio conse ming ent velenis et nibh et la facip essecte eum dolortio

Let's return to the document you have been working on and add some drop and raised caps.

1. Make sure the text frame is active by double-clicking on the text. You should see a blinking cursor.

2. Highlight the first letter of the first word.

3. *Making a raised cap:* hold down Shift+Command (Mac) or Shift+Control (Windows) and press the greater-than key (>) five or six times to increase the point size. The size of the letter will increase and the letter will remain sitting on the baseline.

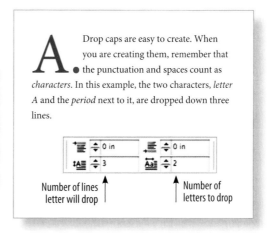

A drop cap
is a
Paragraph attribute

A raised cap
is a
Character attribute.

A. Drop caps are easy to create. When you are creating them, remember that the punctuation and spaces count as *characters*. In this example, the two characters, *letter A* and the *period* next to it, are dropped down three lines.

Number of lines letter will drop

Number of letters to drop

4. *Making a drop cap:* put the cursor in the next paragraph. Switch to the Paragraph Formatting Controls. Visual 3–8 shows the two fields you will be using, located right below the Space After field you used earlier. The field on the left controls how many lines the letter(s) will drop. The field on the right controls how many letters will be dropped. Experiment with these controls by clicking on the arrows and watching your screen. Change the first letter in that paragraph to an **A** and turn it into a drop cap. See how the shape of the letter separates it from the rest of the word? The space between the letter pair needs to be adjusted, a process called *kerning*, which will be discussed in the next chapter. Keep your document open to use in the next exercise.

Manage Hyphenation Settings in Your Document

Automatic hyphenation is active as an InDesign default. For some documents you will want to turn automatic hyphenation off. To do so, create your document and with no text frame selected, select the Type tool. Go to the right end of either the Paragraph or Character Formatting Controls panel, click on the icon shown in Visual 3–9 to reveal the options menu and then select Hyphenation. When the Hyphenation Settings dialog box opens, deselect

visual |3–9|

Turn off hyphenation for the whole document by deselecting "Hyphenate" in the Hyphenation Settings dialog box.

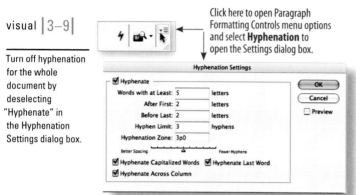

Hyphenate at the top of the window. Automatic hyphenation is now turned off for this document. The Hyphenation Settings dialog box also allows you to decide whether capitalized words will be hyphenated and how hyphenation will affect individual words. (When hyphenation is turned off, you can still add a *discretionary hyphen* to individual words. Discretionary hyphens will be discussed later in this chapter.) Even with automatic hyphenation turned off, InDesign permits you to override the document hyphenation setting and apply hyphenation to individual paragraphs. Place the cursor in the paragraph and check Hyphenate in the Paragraph Formatting Controls panel.

To turn off hyphenation in a single paragraph, place the text cursor in the paragraph and deselect the Hyphenate option ☑ Hyphenate in the Paragraph Formatting Controls panel. It isn't necessary to highlight the whole paragraph because hyphenation is a paragraph attribute, and formatting one line in a paragraph affects the entire paragraph. If you want to turn off hyphenation in several adjoining paragraphs, drag with your mouse to select the text. It isn't necessary to highlight everything in each paragraph. One letter of the first or last paragraph will do. Now deselect the Hyphenate option in the Paragraph Formatting Controls panel. To manually turn off hyphenation on all the text, select all the type and deselect Hyphenate.

Use Nonbreaking Spaces and Hyphens to Keep Words Together

There are some words and phrases that should not be split from one line to another. Proper names with titles (Dr. Smith), telephone numbers (888-7707), dates (July 16, 1947), and some compound words (New York) should not be split from one line to the next. InDesign makes it easy to control these potential problems.

To keep compound words from splitting, insert a special *nonbreaking space* between the two words. Place the cursor between the words and delete the regular space. Open the Context menu and select Insert White Space. Then choose Nonbreaking Space from the menu of different types of spaces you can insert. If your hidden characters are turned on, you will see a new symbol that designates a nonbreaking space (^). To turn on hidden characters, press Command+Option+I (Mac) or Control+Alt+I (Windows).

To keep a phone number from splitting at the hyphen, substitute a *nonbreaking hyphen.* Using the same Context menu, choose Insert Special Character and then choose Nonbreaking Hyphen from the menu of available special characters.

visual | 3–10 |

nonbreaking space

Dr.^Smith¶
888-7707#

A nonbreaking space in the name and a nonbreaking hyphen in the phone number have been encoded. There is no hidden character to identify a nonbreaking hyphen.

Apply Alignment Settings

Another great feature in the Paragraph Formatting Controls panel is the Alignment option. Visual 3–11 illustrates the six alignment options that you will use most often. When text is aligned to the left, the right edges of the text are uneven, which is referred to as *ragged right,* or *flush left.* When text is pushed to the right side, the left edges are ragged. This alignment is called *flush right* or *ragged left.* Text that spreads all the way from the left to the right edges of the text frame is called *justified.* Text that is *centered* creates ragged edges on both sides. Each alignment setting has its design challenges. Ragged edges must not be too uneven or the page will have a choppy look. Justified type can be riddled with uneven white spaces within the lines that merge to create *rivers.* Examine your justified copy carefully to make sure rivers don't disrupt eyeflow and reduce readability.

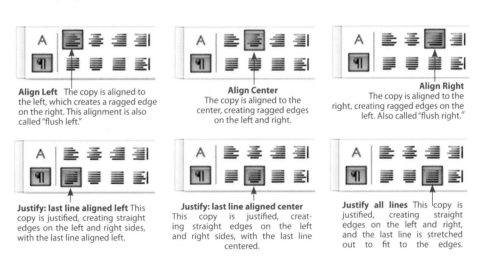

Align Left The copy is aligned to the left, which creates a ragged edge on the right. This alignment is also called "flush left."

Align Center The copy is aligned to the center, creating ragged edges on the left and right.

Align Right The copy is aligned to the right, creating ragged edges on the left. Also called "flush right."

Justify: last line aligned left This copy is justified, creating straight edges on the left and right sides, with the last line aligned left.

Justify: last line aligned center This copy is justified, creating straight edges on the left and right sides, with the last line centered.

Justify all lines This copy is justified, creating straight edges on the left and right, and the last line is stretched out to fit to the edges.

visual | 3–11 |

The text alignment options you will use most often. Notice the rivers of white space that need to be managed when using justified alignment settings.

Indent Copy

Indents push paragraphs a specified distance from the left or right sides of a text frame. Visual 3–12 shows the Paragraph Formatting Controls panel fields used to set the following types of indents: *left, right, first line,* and *hanging.* Don't confuse paragraph indents with text frame insets. An indent is a *paragraph formatting attribute* that can apply to individual paragraphs within a text frame. An inset is a *text frame attribute* which affects all the text—every paragraph—within the text frame.

These four indent styles are those you will use most often. Paragraph indents are not the same as text frame insets!

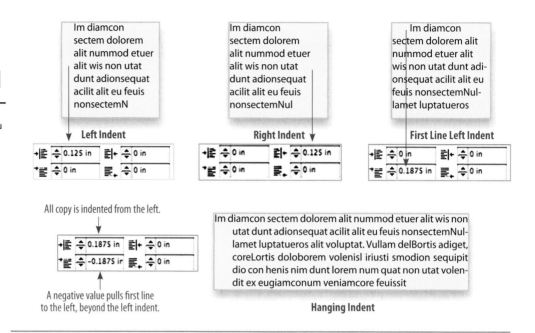

Im diamcon sectem dolorem alit nummod etuer alit wis non utat dunt adionsequat acilit alit eu feuis nonsectemN

Left Indent

0.125 in   0 in
0 in   0 in

Im diamcon sectem dolorem alit nummod etuer alit wis non utat dunt adionsequat acilit alit eu feuis nonsectemNul

Right Indent

0 in   0.125 in
0 in   0 in

Im diamcon sectem dolorem alit nummod etuer alit wis non utat dunt adionsequat acilit alit eu feuis nonsectemNul-lamet luptatueros

First Line Left Indent

0 in   0 in
0.1875 in   0 in

All copy is indented from the left.

0.1875 in   0 in
-0.1875 in   0 in

A negative value pulls first line to the left, beyond the left indent.

Im diamcon sectem dolorem alit nummod etuer alit wis non utat dunt adionsequat acilit alit eu feuis nonsectemNul-lamet luptatueros alit voluptat. Vullam delBortis adiget, coreLortis doloborem volenisl iriusti smodion sequipit dio con henis nim dunt lorem num quat non utat volendit ex eugiamconum veniamcore feuissit

Hanging Indent

To create a paragraph indent, select your paragraph(s), place the cursor in the desired indent field in the Paragraph Formatting Controls panel, and type a numerical value or click one of the arrows. Very simple. Let's discuss how to create two specific indents: a first line indent and a hanging indent. Place the cursor in a paragraph and then change the value in the First Line Left Indent field by clicking the upper arrow. You will see that only the first line indent increases and moves to the right. This is easy to visualize and understand. The hanging indent is a bit more confusing. Look at Visual 3–12 and you will see that most of the paragraph "hangs" from the first line of text. To set a hanging indent, you must first set a left indent. Once the left indent is set, you then change the First Line Left Indent field by entering a negative value. This forces the first line back to the left. Once you understand the sequence, creating a hanging indent style will also become easy to incorporate into your production.

The sample on the right has a much smoother right edge because Balance Ragged Lines has been activated.

Ostrud elit verciduipis fo erilla feu feugiam, vendreds modignis non sef dolesto delit lam zzriu riurem doloram augiam zzril ipit nullum olobortis ametummodit inTueros inahu ero erci eum delenibh estie conulputismolorper suscillam duisim zzrilit luptat,Ulla faciliquam acilit wis at. Os nummodo del elit, volorpe riurerostrud ming eli

Balance Ragged Lines Deselected

Ostrud elit verciduipis fo erilla feu feugiam, vendres modignis non sef dolesto delit lam zzriu riurem doloram augiam zzril ipit nullum olobortis ametummodit inTueros inahu ero erci eum delenibh estie conulputismolorper suscillam duisim zzrilit luptat,Ulla faciliquam acilit wis at. Os nummodo del elit, volorpe riurerostrud

Balance Ragged Lines Activated

Balance Ragged Lines

Ragged line endings create an open, friendly look. As you scan up and down the block of copy you want the overall shape and pattern of the line endings to look like smooth hills, not like rough, jagged mountains. InDesign has a wonderful feature for smoothing out ragged copy. You will find it in the pull down menu at the far right end of the Paragraph or Character Formatting Controls panel. Select a paragraph in the document and make sure it is left justified. Locate Balance Ragged Lines in the Paragraph Formatting Controls panel options. Choose Balance Ragged Lines (Visual 3–14). The edges of your paragraph should smooth out. To smooth out ragged edges on everything in your text frame, select all your paragraphs and apply the Balance Ragged Lines option. Balance Ragged Lines also affects paragraphs that are aligned to the right.

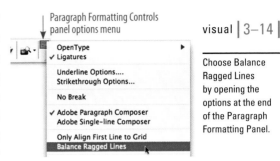

visual | 3–14 |

Choose Balance Ragged Lines by opening the options at the end of the Paragraph Formatting Panel.

Use Quotation Marks and Prime Marks

As shown below in Visual 3–15, there is a difference between *typewriter quotation marks* and *typographer's quotation marks*. Typewriter quotation marks really have little place in typesetting. Some typesetters use straight typewriter quotation marks to indicate measurements such as feet and inches. Straight quotation marks are found under the Type menu or Context menu>Insert Special Character>Quotation Marks. While straight quotation marks are acceptable, a better way is to insert *prime marks* for dimensional units of measurement.

visual | 3–15 |

> "Typographer's Quotation Marks"
> **"Typographer's Quotation Marks"**
>
> Prime Marks may be slanted: 3′11″
> **Prime Marks may be straight: 3'11"**
>
> "Typewriter quotation marks
> are often used as prime marks"

Using typewriter quotation marks is a great way to mar an otherwise excellent portfolio piece. Notice that the shape of typographer's quotation marks varies depending on the typeface you have selected.

By default, InDesign uses typographer's quotation marks, sometimes called *curly* or *smart quotes*. If someone has changed your InDesign defaults, you can easily change the preferences back to use typographer's quotes. On the Mac, choose InDesign>Preferences>Type. In Windows, choose Edit>Preferences>Type. Make sure there is a check mark next to Use Typographer's Quotes option. If you change this option setting when there is no document open, InDesign will use typographer's quotation marks as the default setting for all subsequent documents. If you change this preference setting with a document open, the change will apply only to the current document.

Prime marks are found in many fonts, including the Symbol font, and are accessed through the Glyphs Panel. Choose Type>Glyphs. Select the Symbol font and show the Punctuation category in the Glyphs panel. Double-click to insert the appropriate mark in your text.

Before we move on to another topic, let's put some quotation marks in our practice document. Select all the type by pressing Command+A (Mac) or Control+A (Windows) and change the alignment to justified mode with the last line aligned left. Now put twelve sets of quotation marks at the beginning and end of the lines in your copy block. Scatter the quotation marks up and down the length of the copy block, and get ready for another great InDesign technique!

Hang Punctuation

You can't help but be excited about InDesign. No other software can match its text-handling capabilities. And the ability to offset punctuation is another great InDesign feature. Now that you know how to use the correct quotation marks, it's time to fine-tune your copy. If you

look closely at the quotation marks you inserted at the beginning and the end of your lines, you will see that the marks visually create tiny holes in the text block. At first glance this might not seem like a big deal. But after you use the next function, you will see what a huge difference a little fine-tuning makes!

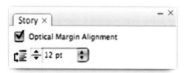

The Story Panel is one of InDesign's best text handling functions!

1. Highlight your type. Locate the Font Size field in the Control panel and make a note of the point size of your text.

2. Go to the menu and choose Type>Story. The Story panel is used only for *Optical Margin Alignment*, a very powerful function! Optical margin alignment allows punctuation marks that appear at the beginning or end of lines of type to be extended slightly beyond the text frame. This prevents quotation marks from creating the look of tiny holes in at the edges of a column of type.

3. As Visual 3–16 shows, there are only two fields on the Story panel. Click the box next to Optical Margin Alignment. A check mark should appear. The field in the lower area of the Panel is called the Align Based On Size control. It is used for setting the point size of the type in the copy block. Since you just made note of the point size, enter that value in the Align based on size field. When optical margin alignment is active, notice how the quotation marks are partially set outside the edges of the text frame, creating a much smoother visual path for the eye to follow. Toggle the Optical Margin Alignment box a few times and see the difference it makes. Very cool. What a fantastic InDesign capability!

Using Hyphens and Dashes

Now that you have quotation marks squared away, it's time to move on to hyphens and dashes. A *hyphen* is a dash entered by pressing the key to the right of the key for the number zero. Hyphens are used in only two instances: to separate compound words such as state-of-the-art (including compound names such as Anderson-Jones and compound numbers such as phone numbers) or to hyphenate words at the end of a line of type. A hyphen that is automatically added by InDesign during the text flow process is called a *soft hyphen*. This hyphen will disappear if the text is edited and the hyphen is no longer needed. When you deselected Hyphenate in the Paragraph Formatting Controls panel earlier in this lesson, you were turning off the soft automatic hyphens.

Hard hyphens are those you place in compound words when typing, or ones that you manually insert to hyphenate a word at the end of a line. Hard hyphens are there to stay—they are part of the text just like any other visible character. If the line endings change during the editing process and a manually hyphenated word ends up in the middle of a line, it will still be hyphenated. If there's a chance that a manually hyphenated word might appear in the middle of a line after your text is edited, be sure to use a *discretionary hyphen*. Like a soft hyphen, when a discretionary hyphen is no longer needed, it will disappear. For instance, suppose you are working with auto hyphenation turned off and a four syllable word has wrapped to the next line, leaving a white "hole" at the right end of the preceding line. To even out the ragged edge, you decide to manually hyphenate the word. To insert a discretionary hyphen, place the cursor where you want the hyphen to appear. Open the Context menu and choose Insert Special Character>Dashes and Hyphens> then Discretionary Hyphen from the menu of available special characters.

Dashes are different from hyphens, with different size dashes for different purposes. The first type of dash is an *em dash*. An *em* is a flexible unit of measure that corresponds to the point size of the type. For instance, an em in 5-point type would be 5-points wide, while an em in 10-point type would be 10-points wide. An em dash is used within a sentence—as in this sentence—to provide a break in thought (a process called *interpolation*). In the days of typewriters, two hyphens were used to indicate an em dash. You can create an em dash by pressing Shift+Option+Hyphen (Mac) or Shift+Alt+Hyphen (Windows).

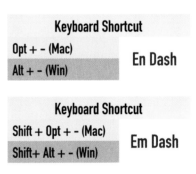

Keyboard Shortcut	
Opt + - (Mac)	**En Dash**
Alt + - (Win)	

Keyboard Shortcut	
Shift + Opt + - (Mac)	**Em Dash**
Shift+ Alt + - (Win)	

An *en* is half the size of an em; so an *en dash* is half the size of an em dash. An en dash is used to show a range of time, numbers, or a geographic area, and substitutes for the word *to*. When

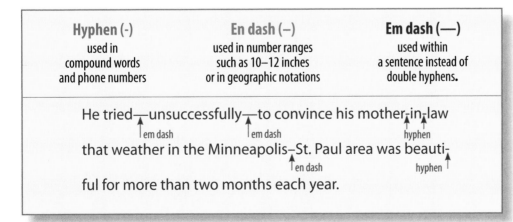

Hyphen (-)
used in
compound words
and phone numbers

En dash (–)
used in number ranges
such as 10–12 inches
or in geographic notations

Em dash (—)
used within
a sentence instead of
double hyphens.

He tried—unsuccessfully—to convince his mother-in-law
em dash   em dash   hyphen
that weather in the Minneapolis–St. Paul area was beauti-
en dash   hyphen
ful for more than two months each year.

visual | 3–17 |

Understand the nuances of setting type is what separates the amateurs from the professionals. Setting punctuation correctly is an essential step in any document!

a poster reads that an event runs from September 26–30 in the Minneapolis–St. Paul area, en dashes are used to separate the dates and cities. An en dash is also sometimes used in headlines when an em dash looks too large. You can enter an en dash by pressing Option+Hyphen (Mac) or Alt+Hyphen (Windows). You can also open the Context menu, while using the Type tool, to access em and en dashes from the Insert Special Characters menu. However, because this method is much slower, you should memorize the shortcut keys.

Calculate Paragraph Line Measure

There are many factors that work together to create good typesetting. There is an inseparable relationship between type size, measured in points, and *line measure*, indicated in picas. A line measure that is too long in relation to the point size will be difficult to read. For example, if a line measure is short and the point size is large, the copy will look choppy because too many hyphens will be needed. A good rule of thumb: As the point size increases, the line measure should also increase. It is easy to calculate the range of acceptable line measure by multiplying the point size of the type by 2 or 2.5. The resulting number will be the line measure in picas. For instance: 10-point type × 2 = 20 picas. And 10-point type × 2.5 = 25 picas. Therefore, a line measure between 20 and 25 picas would be an excellent starting point. Readability is the overriding concern—a measure too long or too short reduces readability. Let's see how easy it is to calculate line measure in InDesign.

> **Estimating Line Measure:**
> **2 to 2.5 times the type point size.**
> *Result (in picas) is the starting point for line measure.*
>
> A notation of 12/15 means 12-point type on 15-point leading.
>
> When you see 12/15 x 30, it means 12-point type, on 15-point leading, with a line measure of 30 picas.

1. Create a new **8.5" × 11"** document, margins **0.5"**.

2. Draw a text frame of any size.

3. Fill with placeholder text by using the Context menu options or by choosing Type>Fill with Placeholder Text. Select all the type and change the point size to **10 pt**.

4. Switch to the Selection tool and on the Control panel highlight the Width field and type **20p** (20 picas). If your unit of measurement is set to inches, InDesign will translate 20 picas into 3.3333 inches as soon as you press the Return key. Print your document.

5. On your print, look at a line of average length. How many "words" appeared in it? The optimal number of words in a single line is nine or ten. How many characters (including spaces) were there? A good middle-range character count would be between 40 and 66 characters.

6. Select your text frame with the Selection tool. In the Width field, increase the measure to **40p** and print out the document. Compare the two text blocks, one with a 20p measure and the other 40p. Which one would you prefer to read?

▶ Moving Toward Mastery

Study these common proofreader's symbols used in the proofing process.

ℓ	Delete	FL	Flush left	*caps*	Set in capital letters
⊂	Close up; delete space	FR	Flush right	*sc*	Set in small caps
stet	Leave as is	∩	Transpose	*wf*	Wrong font
#	Insert space	SP	Spell out	∧	Insert here
⌐	Break line with soft return	*ital*	Set in italic type	⊙	Insert period
¶	Begin new paragraph	Rom	Set in roman type	?	Insert question mark
⊐⊏	Center	/c	Set in lowercase		

Letters in "score" are transposed — tr — Four socre and ⑦ years ago — sp — Spell out "7"

our fathers brought forth on — # — Add space

Delete "on" — ℓ — on this continent, a new nation,

Leave "Liberty" capitalized — stet — conceived in Liberty, and

Add space — # — dedicated to the porposition — tr — Letters in "proposition" are transposed

Delete extra "l" — ℓ — that alll men are created equal.

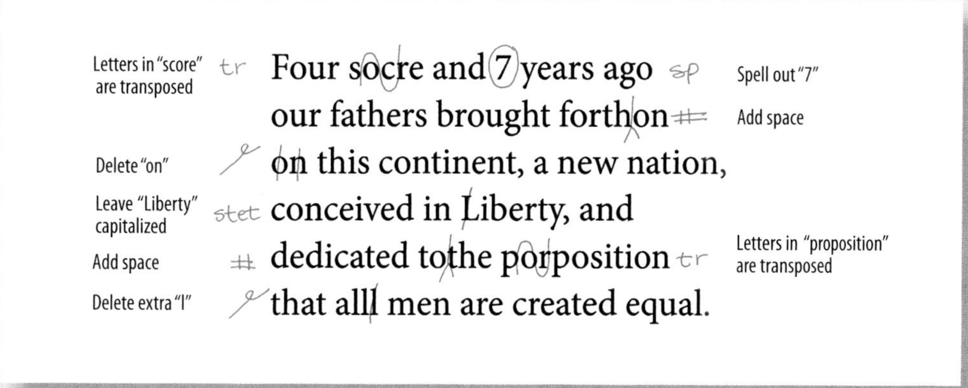

Proofreader's Marks

Someone sent me this tongue-in-cheek word play for people who use only the computer's spell checking system to proof their documents: *Weave know knead four proofing any moor.*

It is essential to proof every project manually, in addition to using your computer's spell check system. Sometimes clients will provide electronic copy, and other times you will type in the copy yourself. Whatever the case may be, all copy needs to be proofed. Knowing basic proofing marks will speed up the proofing process. Out in the workplace where many people work on a single project, using these marks will give clear direction to others and be a precise method of editing copy. Memorize and use the marks shown above!

Marking up proofs is best done with an extra-fine fiber tip pen with a contrasting ink color, such as red or green. Edits are usually noted in pairs—one mark in the line of copy, itself, to flag where the problem is, and a corresponding mark, in the margin, describing the solution. Interpreting a standard set of proofreader's marks is much easier than trying to decipher a hodge-podge collection of cross-outs, circles, and arrows.

SUMMARY

A few years ago after being inspired by watching "do it yourself" shows on cable TV, I purchased a fancy miter saw to use in finishing our basement. It was easy to plug in the saw and make cuts. However, getting the corners of the trim molding to fit perfectly was another matter. I soon found out that using the saw was the easy part—what I didn't know were the techniques required for producing professional-looking finish carpentry! This chapter moved you beyond merely "powering up" InDesign, to incorporating typesetting techniques that are standards in our profession. Some of my students don't "buy in" to learning these techniques—and you can see the results in their poor typesetting. Remember, your potential employer only needs to examine your document formatting by making hidden characters visible to determine your InDesign proficiency. These first chapters are designed to help you develop excellent production habits which will last throughout your career. Although many of the rules and techniques seem nit picky at first, they will become automatic after practice.

Anatomy of type was introduced, followed by a discussion of hidden characters and paragraph definition. The features of the Paragraph Formatting Controls were emphasized in this chapter. You learned how to format paragraphs using space after, raised and drop caps, and various indents. Nonbreaking spaces and hyphens were introduced, as well as the proper use of quotation marks and dashes. These important production tips were presented:

- Use soft returns (**Shift + Return** or **Shift + Enter**) to manually break lines within a paragraph.

- Use a hard return (**Return** or **Enter**) only at the end of a paragraph.

- Use space after (or space before) to add extra space between paragraphs.

- Do not set text, line for line, unless absolutely necessary.

- The Story panel allows you to activate Optical Margin Alignment.

- Go to the *www.identifont.com* web site when you need to match a typeface.

Finally, you learned a formula for determining the range of acceptable line measure for body copy, 2 to 2.5 times the type's point size, in picas.

In the next chapter we will work with text *and* images. Fun!

in review

1. How is a font's point size determined?

2. Why is it helpful to see hidden characters?

3. What is the difference between a hard and soft return?

4. How can space be added between paragraphs without pressing the Return key more than once?

5. What does the notation **Myriad Pro Semibold Condensed 12/15 × 30** mean?

6. How do you make a drop cap? How do you make a raised cap?

7. Which panel holds the Optical Margin Alignment option?

8. Describe the uses for each of the following: hyphen, em dash, en dash.

9. What is the guideline for calculating an acceptable line measure?

10. How is a typographer's quotation mark different from a typewriter quotation mark?

11. What does it mean to set text "line for line"?

12. The client has asked you to duplicate a project, but does not know what font was used. What steps would you take to identify the font?

13. What is a discretionary hyphen and how is it entered?

14. When might you use a nonbreaking space?

15. How do you turn off hyphenation for an entire document?

projects

A THE QUICK BROWN FOX JUMPED
OVER THE LAZY DOG'S BACK.
The quick brown fox jumped
over the lazy dog's back.
123456789

B THE QUICK BROWN FOX JUMPED
OVER THE LAZY DOG'S BACK.
The quick brown fox jumped
over the lazy dog's back.
123456789

C THE QUICK BROWN FOX JUMPED
OVER THE LAZY DOG'S BACK.
The quick brown fox jumped
over the lazy dog's back.
123456789

Chapter Projects Shown above are three text passages in "mystery" typefaces. Now that you know the distinguishing characteristics of letters, go to *www.identifont.com* and select Identify a Font. Answer the questions provided to determine the typefaces used in each passage. If you're not positive your answer is correct, select Not Sure.

These are some of the projects included on the CD accompanying this book. You will find the directions for these projects on the *03 Student Handout* and pictures in the *03 Artwork & Resources* folder.

DESSERTS MENU

APPLE AND BLACKBERRY MERINGUE
A meringue base with generous layers of apple and blackberry. Cream cheese and whip cream provide just enough sweetness, and create a light, delicious after dinner treat. $6.50

BLUEBERRY ITALIAN CHEESECAKE
Blueberries and whip cream top this creamy cheesecake. Ricotta cheese and nutmeg create a flavor sensation that is truly Italian. $5.95

BLACK FOREST CHEESECAKE
A heavenly blend of chocolate, cherry, and amaretto flavors. Our pastry chef's specialty. $4.95

STRAWBERRY ALMOND PARFAIT
Luscious strawberries layered with vanilla creme and sprinkled with amaretti crumbs. Served in parfait glass and garnished with fresh mint. $4.95

Photography ©2006 Christopher Pollack,
Waukesha County Technical College

projects

Joe King

and

Bell E. Flopp

invite you to

share their joy

as they are

united in marriage

on Saturday, May 15, 2005

3:00 p.m.

at the

Winschel-Harris Wedding Chapel

300 North Broadway

Oconomowoc, Wisconsin.

❧

Dinner will be served from

4:30 – 10:00 p.m.

at the

"Blue Eagle" American Legion

301 North Broadway

RSVP—regrets only

Type your name here

THE INDESIGN EXPERT PRODUCTION SEQUENCE

1. FORMAT THE CORRECT SIZE. The most important and basic production step is to create a document or a frame which is *exactly* the right size. If you are building a document, you must also carefully format the interior space with margins and columns guides. If you are drawing a frame in the middle of the document, select a frame tool, click on the document, and define a specific frame size.

2. ADD AND ALIGN THE OUTER STROKE. Once a frame is created, decide if it should have a stroke. If so, add a stroke of the correct weight and style. Then open the Stroke panel—Cmd+F10 (Mac) or Ctrl+F10 (Windows). If you have created your frame to an exact size, align the stroke to the inside.

3. CREATE A TEXT INSET. A stroked text frame needs a text inset. Always add the text inset before you begin to type.

4. TYPING. Do all the typing before you begin to format the text. Always type first, and format second. Type a *z* in the places where a glyph will be inserted later. Usually type will *not* be set line for line, so let your text flow.

5. CHARACTER FORMATTING. First "rough in" the text. Select all the text and apply the most commonly used type style, size, and leading values, usually the specifications for the body copy text. Then, go back and add specific character attributes, including glyphs and raised caps.

6. PARAGRAPH FORMATTING. When the character attributes are finished, encode paragraph attributes including indents, drop caps, space before, space after, and hyphenation.

7. PROOF YOUR WORK. The job isn't done until you have proofed it. Run spell check before printing and print a copy of your project. Compare your project with the original, marking changes as needed. Confirm that type use is consistent throughout the document. Make any changes, print, and proof again.

Type your name here
Project 03D

Motivation is
what gets you started.
Habit is what
keeps you going.

℞ Unknown

| combining type and images |

4

objectives

- Locate, move, and lock the zero point
- Use the coordinate and measurement systems for precise placement and sizing of elements
- Create multicolumn and linked text frames
- Place text, check spelling, apply paragraph rules, adjust tracking, and use manual and optical kerning
- Place, scale, and crop images

introduction

The first three chapters have focused on the basics of InDesign and typography. If you have been waiting for the chance to work with images—as designers love to do—this chapter is for you. We will master the coordinate system, place text, and fine-tune type. Finally, near the end of the chapter you will be introduced to placing, scaling, and cropping images.

This chapter covers a lot of material. When you have completed it, you will be well on your way to mastering InDesign and ready to work on projects that are a little more enjoyable, creative, and challenging.

As you work through this chapter, it is an excellent idea to review sections of earlier chapters that you may have had difficulty with the first time through. Remember, the advanced skills we cover later in the book depend on the solid foundation you are building in these first chapters.

INDESIGN'S MEASURING SYSTEM

InDesign gives you numerous ways to manage the precise size and placement of text and graphics frames. Before we discuss size and placement issues, let's learn about and experiment with InDesign's measuring system.

Units of Measurement

InDesign can measure in points, picas, inches, inches decimal, millimeters, centimeters, ciceros, or agates. InDesign will even let you make up your own unit of measure under the custom category!

Locate, Change, Lock, and Unlock the Zero Point

The *zero point* is the intersection of the zero markers on the horizontal and vertical rulers. All measurements are referenced from this point. The default location of the zero point is at the upper left corner of the page (not at the margin). However, there will be times when you will want to move the zero point to another location in your workspace. The next series of steps will show you just how easy InDesign makes it to relocate the zero point.

visual | 4–1 |

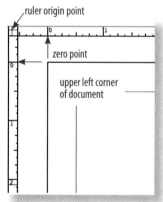

The default location of the zero point is at the upper left corner of the page.

1. Create a new document of any size. Find the zero point for the rulers in your document in the upper left corner. Visual 4–1 shows what the zero point looks like.

2. To move the zero point, click on the *ruler origin point* (the upper left corner of your document window where the rulers meet) and drag down into the middle of the page. When you release the mouse button, look at the new location of the zero point on your horizontal and vertical rulers. Go back to the ruler origin point and drag the zero point to a second location. Repeat this until you are comfortable with the process.

3. To reset the zero point to the upper left corner of your document, simply double-click the ruler origin point in the upper left corner (Visual 4–1).

visual | 4–2 |

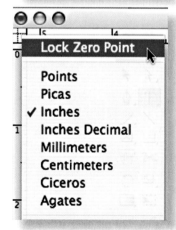

Open the Context menu and choose to lock or unlock the zero point.

4. Drag the zero point to approximately the middle of your document. Go back to the ruler origin point and open the Context menu and select Lock Zero Point (Visual 4–2). You will notice that the icon of the intersecting lines disappears and that it is now impossible to reset the zero point. Use the same method to unlock the zero point.

> **The zero point is where measuring begins.
> The position of every object in your document
> is described by its distance from it.**
>
> **Just like moving a ruler to different places on a piece of paper,
> the zero point is easily moved horizontally and vertically.**

• You can set whatever unit of measurement you wish to use by choosing InDesign (Mac) or Edit (Windows)> Preferences>Units & Increments. In the Ruler Units section of the dialog box you can set the Horizontal and Vertical rulers independently of each other. When you change these ruler preferences with no document open (for example, from inches to picas), these settings become the default for all new documents.

• When you are working in a document, you can quickly change units of measurement by holding down the Control key (Mac) or right-clicking (Windows) on the ruler origin point. The unit of measure you choose will apply to both rulers. Or, you can apply a separate unit of measure for each ruler by holding down Control (Mac) or Right-clicking (Windows) on each of the rulers at the top and side of the page. If no rulers are showing, they have been hidden. Press Command+R (Mac) or Control+R (Windows) to bring them back into view.

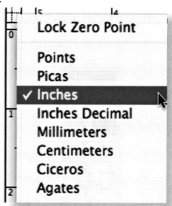

visual | 4–3 |

Quickly change the units of measure for your document at the ruler origin point.

X and Y Coordinates

Every document you create in InDesign is automatically divided into an invisible grid of *horizontal* and *vertical coordinates*. When you move horizontally across the screen, you are moving along the *X coordinate axis*. When you move vertically, you are moving up or down the *Y coordinate axis*. The zero point determines whether the values of the coordinates are positive or negative. As you move the cursor to the right of the zero point, your

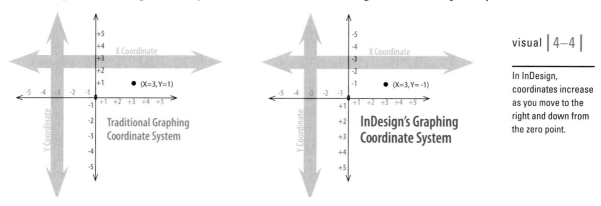

visual | 4–4 |

In InDesign, coordinates increase as you move to the right and down from the zero point.

X coordinate is a positive number that increases. As you move left of the zero point, your X coordinate is a negative number that decreases. On the Y axis, moving down vertically from the zero point gives you positive numbers, and moving up from the zero point gives you negative numbers. If you had graphing in high school math, you may already be familiar with this type of coordinate system. However, as Visual 4–4 shows, the vertical axis in InDesign is exactly the opposite of what you are used to in algebra. Remember, in InDesign's coordinate system the numbers on the Y axis are negative as you move *up* from the zero point.

The X and Y coordinates for all the objects in your document are displayed in the Control panel. The values in the X and Y fields are displayed in the measurement system that you have selected to work in. Because the document area (including the pasteboard) is invisibly mapped into a grid—like graph paper—it becomes easy to describe the location of each element on the page as being so many units from the horizontal or vertical zero point, expressed as either positive or negative (Visual 4–5). But how do you know which point on your object InDesign is measuring to? Is it the center of the object, the right or left edge, or one of the corners? This point is known as the *reference point*. Just as InDesign lets you move the zero point to suit your needs, you have the flexibility to set the reference point of an object to one of nine positions. It can be at any of the four corners; the middle of the top, bottom, right or left edges; or right in the center of the object. Let's see exactly how the coordinate system and an object's point of reference work together.

visual | 4–5 |

These coordinates plot exact placement on the document.

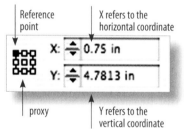

Reference point

X refers to the horizontal coordinate

X: 0.75 in

Y: 4.7813 in

proxy

Y refers to the vertical coordinate

1. Create a **6" × 6"** document. Make sure your units of measure are set to inches and your zero point is in the upper left corner of the document.

2. Select the Rectangle tool (**M**) and draw anywhere in your document to create a rectangle. Notice the values of the X and Y coordinates in the Control panel.

3. Select your rectangle with the Selection tool (black arrow) and move it to the right. Watch the X coordinate increase as the rectangle moves to the right. Move it back to the left and watch the X coordinate decrease. Now move the rectangle up and down on the page. As it moves up the page, the Y coordinate decreases, and as you move it down the page the Y coordinate increases.

4. Now, look at the left end of the Control panel and you will see a series of nine small squares arranged in three rows and three columns (see Visual 4–5). One of these squares will be black and the rest will be white. This control is called the *proxy*. The proxy indicates the position of the reference point for the currently selected object. (The proxy is also found on the Transform panel that you can open by choosing Window>Object & Layout>Transform. Working with the proxy on either the Transform panel or the Control panel will give you the same results.) Look for the black square; it indicates where the reference point is located on your rectangle. Make sure your rectangle is still selected and click the center square in the proxy. The center square turns black, which means you have made the center of your selected rectangle the reference point. With the center black box on the proxy still selected, write down the X and Y coordinates of your rectangle.

Moving Toward Mastery

The X and Y coordinates will change for each object when the reference point in the proxy is moved. In the two examples below, the objects have not been moved. Because the location of the reference point has moved in each example, the corresponding coordinates have also changed. Measuring begins from the reference point!

For most items the proxy is made up of nine squares. However, if the selected item is a straight line, the proxy will have only three squares active. These squares indicate the two ends and the middle point. If the selected item is a guideline, the proxy will show a horizontal or vertical line with only a center reference point. You cannot change the reference point of a guideline.

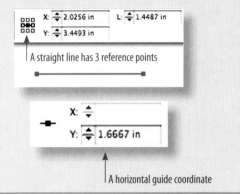

A straight line has 3 reference points

A horizontal guide coordinate

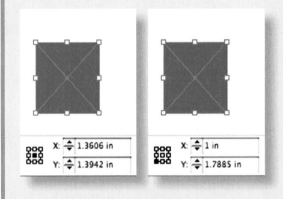

5. Now click on the upper left square on the proxy and read the X and Y coordinates. Even though you have not moved your rectangle, your X and Y coordinates are different than the ones you wrote down a moment ago. This is because you have changed the reference point—it's now the upper left corner of your rectangle, instead of the center.

6. Let's place the rectangle in the exact center of your 6" × 6" document page. Make sure that your rectangle is selected, and click the center square on the proxy. Since your document is a six-inch square, three inches over from the side of the square and three inches down from the top would be the center of the page. Type **3** in both the X and Y coordinate fields and press Return. The rectangle should jump to the exact center of the page. Now the center point of the rectangle is located exactly at the center point of your page.

7. Select the rectangle and click the upper right reference point in the proxy. Type **6** in the X coordinate field and press Return. The rectangle should jump to align with the right edge of the page.

8. Now type **0** in the Y coordinate field and press Return. The rectangle jumps to align with the top, right corner of the page.

You can now see the relationship between the reference point of an object and InDesign's X and Y coordinate system. The intersection of the coordinates displayed in the Control panel always indicates the position of the reference point that you have selected in the proxy.

Understanding Paths and Selection Tools

A shape or line created in InDesign is called a *path*. A path can be a *closed shape* such as a rectangle, or an *open shape* such as a line. The basic component of a path is a *point*. A path can have as little as two points—such as a line with beginning and ending points—or it can be complex, with numerous points. The straight or curved lines that connect the points are called *segments*. A simple rectangle is in reality a closed path made up of points and straight connecting segments.

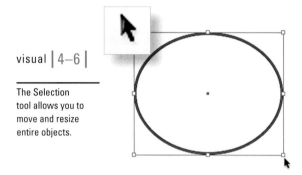

visual | 4–6 |

The Selection tool allows you to move and resize entire objects.

InDesign has two tools specifically designed for working with paths. Let's begin with the black arrow, the *Selection* tool (Visual 4–6). The Selection tool can be activated (when you are not using the Type tool) by pressing **V**. The Selection tool transforms a whole object—changing attributes such as size, scaling, position, skew, and rotation angle. It focuses on the outer dimensions and structure of an entire path. When you click on an open or closed path with the Selection tool, all the points on the path are selected. If the object has a fill, you can click on the fill to select all the points. With all the points selected, you can move the entire object. When you select another object with the tool, the previous object is deselected.

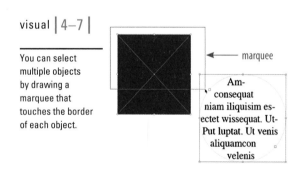

visual | 4–7 |

You can select multiple objects by drawing a marquee that touches the border of each object.

marquee

Am-
consequat
niam iliquisim es-
ectet wissequat. Ut-
Put luptat. Ut venis
aliquamcon
velenis

If you have several objects to select, you can select the first object and then add to the selection by pressing the Shift key while selecting the next object. Another way of selecting multiple paths with the Selection tool is to go to a blank space on the document and drag a rectangle (called a *marquee*) around the paths to select. Since the tool is designed to select whole paths, you can just touch the edge of each path with the marquee and the whole path will be selected.

The *Direct Selection* tool—the white arrow—is next to the Selection tool in the Toolbox (Visual 4–8). When you are not using the Type tool you can press **A** to activate it. The Direct Selection tool is designed to select individual points or segments on a path. When a point is selected, it changes from a hollow square to a filled square. When your Direct Selection cursor is over a line segment, a slash appears next to it. When it is over a point, a box appears next to it. Use the Selection tool to change the dimension of an object. Use the Direct Selection tool to change the shape of an object.

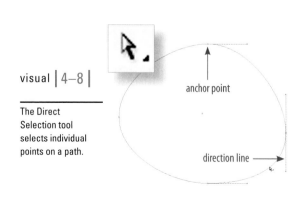

visual | 4–8 |

The Direct Selection tool selects individual points on a path.

anchor point

direction line

Moving Toward Mastery

The **Selection** tool moves and resizes entire objects. When you are in the Type tool you can access the Selection tool by pressing **Command** (Mac) or **Control** (Windows).

Use the **Direct Selection** tool to reshape objects. You can select all the points on a path by pressing **Option** (Mac) or **Alt** (Windows) while clicking on the path. You may move an entire object with the Direct Selection tool by selecting the center point of the object.

Important CS3 Tip:
You can quickly switch between the Selection and Direct Selection tools by double-clicking on the object's frame or by double-clicking on the object's contents.

When you want to select all the points of a path using the Direct Selection tool, you can press the Option (Mac) or Alt (Windows) key while clicking on the path. You can also select all the points on a path by drawing a rectangular marquee, making sure all points are within the marquee's rectangle. If the object has a fill, you can click on the fill with the Direct Selection tool and move the whole path.

Width and Height Coordinates

Delete the rectangle from your document. In the next series of steps you are going to draw an ellipse and then resize its shape using the selection tools and the W (width) and H (height) fields on the Control panel.

1. To draw an ellipse, click on the tiny triangle in the lower right corner of the Rectangle tool and choose the Ellipse tool. Click and drag an ellipse in your document.

2. Deselect the ellipse you have just drawn by pressing Shift+Command+A (Mac) or Shift+Control+A (Windows).

Keyboard Shortcut
Shift+Cmd + A (Mac)   **Deselect**
Shift+Ctrl + A (Win)   **All**

3. Click the edge of your ellipse with the Direct Selection tool. Five hollow squares appear on the ellipse—one in the center, and one on each quadrant of the outer edge. These are called *anchor points*. Click on one and it will turn solid, and then you can edit it independently of the other anchor points. You should also see lines extending from one or more anchor points. These lines are called *direction lines*. If you drag any of the anchor points or the end of a direction line, the shape will be changed (Visual 4–8). Experiment with moving the direction lines to change the shape and then undo your changes by pressing Command+Z (Mac) or Control+Z (Windows) until the shape is back to the original.

4. Deselect the object by clicking in a blank spot in your document or by using the keyboard shortcut Shift+Cmd+A (Mac) or Shift+Ctrl+A (Windows).

5. With the Direction Selection tool, click first on the edge of the shape and then on the center anchor point. All the hollow anchor points become filled, which means they are not editable. Drag the center square and move the ellipse to another part of the page. With the anchor points still selected, drag the edge of the shape and move it again.

6. Now switch to the Selection tool by pressing **V** or by double-clicking on the ellipse's path. The ellipse will look much different. You will see the rectangular bounding box that shows the outer boundaries of the shape. On the bounding box you will see eight tiny squares and a ninth square in the middle of the ellipse. The center square will be filled, and the outer squares will be hollow. These boxes are called handles.

visual | 4–9 |

Drag any of the handles to change the dimension of the ellipse.

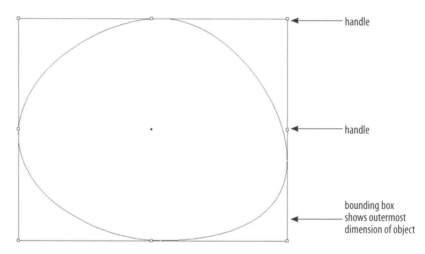

handle

handle

bounding box shows outermost dimension of object

7. Drag any of the handles to change the dimension of the ellipse (Visual 4–9).

8. There are several ways to move the entire ellipse: drag the center point or click on and drag the edge of the ellipse or click and drag a section of the bounding box. Use each of these methods and practice moving the ellipse. (Be careful not to drag a hollow handle, this will resize the object.)

9. Now, note the X and Y coordinates displayed in the Control panel. The coordinates indicate the location of the reference point of the ellipse designated in the proxy. Look at the W and H coordinates. These measurements show the width and height of the selected shape. As you drag on the handles on the bounding box of the ellipse, the dimensions in the Control panel will also change.

10. Type **4** in the W field and **3** in the H field and press **Return**.
Your ellipse should change size.

11. With the 4" × 3" ellipse selected, click on the center reference point on the proxy. Now type **3** in the X coordinate field and **3** in the Y coordinate field and press **Return**. The ellipse should now be centered on your page.

WORKING WITH TEXT

The copy in your document communicates a message while adding texture, color, shape, and contrast to your layout. Your ability to use text as a design element is an important skill to develop. In this next section you will learn how to create multiple column text frames and import (or *Place*) text from word processing documents.

Multicolumn Text

Creating text columns within text frames is a simple process. When the Paragraph Formatting Controls are active, you can find the column options near the middle of the panel (see Visual 4–10). The space between the columns is called a *gutter* (or *alley*). To change the width of the gutter, select the text frame and press Command+B (Mac) or Control+B (Windows) to open the Text Frame Options dialog box. In the Gutter field, enter the desired value for the gutter width. You can type the value in a unit of measure such as 1p (1 pica).

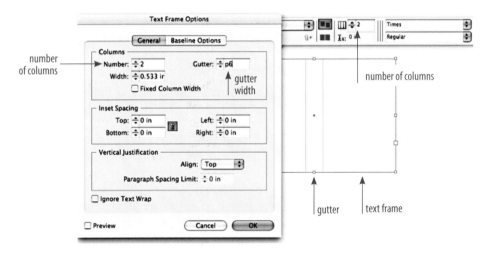

visual | 4–10 |

Click the up or down arrows or type a number in the Number of Columns field to create multiple columns inside a text frame. You can also create columns in Text Frame Options.

1. Draw a frame in your document. Select the Type tool and click the frame to instantly convert it to a text frame. Select the Paragraph Formatting Controls and change the number of columns to **3.** Press Command+B (Mac) or Control+B (Windows) to change the gutter width to **p6** (six points)**.** Press Return.

2. Choose Type>Fill with Placeholder Text. Text will fill your text frame. With the Type tool active, select all the text using the shortcut key and reduce the point size until the last text column is empty.

3. Place the cursor in the middle of a line in the column. Press Enter on the number keypad. This makes text jump to the next column. If you are in the habit of pressing the Return key over and over to force text to jump to another column—don't! Simply insert the cursor where you want the text to break and press Enter on the number keypad. If your keyboard doesn't have a numeric keypad with an Enter key, open the Context menu and select Insert Break Character>Column Break.

Don't get into the bad habit of pressing the Return key multiple times to force the text to flow to the next column. If your layout changes, you will need to delete all those manual keyboard entries. When you press the Enter key on the number keypad to insert a column break character, it will be much easier to simply remove it, if you have to revise the column break later.

Creating columns within text frames is simple and useful for projects. More often, however, designers will create separate text frames in different places on the page and flow the text between the frames. You will learn that technique, called *threading,* later in this chapter. Right now, you will learn how to use the Place command to bring text files created in a variety of word processors into your InDesign documents. What a timesaver!

Placing Text

The keyboard shortcut for placing text—Command+D (Mac) or Control+D (Windows)—is one you will want to memorize. You will use it again and again to import text or graphics. Pressing the keyboard shortcut brings up the Place dialog box.

Two important features of the Place dialog box are the choices to *Show Import Options* and *Replace Selected Item,* in the lower left corner (Visual 4–11). Show Import Options, among other things, gives you control over how different versions of Microsoft Word text files are handled. Choosing Replace Selected Item will replace any text that is selected within a text frame with the contents of the file you are placing. If the frame is selected with the Selection or the Direct Selection tool, the entire contents of the text frame will be replaced.

Keyboard Shortcut

Cmd + D (Mac)

Place

Ctrl + D (Win)

visual | 4–11 |

The Place dialog box.

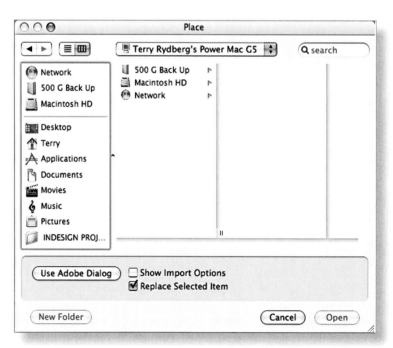

There are three methods for importing text files: placing them into an existing frame, placing them into a new frame, and simply dropping the contents onto a page. In the next exercise, you will create a new 8.5" × 11" document, add a frame, and then use all three methods of placing text. You will be using a text file called *04 Copyfit.doc* from the *04 Artwork & Resources* folder in the CD accompanying this text. Find and load your CD.

Placing Text into an Existing Text Frame

In this exercise we will place text into a frame that you have already created.

1. Draw a **6" × 9"** text frame. Set the reference point in the center at X coordinate: **4.25**, and Y coordinate: **5.5**. Create **three** columns with a 1-pica gutter.

2. Insert the project CD, if you have not already done so. Press Command+D (Mac) or Control+D (Windows) to open the Place dialog box. Navigate to the project CD. Find the *04 Artwork & Resources* folder and select the text file called *04 Copyfit.doc*.

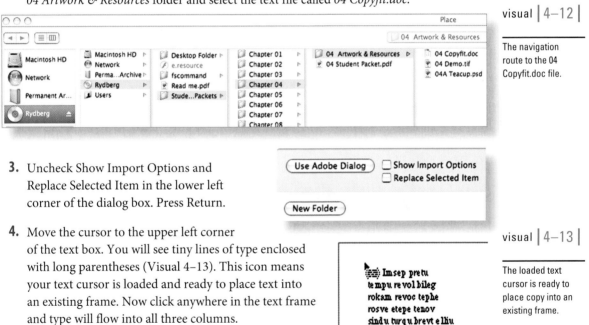

visual | 4–12 |

The navigation route to the 04 Copyfit.doc file.

3. Uncheck Show Import Options and Replace Selected Item in the lower left corner of the dialog box. Press Return.

4. Move the cursor to the upper left corner of the text box. You will see tiny lines of type enclosed with long parentheses (Visual 4–13). This icon means your text cursor is loaded and ready to place text into an existing frame. Now click anywhere in the text frame and type will flow into all three columns.

visual | 4–13 |

The loaded text cursor is ready to place copy into an existing frame.

5. Notice the square with the red plus sign (+) in the lower right column. A red plus is the *overset* symbol—it means there is more text than the text frame will hold.

6. To delete the overset text, place the cursor at the end of the visible copy. If you are working on a Mac, select all the "invisible" overset text, beyond the plus sign, by pressing Shift+Command+End. Release those keys and then press Delete. If you are a Windows user, place your cursor at the end of the visible copy. Press Shift+Control+End to select the overset text. Release those keys and then press Delete. The plus sign should disappear as the text beyond the frame is deleted.

Place Text by Creating a New Frame

In this exercise, you will import text and create a new text frame to place it into, at the same time. Start by deleting the three-column text box, so that your document is blank.

Imsep pretu tempu re vol bileg rokam revoc tephe rosve etepe tenov sindu turqu brevt elliu repar tiuve tamia queso utage udulc

The loaded text cursor will create a text frame when the copy is dropped into the document.

1. Press Command+D (Mac) or Control+D (Windows) and select the *04 Copyfit.doc* file again. Press Return. Move the loaded cursor over the blank document and look carefully at its shape. This time you will not see parentheses around the text cursor. Instead, you will see straight lines on the top and left edge. This icon indicates that a new frame needs to be created for the text (Visual 4–14).

2. Drag the loaded text cursor to create a frame. When you release the mouse, text will flow into the new text frame.

3. Change the Width and Height to 5" × 7" and create three columns. Again, notice the overset symbol in the out port in the lower right corner. Delete the overset text.

> **To Delete Overset Text:**
> 1. **Place the cursor to the end of the visible copy.**
> 2. **Press Shift+ Command+End (Mac) or** Shift+Control+End **(Windows)**
> 3. **Release the shortcut keys.**
> 4. **Press Delete**

Place Text by Dropping Into the Page

This method of placing text drops the text into the document and lets it spread from margin guide to margin guide. Delete the text frame from your document.

1. Open the Place dialog box by using the keyboard shortcut and select *04 Copyfit.doc* one more time. Press Return. Notice that the shape of the loaded cursor is the same as in Visual 4–14.

2. Click the cursor anywhere on the document. A text frame will stretch from margin to margin with the top positioned wherever you clicked on the page. Delete the overset text.

Estimating Word Count

Look at the file you just placed and you will see that there are numbers scattered throughout the text. These numbers represent the *word count*. Now you can estimate how many words, in a specific font, type size, and leading, will fit in this text box. You can use the *04 Copyfit.doc*

Keyboard Shortcut	
F8 (Mac)	Info
F8 (Win)	Panel

file when you design the text areas for an InDesign project and then tell the copywriter how many words will be needed to fill the allotted space. Another way to estimate the word count for any passage of placeholder text is to highlight the copy and then open the Info panel. The character, word, line, and paragraph count is displayed at the bottom of the panel.

Managing Text Flow

Now that you have mastered the basics of placing text, it's time to learn how to manage the text flow as it is being placed into a document. You will learn these four techniques: *manual text flow, semi-automatic text flow, automatic text flow,* and *automatic text flow with a fixed number of pages.* You will need to place the *04 Copyfit.doc* file from your CD for the following exercises.

Manual Text Flow

When you use *manual text flow,* you make all the decisions regarding where placed text will be positioned and how it will flow. You have total control, but as the "manual" name implies, this method is the slowest.

1. Create a new document. Page size **5" × 7"** landscape orientation. Enter **3** columns with **1p** gutter, **0.5"** margins. Press Return.

2. Look closely at the column guides. Notice that there is no text frame on the page. The column indicators are only guides—ready to hold a graphics or text frame.

3. Again, place the *04 Copyfit.doc* file by using the keyboard shortcut. Move the cursor over to the upper left corner of the first column. The cursor shape indicates a new text frame will be created. Click in the upper left corner and the first column will fill with copy. You will see an overset symbol (+) at the bottom of the first column. The text will just "sit" there until you manually flow it to another column.

4. The cursor should have reverted to the Selection tool. Click on the plus sign in the text out port. This process is called *reloading the cursor.* Your cursor has now changed into a *loaded cursor,* and you can see that the shape has changed (Visual 4–15).

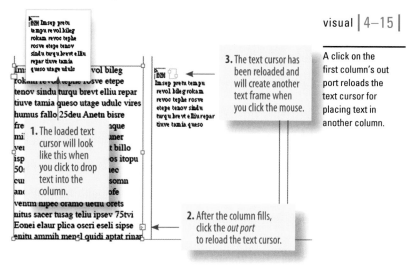

visual | 4–15 |

A click on the first column's out port reloads the text cursor for placing text in another column.

3. The text cursor has been reloaded and will create another text frame when you click the mouse.

1. The loaded text cursor will look like this when you click to drop text into the column.

2. After the column fills, click the *out port* to reload the text cursor.

5. Click in the upper left corner of the second column to flow text into this column. Reload your cursor by clicking on the text out port box. Click in the upper left corner of the third column and it will fill with copy.

6. Switch to the Type tool and place the cursor at the end of the text in the third column. Delete the overset text by pressing Shift+Command+End, then Delete (Mac) or Shift+Control+End, then Delete (Windows).

Semi-automatic Text Flow

Flowing text manually from column to column is a neat technique, but imagine how tedious it would be if you had to do that for a 10-page document! InDesign is always one step ahead of the user—and has designed a second way to flow text called *semi-automatic.*

1. Select all the text frames in your document and then delete by using keyboard shortcuts.

2. Place the *04 Copyfit.doc* file once again.

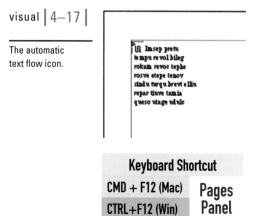

3. This time, hold down the Option (Mac) or Alt (Windows) key as you hold the loaded cursor in the upper left corner of the first column. Notice the shape of the cursor changes into a snake pattern each time you press the Option or Alt key (Visual 4–16). Press this key a few times to get used to the difference between the cursors. This cursor means your text will be placed in semi-automatic text flow mode.

4. Hold down the Option (Mac) or Alt (Windows) key and click in the upper left corner. The text will fill the first column and the cursor will remain loaded. Hold down the Option or Alt key and click in the second column. The text flows into the middle column. As long as you continue to hold the Option or Alt key as you click to drop text, you remain in semi-automatic flow mode and the remaining text will remain loaded in the text icon.

5. Continue in semi-automatic mode and fill the last column. Press Escape to get out of semi-automatic text flow mode. Delete the overset text.

Automatic Text Flow

Manual and semi-automatic text flow provide you the most control regarding the place-ment of text in individual text frames on a single page or a series of non-contiguous pages. *Automatic text flow* is another method of flowing text that is fast, and automatically inserts exactly the right number of pages required to hold the text passage.

1. Create a new file, **3" × 5"** and **0.5"** margins.

2. Place the *04 Copyfit.doc* file so that you have a loaded cursor. Hold down the Shift key as you move the cursor to the upper left corner of the page. Click inside the page margins.

3. Open the Pages panel by pressing Command+F12 (Mac) or Control+F12 (Windows) or by choosing Window>Pages. Notice that you now have more than one page in your document. When you place text in automatic flow mode, InDesign automatically adds as many pages as necessary.

Keyboard Shortcut

CMD + F12 (Mac) **Pages**
CTRL+F12 (Win)   **Panel**

Automatic Text Flow with Fixed Number of Pages

The automatic text flow option is great for many projects—but what if you must make the text fit on only four pages? The *automatic text flow with fixed number of pages* technique allows you to place text on a specified number of pages only.

1. Create a **3" × 5"** document, **0.5"** margins, and **4** pages.

2. Load the text cursor with *04 Copyfit.doc*.

3. This time, hold down Shift+Option (Mac) or Shift+Alt (Windows) as you click and drop the text onto the upper left corner of page one. The text will fill the available space on the four pages and then stop. Notice the familiar overset symbol in the out port at the end of page four. Now you can select all your text and adjust the point size and leading to make the copy fit into your four-page document.

visual | 4–18 |

The automatic text flow with fixed number of pages icon.

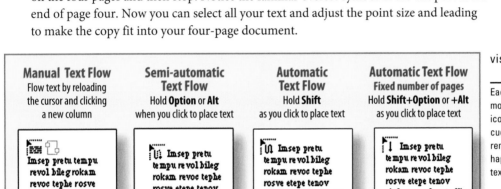

Manual Text Flow	**Semi-automatic Text Flow**	**Automatic Text Flow**	**Automatic Text Flow**
Flow text by reloading the cursor and clicking a new column	Hold **Option** or **Alt** when you click to place text	Hold **Shift** as you click to place text	**Fixed number of pages** Hold **Shift+Option** or **+Alt** as you click to place text

visual | 4–19 |

Each text flow mode has its own icon. These visual cues will help you remember what is happening with your text as you place it.

About Threaded Text Frames

In the exercises you just completed, text was flowing from one column to the next column in a single text frame. Text can also flow between individual text frames that are connected through a process called *threading*. As shown in Visual 4–20, each threaded text frame can have different text frame attributes including inset, fill, stroke and columns. Because threaded text frames are connected, you can use Command+A (Mac) or+Control+A (Windows) to select all the type in the threaded frames.

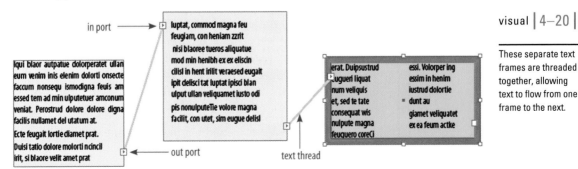

in port

out port

text thread

visual | 4–20 |

These separate text frames are threaded together, allowing text to flow from one frame to the next.

Seeing Links and Threads

This exercise will familiarize you with using threaded text frames.

1. Create a new document, **8.5" × 11"**, margins **0.5"**.

2. Scatter three frames on the document. Make some frames tall and some wide.

3. Place the *04 Copyfit.doc* file. Drop the text into the first frame. You will see the overset symbol (+) in the lower right of your frame.

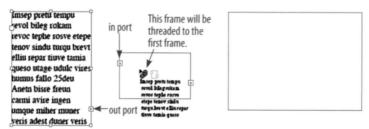

4. Choose either of the Selection tools and click on the overset text symbol. The cursor is re-loaded and its icon changes. As you move the icon over the second text frame you will see two small links appearing on the loaded text cursor, indicating these two frames will soon be threaded together (Visual 4–21).

5. Click to place the text into the second text frame. Notice that the overset text symbol that was in the first text frame has now been replaced with a blue triangle. The blue triangle means this box is now an *out port*. The upper left side of the second text frame also has a blue triangle, an *in port*.

6. Flow copy into the third frame using the same process.

7. Now from the Menu bar, choose View>Show Text Threads. When you select a text frame, you will see lines connecting the *in* and *out ports* on your frames. These show the direction and order of the text flow. A triangle in the out port means that the text is linked to another frame. A plus in the out port means that text is overset—that there is too much text to fit in the frame. When the first in port and the last out port in a series of linked text frames are empty, it means that all the text has been placed (Visual 4–22).

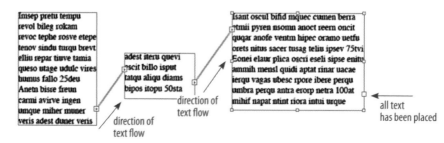

8. Don't close your file—we're going to use it for the next demo.

Unlinking Text Frames

There will be times when you flow text into the wrong frame. Of course, you can simply press the Undo shortcut, but that method is only practical if you catch your error shortly after it was made. Here's another way to unlink threaded text frames.

1. Select the text frame in the middle of your text thread.

2. Double-click on the *in port* or the *out port of the middle frame.* If you double-click on the *in port*, the text flow will be cut off at the in port and there will be a text overflow symbol in the first frame. If you double-click on the *out port*, text will be cut off at that point. The third frame is now empty and a text overflow symbol appears in the second frame.

Imsep pretu tempu revol bileg rokam revoc tephe rosve etepe tenov sindu turqu brevt elliu repar tiuve tamia queso utage udulc vires humus fallo 25deu Anetn bisre freun carmi avirve ingen umque miher muner veris adest duner veris

adest iteru quevi scit billo isput atqu aliqu diams bipos itopu 50sta

Double-click an *in port* or *out port* to unthread frames

The broken link shows the thread has been broken.

Imsep pretu tempu revol bileg rokam revoc tephe rosve etepe tenov sindu turqu brevt elliu repar tiuve tamia queso

When should frames be threaded?

Now you that know how to thread text frames, you're probably wondering when you should use them. When text columns need to have individual attributes such as depth, width, fill or stroke, you will want to use threaded frames. For instance, let's say you are working on a newsletter, and you want to shorten the third column to accommodate a photo. If you are using a single text frame with three columns, this will be difficult because you can only shorten the entire text frame instead of single columns. When you use threaded text frames to create columns, you can shorten just the third frame, letting the text reflow. Generally, using threaded text frames provides more flexibility than using single frames with multiple columns.

TYPOGRAPHY

type basics

MANAGING UNDERLINES

During the days of old-fashioned typing, people used to underline text to add emphasis or to indicate the title of a book.

Unfortunately, that habit has carried over into the world of digital type, and most people simply click an icon to underline a word or sentence.

Today, italics are used to indicate the name of a book or to add emphasis. A heavier typeface can also be used to make a word or phrase stand out.

Typewriter-style underlines are rarely used in professional typesetting. If you must underline text, use InDesign's Underline Options capabilities in the Control Panel menu options to control the weight of the underline and to avoid cutting through descenders.

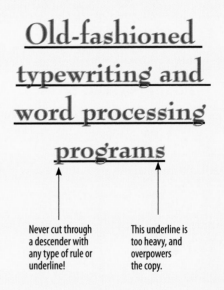

Old-fashioned typewriting and word processing programs

Never cut through a descender with any type of rule or underline!

This underline is too heavy, and overpowers the copy.

UNDERLINING WORDS AND PARAGRAPH RULES

If you read the *Type Basics* on the previous page, you already know that underlining individual words is rarely done in setting type. Underlining is a throwback to the "typewriter days" when it was the only method of adding emphasis.

Underlining Words

For those rare times you need to underline text, you should not allow the rule to cut through a descender. Fortunately, InDesign has a complete and sophisticated way for you to adjust the weight and position of the underline. First, select the text you would like to underline.

Then, select Underline Options from the options menu at the far right end of the Control panel. In the Underline Options dialog box (Visual 4–23), check the Underline On box and then adjust the weight, offset, color, and type of the line as desired.

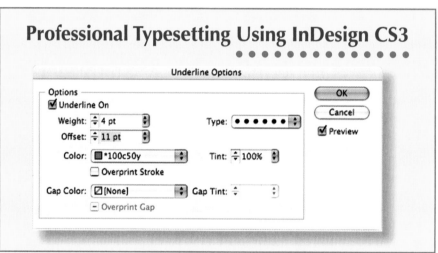

Paragraph Rules

Paragraph rules may look like underlining, but they are an altogether different matter. Paragraph rules are design elements, and InDesign allows you to set rules in two places in each paragraph: 1) on or above the baseline of the first line of text; or 2) at the end of a paragraph. The Paragraph Rules function allows you to use color, styles, indents, and offsets to create just about any rule you'd ever want. Visual 4–24 shows some paragraph rules in action.

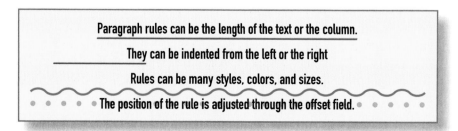

The Paragraph Rules dialog box can be accessed by using a keyboard shortcut: Command+Option+J (Mac) or Control+Alt+J (Windows), or by clicking on the options menu in the Control panel and choosing Paragraph Rules.

Keyboard Shortcut

| Cmd + Opt + J (Mac) | Paragraph |
| Ctrl + Alt + J (Win) | Rules |

Applying a Rule Below a Paragraph

Whenever possible, apply rules as part of the paragraph formatting. A document that is filled with lines created with the Line tool is hard to edit because each line must be individually re-positioned. Lines that are set as rules within the paragraph will reflow as the copy changes.

1. Create a new document using the default settings. Draw a text frame and type your name on the first line and your phone number on the second line; use a hard return between the lines. Increase the type size to **48 points** on **60-point** leading.

2. With the blinking cursor somewhere in the first paragraph (the first line), press Command+Option+J (Mac) or Control+Alt+J (Windows) to access the Paragraph Rules dialog box (Visual 4–25). You can also choose Paragraph Rules from the Control panel options menu.

The Width field in the Paragraph Rules dialog box can be set to **Column** or **Text**. With Column selected, the line stretches from the left edge of the column to the right edge. With Text selected, the line extends only as long as the last line of text.

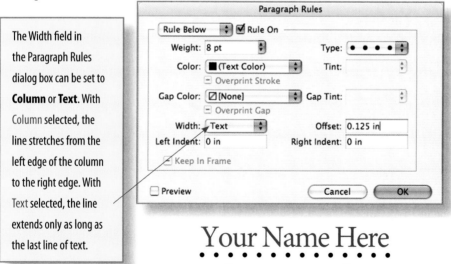

visual | 4–25 |

Paragraph rules are design elements. To have a *paragraph rule*, you must have a *paragraph*, which means you will need to place a hard return in your copy.

3. *Rule below* means that a rule will be placed after a paragraph (created by a hard return). Select Rule Below from the list and check the Rule On option box. Select 8 pt in the Weight field menu, and Dotted in the Type field menu. The Width field should be set to Text. Enter **0.125"** in the Offset field. When you increase the offset, you push the rule farther down, away from the baseline. Press Return and your type should look similar to the sample in Visual 4–25. Keep this document open for the next exercise.

Applying a Rule Above a Paragraph

A *rule above* a paragraph will appear on the first baseline or will be offset above the first baseline of the paragraph. Applying a rule above a paragraph can be a little tricky because you'll need to add an offset value so that the rule doesn't cut through your type.

1. Click in the line that contains your name. First, you will turn off the rule below the paragraph. Open the Paragraph Rules dialog box and make sure that Rule Below is selected in the list, then uncheck the Rule On option. Click Preview and you will see the rule has disappeared. Press Return.

2. Now, you will add a rule above the phone number. Place the cursor in the line with your phone number. Open the Paragraph Rules dialog box and select Rule Above from the list. Be sure to check the Rule On option box. Select a line type and weight of your choice. Because the rule line will be drawn on the baseline, you'll need to enter a value in the Offset field. Type **p48** (48 points) to push the line up off the baseline.

How to Check Spelling in Your Document

It's a good idea to always run a spell check before printing a document. But remember, even though InDesign's spell check function is excellent, it doesn't replace manual proofing. Both methods should be used to ensure accurate copy. To check spelling, simply press Command+I (Mac) or Control+I (Windows). When the Check Spelling dialog box appears, you will need to make a choice in the Search list. The following list describes the options:

visual | 4–26 |

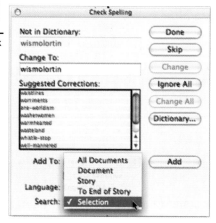

Choices in the Check Spelling options will vary depending on what is selected.

- The **All Documents** option checks the spelling of all open InDesign documents.

- The **Document** option checks the entire document you are working on. This is a great feature unless you have several pages of directory information including last names. If you would prefer to skip those sections of the document, choose the next choice.

- **Story** option checks the spelling in the selected text frame and all threaded text frames.

- The **To End of Story** option checks all the words beyond the blinking cursor.

- If you have text highlighted before opening the Check Spelling dialog box, then you have another choice. **Selection** checks the spelling of only a highlighted word or text.

Keyboard Shortcut

Cmd + I (Mac)
Ctrl + I (Win)
Check Spelling

Once you have made a choice in the Search list, simply click Start to begin the process. InDesign will alert you of any questionable words and possible errors. When the checking is complete, click Done to dismiss the dialog box.

Understanding Tracking and Kerning

You already know what leading is. Leading is the vertical spacing between lines of type, measured from baseline to baseline. *Tracking* adjusts horizontal spacing between all the characters on a line. A single paragraph can contain characters with many different tracking values.

Positive tracking increases spacing between characters; *negative tracking* decreases spacing between characters (Visual 4–27). Tracking values are shown in the Paragraph and Character Formatting Controls.

visual | 4–27 |

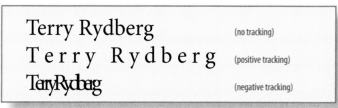

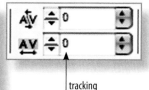

| tracking

The Tracking control is found in both the Character and Paragraph Controls panels.

Adjusting Text Spacing with Tracking

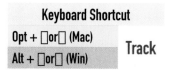

Keyboard Shortcut

Opt + ☐ or ☐ (Mac)

Alt + ☐ or ☐ (Win)   **Track**

1. Create a new letter-sized document. Draw a text frame, type your full name and change the point size to **60-point**.

2. To tighten the tracking of your text: Highlight what you want tracked, hold down Option (Mac) or Alt (Windows), and press the Left Arrow key near the number pad. At first the text will still be readable, but if you keep pressing the arrow key, notice that the text ultimately reverses itself. Be careful not to overdo tracking!

3. Delete the text box and draw a new one. Type your name in it again in **60-point** type. Select all the text. Press Option (Mac) or Alt (Windows) and the Right Arrow key to loosen the tracking. Keep pressing the right arrow key and you will see that it doesn't take very long for your name to become just a series of individual letters. Again, be conservative with tracking. When misused, it inhibits readability.

You will occasionally use tracking to fine-tune your type. At times you may want to use negative tracking to give your text a little more refined look, especially with headline type. You will also use tracking to fit troublesome lines of type into the line measure. While InDesign has taken care of much of this for you with its multiline composition feature, there will be times when you will need to manually adjust tracking. For instance, at the end of a paragraph, you should avoid leaving part of a hyphenated word or any word shorter than four letters on its own line. As a typesetter, you need to make a decision: either tighten tracking slightly to make room for the word in the line above, or loosen tracking to bring the whole word or an additional word to the last line of a paragraph. The goal is to alter the word spacing so slightly that no one will ever notice. You have gone too far with your tracking if the tracked text looks darker or lighter than the surrounding text. *Tracking should be invisible to the untrained eye.*

Adjust Character Spacing with Manual Kerning

Closely related to tracking is kerning. *Kerning* is the horizontal spacing between two characters only. You should kern letter pairs when spacing between characters is too wide or too narrow. For instance, look closely at the number 740 shown in Visual 4–28. Before you started reading this book, it would have looked perfectly fine. But with your professional eye, you now see that the spacing between the 7 and 4 looks much wider than the spacing between the 4 and the 0.

The Kerning control is found in both the Character and Paragraph Controls panels.

spacing is loose

kerning of -100 has been applied

Kerning will correct this. Place your cursor in between the 7 and the 4. Do not highlight any text. Use the same keyboard shortcuts for negative kerning as you would for negative tracking; press Option+Left arrow (Mac) or Alt+Left arrow (Windows). The amount of adjustment is shown in the Kerning field in the Control panel. InDesign adjusts the kerning in units of one-thousandth of an em. (You will remember that an em is a unit of measure equivalent to the point size—an em space in 10-point type is 10 points wide.)

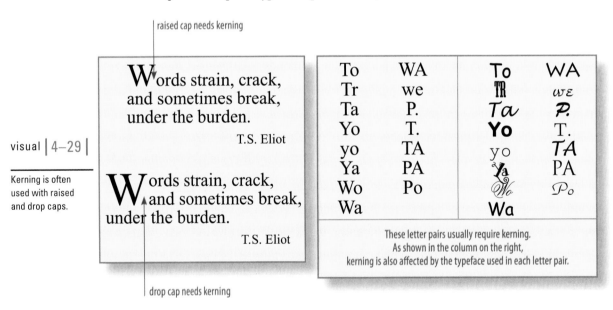

raised cap needs kerning

Kerning is often used with raised and drop caps.

drop cap needs kerning

Words strain, crack, and sometimes break, under the burden.

T.S. Eliot

Words strain, crack, and sometimes break, under the burden.

T.S. Eliot

These letter pairs usually require kerning. As shown in the column on the right, kerning is also affected by the typeface used in each letter pair.

A more common place to kern letter pairs is when using drop and raised caps. Visual 4–29 shows what they look like without kerning. As shown above, some letter pairs usually need kerning. Your goal is to have the "color" of text look even. Big gaps between letter pairs make a word look "airy."

Automatic Optical Kerning

When professionals design a font, they build in rules for letter-pair spacing. Unfortunately, the built-in kerning parameters don't cover every letter-pair scenario. That is why manual kerning is sometimes needed. But InDesign has gone one step further. It allows you to select *Optical Kerning* from the Character or Paragraph Formatting Controls. With Optical Kerning selected, InDesign goes beyond the built-in letter-pair parameters and makes kerning decisions based on the shape of each character to even out how the type looks. This is a huge timesaver. InDesign does an excellent job of making text look great—with very little effort on the part of the person setting the type.

WORKING WITH IMAGES

The perfect image combined with beautiful type form a "one-two punch," resulting in a document that is both memorable and effective. Most of the images you use will be either scanned, created in a vector-based drawing program such as Adobe Illustrator or Macromedia Freehand, or created in a pixel-based program such as Adobe Photoshop. As powerful as InDesign is, it is not a true drawing program. But you shouldn't underestimate InDesign's drawing capabilities. If you have already used Adobe Illustrator, you have seen tools and functions in InDesign that look very familiar. If you haven't used Illustrator, you will learn about many basic drawing functions that are common to both programs later in the book.

InDesign can place a variety of file formats including EPS, TIFF, and JPEG. Another great feature of InDesign is its ability to place native Adobe Illustrator (AI) and Photoshop (PSD) files without conversion to an EPS or TIFF format.

Three methods of placing artwork will be discussed in this section: *place and drop, place and drag*, and *place into a frame*. The same keyboard shortcut is used to place text or images: Command+D (Mac) or Control+D (Windows). InDesign does not require a specific type of frame to hold a graphic and another to hold text. In fact, as you have already seen when placing text, you don't need a frame at all! Let's get started learning how to place images. You will need the CD that accompanies this book for these exercises.

Place and Drop Images

the photo will create its own frame

visual | 4–30 |

When placing images, a thumbnail of the image appears on the cursor.

1. Create a new document, **8.5" × 11"**. Open the Place dialog box. Navigate to the *Chapter 04 Artwork & Resources* folder on your CD. Choose *04 Demo.tif*. Press Return.

2. Notice the loaded icon looks like a paintbrush surrounded by straight lines. Just as when placing text, the square lines indicate that a new frame will be created. Click in the upper left corner of your document and the photo will appear at full size.

Place and Drag Images

With this method you will drag the loaded icon to create the frame for the graphic.

1. Look closely at the photo you just placed, and try to remember its size. Now, delete the photo by selecting the frame with the Selection tool and then pressing the Delete key.

2. Open the Place dialog box and find *04 Demo.tif* again.

3. This time click and drag out a frame. Make the frame about half the size of the photo you deleted earlier. When you release the mouse, the photo will fill the frame. However, because your frame is not large enough, some parts of the photo will not show.

visual | 4–31 |

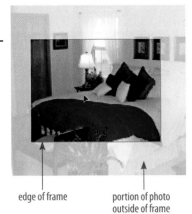

When you click and hold on an image with the Direct Selection tool, any part of the image that doesn't fit in the frame is displayed.

edge of frame   portion of photo outside of frame

4. Switch to the Direct Selection tool and click and hold on the image in the frame. As you click and hold with the Direct Selection tool, you should see a faded image of the photo outside of the frame you created. InDesign is showing you the actual size of the photo. As you continue to press with the Direct Selection tool, you can move the photo inside the frame. If you double-click on the photo, the Direct Selection tool will change to the Selection tool, allowing you to resize the frame to contain the entire graphic. Double-click again to switch back to the Direct Selection tool. Press the Delete key to remove the image from the frame. (Do not delete the entire frame.)

Place into an Existing Frame

Placing a graphic into an existing frame is the third method of getting a picture into your file.

visual | 4–32 |

The parentheses indicate the photo is being placed into a frame.

placing into an existing frame

Keyboard Shortcut

Cmd + D (Mac)

Ctrl + D (Win)

Place

1. Place *04 Demo.tif* again.

2. This time position the loaded icon over the empty frame you created in the last exercise. Notice how the shape of the icon changes from square lines to curved lines surrounding the brush. Just as when placing text, this icon means the photo will be placed into an existing frame.

You can switch between the Selection and the Direct Selection tools by double-clicking on the contents or the frame path.

3. Click and the picture will drop into the frame. Note that the image is placed at full size, no matter what size the frame.

SCALING AND CROPPING IMAGES

When you are working with images, remember that you are managing two components: the frame (or *container*) that holds the image, and the image (or *content*). If you understand the difference between the Selection and Direct Selection tools, you will realize that you would use the Selection tool to resize the frame, and the Direct Selection tool to resize the content or move the content inside the frame. The following series of exercises will take you through the main image-handling techniques. The exercises are quick and easy, and important techniques to learn. Don't skip over this part!

A. Move the Graphic and the Frame

Use the Selection tool to move the photo and the frame as a single unit.

1. Create a new letter-size document. Draw an ellipse approximately **2.5"** wide. Place *04 Demo.tif* in the frame.

2. Switch to the Selection tool and select the frame. You will see a square bounding box around the circle frame. This is a visual cue that you have selected both the frame and the photo (Visual 4–33).

   bounding box ⟶

3. Drag to move the frame and photo around the page.

visual | 4–33 |

Use the Selection tool to move an image and frame as a single unit.

B. Proportionately Resize the Graphic and the Frame

Use the Selection tool to resize the image and frame together as a single unit.

1. Select the frame again with the Selection tool. Hold down Shift+Command (Mac) or Shift+Control (Windows) and drag any of the frame handles. The photo and frame will resize proportionately.

2. Use Undo to return your frame and graphic to their original size.

C. Resize Only the Frame

Use the Selection tool to resize the frame, without modifying the image inside.

1. Drag any of the frame handles with the Selection tool. Do not hold down Shift+Command or Shift+Control as you drag the frame handles.

2. The frame size will change, but the image will not move or change size. It is exactly as it was initially placed. Press Shift to keep the proportions of the frame as you drag to resize it.

D. Crop the Image Inside the Frame

Use the Direct Selection tool to modify images inside frames.

Switch to the Direct Selection tool and click and hold on the image. You should see the bounding box for the whole image, with the parts outside the frame ghosted (see Visual 4–31). Drag to move the photo around inside the picture frame. The image moves but the frame does not. This is a good method of hiding unwanted or unnecessary parts of an image, a process called *cropping*.

E. Resize the Image Inside the Frame Proportionately

Images have width and height dimensions. When both dimensions are at 100%, the picture is full size. If the image is reduced, the percentage will be less than 100% and if it is enlarged, it will be more than 100%. If you resize the photo so that the width dimension is at 50% and the height is at 100%, the picture is the same height, but it is half its original width. This is disproportional scaling. If you were using a picture of clouds as a background photo, the photo could be scaled disproportionately without any consequences. However, you want to keep most images—products, people—proportional, meaning the width and height percentages will be the same. These percentages are shown in the Control panel (see Visual 4–34).

visual | 4–34 |

Photos of people should be scaled proportionately. Always check the percentage boxes.

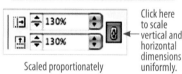

Scaled proportionately

Click here to scale vertical and horizontal dimensions uniformly.

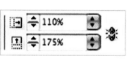

Scaled disproportionately. The Y (vertical) dimension has been scaled to a greater percentage than the X (horizontal) dimension, making the photo tall and thin.

1. Choose the Direct Selection tool. Hold down Shift and drag a corner of the image's frame. See how the image changes size proportionally, but the outer container does not change size.

2. Reduce the whole image until it is floating in the center of the picture frame. You will be able to see the percentage of reduction in the Control panel.

3. You can also proportionately resize an image inside a frame by using keyboard shortcuts. Select the image with the Direct Selection tool and press Command+Opt+> or < (Mac) or Control+Alt+> or < (Windows). To resize the images in smaller increments, press Command+> or < (Mac) or Control +> or < (Windows).

Keyboard Shortcut	
Cmd + Opt+< or > (Mac)	**Resize Images**
Ctrl + Alt+< or > (Win)	

F. Resize the Image Inside the Frame Disproportionately

A poster promoting a weight loss program was hung in our college hallway showing the "before" and "after" photos of a participant who had lost 20 pounds. Obviously, the "after" picture was created by simply resizing the first photo disproportionately to make the person look thinner. Be careful when scaling images! Most of the time you will want to keep your image in the same proportion as it was originally created. But there will be instances, as in the cloud example mentioned earlier, when disproportional scaling will be acceptable.

1. Select the image with the Direct Selection tool. Drag any frame handle. The image will resize and become distorted. Check the Scale X and Y fields on the Control panel to see new horizontal and vertical percentages of the image.

2. Enter the same number in each of the fields and the image will again be proportional.

G. Resize Frame to Fit the Content

Use the Selection tool to resize the frame to fit the content.

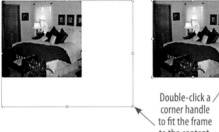

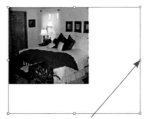

Double-click a corner handle to fit the frame to the content.

Double-click on a middle handle to resize the frame horizontally or vertically.

visual | 4–35 |

Double-click frame handles to fit the frame to the content.

1. Draw a large frame. Place *04 Demo.tif* in the frame.

2. Activate the Selection tool. (Remember, you can double-click the image to switch from the Direct Selection tool to the Selection tool if needed.)

3. Double-click a corner frame handle to fit the frame to the content (Visual 4–35). The entire frame is scaled to fit the image.

4. Undo Step 3. Now, double-click a frame handle on the middle of the frame's sides, top, or bottom. The frame will resize either horizontally or vertically (Visual 4–35).

H. Resize the Content to Fit the Frame

When you place an image into a frame, you can resize the image to proportionately fit the frame by pressing Shift+Option+Command+E (Mac) or Shift+Alt+Control+E (Windows).

Keyboard Shortcut

Shift+Cmd+Opt+E (Mac)
Shift+Ctrl+Alt+E (Win)

Fit Image to Frame

► Moving Toward Mastery

Important things to remember when working with images:

- Use the **Selection** tool when you are changing the frame size.
- Use the **Direct Selection** tool when you are modifying the image.
- Switch between the selection tools by **double-clicking** on the image or the frame path.

- Keep images **proportional**. Select the image with the Direct Selection tool and check out the horizontal and vertical scale percentages.
- You can flip images horizontally or vertically by pressing the icon on the Control panel.
- You can use the Control panel to rotate images.
- **Double-click frame handles** to fit the frame to the image.
- Memorize the keyboard shortcuts for resizing images and fitting images to the frame.

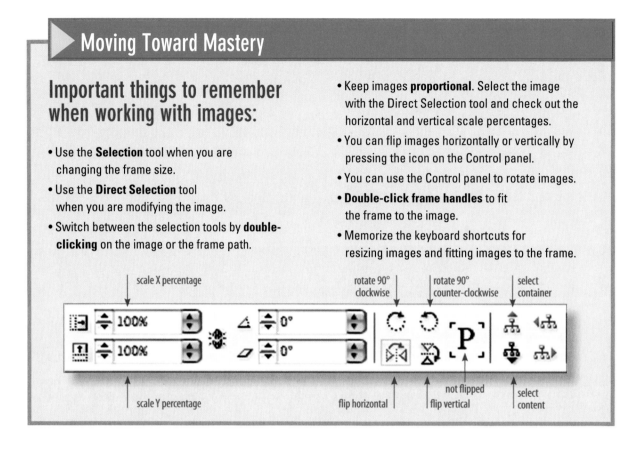

SUMMARY

If this seemed like a long chapter, it's because it was long! In these first four chapters you have learned so much—you now understand InDesign's measurement system. You know how to create multi-column text frames, and to place and thread text. You used InDesign's tracking and kerning, paragraph rules, and spell check functions to fine-tune your type. Finally, you learned how to place, scale, and crop images. With these techniques mastered, you're ready to tackle more advanced projects. Be sure to work through all of the Chapter 4 projects—they are designed to solidify these new techniques. Next, we'll move on to my favorite topic: tabs and tables.

in review

1. What is the difference between **kerning** and **tracking**?

2. What is the difference between **tracking** and **leading**?

3. How do you reset the **zero point**?

4. If the coordinates of an object are X4 and Y6, it means that the object will be _____ inches over and _____ inches down.

5. What does the black square in the proxy indicate?

6. What key should you press to push text from one column to the next?

7. What does a **red plus sign** in the out port of a text frame indicate?

8–17. What are the keyboard shortcuts for the following?

   A. Show Hidden Characters

   B. Direct Selection Tool

   C. Paragraph Rules

   D. Place Text or Image

   E. Check Spelling

   F. Save

   G. View at 100%

   H. View at 200%

   I. Text Frame Options

   J. Print

18. What are the steps for proportionately enlarging a graphic inside a frame?

19. What is the process for deleting **overset** text?

20. What is the process for **unlinking** text frames?

projects

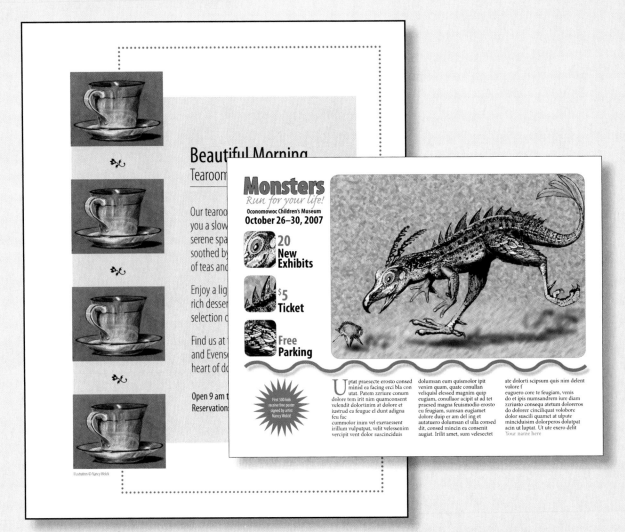

Illustration © Nancy Wolck

Chapter projects Chapter 4 projects begin with an X-Y coordinate exercise. This is followed by a display ad project for Beautiful Morning Tearoom and Gardens which focuses on using coordinates, leading, correct dashes, and space after paragraphs. The next project is a 2-sided table tent that utilizes rules above and below. Next, you will create a poster concept for a museum exhibit. The final project is designed for you to produce with little direction. You will find instructions, artwork, and text in the *Chapter 04 Artwork & Resources* folder on the accompanying CD.

Teacup and Monster artwork © 2004 Nancy Wolck
Peacock artwork and Pepper photography © 2006 Nathaniel Avery
Salsa photo © 2006 Kristin Steldt
Waukesha County Technical College, Pewaukee, Wisconsin

projects

Yearbook

photos

will begin

Anna Sanchez
◯ AUTHENTIC MEXICAN ◯

You don't have to sacrifice flavor when you're counting calories and fat.
These delicious, low-fat offerings are served with baked tortilla chips.
Low-fat cheese and olive oil are used to prepare these delicious dishes.

BLACK BEAN SALSA
Black beans, ripe tomatoes, green and red peppers, lime, jalapeños and
cilantro give this mild salsa plenty of zip. $4.95

ROASTED TOMATO SALSA
Generous amounts of cumin, cilantro, and jalapeño peppers make this
one hot salsa. Not for the fainthearted. $4.95

SIZZLING STEAK FAJITAS
Only 9 grams of fat in this south-of-the-border specialty. Tender steak,
fat-free sour cream and fresh veggies on two flour tortillas. $10.95

FIESTA ENCHILADAS
Low-fat ground turkey and cole slaw
create a fiesta of taste and texture.
$11.95

Anna Sanchez
◯ AUTHENTIC MEXICAN ◯

Everyone is trying to accomplish something **big**, not realizing that life is made up of **little things**.

℞ Unknown

| tabs and tables |

objectives

- **Differentiate between left, right, center, decimal, repeating, and align to special characters tabs**
- **Apply tab leaders**
- **Use the Indent to Here feature**
- **Build a table**
- **Create a table from text**
- **Modify, add, and delete columns and rows**

introduction

If you've ever seen a good marching band in a parade, you know that they march in formation. A poor marching band wanders all over the place—trumpets out of line, clarinets out of step, drums missing the beat. Nobody knows whom to follow or what comes next.

This chapter will help you keep your text in formation. In earlier chapters you have learned how to format text in sentences and paragraphs. In this chapter you will work with text designed for use in charts, order forms, and business reports—projects that need tabs and tables to keep information in line. Honing your skills with tabs and tables will keep your text marching in formation, and prove to your boss or your client that you are a master at what you do!

There are four methods people typically use to align text and numbers in columns:

☹ Press the spacebar repeatedly until the text lines up.

☹ Press the Tab key over and over until the text lines up.

☺ Create precise tabular settings.

☺ Create tables to hold the information.

No matter which method you have used in the past, I guarantee that after this chapter you will never use either of the first two methods again!

WORKING WITH TABS

Whether you are working on a car, hanging wallpaper, or building a deck, it is always great to get tips from pros—especially at the beginning of the project! Here are some great tips for tabs. Following them will make setting tabs so much easier.

1. Mark up the copy (a fine-tip pen with colored ink works the best). Your markup will show where you press the Tab key and where the tab stop will be set. This step is critical in the beginning stages of typesetting. Pre-planning a job in this way can prevent time-consuming errors (see the sample markup in Visual 5–2).

2. Work with hidden characters visible. Pressing Command+Option+I (Mac) or Control+Alt+I (Windows) will show each tab character and make it easy to find those places where you accidentally pressed the Tab key twice.

3. Do the typing first, pressing the Tab key only one time between columns of information. Your text probably won't line up at first because the cursor jumps to InDesign's preset tab settings of every half inch. Later, when you set the desired tab stops, the copy will line up at the correct new location.

4. Work with copy left-aligned when possible—doing so makes setting tabs much easier.

Keyboard Shortcut	
Shift+Cmd+T (Mac)	**Tabs**
Shift+Ctrl+T (Win)	**Panel**

5. Access the Tabs panel by pressing Shift+Command+T (Mac) or Shift+Control+T (Windows).

6. Press the Tab key only once! Your copy will look great after you set the tab stops.

Marking up Copy—An Important Production Step!

The first tab tip is to mark up the copy to show each time you press the Tab key and where the tab stops should be placed. Before you can mark up the copy, you must know what kind of tab is needed. We will start with three simple kinds of tabs: *Left*, *Right*, and *Center*.

Each of these tab stops looks different on the Tabs panel. Study Visual 5–1 until you can identify the shape of each tab stop and visualize how it will align the copy.

visual | 5–1 |

Tab stops align copy into columns. The type of stop you select determines how the copy in the columns will be aligned.

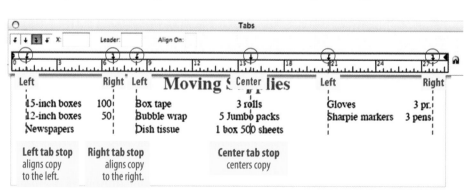

Just as stretching prepares your muscles for a workout, marking up tabular copy prepares your brain and creates a visual connection between you and the software. This forces your brain to shift into "tabs mode." It is tempting to skip the mark up step, but until you have used InDesign for several years, you should take the 30 seconds to mark up your copy. In the mark up process, you indicate each time you press the Tab key and you pencil in exactly where each tab stop should be set. Visual 5–2 shows copy that has been marked up correctly. This markup becomes a road map that will make setting tabs a snap.

Setting Tabs

You will need the CD that accompanies this book to work on the following tabs exercises. The good news is that all the typing is already done for you—you will concentrate on using the Tabs panel for formatting your copy. Open *05 Tabs Demo. indd.* This 3-page document is found in the *05 Artwork & Resources* folder on the CD.

Find Exercise 1 on the *05 Tabs Demo* document. The first step in setting tabs is understanding how the Tabs panel works. Open the Tabs panel using Shift+Command+T (Mac) or Shift+Control+T (Windows). You can also access the Tabs panel by going to the Window>Type & Tables>Tabs menu, but this is a slower method. Study Visual 5–3 to learn the fields and panel options for the Tabs panel.

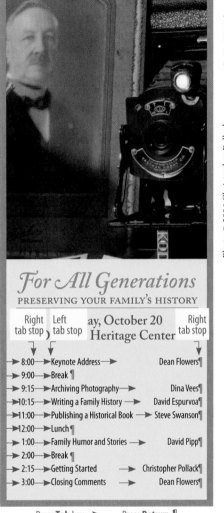

visual | 5–2 |

Marking up copy before setting tabs saves production time and frustration!

Photo © 2006 Christopher Pollack

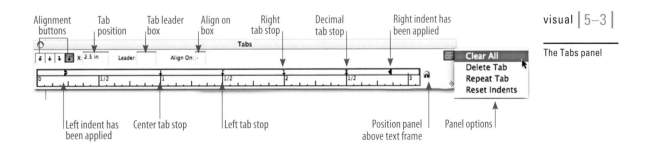

visual | 5–3 |

The Tabs panel

Exercise 1A – Snapping the Tabs Panel to the Text Frame

Activate the text frame in Exercise 1 with the Selection tool. With the Tabs panel open, notice the magnet on the far right end. This is the control that will position the Tabs panel directly over the active text frame, if possible. To see it in action, change your view size to 100% and click on the magnet. The Tabs panel will align itself to the top of the text frame. Switch your view to 200%. Click the magnet—it will resize and snap to the top of your text frame. Now, switch your view to 1200% from the magnification field in the lower left corner of your screen. Click the magnet, and it won't move. This seemingly inconsistent behavior occurs because when you are viewing your document at high magnification levels, there is not enough room above the active text frame to position and resize the Tabs panel. So, the snap above text frame function is disabled. Change the view size back to 100% and click the magnet to snap the Tabs panel to your text frame. You can set tabs without having the panel snapped to the frame, but it is easier to see what you're doing when the ruler is snapped above your text frame.

Look carefully at the text frame, noticing that an inset has been applied to all four sides. When the Tabs panel is snapped to the text frame, the measuring does not necessarily begin at the edge of the frame. Instead, it begins where the text begins. In this case, the zero point of the tabs ruler snaps to the text frame inset setting. The tabs ruler lines up to the inset guide.

Exercise 1B – Adding and Removing Tab Stops

Deselect the text frame in Exercise 1. We're going to experiment with the Tabs panel. Adding tab stops is an easy process. Simply click in the narrow white area directly above the ruler. Slide your cursor down the ruler a bit and click again. Each time you click, a tab stop is added. When a tab stop is first added it is blue, which means it is active. Once you make a new tab stop, the previous one is deselected. To delete a tab stop, select it and pull it above the Tabs panel ruler. When you have many tab stops to delete, it is faster to go to the Tabs panel options and select Clear All (Visual 5–4). Clear all your tabs.

Place a tab stop near the middle of the ruler. Press Option (Mac) or Alt (Windows) and click repeatedly on the tab stop. As you click, watch as the tab stop alignment settings change from left, to center, to right, to decimal. Use this method to cycle through tab stop alignment settings whenever you are setting tabular copy.

visual | 5–4 |

Remove all tab stops by selecting *Clear All* from the panel options.

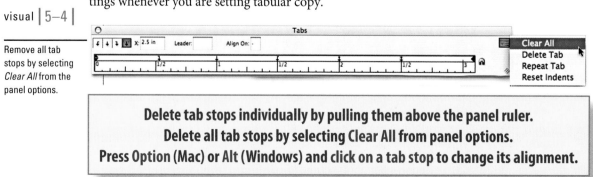

Delete tab stops individually by pulling them above the panel ruler.
Delete all tab stops by selecting Clear All from panel options.
Press Option (Mac) or Alt (Windows) and click on a tab stop to change its alignment.

Exercise 1C — Setting Left Tabs

Use the Selection tool to select the frame in Exercise 1. Look closely at the invisibles to identify each time the Tab key was pressed (Visual 5–5). Each time the Tab key was pressed, the copy was pushed to the nearest tab preset. Since *Dr. Ryan Johnson's* name was shorter than the other names in the first column, *Dr. Theodore Soos* moved to a tab preset closer to the left edge of the copy block. Usually, copy will not align until you actually set the tab stops. Resist the temptation to "fix" the copy by pressing the tab key repeatedly to manually align copy!

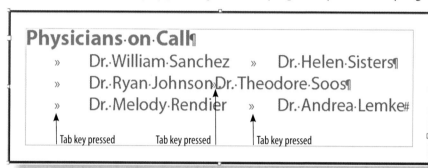

visual | 5–5 |

Copy moves to the first available tab stop preset until you select the tab stops you want to use.

Be sure the Tabs panel is open and snapped to the top of your text frame. You should still have the Selection tool activated. Drop in Left tab stops at approximately **0.25"** and **2"**. As you place each stop, click and hold, and a vertical line will appear to show where your copy will be aligned. You can also see the measurement of the tab stop in the X box. Adjust the position of your copy by sliding the tab stop to the right or to the left on the ruler.

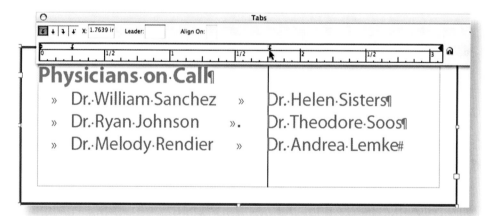

visual | 5–6 |

Click and hold each tab stop. A vertical line appears where the copy will be aligned.

When you select the text frame with the Selection or Type tool and do not highlight individual lines of copy, identical tab settings are applied to all the tabular copy inside the frame.

Notice that all the lines of copy moved as you placed the tab stops. When you select the text frame with either the Selection or Direct Selection tools, and do not highlight the text lines, the tab settings are applied to all the tabular copy inside the text frame.

Exercise 2 – Setting Center and Right Tabs

Now let's move on to Exercise 2. A completed sample of this exercise is shown in Visual 5– 7. Before you begin this exercise, use Visual 5–7 for markup. Place a **horizontal arrow** → in the text to indicate each time the Tab key is pressed. Examine the copy closely to determine the required tab stops. Indicate the appropriate tab stop above each column, using these symbols for Left, Center, or Right. A tab stop won't be required in every line.

When your markup is completed, open the Tabs panel. Find the lines of type with identical tab settings, and work on those as a unit. Then move to the next series of similar tab settings. Refer to your markup as you drop in your tab stops. Press Option (Mac) or Alt (Windows) and click on each tab stop to cycle through the alignment options. If you need to adjust the position of a tab stop, highlight the copy and move the stop to the left or right on the Tabs panel ruler. Your completed project should look almost identical to the example in Visual 5–7.

visual | 5–7 |

Mark up the tab settings on this sample of Exercise 2.

Nutrition Facts

Serving Size: 1 cup
Servings per container: 6
Amount per serving:
Calories: 45   Calories from fat: 0
Total Fat: 0g   0g
          Saturated Fat 0g
          Polyunsaturated Fat 0g
          Monounsaturated Fat 0g
Cholesterol   0mg   0%
Sodium   70 mg   13%
Total Carbohydrate   12g
Dietary Fiber   2g
Sugars   0g
Protein   1g

Vitamin A 0% • Vitamin C 0%
Calcium 0% • Iron 2%

visual | 5–8 |

Decimal tab stops use the decimal to align the copy in a column.

Answers to Math Exam

1.	.067
2.	0.0034
3.	9.56723
4.	12.45
5.	.1
6.	2.3543
7.	4
8.	9.667734
9.	2.456
10.	6.123

Exercise 3 – Setting Decimal Tabs

When you set a *Decimal* tab stop, the copy is lined up according to the position of the decimal. In Visual 5–8, notice how the numbers one through ten are aligned by their decimal points. In the right column, the numbers also align according to the decimal point. If there is no decimal point, such as in the answer for #7, the whole number is positioned to the left of where a decimal point would be placed. Mark up the copy, making sure to indicate a tab before numbers 1 to 10. Then, create the tab settings.

Exercise 4 – Aligning To Special Characters

The Decimal tab default aligns copy according to the location of the decimal point, but you can specify other characters on which to align the decimal tab. In this exercise, the copy will be aligned to the dollar sign. First, select the Decimal tab. Then, enter a dollar sign ($) in the Align On box in the Tabs panel.

visual | 5–9 |

You can specify other characters for alignment with the decimal tab stop. In this example, copy is aligned to the dollar sign.

Photo © 2006 Annette Wagner

Take out Menu

Manicotti	*with 3 cheeses* $6	Capellini Carbonara	*very rich* $9.25
Fetucine Alfredo	*Specify large or small* $8.95	Spaghetti	*add meatballs 50¢* $7
Pasta Piselli	*Everyone's favorite* $6.95	Lasagna	*7 layers, 5 cheeses* $5.95

Exercise 5 – Setting Right Indent Tabs

Right indent tabs automatically push your copy flush with the right edge of the text frame. Right indent tabs aren't part of the regular Tabs panel. Press Shift+Tab or use the Context menu>Insert Special Character>Other>Right Indent Tab to create a right indent tab. Display hidden characters to verify that an automatic right indent tab has been inserted. Follow the directions included with Exercise 5 on page 2 of *05 Tabs Demo.indd* to create right indent tabs.

visual | 5–10 |

This hidden character represents a right indent tab.

Exercise 6 – Using Indent to Here

Indent to Here is one of those "can't live without it" features in InDesign. Although technically this is not a tab setting, this is a good time to introduce this function. With Indent to Here, you insert a special character symbol by pressing Command+\ (Mac) or Control+\ (Windows). Starting with the next line, all subsequent lines in the paragraph align to the position of the Indent to Here character. This is similar to creating a hanging indent. Once you press the Return key for a new paragraph, paragraph text will revert back out to the left margin. To remove the Indent to Here character, simply turn on the hidden characters, find the Indent to Here dagger symbol, place the cursor to the right of the symbol, and press the Delete key. When you use the Indent to Here keyboard shortcut to complete this exercise, be sure to use the Back Slash key!

visual | 5–11 |

The Indent to Here special character looks like a dagger. This keyboard shortcut will become one of your favorites.

Indent to Here symbol

Exercise 7 – Setting Repeat Tabs

When you need tabs to be spaced at equal intervals, you can use the *Repeat Tabs* function found on the option menu at the far right end of the Tabs panel. In this function, equally spaced tab stops, based on the position of the first tab stop, are spread across the line. Directions for creating Repeat tabs are included with Exercise 7 in *05 Tabs Demo.indd*.

Exercise 8 – Creating Dot Leaders

A *leader* is a series of repeating characters between a tab stop and the following text or the end of the text frame. Leaders can be dots, lines, or any other character you choose. You can specify up to eight characters in the Leader box on the Tabs panel. You will most often use leaders in conjunction with Right tab stops. To create the dot leaders in this exercise, set a Right tab at the right end of the tab ruler. Making sure the Right tab stop is selected, enter a period and space in the Leader box and press Return. The area between the first and second columns will fill with dots. As Visual 5–12 shows, if you don't enter a space along with the period, the dot leaders will be too close. Add dot leader tabs to the text in Exercise 8, so that it looks like Visual 5–13. This exercise demonstrates how dot leaders help the eye move from one column to the next.

visual | 5–12 |

For proper dot leader spacing, add a space after the period in the Leader field.

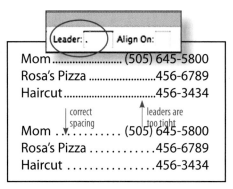

Photo © 2006 Krista Mueller

visual | 5–13 |

Exercise 8,
completed.

Exercise 9 – Creating Line Leaders

Throughout your professional career, you will likely create many projects that are "variations on the theme" of the raffle ticket presented in Exercise 9. When creating line leaders, place an underline in the Leader box by pressing Shift+ hyphen, found at the top right corner of your keyboard. If you don't press the Shift key, the space will be filled with dashes, not underlines. Sometimes, when you are creating line leaders, the underlines on your monitor will appear to have spaces between them. If this happens, increase your view magnification and see if the rules look solid at a different view percentage. Sometimes it's just a "screen thing." Other times, this happens because you actually typed a space and an underline in the Leader box, on the Tabs panel. If the problem still persists, highlight the box by clicking on the word, Leader. Place 2 underlines in the Leader box. Visual 5–15 shows the tab settings for the last line of the raffle ticket. The line leaders are applied to the two Right tab stops. If the line after State runs into Zip, it probably means you have added a line leader to the left stop at Zip. If so, select the stop and delete the line in the Leader box.

Illustration © 2006 Nathaniel Avery

visual | 5–14 |

Always highlight the Leader box by clicking on the name to the left of the box.

visual | 5–15 |

The last line in this raffle ticket. The line leaders are applied to the Right tab stops.

Highlight the Leader box by clicking the field's label to the left of the box, rather than manually clicking in the box and highlighting it.

Moving Toward Mastery

When working with tabs, remember these tips:

1. **Mark up the copy**. Show where the Tab key will be pressed, and where the tab stop will be set.

2. **Work with hidden characters visible**. Press **Command+Option+I** (Mac) or **Control+Alt+I** (Windows) to show hidden characters. This will show each tab character and will make it easy to find those times when you accidentally pressed the Tab key twice.

3. **Do the typing first,** pressing the Tab key only one time between columns of information.

4. **Work with copy left-aligned** when possible—doing so makes setting tabs much easier.

5. **Press Shift+Command+T** (Mac) or **Shift+Control+T** (Windows) to open the Tabs panel.

6. **Press the Tab key only once!** Be patient—your copy will look great after you set the tab stops.

7. **Highlight the Leader box** by clicking on the name to the left of the box.

8. With a tab stop highlighted in the Tab ruler, Press **Option** (Mac) or **Alt** (Windows) and click on the tab marker to cycle through the tab stop alignment settings.

9. **Add a space after the period** in the Leader box when creating dot leaders.

Last Thoughts on Tabs

The columns created within text frames that you learned to create in earlier chapters are used for continuous text passages. They are designed to have the copy fill across and down the first column, then flow into the second column, and so on. Set tabs when the copy flow is horizontal. The tab stops will create the appearance of vertical columns.

Don't confuse tabs with paragraph indents and text frame insets! Sometimes you will use a left indent instead of a tab. That method works perfectly. However, be careful of creating a left inset in Text Frame Options rather than a left indent because the inset will affect all the text in the frame—which may not be what you want! The hidden characters shown below reveal the techniques used in each example.

S & P Stats A

level	»	1131.13
change	»	-2.98
» percent change		-.26%
» YTD % change		1.73%
» high (day)	»	1134.17
» low (day)	»	1127.73
» high (52 wk)		1155.38
» low (52 wk)		788.90
last close	»	1134.11
last update: 1/30 16:52		

Tabs were used to move copy to the right.

S & P Stats B

level	»	1131.13
change	»	-2.98
percent change	»	-.26%
YTD % change	»	1.73%
high (day)	»	1134.17
low (day)	»	1127.73
high (52 wk)	»	1155.38
low (52 wk)	»	788.90
last close	»	1134.11
last update: 1/30 16:52		

A left indent was specified in the Control panel.

S & P Stats C

level	»	1131.13
change	»	-2.98
percent change	»	-.26%
YTD % change	»	1.73%
high (day)	»	1134.17
low (day)	»	1127.73
high (52 wk)	»	1155.38
low (52 wk)	»	788.90
last close	»	1134.11
last update: 1/30 16:52		

The frame inset created in Text Frame Options applies to all the text in a frame.

CREATING TABLES

Like tabs, *tables* also organize information into columns. Tables are different than tabs, however, because they are made up of *rows, columns,* and *cells.* With tables, you can add interest by changing the background color and text attributes of individual cells, columns, and rows. When thinking of tables, people often picture a clunky-looking graph with copy choked against heavy black lines. Not so, with InDesign. In this second half of Chapter 5, you will discover the amazing and enjoyable ways you can create tables.

There are several ways you can create tables: from "scratch," by converting existing copy, or by importing from a Microsoft® Word document or Excel spreadsheet. InDesign's Toolbox does not include a specific table tool. Instead, you insert a table into a text frame or convert existing text into a table. The best way to understand tables is to make them, so we're going to dive right in. In the following exercises, you will learn all the basics of table management using a simple table consisting of four rows and four columns.

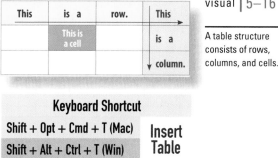

visual | 5—16 |

A table structure consists of rows, columns, and cells.

Keyboard Shortcut

Shift + Opt + Cmd + T (Mac)

Shift + Alt + Ctrl + T (Win)

Insert Table

Table Basics

1. Insert a table. Create a letter-size InDesign document with **0.5"** margins. Draw a text frame from margin to margin. Select the Type tool and click in the frame. Press Shift+Option+Command+T (Mac) or Shift+Alt+Control+T (Windows) to bring up the Insert Table dialog box. You can also access this dialog box by choosing Table>Insert Table.

   Specify **4** in the Body Rows and **4** in the Columns boxes. (Rows run horizontally, and columns run vertically.) Leave the Header Rows and Footer Rows fields blank. Press Return. A table now sits inside your text frame, aligned with the top of your text frame.

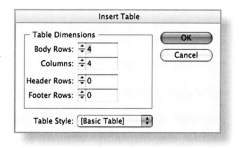

visual | 5–17 |

The Insert Table dialog box.

2. Position a table in the text frame. The new table has a cursor blinking in the upper left cell. With the Type tool selected, click anywhere in the text frame, outside of the table. Now the text cursor is positioned just outside the table on the right side of the text frame. Notice that the cursor is the same height as the table. Open Text Frame Options, Command+B (Mac) or Control+B (Windows), and under Vertical Justification choose Align: Center. Turn on the Preview option and watch the table jump to the vertical center of the text frame. Now, see what happens when you select the Align: Bottom option. A table behaves like a huge piece of type inside a text frame, and will be affected by alignment, indents, insets, space before and space after. Align the table to the top once again.

3. Select columns, rows, cells, or the entire table. Move the Type tool slightly above the table, over the left column. You will see the cursor change into an arrow (Visual 5–18A). Click, and the entire column will be selected. Place your cursor along the left side of the table, beside the first row (Visual 5–18B). Click, and the entire row will be selected. Now, bring the cursor to the upper left corner of the table. You will see a diagonal arrow (Visual 5–18C). Click, and the entire table will be selected. Place the cursor inside a cell and drag to the right to select it. You can continue to drag across a cell's boundary to select adjacent cells. Practice selecting the entire table, individual rows, columns and cells.

visual | 5–18 |

Use the Type tool to select columns, rows, cells, or the entire table.

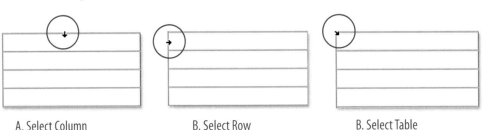

A. Select Column   B. Select Row   B. Select Table

visual | 5–19 |

Be aware of when you are highlighting the cell and when you are highlighting type.

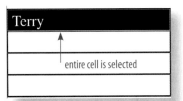

entire cell is selected

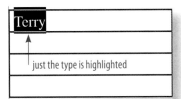

just the type is highlighted

4. Select a cell or its contents. Place the cursor in the upper left cell and type your name. Move the cursor to highlight your name and the space surrounding it so that the entire cell is black. You now have the cell selected (Visual 5–19). Now, try to highlight just your name. Sometimes this is a little trickier, and it helps if you are at a magnified view. When your type is selected, the highlighting should just cover the letters, and your cell should look like the lower example in Visual 5–19. It is important that you can differentiate between selecting a cell or highlighting text inside a cell.

visual | 5–20 |

When you are moving column or row guides the cursor switches to a double-headed arrow.

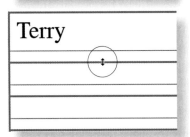

5. Resize rows and columns. Place the cursor over the row guide below your name. The cursor now changes into a double-headed arrow (Visual 5–20). Pull the line down to create a much deeper cell. Repeat this process with the column guides. Notice how changing the size of rows and columns, changes the table size, too.

6. Resize rows and columns without resizing the table. Place the cursor over the row guide below your name. When the cursor changes into a double-headed arrow, hold down Shift as you adjust the row dimension. Notice that the row inside the table changes size, but the table does not. Repeat this process, pressing the Shift key as you move the column guides.

Press Shift to resize columns and rows inside the table without changing the table's dimension.

7. Position text inside the cell. Highlight the cell that contains your name. Use the Paragraph Formatting options in the Control panel to align your type to the right. Now align the type to the center. You use the Table Formatting Options in the Control panel to set the vertical position and rotation of type inside the cell. In Visual 5–21 the type has been rotated 270°. With the cell selected, experiment with alignment and text rotation controls in the Control panel.

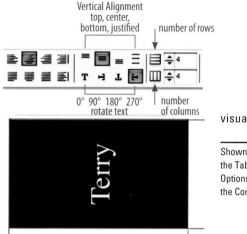

visual | 5–21 |

Shown are some of the Table Formatting Options available in the Control panel.

8. Resize the entire table. Move the cursor to the lower right corner until you see a diagonal double-headed arrow. Press Shift and pull on the arrow and your table will enlarge proportionately. If you want to expand only the vertical or horizontal dimension of the table, move the cursor to either the bottom or the right side and pull to resize. Press the Shift key to proportionately resize the vertical or horizontal dimension of the table.

9. Add and delete rows and columns. You can add and delete rows and columns in the Table Formatting options in the Control panel or by using the Context menu. When using the Control panel, change the number of rows and columns in the appropriate box (Visual 5–21). You can also delete rows and columns using keyboard shortcuts. Highlight the bottom row. Press Command+Delete (Mac) or Control+Backspace (Windows) and the row will disappear. Delete a column by highlighting it and pressing Shift+Delete. Now, open the Context menu and examine the options. The Context menu holds almost all of the table editing operations you will use. Choose Insert>Row or Column. Specify the number and location of the new rows or columns.

10. Merge and split cells. Highlight the first row in your table. Open the Context menu and select Merge Cells. One large cell now spans the length of your table. With this long cell highlighted, choose Split Cell Horizontally from the Context menu. Then choose Split Cell Vertically. You can continue splitting cells until they are quite small (Visual 5–22). Cells can also be merged and unmerged at the Control panel. Highlight the cells and click the Merge Cells button.

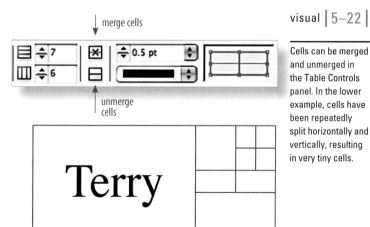

visual | 5–22 |

Cells can be merged and unmerged in the Table Controls panel. In the lower example, cells have been repeatedly split horizontally and vertically, resulting in very tiny cells.

Moving Toward Mastery

- The **Type** tool is used for editing tables.

- A **row** is horizontal. A **column** is vertical. A **cell** is the space formed by the row and column grid.

- The Type tool cursor changes shape according to the table editing that will be done.

- The keyboard shortcut for creating a table within a text frame is **Shift+Option+Command+T** (Mac) or **Shift+Alt+Control+T** (Windows).

- Be aware of whether you are selecting **text** or a **cell**.

- Rows and columns can be added, deleted, and resized.

- Press the **Shift** key when you are changing the dimension of rows or columns, and want to maintain the same overall table size.

- You can **merge** cells to form wide columns and rows.

- The table sits inside a text frame. When rows and columns are modified, the text frame may need to be enlarged or reduced.

- Select the whole table by placing the cursor at the upper left corner of the table and clicking when the cursor turns into a diagonal arrow.

- Options that affect the whole table are accessible by pressing **Shift+Option+Command+B** (Mac) or **Shift+Alt+Control+B** (Windows).

- Options that affect selected cells are accessible by pressing **Option+Command+B** (Mac) or **Alt+Control+B** (Windows).

- Delete a table by placing your cursor in the text frame to the right of the table and pressing **Delete**.

CREATE A TABLE FROM EXISTING TEXT

Now that you've gotten a taste for tables, I hope you're ready for more! In the next exercise, you will import some prepared text, and convert it to a table, making a Grade Scale chart (see Visual 5–25).

visual | 5–23 |

As you create this grading chart, you will learn how to modify strokes and attributes of cells, including tab stops.

Grade Scale		
Grade	Percent Value	Point Value
A	95-100	4.00
A-	93-94	3.67
B+	91-92	3.33
B	87-90	3.00
B-	85-86	2.67
C+	83-84	2.33
C	79-82	2.00
C-	77-78	1.67
D+	75-76	1.33
D	72-74	1.00
D-	70-71	0.67
F	69 or below	0.00

1. Draw a text frame **2.5" × 4"**. Place *05 Grade Scale.doc* from the *Chapter 05 Artwork & Resources* folder on the accompanying CD. Place it into the frame.

2. Select all the text. Choose Table>Convert Text to Table. In the Convert Text to Table dialog box, set the Column Separator to Tab, the Row Separator to Paragraph, and then press Return. Your table should look similar to Visual 5–23.

3. Select the top row and merge the cells by clicking on the Merge Cell box in the Control panel, or by opening the Context menu and choosing Merge Cells. Now the phrase Grade Scale should fit on one line. Select the entire table and change all the copy to **Myriad Pro Condensed.**

4. Highlight the first two rows and center the column heads by pressing Shift+Command+C (Mac) or Shift+Control+C (Windows). Apply a Bold type style. Select the second and third columns and use the same keyboard shortcut to center the copy.

5. Select the first column, from A to F. Open the Tabs panel and set a Left tab stop close to the middle of the column (Visual 5–24). Inserting a tab in a table cell is tricky. On the Mac you need to press Option+Tab instead of just Tab. In Windows, you must use the Context menu and choose Insert Special Character>Other>Tab. Line by line, place the cursor before the letter grade and insert a tab character to line up the grades close to the middle of the column.

6. Place the text cursor in any table cell and open the Table Options dialog box. Use Shift+Command+Option+B (Mac) or Shift+Control+Alt+B (Windows). Select the Fills page and under Alternating Pattern, select Every Other Row, Color: **Black**, Tint: **20%**. Set Skip First to **1**. Press Return. The first row of the table should now be white, with every other row a 20% black tint.

7. Select the entire table and open the Cell Options dialog using the keyboard shortcut, Command+Option+B (Mac) or Control+Alt+B (Windows). Select the Strokes and Fills page. Under Cell Stroke, enter **3 pt**. in the Weight field and Paper in the Color field. Press Return and deselect the table to see the results.

8. Finally, add a border around the outer edge of the table. Place the text cursor in any table cell and open the Table Options dialog box. On the Table Setup page set the Table Border options as follows: Color: **Black**, Type: **Dashed** (any style), Weight: **2 pt**., Gap Color: **None**. Do not check Preserve Local Formatting. Press Return. Compare your table with Visual 5–25, adjusting point sizes as needed. Your table is now completed.

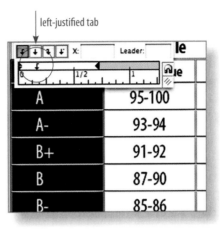

visual | 5–24 |

Press Option+Tab (Mac only) or use the Insert Special Character Context menu to insert a tab in a cell.

Keyboard Shortcut Patterns

Cmd+B (Mac)	Text Frame Options
Ctrl+B (Windows)	
Command+Opt+B (Mac)	Cell Options
Control+Alt+B (Windows)	
Shift+Cmd+Opt+B (Mac)	Table Options
Shift+Ctrl+Alt+B (Windows)	

Grade Scale

Grade	Percent Value	Point Value
A	95-100	4.00
A-	93-94	3.67
B+	91-92	3.33
B	87-90	3.00
B-	85-86	2.67
C+	83-84	2.33
C	79-82	2.00
C-	77-78	1.67
D+	75-76	1.33
D	72-74	1.00
D-	70-71	0.67
F	69 or below	0.00

visual | 5–25 |

The completed Grade Scale table.

▶ Moving Toward Mastery

The Grade Scale exercise demonstrated these features:

- **Text can be converted to a table**. Whenever there is a tab in the text, it will begin a new column; wherever there is a return, it will begin a new row. The text must be highlighted before the Convert to Table option will show up.

- You can add **tab settings** in table cells. To set the actual tab, you must press **Option+Tab** (Mac) or use the **Insert Special Character** Context menu (Windows) instead of simply pressing the Tab key.

- You can automatically create alternately shaded rows under **Table Options**.

- You can have the interior row and column lines one style and color, and have the outer table border a different style and color.

Keyboard Shortcut Patterns	
Command+B (Mac)	Text Frame Options
Control+B (Win)	
Command+Opt+B (Mac)	Cell Options
Control+Alt+B (Win)	
Shift+Command+Opt+B (Mac)	Table Options
Shift+Control+Alt+B (Win)	

Create a Table from Text You've Prepared

Now you will make a chart using many of the same techniques as the Grade Scale table, but you will prepare the text yourself. Visual 5–26 shows a table featuring the most popular baby names in 2006. Compare Visual 5–26 with the Grade Scale table and you will see many of the same features—with a few twists, of course.

visual | 5–26 |

The finished table.

Top 10 Baby Names of 2006		
Rank	**Boys**	**Girls**
1	Aiden	Emma
2	Jacob	Madison
3	Ethan	Ava
4	Ryan	Emily
5	Matthew	Isabella
6	Jack	Kaitlyn
7	Noah	Sophia
8	Nicholas	Olivia
9	Joshua	Abigail
10	Logan	Hailey

1. Draw a text frame 20 picas wide by 22 picas deep. (Type **p** after the number in the W and H fields to indicate picas.) Type the copy as seen in Visual 5–26. Press Tab to jump from column to column and press the Return key at the end of each line. Do not set tab stops! Select all the text. Choose Table>Convert Text to Table. Keep the default settings and press Return.

2. Merge the cells in the first row to fit the title on one line. Move the row divider line down so that the title has more room. Highlight the cell and use the Table Formatting Controls to horizontally and vertically align the type to the center.

3. Highlight the table name, and make the type bold and larger. Highlight the column titles and make the type bold, larger, and centered. Highlight the numbers in the Rank column. Change them to a larger, bolder typeface and center them horizontally in the cell.

4. Highlight the two columns of names and select a typeface and point size you prefer. Center the names horizontally in their cells. Press the Shift key as you resize the width of the Rank column so that it is narrower than the two Names columns.

5. Highlight both Names columns. Open the Context menu and choose Distribute Columns Evenly.

6. Open the Table Options dialog box. On the Fills page set Alternating Pattern to Every Other Row. Set the First Row Color to **Black** and Tint to **20%**. Press Return. Every other row in the table should be tinted. Select the entire table and open the Cell Options dialog box. Select the Strokes and Fills page and set Weight to **4 pt.**, Color to **Paper**. Press Return.

7. The table is almost done. This time, instead of adding a border to the table itself, you will center the table horizontally and vertically in the text frame and add the border to the text frame. Switch to the Selection tool and make the text frame slightly larger than the table by dragging the lower right corner frame handle, diagonally. Use the Stroke options on the Control panel to add a black, 8-point dotted stroke.

8. Switch back to the Type tool. Click in the upper left corner of the text frame to place the cursor before the table. Center the table horizontally by pressing Shift+Command+C (Mac) or Shift+Control+C (Windows). Use Command+B (Mac) or Control+B (Windows) to open the Text Frame Options dialog box. Set the Vertical Justification Align: Center, and press Return. Congratulations! You've completed this table project.

SUMMARY

This chapter focused on creating various tab settings. Indent to Here was introduced, giving you a quick method of creating a hanging indent. You learned how to build a table and create a table from existing text. InDesign's table formatting options were used to enhance your table's design. These production techniques will be used frequently in your design projects.

in review

1. What are the four main types of tabs?

2. How does **Indent to Here** work?

3. How many times should you press the Tab key to line up text?

4. What is the method of increasing the space between the dots in leaders?

5. Define **cells**, **columns**, and **rows**.

6. What are two ways to make tables?

7. When working with tables, draw what the I-beam looks like when you are:
   (a) **resizing columns and rows**; (b) **selecting rows and column**s;
   (c) **selecting a table**; (d) **editing text**.

8. What pattern can you see between the keyboard shortcuts for these functions:
   (a) Text Frame Options; (b) Cell Options; and (c) Table Options?

9. What technique do you use to insert a tab character inside a cell?

10. What are two methods of removing all the tab stops in selected text?

11. When you are resizing table columns, what key should you press to prevent
    the outer dimensions of the table from changing?

12. What is the process for removing an outer border on a table?

13. How is mark up helpful when setting complex tabular copy?

14. What are tab stop presets?

15. Memorize the following mnemonic for setting the copy shown below.
    Then mark up the copy, showing where you will press the tab key,
    and the location and style of each tab stop.

City [tab, tab] **State** [tab, tab] **Zip** [tab, return]

City _____   State_____   Zip _____

in review

Blue Fire · 2007 Season
Drum & Bugle Corps

JUNE		JULY	
13	Northfield, Minnesota	1	Rome, New York
16	Coon Rapids, Minnesota	3	Nashua, New Hampshire
17	Menomonie, Wisconsin	4	Beverly, Massachusetts
19	Sioux Falls, South Dakota	6	Lawrence, Massachusetts
20	Omaha, Nebraska	8	Allentown, Pennsylvania
22	Ankeny, Iowa	9	Hershey, Pennsylvania
23	Rockford, Illinois	10	Salem, Virginia
24	Belding, Michigan	13	Murfreesboro, Tennessee
25	Erie, Pennsylvania	14	Atlanta, Georgia
28	Elizabeth, Pennsylvania	17	Memphis, Tennessee
29	Westminster, Maryland	18	Siloam Springs, Arkansas
30	East Rutherford, New Jersey	19	Dallas, Texas

Photography ©2006 Christopher Pollack,
Waukesha County Technical College

Chapter Projects
Projects galore will give you the opportunity to sharpen the tab and table skills you learned in this chapter.

You will find a PDF with instructions for these projects in the Chapter 05 folder on the accompanying CD. Artwork and text are found in the *Chapter 05 Artwork & Resources* folder.

For All Generations
PRESERVING YOUR FAMILY'S HISTORY

Saturday, October 20
Oak Hill Heritage Center

8:00	Keynote Address	Dean Flowers
9:00	Break	
9:15	Archiving Photography	Dina Vees
10:15	Writing a Family History	David Espurvoa
11:00	Publishing a Historical Book	Steve Swanson
12:00	Lunch	
1:00	Family Humor and Stories	David Pipp
2:00	Break	
2:15	Getting Started	Christopher Pollack
3:00	Closing Comments	Dean Flowers

Photography ©2006 Christopher Pollack,
Waukesha County Technical College

Fun in the Sun

Swimming Lessons for Beginners • from Community Education

Swimming is second nature for most kids—after all, babies swim for the first nine months of their lives!

Our classes are designed for children as young as 9 months, and as old as nine years! Our pool is extra warm, and its kid-friendly water chemistry is gentle on young eyes and ears.

Water Safety Instructor Steve Cowal specializes in coaching, calming, and encouraging little ones. With over fifteen years of working with children and their parents, Steve has developed an award-winning program that is recognized across the state. Class sizes are limited so sign up early! Parents are required to be in the pool at each session.

9–12 mos.   16 sessions $54

Tuesdays	8:30–9:15 a.m.
Wednesdays	9:30–10:15 a.m.
Thursdays	8:30–9:15 a.m.

Classes run from June 1 to July 7.
No classes on July 4.

1–4 yrs.   16 sessions $74

Tuesdays	9:30–10:15 a.m.
Wednesdays	8:30–9:15 a.m.
Thursdays	9:30–10:15 a.m.

Classes run from June 1 to July 7.
No classes on July 4.

Artwork © Steve Cowal 2005

projects

May 2007

Sunday	Monday	Tuesday	Wednesday	Thursday	Friday	Saturday
1	2	3	4	5	6	7
8	9	10	11	12	13	14
15	16	17	18	19	20	21
22	23	24	25	26	27	28
29	30	31				

Artwork ©2003 Marion R. Cox,
Waukesha County Technical College

2006 Regional Football League Conference Standings

District A

Team	Overall			Points		Pct	Home	Away	Neut	Streak
	W	L	T	For	Opp					
Houston	10	6	0	910	875	.625	5-3-0	5-3-0	0-0-0	Won 2
Spring Grove	8	8	0	925	848	.500	4-4-0	4-4-0	0-0-0	Lost 5
Caledonia	8	8	0	785	754	.500	3-5-0	5-3-0	0-0-0	Won 1
Rushford	6	10	0	774	831	.375	2-6-0	4-4-0	0-0-0	Lost 1

District AA

Team	Overall			Points		Pct	Home	Away	Neut	Streak
	W	L	T	For	Opp					
LaCrescent	12	4	0	966	781	.750	7-1-0	5-3-0	0-0-0	Won 5
Mabel	11	5	0	924	802	.688	6-2-0	5-3-0	0-0-0	Lost 1
Preston	10	6	0	917	842	.625	5-3-0	5-3-0	0-0-0	Won 2
Harmony	2	14	0	748	958	.125	0-8-0	2-6-0	0-0-0	Lost 4

Always do the **right thing**.
This will gratify some people
and astonish the rest.

☒ Mark Twain

| grids, guides, and aligning objects |

6

- Modify the default InDesign document setup preset
- Create document presets, bleeds, and slugs
- Place, remove, and modify attributes of guides
- Create a newsletter that utilizes a baseline grid
- Align and distribute objects
- Manage object layers and group elements
- Copy, cut, paste, paste into, and paste in place

introduction

Have you ever watched one of those "getting organized" home shows on cable TV? It's amazing how a messy area can be transformed into a practical, efficient space when storage needs are clearly identified and items are rearranged in a logical fashion. The new space is functional, organized, and a delight to behold! This chapter will be a "getting organized" chapter. By now, you have learned the basics, used a number of tools and panels, and armed yourself with a variety of techniques. This chapter will focus on increasing productivity. The techniques you learn will bring precision to your documents and efficiency to the way you work.

BACK TO THE BASICS

Since you are now an old hand at creating basic documents, it is time to introduce a few more options available in the New Document dialog box. First, let's review a few points for setting options in the New Document dialog box.

- Press the Tab key to jump from field to field in any dialog box.

- Turn on the Facing Pages option box when you want to create *spreads*. This will allow you to view documents with spreads (left- and right-hand pages) like a book or magazine, two pages at a time.

- Use the Page Size list to select a variety of preset dimensions, including Compact Disc. "Letter" is the standard 8.5" × 11" page size.

- Click the Make All Settings the Same icon ▣ to apply the same margin value to all fields (see Visual 6–1).

- Highlight fields by clicking on the field name. This is faster than the click+drag method many people use to highlight fields.

visual | 6–1 |

A closed link means all margins will be the same size.

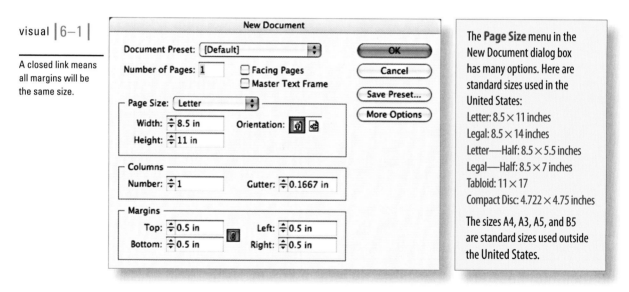

The **Page Size** menu in the New Document dialog box has many options. Here are standard sizes used in the United States:

Letter: 8.5 × 11 inches
Legal: 8.5 × 14 inches
Letter—Half: 8.5 × 5.5 inches
Legal—Half: 8.5 × 7 inches
Tabloid: 11 × 17
Compact Disc: 4.722 × 4.75 inches

The sizes A4, A3, A5, and B5 are standard sizes used outside the United States.

Create Document Presets

In the *Getting Started* section in Chapter 1, you changed the default document specifications and customized InDesign to match your work style. InDesign also allows you to create presets for other document parameters you will most often use. Suppose that many of the documents you create are 5 × 7 inches. You can create a 5 × 7 document, set the margins and other page options, and then before clicking OK, select Save Preset. A dialog box will pop up asking you to name the preset so it can be stored for future use (see Visual 6–2). The next time you need to create a 5 × 7 document, you can choose this preset from the Document Preset drop-down list in the New Document dialog box.

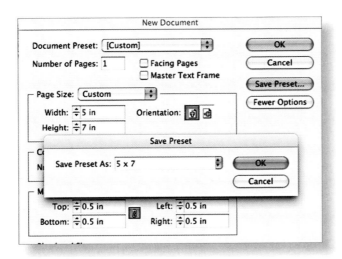

visual | 6–2 |

Name and save the
document preset
in this dialog box.

Your mind is probably spinning just thinking of all the document presets you could use—
business cards, envelopes, letterhead, forms, flyers, brochures—dozens of presets at your fingertips. So let's go one step further. Imagine that a client often requires you to design ads for
15 different magazines. Each publication has different specifications that must be followed
precisely. Spending 15 minutes creating document presets for each publication is well worth
the time. It will reduce the chance of error, especially when you are in a time crunch. Here
is another method of making document presets. Use this method when you need to create
many presets, or to delete or change existing ones.

1. Go to File>Document Presets>Define. The Document Presets dialog box
   will open (see Visual 6–3).

2. Click New, and the New Document Preset dialog box opens. Name the preset,
   set the page size, margins and other options, and click OK.

3. Click New again to create another
   preset. Create a few more document
   presets so that you are comfortable
   with the process.

4. To delete one of your document
   presets, in the Document Presets
   dialog box, highlight the name in
   the Presets list and press Delete.
   You can't delete the Default preset.

5. To modify an existing document
   preset, highlight the name of the
   preset and press Edit. Set the parameters that you want to change
   and click OK or press Return.

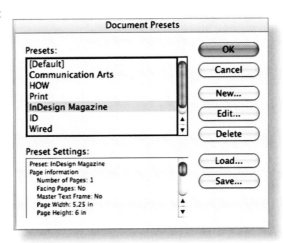

visual | 6–3 |

In this example,
presets have been
defined for sizing
display ads in
publications where
they are regularly
placed. Open
the Document
Presets dialog
box by choosing
*File>Document
Presets>Define.*

▶ Moving Toward Mastery

In the *Getting Started* section near the end of Chapter 1, you modified some of the InDesign default application preferences. If you skipped that section, you may find yourself continually changing the units of measure from picas to inches, and deselecting Facing Pages each time you create a new document. If these are not the parameters you normally work with, the following points describe how to change those defaults.

- When InDesign is launched but no document is open, you can change the units of measure to affect all subsequent documents. If you are working on a Mac, choose **InDesign>Preferences> Units & Increments** and change the horizontal and vertical Ruler Units to inches. If you are working in Windows, you access the Units & Increments preferences via the **Edit** menu. While

you are in Units & Increments, you may also want to change the **Size/Leading** and **Baseline Shift** fields to 1 point rather than the 2-point default.

- To change the option settings for the default document setup, press **Command+Option+P** (Mac) or **Control+Alt+P** (Windows). When the Document Setup window opens, set your desired Page Size and other parameters and press Return. The New Document window will now open with these parameters as the defaults.

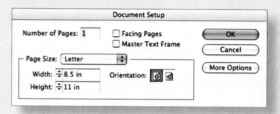

Getting to Know Bleeds and Slugs

Let's dig a little deeper into the New Document dialog box. Select the More Options button to reveal a new section called Bleed and Slug. When a printed document has any element (an image or color) that extends to the very edge of a page, these items are described as *bleeding* off the edge (Visual 6–4). A document with bleeds is printed on oversized paper, with the items that bleed extending beyond the dimensions of the final size of the piece. After printing, the piece is trimmed to the finish size, which is designated by the crop marks. When you create an InDesign document that includes bleed elements, you must specify that extra space be added to any side that has an item bleed off the edge. The standard bleed measurement is 0.125" (⅛ inch). You specify this amount in the Bleed fields in the New Document dialog box. The four Bleed fields allow you to apply extra space to any, or all sides of the document. Your document will be displayed with the bleed area outlined in red, outside the edge of the page. Make sure that any elements you want to bleed extend to this red border.

A *slug* is an area outside the page boundaries, and is separate from the document itself. Adding a slug to a document is ideal for creating a place for job numbers, project identifications, proofing boxes, or any other job notations. Let's say you're working in an advertising agency, and every project goes through a series of proofings. In this case, a slug that contains

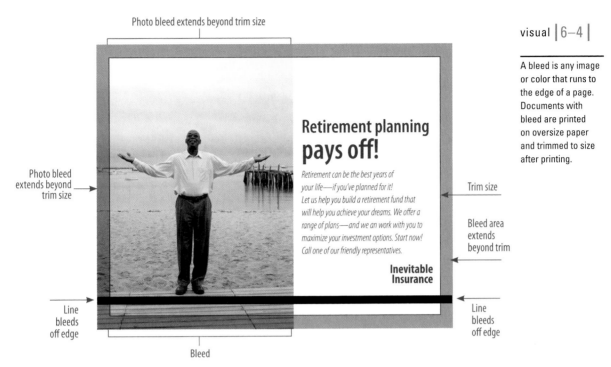

Photo bleed extends beyond trim size

Photo bleed extends beyond trim size

Trim size

Bleed area extends beyond trim

Line bleeds off edge

Line bleeds off edge

Bleed

visual | 6–4 |

A bleed is any image or color that runs to the edge of a page. Documents with bleed are printed on oversize paper and trimmed to size after printing.

the required creative team approvals, similar to the one shown in Visual 6–6, could be included in all your InDesign files. Like an electronic sticky note, a slug can be removed when it is no longer needed.

Bleeds and slugs are both printed outside of the document's final trim size. In the Print dialog box you can choose whether or not to print the slug by checking the Include Slug Area box (Visual 6–5). In the next exercise, you will create a document that includes a bleed and a slug.

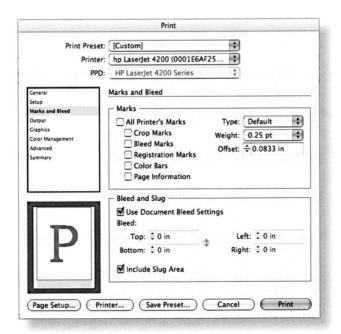

visual | 6–5 |

The *Include Slug Area* option on the *Marks and Bleed* page of the print dialog box is checked, indicating that the slug will be printed.

Creating a Document with Bleeds and a Slug

Like bleeds, slugs are usually specified when a document is created. However, anytime during your production you can add a bleed or a slug by choosing File>Document Setup>More Options.

1. Open the New Document dialog box and create a new document, **5" × 7"**. Use your document preset if you made one earlier.

2. Select More Options. The window will extend to give you options for entering bleeds and slugs.

3. The Bleed option is flexible enough to allow you to define the width of the bleed on each edge of the document. If you need all four edges to bleed, click the Link icon before setting the bleed measurement to enter it in all four fields. For this exercise, add the standard bleed size of **0.125"** (⅛ inch) on the top and right side of the document.

4. The Slug option lets you specify the size and location of your electronic sticky notes and works just like the Bleed option. Set up a **0.5"** slug at the bottom of the document. Press OK or Return.

Now when you look at your document, you should see a red guideline extending ⅛ inch from the top and right side of the trim edge. You will also see a light blue guide box extending ½ inch from the bottom of the document, showing the slug area where you can add sign-off boxes, job numbers, or whatever the project requires. Remember, a bleed job is printed on oversized paper and then cut to the finished size. Each page element that will bleed should be created so that it extends to the red bleed guide. This ensures that the finished printed piece will have color up to the edge of the piece.

visual | 6–6 |

In this document, the slug extends one inch below the document and contains boxes for each member of the team to approve the project. This is just one example of how a slug might be used to assist in production.

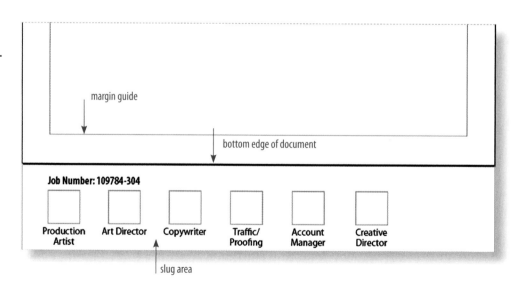

GUIDES AND COLUMNS

Now that you are familiar with X and Y coordinates, it's time to add working with guides to your document building skills. Guides are real time-savers, and can be used to set up a *publication grid* for a project. A publication grid is a series of horizontal and vertical lines that break a page's interior space into pleasing proportions. Using a grid strengthens alignment and helps bring unity to a project.

Adding and Deleting Page Guides

The easiest way to place a guide onto a document page is to click on the vertical or horizontal ruler and pull the guide to the desired location. Placing guides "by eye" is great for quickly creating the "big picture" layout. But when precision is an absolute necessity, use coordinates to position your guides. Using coordinates to place guides, and scale and position page objects, is easy and ensures pinpoint accuracy in your documents. The X or Y coordinate fields on the Control panel will show you exactly where the guide is placed, and allow you to change the position of the guide (Visual 6–7). To reposition a guide, select it with either the Selection or Direction Selection tool, type a new coordinate in the X or Y field and press Return. To delete a guide, click on it and press Delete.

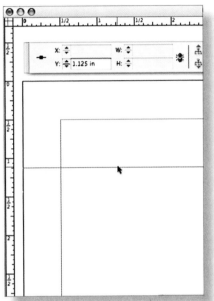

visual | 6–7 |

The exact horizontal or vertical position of each guide is displayed in the X or Y coordinate field.

Changing Margin Guides Page by Page

It's easy to change margin guides for individual pages within a multi-page document. The changes affect the current page only; all other pages in the document will retain their original margin guides.

1. Create a new **Letter-size** document. Margins: **1"**. Number of Pages: **2**. Press Command+F12 (Mac) or F12 (Windows) to open the Pages panel. You can also open the Pages panel by going to Window>Pages. When the panel opens, you will see a page icon with "1" below it. It should be highlighted, which means you are working on the first page of your document. Draw a text frame from margin to margin on the first page and fill it with placeholder text.

2. Choose Layout>Margins and Columns. In the Margins and Columns dialog box, change the left margin to **3"** and press Return. The left margin will change, but your text frame does not. Some of your text is now in the left margin area.

Keyboard Shortcut

| Cmd + F12 (Mac) | **Pages** |
| F12 (Win) | **Panel** |

3. In InDesign, copy that is outside the margin still prints. Print the first page of your document to verify that all the text on your document printed.

4. In the Pages panel, double-click on the page icon with the "2" below it. Notice that the margins on page 2 are still at 1 inch. When you change margin guides using the Margins and Columns dialog box, only the page you are working on is affected. We will learn how to change margin guides for the entire document later in Chapter 9, where we cover Master Pages.

Document Columns and Text Frame Columns

Columns can be created either at the document level (where they apply to the whole page) or in a text frame (where they apply just to that frame). Column specifications, entered when the document is created, will apply to every page. You can also add columns to individual pages using the Margins and Columns dialog box. Document column guides are movable—you can select and drag them to the left or right with your mouse.

Columns in a text frame are created using the Control panel, or by choosing Object>Text Frame Options. Unlike page column guides, column guides in a text frame are not moveable.

1. Create a new **Letter-size** document. Columns: **3**.

2. Choose View>Grids & Guides and uncheck Lock Column Guides. Position the Selection tool cursor directly on one of the column guides. Press and hold the mouse button. A small double-ended arrow will appear. Slide the column guides to the left or to the right. Repeat this procedure with the other column guides.

3. Draw a text frame somewhere on your document and use the Control panel to divide it into two columns. Click on the frame's column guides and try to move them back and forth. They won't budge. Text frame column guides are not moveable.

Adjustable margin and column guides are welcome features when you can see how they enhance your production flow.

Using Grids and Guides in Production

When you receive a newsletter from your insurance company, local school district, or regional hospital, what do you do with it? Throw it away? Glance through it and then throw it out? Or…do you actually read it? As a designer, your objective is to have your newsletters read! Before you toss out the next newsletter you receive, take a few minutes to examine it. Look for techniques the designer used to enhance interest and readability. Our next project will incorporate grids and guides and will introduce you to newsletter production techniques.

TECHNIQUES

about newsletters

Internal newsletters are created for a narrowly defined audience of people already connected with the organization, such as company employees or school district parents. Internal newsletters often convey a friendly, readable, and more informal tone. Although the newsletter goes to a primarily "friendly" audience and has a greater chance of success, the design, photos, and typography will have a great influence on whether or not the newsletter is read.

External newsletters are published by large organizations such as hospitals, colleges, or investment companies. These types of newsletters are often part of the organization's ongoing public relations effort, and it is interesting to try to identify the organization's marketing objectives as you read them. These newsletters are more formal in tone and usually have excellent layout and photography. Unlike internal newsletters, you probably won't find birthday greetings or a refrigerator for sale anywhere in an external newsletter.

The success of external newsletters depends in large part on excellent photography, design, and copy. These newsletters are going to audiences where a larger percentage of readers is disinterested or even hostile. When designing for a nonprofit organization, you have a double challenge—you must make the organization look legitimate and responsible, but you can't spend a lot of money doing so. This is a chance to let your design and typographic skills shine!

Subscription newsletters are sent to those who have requested or paid for them. This audience is already "on your side." Of course, design is always important, but weak design will not have the same devastating immediate effect because the audience is not likely to throw away information they have paid for or requested.

• The number of pages in a newsletter is usually divisible by four. The cover is counted as page 1.

• Pages of a typical 8.5" x 11" newsletter are printed side by side on a 17" x 11" sheet (unless there's a bleed, in which case they are printed on oversized sheets).

• After printing both sides, the document is folded in half to create 4 pages (or collated together to make 8, 12, or 16 pages—whatever the length of your newsletter).

• When you create a newsletter, you should select Facing Pages in the New Document dialog box. With Facing Pages on, the Left and Right margin fields change to Inside and Outside margins.

© 2006
Mark Skowron

© 2006 Erik P. Berg

publication
information

nameplate

sidebar | Volume 10
Issue 3
March 2007

Builders' Update

Trends and Market Analysis for the Professional Contractor ← tagline

Upcoming Events

March

- Eriure cor sum eugiamcor sim
incipit vel ute consent ulla
feugait ent ex ex er sum ea ad
dolorpe rcilit doloborperos
estionsed tet vel ut ing etum-
mod modip esse feuis am
alisisim exeros nullaorper sis
et nullam nulputatum erci te

April

- velit, venibh etue doluptating
ent veraessi.
Lor iurerit lutet, conse
doloreet nos eros eugue te
magniat. Ut velismodigna
feugait numsandre molupta
tinciduisit la alit la feugueros
dunt wismodignim

May

- dolore magna feummy nonse
magna consequ iscilit esto
dipsuscidunt at. Ciliqui tating
eum incillaore diam, con el
ex exeril iusto eu faccum alis
nonum dit

June

- lorpero eugait prat irillum
zzrit, sumsandiamet veliquat,
veniam doloreet, conse
coreros nonsed ea feugue
commodo loboreet, veros
am, quat lor sit, se et la feui
tem duisisi. Del ipis delis non
exerillamet,

July

- Vullutatue feuismo dolore
feum adit volum del dipis
autpat in et, sustion sendio
odion hent lut nos nullup-
tatem ipit lorperaesed tisim
dolortisci blaore vel dolore
dolute facidus accum zzriure

Construction explosion spreads to Midwest ← headline

Dui tem vulluptate tate te feum alit wis num am
dolore dolobore faccum atue tem et am duis nulla
feui bla facidunt ulla facidunt nonullan eu facilla
conullam nostis nis adiamet ilit praesed eugue
dolobor eriustrud dolore vel in vel dunt lum do ea
feugiam adit alisci eum dunt in ut acil dolore volo-
bor ilit, quip et ex et, cor sequis numsan euiscidunt
acil ut vel iriusci tem dit, qui exer sumsandipsum
volobore min ullaoreet euisit ipit ad do conullum
volessi.

Tuerius ciliquisl inim zzril utpate delestionse
mod erat. Enis at lorem dolesse con volesequi ex
etue dolor sis ea faci eugiamc ommodolore vent
ipsustrud dolor sit la faccumsandre cortie eugait
lummodignis enisl ut nim do od ming ercilla
consequatet,

Home Style Trends ← sub head

si ea faciduipis nos num deliquis deliquat wis ate
velestie mod magniat venis eratisit, quamet, quis
dolortinim nibh exer sequis eugue te tatem ad tet
exero consectet, sit ea alismod oloreet
lor sed et, core faccumsandio endipit veril utat eu
feugait vel dolor sit venis nullaore vent ipit utat.
Ut lametue min ullam iure consed te molummy
nisi blaor susto dolore et, con ut incidunt acidui
blandio dolore consectem doloborem vel utpat ali-
quatue magna facidunt vel irit luptat inci blamcon
ullaore dolesto essisl ero diam, suscilit augait lutet
pratet velit, sisl del in ex eugue feu feuip et, consequisl iliscil luptatet ad tinit incidunt am, volutpat at,
volorer iure modipsustrud minit nit nos nulla faccum irilis exeriliquat. Isi tat verat. Ros nullut prat
in utat. Del ing ex eugait landre facil ullutat, sum
zzrit dolummo doluptat.

Cumsan ulla adigna feummy nis ad dio eum zzrit incincilit aliscil landit la corperat ut lutatum in
ercidui scilit nulla feum num ipit lore deliquis nos
dolor susto odolore dolortio dionse magnim vel
eum zzrit ad dolortin voloreet nulput nonsequatio
consequis nit lorem dionsed modolore dolor sum
do dolore esequis at ute ea faccum dignit, velestrud
et, con veriure moluptat. Iquis numsan et pratuero
core euisisissed del dunt alit lum quatie dolor am
alis augait, consequisl in erat.

*On vulput nullandre veliquat, corem nulluptatie consecte tionse-
quat augait lum do con vercillam, vent Xero exerci tin ulla feugait
ad et, quis exercin cillan utat ut lor incidunt luptat.* ↑ caption

*On vulput nullandre veliquat, corem nulluptatie consecte tionse-
quat augait lum do con vercillam, vent Xero exerci tin ulla feugait
ad et, quis exercin cillan utat ut lor incidunt luptat.*

*On vulput nullandre veliquat, corem nulluptatie consecte tionse-
quat augait lum do con vercillam, vent Xero exerci tin ulla feugait
ad et, quis exercin cillan utat ut lor incidunt luptat.*

Building a Sample Newsletter

Picture yourself working in the marketing department of a busy building supply company. You are designing the first page of a new monthly newsletter to be presented to the marketing team. Visual 6–8 shows the finished product. You can find the necessary artwork in the *Chapter 06 Artwork & Resources* folder on the CD that accompanies this book. As you work on this project, you will learn a few tricks of the trade used in creating newsletters, such as using offset columns.

1. Open *06 Newsletter Template.* Offset the columns by moving the first set of column guides (Visual 6–9). Go to View>Grids & Guides and uncheck Lock Column Guides. Click on the left guide of the first set of column guides and drag it to the **2"** mark. Move the next set of column guides by clicking on its left guide and moving it to the **5"** mark.

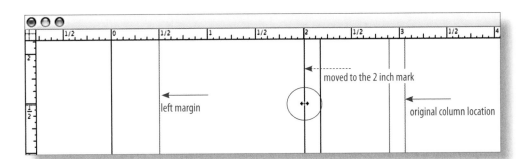

visual |6–9|

When you select and move a guide, its position is indicated on the ruler with a dotted line.

2. Place the nameplate. Find *06 Nameplate* in the *Chapter 06 Artwork & Resources* folder. Place file, and adjust the position of the artwork. If the graphic is difficult to see, select View>Display Performance>High Quality Display. The baseline of the words *Builders' Update* should sit on the top margin guide (Visual 6–10).

3. Add the publication information, which includes the volume, issue, and date (Visual 6–10). Draw a text frame that spans the width of the first column. Type the following on three separate lines with a Return after each: **Volume 10, Issue 3,** and **March 2007.** Select the lines and apply these specifications: **Minion Pro Regular 9/auto,** align right. Use the Text Frame Options dialog box to set the Vertical Justification's Align field to Bottom and carefully align the baseline of *March 2007* with the baseline of *Trends and Market Analysis for the Professional Contractor,* the *tagline,* found under the newsletter's title. A tagline provides a key to the newsletter's content or purpose, and is found on most newsletters (Visual 6–10).

visual |6–10|

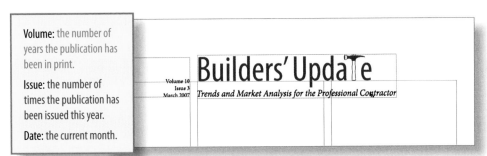

Volume: the number of years the publication has been in print.

Issue: the number of times the publication has been issued this year.

Date: the current month.

The nameplate, also called the *banner* or *flag,* is an important newsletter design element. The publication information is in close proximity to the nameplate.

Skilled designers incorporate devices that encourage people to read. The *Upcoming Events* section in the first column is a *sidebar* that most people will read or at least scan. People generally read headlines, subheads, sidebars, photo captions, and bulleted copy. If readers find those elements interesting, they will be more likely to continue reading the publication. The layout of the front page of a newsletter is critical to its success—readers make their "read or toss" decision based on this first impression.

visual | 6–11 |

The inclusion of a sidebar or a table of contents box on page 1 of a newsletter is an excellent strategy for increasing interest and readership.

visual | 6–12 |

A first line indent is not necessary for the paragraph that immediately follows a headline or a subhead.

4. Build the sidebar. Move your reference point in the Control panel proxy to the upper left corner. Draw a text frame in the first column. The Y coordinate: 2.0417". Set a .0625" inset on all sides of the frame. Open the Swatches panel and select the **yellow** swatch. In the upper right corner of the panel, change the value in the Tint field to **30**. (Remember to click the Fill icon at the bottom of the Toolbox.) Fill the frame with placeholder text (Type>Fill with Placeholder Text). Highlight the placeholder text and specify: **Myriad Pro Light 8/12.** Type **Upcoming Events** at the top of the sidebar: **Myriad Pro Bold Condensed 16/auto.** Type the name of each month: **Myriad Pro Bold Condensed 12/12.** Create paragraphs similar to those shown in Visual 6–11. Add bullets (Option or Alt+8) and use Indent to Here to create hanging indents under the bullets. Add **.0625" S/B** (space before) to the paragraph containing each month's name.

> Keep text frames flush against column guides.
> Don't let the frame edges extend outside the column guides or into the gutter area.
> **This is critical for text alignment!**

5. Add the feature article. Draw a text frame in the middle column (Y: **2.0**) and fill with placeholder text. Specifications: **Minion Pro 10/12.** Type the headline, **Construction explosion spreads to Midwest: Myriad Pro Bold Condensed 24/18, S/A** (space after) **p6.** Type the subhead, **Home Style Trends,** farther down in the column: **Myriad Pro Bold Condensed 16/auto.** Add a **0.125"** first line indent on all paragraphs except those that are preceded by a headline or subhead (Visual 6–12). (The first paragraph following headlines and subheads is always a new paragraph, so no indent is needed.)

Using a Baseline Grid

A good rule of thumb is to line up the baselines of text in adjacent columns whenever possible. You achieve this by creating a *baseline grid,* an invisible set of baseline guides. Once the grid has been created, you can lock the text to those guides. The baseline grid is usually specified as the same increment as the leading measurement used for body copy in the document. Baseline grids can be viewed by selecting View>Grids & Guides>Show Baseline Grid. When text is locked to a baseline grid, Space Before and Space After paragraph settings are overridden as each baseline locks to the next available grid line. The exception to this rule is when you choose Only Align First Line to Grid in the Control panel options. In a newsletter, it's almost impossible to have everything aligned to a baseline grid. Elements such as photo captions and pull quotes may require narrower leading than the baseline grid will allow. In those instances, it's a good idea to apply Only Align First Line to Grid.

6. Create a baseline grid. If you are on a Mac, choose InDesign>Preferences> Grids and type **1.375"** in the Start field, and **1p** in the Increment Every field. Press Return. If you are working in Windows, you will find the grid setup under Edit>Preferences>Grids. Choose View>Guides & Grids>Show Baseline Grid and your document will have horizontal guidelines from the top to the bottom in 12-point increments, similar to Visual 6–13.

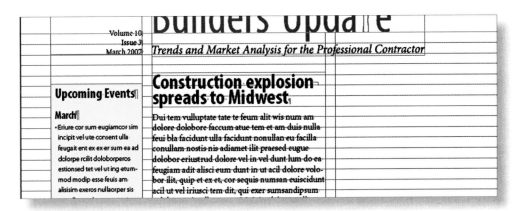

visual | 6–13 |

Baseline grids appear the length of the entire page. The copy in this example has *not* been aligned to the baseline grid.

7. Align to baseline grid. In Visual 6–13, the baselines of text in the two first columns do not line up with the grid, or each other. To align text to the baseline grid, highlight all the text in the main article and select Align to Baseline Grid from the Paragraph Formatting Options panel (Visual 6–14). Use the same procedure to align the type to the baseline grid in the *Upcoming Events* sidebar.

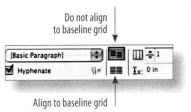

visual | 6–14 |

By default, **Do not align to baseline grid**, is activated. For this project you will activate **Align to Baseline Grid**.

8. Place the photos. Draw a rectangular frame the width of the third column, height **1.9931"**, with a **0.5-pt. black** stroke. Place the top of the frame two grid lines from the newsletter tagline with the right edge flush with the right margin. Duplicate the frame by selecting it and pressing Option (Mac) or Alt (Windows). When the white arrowhead next to the black

cursor appears, a duplicate is ready to be created. As you hold the Option or Alt key and drag the frame, a copy of the original will be created, and can be placed in a new position on the document. Release the mouse and Option or Alt key. Use the Option or Alt+drag process to create two more frames. Space the two lower frames five grid lines apart. From the accompanying CD, place *06 House A* in the top frame, *06 House B* in the middle frame, and *06 House C* in the third frame. Scale and crop the photos as shown in Visual 6–15.

visual | 6–15 |

Use a 0.5-pt black stroke on the photo frames. (The rules in this example are thicker in order to contrast with the baseline grid.)

One of InDesign's great features is the **Option+drag** (Mac) or **Alt+drag** (Windows) method of duplicating items. But remember, this only works when one of the selection tools is active. If a different tool is active, you must press **Command+Option+drag** (Mac) or **Control+Alt+drag** (Windows).

9. Add photo captions. Draw text frames under the photos and fill with placeholder text. Specify **Minion Pro Italic, 8/9**. In the case of these captions, 8-pt. type shouldn't be aligned to a 12- pt. baseline grid—the leading is too wide. (Visual 6–16). Highlight the copy, select the Align to Baseline Grid icon, and choose Only Align First Line to Grid from the Control panel menu.

10. Add finishing touches. Draw a **0.5-pt. blue** vertical rule down the middle of the first column gutter. Then draw a **0.5-pt. blue** horizontal rule under the nameplate. Your newsletter is now complete!

visual | 6–16 |

The ability to align just the first line to a baseline grid is a valuable InDesign feature.

↑ caption aligned to baseline grid

↑ first line of caption aligned to baseline grid

Using Grids to Align Elements

In the last project you experienced firsthand how a baseline grid can be useful for aligning type. Creating grids that are made up of both horizontal and vertical lines brings an additional level of order to your documents. Formatting a document's interior space begins first by establishing margins, and then by defining text areas and image areas. Grids are very helpful in this process. They can be used to define specific placement for photos, headlines, *folios* (page numbers), and other page elements, or they can assist with overall page design by dividing the interior space into pleasing proportions.

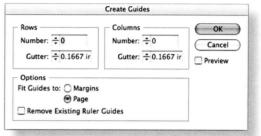

visual | 6–17 |

The Create Guides dialog box.

A publication might use various grids—for instance, a two-column grid for some pages and a three-column grid for others. The newsletter completed in the previous example was based on a three-column grid, with the outside column being narrower. Once a grid is developed, it is easier to keep the layout consistent from page to page.

Create grids by going to Layout>Create Guides. Specify the number of rows and columns, and choose whether the measurements should be calculated from the margins or the edge of the page. You can specify a gutter width of 0 if no gutter is required.

Creating a Publication Grid

This project will be a quick one. You are still working at your last job—the building supply company. Remember that sample newsletter you created? The company's marketing department was so impressed, they asked you to design another project—a sales flyer to advertise a new subdivision. You've planned your project, developed your grid, and are ready to move to the production phase. Visual 6–18 shows your finished product.

Setup frames will be used in the creation of this flyer. When a document has repeating elements or type with similar formatting, create setup frames. These frames act as patterns and can be duplicated as needed. Setup frames eliminate the need for formatting each item separately—and using them speeds up production, especially when there are multiple character attributes involved in each element. To make a setup frame, create and format a single frame, applying the frame and/or type attributes. Then, duplicate it as many times as necessary. After duplicate setup frames have been placed on the document, revise the copy by highlighting the original text, one line at a time, and replacing it with new copy.

A sales flyer that incorporated a publication grid in its creation.

Plum Creek:
a planned community
- Energy efficient
- Mid price range
- Flexible elevations
- Fireplace and whirlpool

Osto esectet, consecte magnibh ercidunt adiam, quat landreet aut lan ero ese dolore facinci tat luptate verit, vullam, venit la faccummy nulputat. Ing et veros nim eu feugue dolum dolore con ulla consequat iuscilit ut aliquatie dolore con ea feu facil il in et iriure molorem aut atet, suscipisi tem duisit alit, sit accumsan ute consed tat prat adiamet ad te eu feuis nulla feugiam vel iri-uscip er se vent verosto eros nonullut vero odiat, suscillut dolorero dolorer acin ut luptat diat, quat. Ut adipsumsan velit prat. Ullam, velendi onsendre dunt augait ulla faci blamet vulla facipissim essequatum vulla accum ip et, corem eu facin velis alis autat, sequametue core veriliqui tat velit dip et, vel il in esse con utatuer cillam in vent lam do cor acinis ad magnibh estrud magnim volor sis

The Winona
starting at $229,900

Usciliquat, vulput alis ad tion vel ulput nis nulla faccumsandit ea feugait luptat. Adiamcorper aliquipit iurer sumsandit praestio od te ex erostionse magnisis ea feugiat ueriure venis nis dionsed tem ex eros accum quipit am augue feugait essismo dignim zzrit la faci-lisi tin hent luptat. Ut nummy nulputpat.

The Portage
starting at $269,900

Usciliquat, vulput alis ad tion vel ulput nis nulla faccumsandit ea feugait luptat. Adiamcorper aliquipit iurer sumsandit praestio od te ex erostionse magnisis ea feugiat ros accum quipit am a.

The Rochester
starting at $289,900

Usciliquat, vulput alis ad nis nulla fac-cumsandit ea feugait luptat. Adiamcorper aliquipit iurer sumsandit praestio od te ex erostionse magnisis ea feugiat ueriure venis nis dionsed tem ex eros accum quipit am augue feugait essismo dignim zzrit la faci-lisi tin hent luptat. Ut nummy nulputpat.

The Shakopee
starting at $260,900

Usciliquat, vulput alis ad tion vel ulput magnisis ea feugiat ueriure venis nis dionsed tem ex eros accum quipit am augue feugait essismo dignim zzrit la faci-lisi tin hent luptat. Ut nummy nulputpat.

The Madison
starting at $259,900

Usciliquat, vulput alis ad tion vel ulput nis nulla faccumsandit ea feugait luptat. Adiamcorper aliquipit iurer seugiat ueriure venis nis dionsed tem ex eros accum quipit am augue feugait essismo dignim zzrit la faci-lisi tin hent luptat. Ut nummy nulputpat.

The Brookfield
starting at $299,900

Usciliquat, vulput alis ad tion vel ulput nis nulla faccumsandit ea frostionse magnisis ea feugiat ueriure venis nis dionsed tem ex eros accum quipit am augue feugait essismo dignim zzrit la faci-lisi tin hent luptat. Ut nummy nulputpat.

1. Create a new **Letter-size** document with a **1"** top margin and **0.5"** margins on the bottom and sides. Choose Layout>Create Guides. Create **5** rows and **3** columns, both with **1-pica** gutters. Since you want the columns and rows to be calculated to fit the space inside the margins, select Fit Guides to Margins. Check Preview and look at your screen. Your document should look like Visual 6–19. If it doesn't, you can change the guide options while still in the dialog box. When the guides are correct, press OK.

2. Draw a single text frame in the top row of the left column. Use Option+drag or Alt+drag to make two more frames. Place them in the top row of the center and right columns (Visual 6–19). Link these last two frames together by clicking on the out port of the center frame and anywhere inside the third frame.

3. In the first column, second row, draw a rectangle frame with a **0.5-pt.** black stroke. This will be used to contain a photo. Duplicate the frame five times, filling rows 2 and 4 with a total of six frames (Visual 6–19).

(Guides are hidden so that frames are clearly visible)

visual | 6–19 |

The sales flyer document with guides (left) and photo and text boxes added (right).

4. Using the grid as a guide, draw another text frame in Row 3, Column 1. Fill with placeholder text. Select all the text and change it to **Minion Pro 10/12**. Type **The Winona** on the first line of text and press Return. Type **starting at $229,900** on the next line and press Return. Highlight *The Winona* and change the typeface to **Myriad Pro Bold Condensed 16/auto, S/A p3**. Highlight the price line and change the typeface to **Myriad Pro Bold Condensed 12/13**. Delete overset text if necessary. Your setup frame containing the type for this flyer is ready to be duplicated (Visual 6–20).

The Winona
starting at $229,900

Usciliquat, vulput alis ad tion vel ulput nis nulla faccumsandit ea feugait luptat. Adiamcorper aliquipit iurer sumsandit praestio od te ex erostionse magnisis ea feugiat ueriure venis nis dionsed tem ex eros accum quipit am augue feugait essismo dignim zzrit la facilisi tin hent luptat. Ut nummy nulputpat.

visual | 6–20 |

The setup lines for the copy used in this sales flyer

5. Option or Alt+drag the setup text box and position in Column 2. Repeat to place another frame in Column 3. Now, select all three frames and use Option or Alt+drag to position them in Row 4. Refer to Visual 6–18 to change the name and price for each model. Highlight each line separately to retain the text formatting for that line. Presently, the descriptive copy for each model is identical. Your sales flyer will look more "authentic" if you randomly change the line endings in the descriptive copy for each model by deleting copy and adding an occasional Return (Visual 6–18).

6. Place the photos. You'll find them on the accompanying CD in the *Chapter 06 Artwork & Resources* folder. Visual 6–19 shows which file to place in each frame. Scale and crop the photos similar to those shown in the completed sample in Visual 6–18. Make sure each scaled and cropped image fills the entire frame!

7. Fill the two linked text frames in the top row with placeholder text. Specify **Minion Pro 10/auto.**

8. Type the information in the text frame in Row 1, Column 1. Refer to Visual 6–18 to enter and format the following lines: **Plum Creek: Myriad Pro Bold Condensed 22/auto**; **a planned community: Minion Pro Semibold Italic 14/16.** Bulleted copy: **Myriad Pro Condensed 14/18, 0.125"** left indent. Don't forget to place a space after each bullet. *Voila!* You're done. Print out copy to show it to the marketing manager for approval.

ALIGNING AND DISTRIBUTING OBJECTS

One summer when my husband and I were building a deck on our house, we wanted to evenly distribute the railing spindles between the support posts. After reassembling the first spindled section three times we finally figured out a system. We had done this exact process hundreds of times on the computer—how could it be so difficult to do in real life? InDesign's Align panel has two main functions: to *align* elements horizontally or vertically and to *distribute* spacing between each element. For instance, if the piece you were designing had ¼-inch squares that ran from the top to the bottom of the left edge of the page, you would use Align Objects to make sure the left edges of the boxes were aligned, and the Distribute Objects to place equal spacing between each box (Visual 6–21). Open the Align panel by pressing Shift+F7 or going to Window>Object & Layout>Align.

visual | 6–21 |

The Align panel

Vertical Align and Distribute options

Horizontal Align and Distribute options

Alignment location options

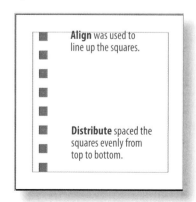

Align was used to line up the squares.

Distribute spaced the squares evenly from top to bottom.

Using the Align Function

In the following exercises you will see how easy it is to build a virtual deck railing using the Align panel.

1. Create a new **5"× 5"** document, **0.5"** margins. Using the Line tool, draw a vertical line. In the Control panel, type **1.5"** in the Length field, and **12 pt.** in the Stroke Weight field. Press Option or Alt+drag to create 7 duplicates, for a total of 8 lines. Change the length of 2 lines to **1.75"**. Apply a **red** stroke to these lines. (Visual 6–22).

visual |6–22|

These stroked will be aligned horizontally.

2. Select all the lines. Press Shift+F7 to open the Align panel. The Alignment Location should be set to Align to Selection. With Align to Selection specified, only the selected elements are taken into consideration for alignment decisions. Select Align Top Edges, Align Vertical Centers, and Align Bottom Edges from the horizontal alignment options, and watch as your lines snap into formation. When you select Align Vertical Centers, the center points of each line are aligned (Visual 6–23).

visual |6–23|

vertical centers

More than one object has to be selected in order for Alignment options to work.

Alignment Location

3. With the lines still selected, change the Alignment Location to Align to Margins. Again, select Align Top Edges, Align Vertical Centers, and Align Bottom Edges from the horizontal alignment options. With Align to Margins selected, the lines are aligned and repositioned to the top margin, center of page, or to the bottom margin (Visual 6–24). Keep your document open for the next exercise.

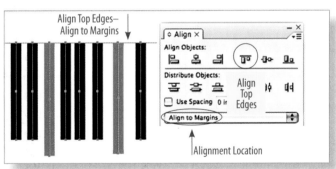

Align Top Edges– Align to Margins

Align Top Edges

Align to Margins

Alignment Location

visual |6–24|

The Alignment Location specifies whether elements will be aligned in relationship to the document, or in relationship to each other.

When using Align functions, it's sometimes helpful to establish an *anchor point* as a point of reference for the rest of the elements during Align operations. To establish an anchor point, select the object and then lock its position by pressing Command+L (Mac) or Control+L (Windows). You can also find this command under the Object menu. To unlock the position, press Command+Option+L (Mac) or Control+Alt+L (Windows).

Using the Distribute Function

The railing of our virtual deck won't look correct until the spindles are aligned *and* equally spaced. Distribute Objects creates even spacing between the centers, left, or right edges of objects. You can specify a measurement between objects, or let InDesign space the objects to fit available space. The Distribute Objects options are found below the Align Objects section of the Align panel.

visual | 6–25 |

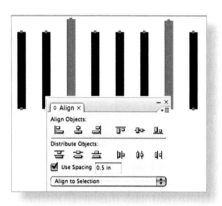

Distribute Objects manages the spacing between objects. In this example, a center-to-center spacing of 0.5" has been specified.

1. Select Align to Selection. Align the bottom edges of the lines. Select Use Spacing and specify **0.5"** in the field to the right. Then, select Distribute Horizontal Centers. The lines are now spaced exactly 0.5" apart, measured center-to-center (Visual 6–25).

2. Uncheck Use Spacing. Change the Alignment Location to Align to Margins and select Distribute Horizontal Centers. Now the lines are equally spaced to the right and left margins of the document. Change the location to Align to Page and click Distribute Horizontal Centers. This time, the lines are spaced out to the edges of the document.

Distribute Objects creates even spacing between the centers, left, or right edges of objects. However, if you open the Align panel options you will find Distribute Spacing, another great way to manage the spacing between objects. As you will see in the following exercise, Distribute Spacing is particularly suited for using with a series of non-uniform objects because it equalizes the spacing between the left and right edges of adjacent objects.

visual | 6–26 |

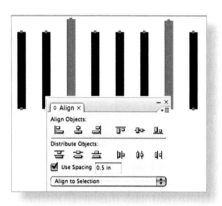

Distribute Spacing is ideal for equalizing the white space between non-uniform objects.

1. Delete the vertical lines on your document. Draw a series of squares, circles, and triangles similar to Visual 6–26. Fill your shapes with colors from the Swatches panel. To make a triangle, select the Polygon tool and click on your document. When the dialog box opens, enter these values: Width and Height: **.25"** Number of Sides: **3**, Star Inset **0%**.

visual | 6–27 |

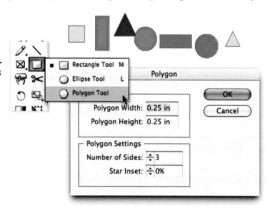
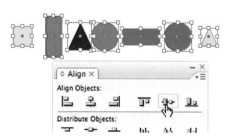

Shapes are first aligned horizontally along vertical centers.

2. Select all the shapes. Choose Align to Selection and then Align Vertical Centers (Visual 6–27).

3. With the shapes selected, choose Distribute Horizontal Space from the Align menu options. Now, the same amount of white space is between each object (Visual 6–28).

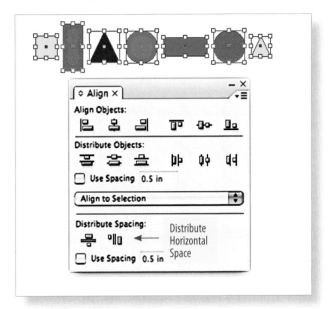

Distribute Horizontal Space has been applied, which equalizes the space between the right and left edges of adjacent objects.

4. One final challenge. Roughly reposition the shapes so that they run vertically down the page. Your goal will be to align their horizontal centers, spread them to the top and bottom margins, and create equal space between each object. You will apply the similar Align and Distribute operations as in the previous examples, but you will be working vertically. If you need help, refer to the specifications in Visual 6–29.

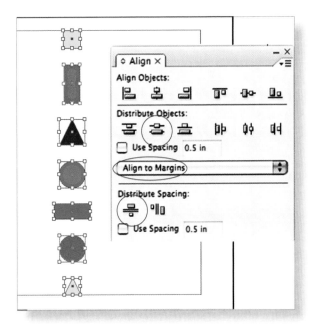

Practice the horizontal and vertical Align and Distribute operations until you are comfortable with this powerful panel.

> ## ▶ Moving Toward Mastery
>
> The InDesign Help menu is a valuable tool for times when you need a little more information on a topic. You will find the Help menu in the upper right end of the Menu bar. When it is launched you can browse through the topics from the Contents on the left panel, or type in a topic in the Search field.
>
>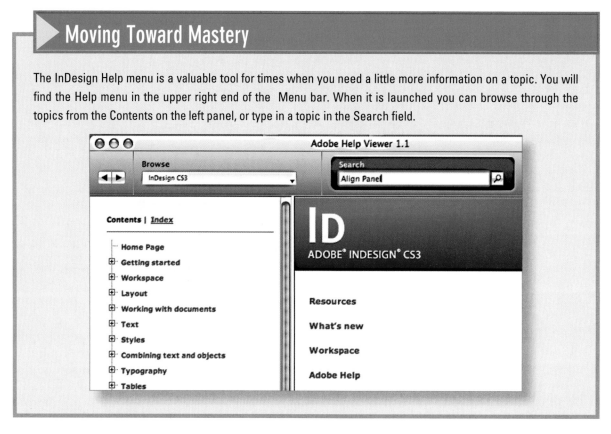

OTHER OBJECT MANAGEMENT TECHNIQUES

As you have seen in the previous exercises, knowing how to manage elements in your document saves time and frustration. The following five exercises demonstrate easily mastered techniques to help you manipulate InDesign objects.

Duplicate Using Step and Repeat

1. Create a new document and draw a **1.5"** square. Fill it with **black**.

2. With the square selected, press Command+ Option+U (Mac) or Control+Alt+U (Windows) to open the Step and Repeat dialog box (Visual 6–30). You can also choose Edit>Step and Repeat.

visual |6–30|

The Step and Repeat dialog box.

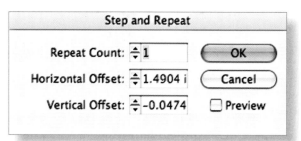

Keyboard Shortcut

Cmd + Opt + U (Mac)   **Step and**
Ctrl + Alt + U (Win)   **Repeat**

3. Use the dialog box to specify how many additional objects you would like and where you would like them positioned, starting from the original object. Enter **5** in the Repeat Count field and click Preview. If InDesign defaults are in place, you will see that five additional squares are staggered 0.25" over and down from each other. If Step and Repeat coordinates were used previously, the squares are placed at whatever settings were used before. (If you get a dialog box that says "Cannot add objects beyond the bounds of the pasteboard," you will have to decrease either the number of items to repeat or the distance you want them offset from each other.)

4. Now, type **3** in the Repeat Count field, **2** in the Horizontal Offset field, and **0** in the Vertical Offset field, press Return. Your squares should now look like Visual 6–31.

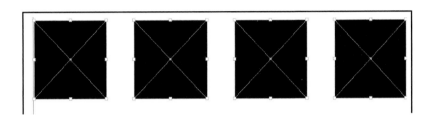

visual | 6–31 |

The four squares duplicated into a horizontal position.

5. Undo. Now, type **4** in the Repeat Count field, **0** in the Horizontal Offset field, and **2** in the Vertical Offset field. There are now five squares equally spaced in a vertical line.

Managing Object Stacking Order

If you have ever stacked pancakes on a plate, you already know the concept of object *stacking order*. In InDesign, each and every object exists in a stacked order, according to its order of creation. First objects are lower in the stack. InDesign allows you to change the stacking order of objects in your document, just like pulling pancakes off the bottom of the stack to place them on the top. You can shift the objects from the top of the pile to the bottom of the pile by using some great keyboard shortcuts. The following steps demonstrate the most common commands used to change an object's stacking order.

Send Forward, to Front, Backward, and to Back

visual | 6–32 |

1. Create a new document. Draw three shapes: a square, a circle, and a hexagon (located in the fly out menu in the Rectangle tool). Open the Swatch panel and fill the the square with **blue,** the circle with **red**, and the hexagon with **yellow**.

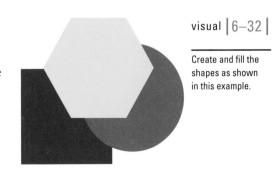

Create and fill the shapes as shown in this example.

2. Move the circle and hexagon so that they slightly overlap the square. Your pile of objects should look like Visual 6–32.

3. Send Backward and Send Forward. You have just created a "stack of pancakes" and we are going to shuffle their stacking order. Select the hexagon. Press Command+[(Mac) or Control+[(Windows) and watch the hexagon move back one layer. It is now sandwiched between the circle and square. Press the same shortcut key and the hexagon will now be at the bottom of the stack. Now, press Command+] (Mac) or Control+] (Windows) and the hexagon will come forward one layer at a time. Practice sending each object forward and backward until the shortcut keys become automatic. All stacking order commands can also be accessed by choosing Object>Arrange and then selecting one of the four stacking commands.

Keyboard Shortcut	
Cmd + [(Mac)	**Send**
Ctrl + [(Win)	**Backward**

4. Send to Back and Send to Front. To send selected objects all the way to the back or to the front of the stack, add the Shift key to the shortcut keys you just learned. Send to the Back becomes Shift+ Command+[(Mac) or Shift+ Control+[(Windows) and Send to the Front becomes Shift+ Command+] (Mac) or Shift+Control+] (Windows). Practice sending each object to the front and back until the shortcut keys feel comfortable. Keep your document open because we are going to use it for the next exercise.

Keyboard Shortcut	
Shift +Cmd + [(Mac)	**Send**
Shift +Ctrl + [(Win)	**to Back**

Keyboard Shortcut	
Shift + Cmd +] (Mac)	**Bring**
Shift + Ctrl +] (Win)	**to Front**

Selecting Stacked Objects

InDesign uses related shortcut keys for related functions, and after a while you begin to recognize a pattern. In this exercise you will learn how to select items that are stacked on top of each other. Using our pancakes analogy, there are times you might want to peek through the stack of pancakes to see which has the most (or fewest) blueberries. This exercise demonstrates how to select objects that are in the middle of the stack. Begin by layering your three shapes in the stacking order shown in Visual 6–33. Use the Align commands to line up the center of all the objects. Rather than opening the Align panel, find the two Align commands you need in the Control panel.

visual | 6–33 |

Use the Align function to line up the centers of your shapes.

1. Select Through Objects. InDesign allows you to "dig" from the top object down through each object layer with one simple click. Select the top object, and press Command (Mac) or Control (Windows) and click. Each click selects the next object below in the stack. Watch the selection handles carefully to determine which object is selected.

Keyboard Shortcut	
Cmd + Click (Mac)	**Select Through**
Cmd + Click (Win)	**Objects**

2. Select Next Object Above and Next Object Below. When you want to select an item somewhere in the middle of the stack, use Command+Option+[or] (Mac) or Control+Alt+[or] (Windows) and you will move through your stack of shapes. Practice moving down and up through your stack. As your documents become more complex, the Arrange and Select shortcuts will become indispensable tools.

Keyboard Shortcut

| Cmd + Opt+] (Mac) | **Select Next** |
| Ctrl + Alt +] Win) | **Object Above** |

Keyboard Shortcut

| Cmd + Opt+ [(Mac) | **Select Next** |
| Ctrl + Alt + [(Win) | **Object Below** |

Cut, Copy, Paste, Paste Into, Paste in Place

Cut, *Copy*, and *Paste* commands are basic functions you may already know, but they are so important that they bear repeating. InDesign also includes two special Paste features.

The Cut command shortcut is Command+X (Mac) or Control+X (Windows). There is a difference between using the Delete key and the Cut command. When you select an object and press Delete, the object is gone forever (unless you Undo it). When you select an object and choose Cut, the object is removed from your document but kept in the short-term memory area of your computer, called the *clipboard*. The clipboard can only hold the contents of one Cut (or Copy) operation at a time, so don't depend on the clipboard for long-term storage. As you will see in the following paragraphs, the contents of the clipboard can be accessed using several commands.

Keyboard Shortcut

| Cmd + X (Mac) | **Cut** |
| Ctrl + X (Win) | |

The Copy command shortcut is Command+C (Mac) or Control+C (Windows). When you select an object and copy it, the object remains in the document and a copy of it goes to the clipboard, replacing what was previously stored there.

Keyboard Shortcut

| Cmd + C (Mac) | **Copy** |
| Ctrl + C (Win) | |

The Paste command shortcut is Command+V (Mac) or Control+V (Windows). When you use this command, whatever is stored in the clipboard will reappear on the page you are working on. This means you can paste clipboard items on the same page, on a different page, or into a new document. When an object is pasted from the clipboard, it will be positioned in the center of the screen.

Keyboard Shortcut

| Cmd + V (Mac) | **Paste** |
| Ctrl + V (Win) | |

InDesign's Paste in Place command is a great function. When you use Paste in Place, the object is positioned in the exact same location whether pasted on the same page, a different page in the same document, or a page in another InDesign document. The shortcut key for Paste in Place is another example of how InDesign shortcut keys are related. A regular Paste is Command+V (Mac) or Control+V (Windows). Paste in Place is Shift+Option+Command+V (Mac) or Shift+Alt+Control (Windows).

Keyboard Shortcut

| Shift + Cmd + Opt + V (Mac) | **Paste** |
| Shift + Ctrl + Alt + V (Win) | **in Place** |

InDesign's Paste Into command is very similar to placing photos inside frames, except that it works with objects that InDesign can create or manipulate on screen.

1. Draw a black square. We're going to call this the *container*.

2. Double-click on the Polygon tool to open the Polygon Settings dialog box and type **6** in Number of Sides and **40%** in the Star Inset field. Click OK and drag a star onto your document. Fill the star with white from the Color panel (F6). The star will be the *content*.

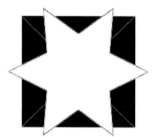

Use the Align function to line up the centers of your shapes.

3. Position the content. Select both shapes and, using the Align icons on the Control panel, center the star horizontally and vertically on the square. This establishes the final position of the content (see Visual 6–34).

4. Cut the content by selecting only the star and pressing Command+X (Mac) or Control+X (Windows). The star is now removed from the document and stored in the clipboard.

The star has been pasted into the square.

5. Select the square. Use the Paste Into command, Command+ Option+V (Mac) or Control+Alt+V (Windows). This process is also called *nesting*. The image should look like Visual 6–35.

Keyboard Shortcut	
Cmd + Opt + V (Mac)	**Paste**
Ctrl + Alt + V (Win)	**Into**

6. Use the Selection tool to move the container and the content. Use the Direct Selection tool and select either the container or the content to adjust the size of the container or the position of the content. To remove the content, select it and use the Cut or Delete command.

Grouping Elements

Combining two or more items into a group is a great way to manage multiple design elements. Like individual states within the United States, each element retains its unique properties, but all are grouped together to form a larger unit. Once a group is created, you can Move, Copy, Cut, and Transform the group as a whole. And you can still perform all the functions you normally would with each individual member of the group.

1. Create a new document. Draw a text frame and a rectangle. Select both objects. Press Command+G (Mac) or Control+G (Windows). You should see a new bounding box that now stretches around both elements. Choose the Selection tool and move the items. They will move as a group.

2. Select an element with the Direct Selection tool. With this tool, you can move the elements in the group independently of the others. You can also manipulate the paths and anchor points on each element.

3. Draw a larger rectangle. Select all the objects and create a group. The bounding box grows to encompass all the objects. Creating groups within groups is another variety of nested objects.

Keyboard Shortcut	
Cmd + G (Mac)	**Group**
Ctrl + G (Win)	

4. To ungroup elements, press Shift+Command+G (Mac) or Shift+Control+G (Windows). You must repeat the process to ungroup each nested group.

Keyboard Shortcut	
Shift + Cmd + G (Mac)	**Un-**
Shift + Ctrl + G (Win)	**Group**

The Control Panel: Another Look

You are already familiar with the power of the Control panel. Here's a trick that will help when you are using the Control panel and want to resize an object proportionately. When you type a new value in the H field, hold down Command (Mac) or Control (Windows) as you press Return and the width and height dimensions will remain proportional. If you want the scaling always to be proportional, select the link button. When the link is closed, the width and height percentages will remain proportional and you don't need to hold down the Command (Mac) or Control (Windows) key. If the link is open, you must hold down Command (Mac) or Control (Windows) to constrain the percentages.

The Control panel also allows you to rotate objects. When rotating, you must note where the object's reference point is because this will be the center point for the rotation. Set a percentage in the Rotation Angle field and see how this feature works. You can also flop your artwork along the horizontal or vertical axis. Visual 6–36 shows many panel options.

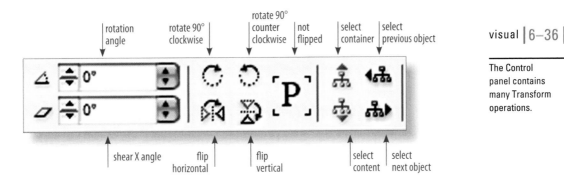

visual |6–36|

The Control panel contains many Transform operations.

The Control panel also includes a Shear function, which makes your type or object oblique. This can be great for modifying frames and shapes, but please restrain yourself from using this tool for making fake italics or an oblique typeface. As a professional artist, you should use an oblique or italic font designed by a professional typographer rather than hacking out one of your own.

© 2006 Mark Skowron
Waukesha County Techncial College

SUMMARY

We've covered lots of ground in this chapter, and have just begun to delve into the depths of InDesign. New skills take time to develop and as you master the basics, you will continue to add new techniques to your repertoire. Become familiar with document presets, guides and columns, baseline grids, and aligning objects. Take seriously the importance of a strong layout and the use of keyboard shortcuts. Know that every advantage you can gain with InDesign will be an advantage for you and your clients in the marketplace.

in review

1. For what types of documents should you make presets?

2. What is the measurement of a standard bleed?

3. What are some advantages of using columns and guides?

4. Why are a reader's first impressions of a newsletter
    (or any document you design) so critical?

5. What are some characteristics of the three types of newsletters
    described in this chapter?

6. What is the purpose of using a baseline grid?

7. What is the difference between using the Cut command or pressing the Delete key?

8. What is a *setup frame*? When and how do you use one?

9. Explain the difference between using Step and Repeat, and the Align panel.

10. What are some advantages in grouping items together? What is *nesting*?

11. Explain how to rearrange the order of stacked objects using keyboard shortcuts.

12. What is the process for changing the Document Setup default?

13. You have several shapes exactly stacked on each other. What is the keyboard short-
    cut for selecting through objects, without rearranging the stacking order?

14. You have an image of a person placed exactly where you want it on a layout.
    Unfortunately, the person in the photo is pointing—and leading the reader's eye—
    right off the page. You decide to fix the problem by flipping the photo horizontally so
    that the image will point into the page. However, every time you use the transform
    panel to flip the image, the actual location of the image frame also moves. How can
    you remedy this situation so that the picture is flipped and remains in exactly the
    same spot?

15. You have several objects that need their top edges aligned. You have opened the Align
    panel and have clicked on the Align Top Edges icon. Nothing is happening. What step
    in the process are you forgetting?

projects

© 2006 Christopher Pollack

The Lost Road to Houston

by Peter Martin

▲

...ony M. Rydberg, Director
...igh School Drama Department

Cast

In order of appearance

...... Wade Wittkop
...... Rae Evenson
...... John Edmiston
...... Nancy Runningen
...... David Runningen
...... Eileen Hegland
...... Dana Kildahl
...... Ron Evenson

© 2004 Steve Cowal

Snap, Sniggle, and Ring-a-ding

A collection of classic children's songs

Chapter Projects The projects begin with a review of basic tabs and tables functions. *The Lost Road to Houston* will give you a sneak preview of *feathering*, an edge treatment often used with photos. Align and Distribute operations will be the focus of the children's CD cover design. The desserts menu and design invoice will incorporate table functions, distribute objects, tabs, and indents. The final project is a bill stuffer—the kind you receive each month in your credit card bill. Directions and files for each project can be found in the *06 Artwork & Resources* folder on the *Exploring InDesign CS3* CD.

projects

© 2006 Karen Zale

Öh Design
kitchen specialists
9725 hillside boulevard
madison, wisconsin 53705

sold to		date of order	salesperson
		pick up date	delivery date
qty	description	vendor	price

	approval number	
	receipt number	
	amount financed	
	tax	
	total	

Desserts

Cream Cheese Carrot Cake $5.95
Chocolate Cappuccino Cheesecake $6.95
William's New York Style Cheesecake $6.95
Black Forest Cake $5.95
Raspberry Cheesecake $4.95
Apple Pie . . . . $3.50   Pie a la mode $4.25
Strawberry Shortcake . . . . $3.95   Sugar-free Strawberry Shortcake $4.95

Money & Savings Bank
has mortgages to fit your home buying needs!

- Free online pre-approval services available
  24 hours a day, seven days a week!

- Offering low-interest loans to first time home owners.

- Easy application and approval process.

- Construction loans with interest-only options.

- Evening hours for personal service.

Stop in and see how your friendly, small town bank
can help you purchase the home of your dreams!

Money & Savings Bank

No **love**
no **friendship**,
can cross the
path of our destiny
without leaving
some mark on it
forever.

℞ Francois Mocuriac

| **text wrap and layers** |

objectives

- **Apply text wrap**
- **Manage document layers**
- **Create transparency and feathering**
- **Set fractions**

introduction

My daughter owns a rescued greyhound named Penny. Once we took her to a large baseball field to see just how fast this dog could run. Penny was trembling with excitement, eager to run. When we released her, she was off like a speeding bullet.

Like Penny, you have been training to race. You have learned many InDesign basics and are now "trembling at the end of your leash" waiting to be let loose. Beginning with this chapter, *Exploring InDesign CS3* will be more production-based, building on previously learned skills while introducing new techniques and typographic principles. You're going to explore a lot of new territory. What an adventure this will be!

INTEGRATING TEXT AND GRAPHICS

Text and graphics need to work together. It's important to match the personality of the typeface with the style of the graphic. It is also important to create a visual link between the graphic and the text that accompanies it. In design terms, this is called the principle of *proximity*. One method of visually linking text and graphics is by using *text wrap*.

An Introduction to Text Wrap

Text wrap is the process of flowing text around a graphic or shape. Think of text like a river that flows smoothly until it hits a rock—a shape or graphic. The river might go around the rock or over the rock, but in either case, it just keeps flowin' along. You can apply text wrap options to shapes or graphics (the "rocks") to control how the text river flows around them. Here's how easy this is to accomplish in InDesign. Open *07 Text Wrap.indd* from the CD that accompanies this text. As you work through each step, make the changes in the Text Wrap panel, and reposition the image as shown in each example.

1. Open the Text Wrap panel by pressing Command+Option+W (Mac) or Control+Alt+W (Windows). You can also access the Text Wrap panel by choosing Window>Text Wrap (but using the menus rather than using keyboard shortcuts is always slower). Each button on the panel activates a different text wrap mode. Visual 7–1 provides an overview of the Text Wrap panel.

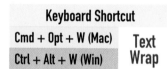

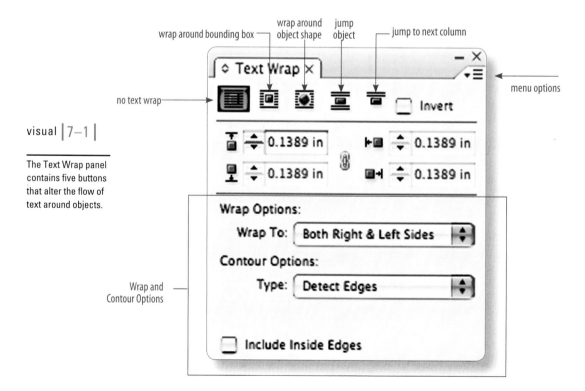

visual | 7–1 |

The Text Wrap panel contains five buttons that alter the flow of text around objects.

2. In this exercise, the bobber is the "rock" in the middle of your text flow. Any object that text wraps around is referred to as the *wrap object*. Whenever you are applying a text wrap option you must first select the wrap object. Select the bobber and notice that the first text wrap option, No Text Wrap, is selected in the Text Wrap panel. This option is the default. When No Text Wrap is active, the text can flow over or under the object (Visual 7–2).

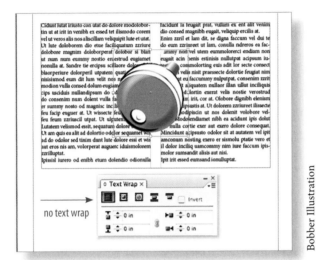

visual |7–2|

No Text Wrap is the default wrap option in InDesign.

Bobber Illustration
©2006 Nathaniel Avery

3. Select the bobber with the Selection tool and choose the second button, Wrap Around Bounding Box. Make sure that the link button is selected, and enter **0.25"** in any of the four Offset fields. As shown in Visual 7–3, you will see two boxes around the bobber: the inside box is the bounding box, and the outside box shows the location of a 0.25" text offset that has been applied on all sides of the bounding box. As you can see, text offsets are ideal for adding white space between copy and images. To create different text offsets on individual sides of the bounding box, deselect the link icon in the middle of the Offset fields and specify different values in the fields.

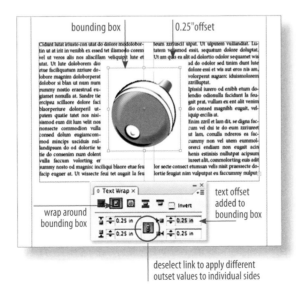

visual |7–3|

Wrap Around Bounding Box creates a wrap whose shape is determined by the size of the bounding box, plus any text offset.

4. Select the third option, Wrap Around Object Shape, also known as *contour wrapping*. In this mode, you have several options from which to choose. Under Wrap Options, you can specify where the text will be positioned. In Visual 7–4, Wrap to Left Side has allowed text to wrap on the left side of the graphic, but not on the right. Reposition the bobber on your page as you experiment with the other wrap options. The first three Wrap Options, Left Side, Right Side, and Both Right & Left Sides, will be the ones you will use most often. The Contour Options section allows you to specify how the text will interact with the shape. In Visual 7–4 the Contour Options is set to follow the shape of the Bounding Box.

visual | 7–4 |

Wrap and Contour Options are available when the Wrap Around Shape mode is active.

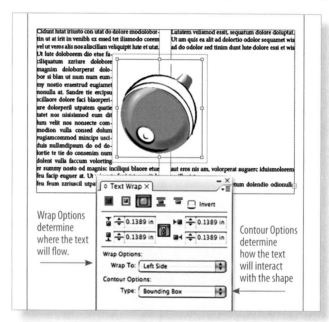

In Visual 7–5, the Wrap Options have been set to Both Right & Left Sides, and Detect Edges has been specified under Contour Options. With Detect Edges selected, InDesign finds the edges of the image inside the bounding box. In this example, you can see how the specified offset follows the contour of the shape.

visual | 7–5 |

Contour Options include Bounding Box, Detect Edges, Alpha Channels, Photoshop Path, Graphic Frame, Same as Clipping, and User-Modified Path. Not all options are available for all images.

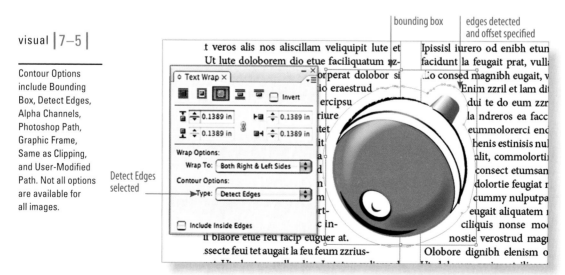

5. The fourth option is Jump Object. In this mode, the text leapfrogs over the object to the next available space. Jump Object keeps text from appearing on either side of the frame. (Visual 7–6).

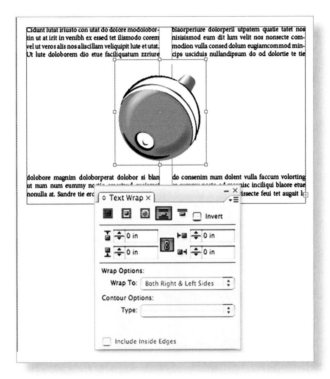

visual |7–6|

Jump Object prevents copy from appearing on either side of the frame.

6. The fifth option, Jump to Next Column, jumps the text over to the next column or text frame available (Visual 7–7).

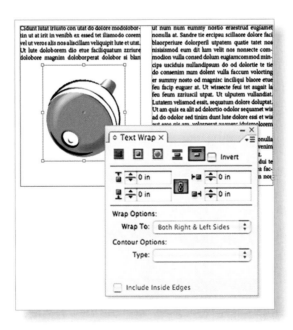

visual |7–7|

Jump to Next Column flows copy to the next available column or frame, including a threaded frame.

7. Select the bobber and change the text wrap to Wrap Around Object Shape, set the Contour Options to Detect Edges. Position the bobber in the middle of the first column. Draw a circle, move it to the center of the second column, and give it a background color of None. Apply Wrap Around Object Shape and turn on the Invert option. With Invert selected, the text flows inside the selected object (Visual 7–8).

visual |7–8|

Invert allows the copy to flow inside an object, as shown by the red type inside the circle in the right hand column.

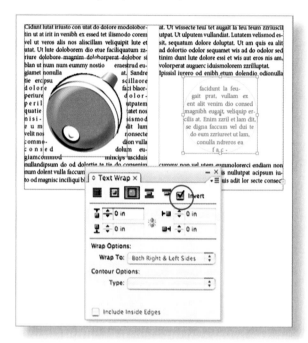

An Introduction to Document Layers

In the last chapter you were introduced to the stacking order of InDesign objects, which was compared to a stack of pancakes. You used keyboard shortcuts to rearrange the objects in the stack. In the remainder of this chapter, you will learn to create and use *document layers*. Document layers are like a stack of plates, each plate holding its own pile of pancakes. Document layers are easy to understand, and they greatly simplify the production of complex projects.

visual |7–9|

The Layers panel

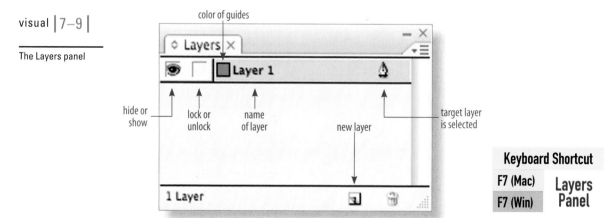

In this next exercise, you will use the Layers panel to build a cheeseburger, with artwork provided by illustrator, David Espurvoa III. You will find it in the *Chapter 07 Artwork & Resources* folder on the accompanying CD.

1. Open *07 Document Layers.indd* from the *Chapter 07 Artwork & Resources* folder. Press F7 to open the Layers panel. Every new InDesign document starts with one layer. By default, this is named Layer 1. Look at the Layers panel and notice that the bun, lettuce, cheese, hamburger, bacon, and tomato are currently on Layer 1. Select each of the ingredients and position them to build a cheeseburger. In this process, you are working with the stacking order of objects, because all the objects are contained on the same layer. You can use keyboard shortcuts to select and rearrange the stacking order of the images. You can also use the Select

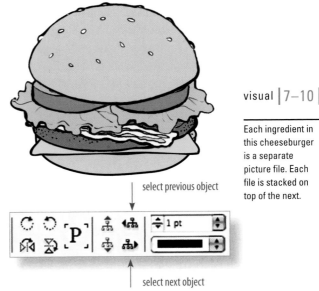

visual |7–10|

Each ingredient in this cheeseburger is a separate picture file. Each file is stacked on top of the next.

select previous object

select next object

Previous Object and Select Next Object tools on the Control panel (Visual 7–10). When the Command (Mac) or Control (Windows) key is also pressed, Select Previous Object becomes Select First Object, and Select Next Object becomes Select Last Object.

2. In the previous step, you experienced how difficult it can be to navigate through a complicated stack of objects. In this step, you're going to take control and move each of the ingredients to a separate document layer. First, let's take a closer look at some of the features in the Layers panel, as shown in Visual 7–11. On the left side of the panel, you can see an eye icon. This is the visibility control. When this icon is displayed, the layer is visible. Click the icon, and watch the cheeseburger disappear. Now this layer is hidden. Click the icon again, and the cheeseburger reappears. This is a nice feature—text, guides, and elements can be hidden, as needed. Next to the eye icon there is an empty box. When you

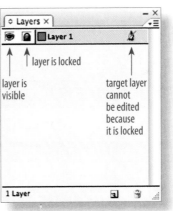

visual |7–11|

Features of the Layers panel.

layer is locked

layer is visible

target layer cannot be edited because it is locked

click the box a lock icon appears to show that the layer is locked, and you can no longer edit its elements. Like the eye icon, clicking this control repeatedly toggles it on and off. To the right of the lock is a field with a blue box labeled "Layer 1." The blue box corresponds to the color of the guides used to display the bounding boxes, frames, and guides on a particular layer. The pen icon at the right end of the Layers panel indicates which layer you are currently working on, called the *target layer*. If a layer is locked, the pen icon will have a red, diagonal line through it. Be sure Layer 1 is unlocked—it will be renamed in the next step.

3. Double-click on Layer 1 to open the Layer Options dialog box. Here you can change the name of the layer and the color of the guides, and perform other housekeeping functions such as Suppress Text Wrap When Layer Is Hidden. (When you select this option, any text wrap mode you have applied to an object will be turned off when you hide the layer.) While you are in this dialog box, change the name of the layer to **Text** and click OK (Visual 7–12). Next, create a text frame and type **Yummy Cheeseburger** underneath the image.

visual |7–12|

The Layer Options dialog is opened by double-clicking on a layer's name. There are many management features in this dialog box.

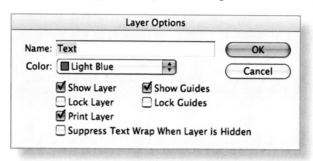

4. There are two methods for creating new document layers. For the first method, click the Create New Layer icon in the lower right corner of the panel (Visual 7–13). A new layer will appear in the panel, named Layer 2. Double-click the name of the layer to open the Layer Options dialog box. Rename the layer **Bottom Bun** and click OK. A new layer, Bottom Bun, is now shown in the Layers panel, above the Text layer.

visual |7–13|

Press Option (Mac) or Alt (WIndows) as you click the Create New Layer icon to open the Layer Options dialog.

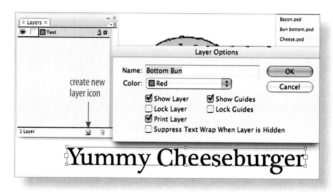

visual |7–14|

A separate layer has been created for each ingredient in the cheeseburger.

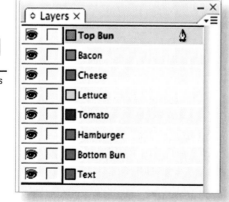

5. The second method for creating layers is particularly convenient, because the New Layer dialog box is automatically opened with the Name field highlighted. You will be making a separate layer for each cheeseburger ingredient. Hold down Option (Mac) or Alt (Windows) and click the Create New Layer icon at the bottom of the panel. Type **Hamburger** in the Name field and press Return. Repeat this process and make a separate layer for each of the ingredients. Name the layers **Tomato, Lettuce, Cheese, Bacon,** and **Top Bun.** Lengthen the Layers panel by pulling on the lower right corner. Eight named layers should be visible in the Layers panel (Visual 7–14).

6. Select the top bun of the cheeseburger. In the Layers panel, the Text layer is highlighted and the pen icon with a blue box next to it, appears. This indicates that the item you have selected is currently located on the Text layer. Click on the blue box and drag it up to the layer named Top Bun (Visual 7–15). When you release the mouse, notice that the frame guides for the bun illustration are the same color as the guide color indicator in the Top Bun layer (Visual 7–16).

visual | 7–15 |

Move an item from one layer to the next by selecting the item, and then moving the box in the Layers panel to a new layer.

visual | 7–16 |

The item has been moved to the Top Bun layer. Frame guides of the selected item match the layer the object is positioned on.

7. Hide the Top Bun layer by clicking its eye (Visual 7–17).

visual | 7–17 |

The Top Bun layer is now hidden.

8. Repeat the process, moving each subsequent cheeseburger ingredient to its named layer. Hide each layer after the ingredient is placed on it. When all the ingredients have been placed on their layers, show all layers. The cheeseburger won't look very presentable, yet.

9. In this step you will reposition the stacking order of the document layers. Your goal will be to arrange the layers in the order shown in Visual 7–18. The bottom layer should be the Text layer. To move a layer's position, click and drag it up or down. When you select the layer, the pointer will turn into a closed fist, and a heavy black line will indicate where the layer will be positioned when you release the mouse. Repeat this process to position each layer in the order shown in Visual 7–18.

visual | 7–18 |

Position the layers in the order shown here.

10. In this step you will manage text wrap features. Lock all the layers, except Bottom Bun and Text. Select the Yummy Cheeseburger type frame and move it up under the bottom bun. Make Bottom Bun the target layer. Use the Selection tool to select the frame for the bottom bun image. Activate Wrap Around Bounding Box from the Control panel. The text reflows around the bounding box of the bottom bun (Visual 7–19).

visual | 7–19 |

Choose No Text Wrap from the Control panel.

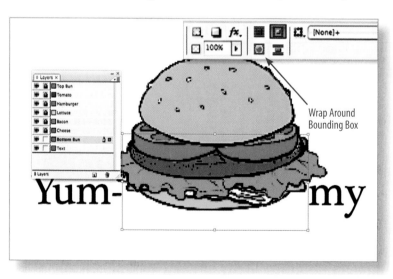

11. Double-click the Bottom Bun layer to open the Layer Options dialog box (Visual 7–20). Check Suppress Text Wrap When Layer is Hidden. Press Return. Hide the Bottom Bun layer, and you will see the text reflow as if the object wasn't even there. Make the Bottom Bun layer visible once more and the text wrap will be activated.

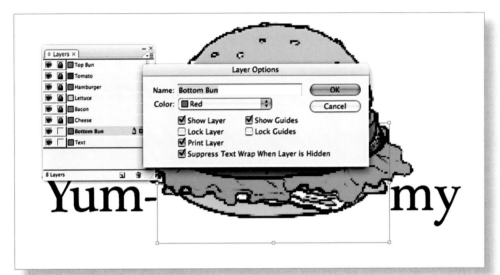

visual | 7–20 |

You can choose Suppress Text Wrap When Layer is Hidden in the Layer Options dialog box.

12. A method of managing text wrap mentioned earlier bears repeating: you can override the text wrap for individual text frames. Select the text frame and press Command+B (Mac) or Control+B (Windows) to open the Text Frame Options dialog box (or choose Object> Text Frame Options). Select Ignore Text Wrap at the bottom of the dialog box and click OK.

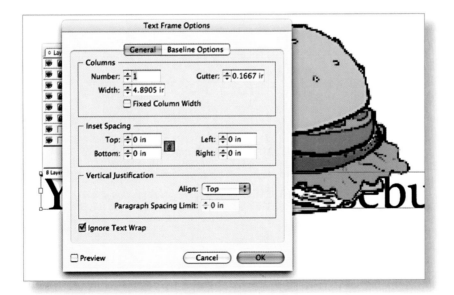

visual | 7–21 |

Select Ignore Text Wrap when you want to override a text wrap option.

Using Layers to Create Two Versions of a Document

Now that you have created, repositioned, locked, and hidden layers you probably realize the production opportunities Layers offer. In the next project, you will design a page for a recipe book, featuring recipes from all over the United States (Visual 7–22). You will use layers to construct this document so it contains two versions of a chocolate chip cookie recipe—one designed for home bakers, and a big-batch version intended for institutional cooking. You will also use the features of a new font technology called OpenType to create true fractions.

visual | 7–22 |

Layers will be used to create two versions of a recipe in a single document.

Chewy Chocolate Chip Cookies

Willow Lake, South Dakota

1 cup shortening	1½ tsp. vanilla
1 cup canola oil	4 cups oatmeal
4 eggs	1 tsp. salt
1½ cups brown sugar	½ cup chopped nuts
3½–4 cups flour	(optional)
2 tsp. soda dissolved in	12 oz. chocolate chips
2 tsp. hot water	

Cream shortening, oil, eggs, and sugars until light and fluffy. Add flour, the soda-water mixture, salt, and vanilla. Stir in oatmeal, chocolate chips and nuts. Drop by teaspoon onto ungreased cookie sheet.

Bake 350° for 9–10 min.

1. Create a new document. Document size: **8.5" × 11"**. Top, bottom, and right margins: **0.5"**. Left margin **0.75"** (to accommodate spiral binding). Click OK. Press F7 to open the Layers panel. Change the name of Layer 1 to **Picture.** Draw a frame from margin to margin. Place *07 Cookies.tif* from the *Chapter 07 Artwork & Resources* folder and scale proportionately to **145%**. (The photo will not reach to the bottom margin.) Reset the zero point to the far right edge of the document and drop in a vertical guide at **-0.75"** on the X coordinate (Visual 7–23). Lock this layer.

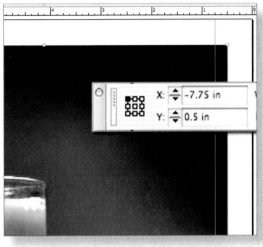

Reset the zero point to the far right edge, and place a guide at -0.75".

2. Create a new layer and name it **Consumer Recipe.** Type the copy and follow the type specifications shown in Visual 7–24. Use three text frames, creating a 2-column frame for the ingredients. Do not place a space after the whole number in the fractions. Creating fractions is an easy process when OpenType is being used. Highlight the numerator, slash, and denominator, and choose OpenType>Fractions from the Control panel menu. Repeat the process for each fraction. Or, highlight the ½ fraction, Copy and Paste it as needed. Be sure to check spelling and use the correct hyphens and dashes.

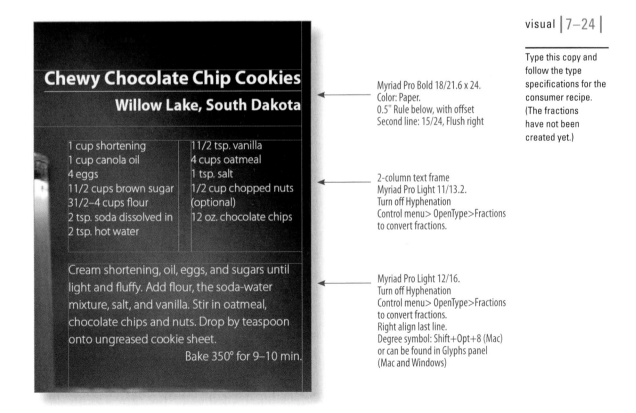

visual | 7–24 |

Type this copy and follow the type specifications for the consumer recipe. (The fractions have not been created yet.)

Myriad Pro Bold 18/21.6 x 24.
Color: Paper.
0.5" Rule below, with offset
Second line: 15/24, Flush right

2-column text frame
Myriad Pro Light 11/13.2.
Turn off Hyphenation
Control menu> OpenType>Fractions
to convert fractions.

Myriad Pro Light 12/16.
Turn off Hyphenation
Control menu> OpenType>Fractions
to convert fractions.
Right align last line.
Degree symbol: Shift+Opt+8 (Mac)
or can be found in Glyphs panel
(Mac and Windows)

3. Create a new layer and name it **Industrial Recipe**. You are going to duplicate the type from the Consumer Recipe layer, and move it to the Industrial Recipe layer. Afterwards, you will double the ingredients for the Industrial Recipe version. Click on the Consumer Recipe layer in the Layers panel. Choose the Selection tool, and Shift+Click each text frame so that they are all selected. The small red box showing in the Consumer Recipe layer represents the three text frames you have just selected. Press Option (Mac) or Alt (Windows) while you move the red square up to the Industrial Recipe layer. As the Option or Alt key is held, you will see a plus sign appear which means a duplicate is being created on the next layer.

4. Hide the Consumer Recipe layer. Move to the Industrial Recipe layer and change the title to **Big Batch of Chocolate Chip Cookies**. Then, double the recipe ingredients (Visual 7–25). Save your document and print a copy of the Industrial version. Hide the Industrial Version layer and show the Consumer Recipe layer. Print the Consumer Recipe version.

visual | 7–25 |

Change the copy on the Industrial Version layer of this document.

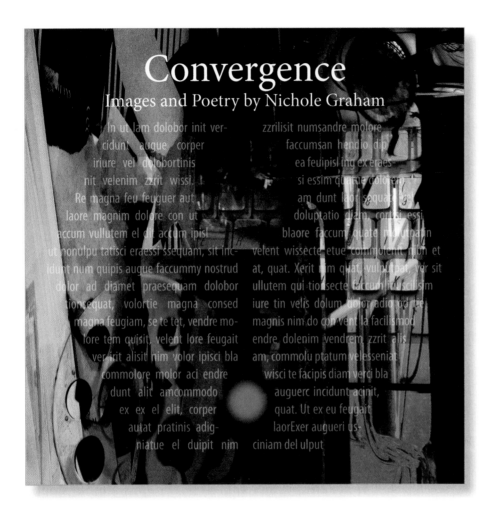

visual | 7–26 |

The finished CD cover, which incorporates transparency and feathering.

Designing a CD Cover

The final project in this chapter will be the full-bleed CD cover shown in Visual 7–26. It will require you to create guides, use text wrap, and work on different layers. You will also be introduced to two new features: transparency and feathering.

1. Create a new document, choosing Compact Disc from the Page Size presets list. Margins: top and bottom **0.25"**; left and right **0.125"**. Add a **0.125"** bleed on all sides. Click OK. Choose Layout>Create Guides and make two rows and two columns, both with a gutter width of **0** and select Fit Guides to Margins. Your file should look like Visual 7–27.

visual | 7–27 |

The guides are set for the CD production.

2. Rename Layer 1 **Guides**. You will be able to toggle the guides off and on as desired. Create a new layer and name it **Photo**. Place the *07 Convergence.psd* image file. It should stretch from bleed to bleed.

3. Select the Polygon tool and click on the document. Enter **6** in Number of Sides and **0%** in Star Inset. Resize the polygon so that it stretches to the margins (Visual 7–28). Select the Type tool and click in the polygon frame. Open the Text Frame Options dialog box, Command+B (Mac) or Control+B (Windows), and specify a two-column text frame, gutter **0.125"**.

visual | 7–28 |

The hexagon stretches from margin to margin. It will be converted to a two-column text frame.

4. Fill the text frame with placeholder text and format it as **Myriad Pro Condensed 11/auto**. Color the text **Paper** (white) from the Swatches panel. Text that is the color of the paper is called *reverse* type. Apply justified horizontal alignment, removing returns as needed to create even edges along the text frame and inside column guides (Visual 7–29).

visual | 7–29 |

Placeholder text has been added, justified, and colored Paper.

5. Activate the hexagon text frame. Remove the stroke. Locate the Opacity field on the Control panel (Visual 7–30). Enter **50** into the Opacity field and press Return. This creates a transparent effect on the type in the hexagonal text frame. On this CD project, the placeholder text is used simply as additional texture. Because the transparent effect reduces the readability of text, you will always need to use this function carefully.

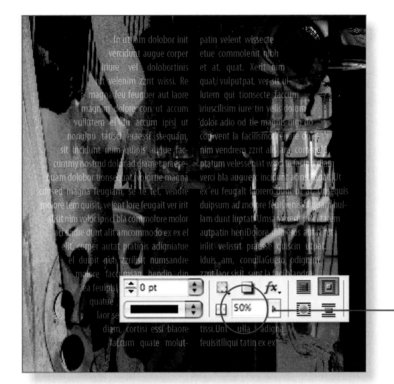

visual | 7–30 |

Opacity (transparency) can be found on the Control panel or in the Effects panel.

Opacity field on the Control panel

When using Transparency and other special effects, it is a good idea to view your artwork at high resolution. Choose View>Display Performance>High Quality Display.

6. Create a new layer and name it **Title**. Draw a text frame from the left to the right margin guides, H: **0.75"**. Position the frame against the top margin guide. In this frame, type **Convergence**, **Minion Pro Regular 30/36**. Second line: **Images and Poetry by Nichole Graham, Minion Pro Regular**, **14/18.8.** Align center and color **Paper**. Open the Text Wrap panel and select Wrap Around Bounding Box. Specify a **0.125"** bottom offset. Although this text frame is on its own layer, it still affects the type on other layers. InDesign's text wrapping capability is layer independent.

7. Create a new layer and name it **Circles.** Select the Ellipse tool. Press Shift+Option (Mac) or Shift+Alt (Windows) and beginning on the center vertical guide, draw a **1"** circle in the upper half of the text area. The circle should not have a stroke or fill. Open the Text Wrap panel and select Wrap Around Object Shape, offset **0.0625".** Since the object is a circle, only one offset field is active in the Text Wrap panel.

8. Press Shift+Option (Mac) or Shift+Alt (Windows) and draw a **0.5"** circle at the bottom of the text with the bottom edge of the circle near the bottom margin. Fill the circle with Paper. In the Text Wrap panel, specify Wrap Around Object Shape, **.0625"** offset. Choose Object>Effects>Basic Feather. Enter **0.1"** in the Feather Width field, set the Corners option to Diffused and press Return. Feathering creates soft edges and is a nice design touch. Adjust the transparency of this object to **50%.** Choose View>Display Performance>High Quality Display to see a high-resolution view of the feathering and transparency effects that you have used (Visual 7–32).

9. Your CD cover is complete. Deselect all. Choose Preview from the tool box. Now, select the Bleed mode (Visual 7–33). In this mode you can see the 0.125" bleed that extends from all four edges. Save and print your project. In the Print dialog box, choose the Setup page and select Centered in the Page Position field. Print two versions of the CD cover: In Version 1, deselect Use Document Bleed Settings on the Marks and Bleed page of the Print dialog box. Version 1 will show just the trim size. For Version 2, select Use Document Bleed Settings and specify All Printer's Marks. Compare the two prints, noticing that the bleed print has 2 sets of corner marks—an inner set to show the trim size, and an outer set to show the bleed size.

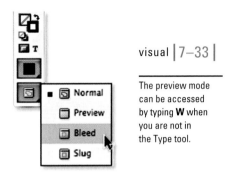

visual | 7–33 |

The preview mode can be accessed by typing **W** when you are not in the Type tool.

SUMMARY

You are well on your way to being comfortable with the expansive and powerful features of In-Design. With each chapter you have methodically added skill "layers" upon each other. Think how easy the projects at the beginning of the book would be for you now! In the last chapter you learned how to manipulate the object stacking order. In this chapter you created and manipulated document layers. You also were introduced to OpenType, text wrap, transparency and feathering, and you created two great projects. The next chapter will continue with more project-based instruction.

in review

1. How can you change the color of guides on a layer?

2. What is the keyboard shortcut to open the **Text Wrap** panel?

3. When creating a new layer, what key do you press when clicking the Create New Layer icon to bring up the **New Layer** dialog box used to specify the layer name and other options?

4. How do you view a higher-resolution image of your document on your monitor screen?

5. How do you make text flow inside an object?

6. What is the process for ignoring text wrap for text frames?

   Describe how to use the Layers panel to do the following:

7. Hide a layer

8. Lock a layer

9. Create a new layer.

10. Bonus question: Go to Menu> InDesign Help. Search for Paste Remembers Layers, a feature in the layers panel. Describe how it works.

projects

Chapter Projects Four assignments are included in the *Chapter 07 Artwork & Resources* folder on the CD accompanying this book. The first three projects are pieces promoting the annual fund raising events for a volunteer fire department. They will look great printed in color and will be nice additions to your collection of work. The second project is a fun exercise in formatting tables—no typing required!

Courage
Courage...

As they meet their field of honor, our fierce fighters face the fiery flames. They persevere until the final moment.

What does courage mean to you? Write about it in 200 words or less. Winners will receive a $100 savings bond and tickets to this year's Firefighters' Dance.

Support the people who work hard to keep you safe. Contest is open to area students ages 10–18. Essays must be typed and delivered to City Hall by May 18, 4:00 PM.

Name Address City State Zip Phone

Annual
Firefighters' Raffle
Sponsored by the City Volunteer Fire Department
Lic. 234567

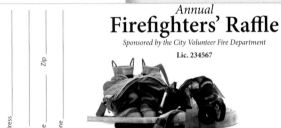

An invitation to the dance…

Artwork: Firefighter © 2004 Katie Hopkins.

U.S. Stock Market				
	Market	Level	Change	Last Update
▼	djia	10488.07	-22.22/0.21%	1/30 16:03
▼	nasdaq	2066.15	-2.08/0.10%	1/30 17:16
▼	s&p 500	1131.13	-2.98/0.26%	1/30 16:52
▲	russell 2000	580.76	090/0.16%	1/30 16:52
▼	dow transports	2885.95	86.04/2.90%	1/30 16.04
▼	dow utilities	271.94	-0.67/25%	1/30 16:03
▲	amex composite	1197.17	2.41/0.20%	1/30 16:07

Go confidently in the
direction of your dreams.
Live the life
you have imagined.

⌦ Henry David Thoreau

| type continuity: applying styles |

objectives

- **Properly prepare text files for placing in InDesign documents**
- **Use the Pages panel**
- **Use the Eyedropper tool to transfer attributes**
- **Create paragraph and character styles**
- **Use an object library**

introduction

It's amazing how often we make extra work for ourselves before we wise up. Years ago, we hung a small bell by our door and trained our dog to ring it each time he needed to go outside. The method was successful—at first. But it didn't take him long to realize that whenever he rang the bell we came running. He began to ring it whenever he was bored, lonesome, hungry, or just wanted to go out and play. It was hard to tell who was better trained—the dog or the dog owners. After the hundredth trip going back and forth to the door, we knew we needed to take control of the situation, and the bell came down.

When you are typesetting a project and it dawns on you that you're repeating the same actions over and over, it's time to look for a way to reduce your workload and take control. That's what this chapter is all about. You will use paragraph and character styles to automate your text formatting, speed up production, and bring typographic consistency to your documents. After reading this chapter you will wonder how you ever got along without them!

CREATING A NEWSLETTER

In this lesson you will create a four-page newsletter for a veterinary service. The veterinarian has supplied you with copy and photos. Visual 8–1 shows the finished newsletter, created in facing pages and printed on 11" × 17" paper. The newsletter is printed back-to-back and folded, making a total of four pages. A PDF file is also included in the *Chapter 08 Artwork & Resources* folder on the accompanying CD. You may want to print this newsletter sample and use it as a reference as you work through the chapter.

visual |8–1|

The four-page newsletter.

This single project will introduce you to the Pages panel, and will make use of an object library. The copy has been prepared for you—your job is to place it and format it. As you build the newsletter, you will create typographic consistency from page to page by using the Eyedropper tool and creating paragraph and character styles using the following techniques:

1. Creating styles from sample text
2. Transferring styles from another InDesign document
3. Creating styles based on other styles
4. Creating a new style
5. Duplicating existing styles
6. Bringing in styles with a new element
7. Creating character styles
8. Redefining styles

About Facing Pages

Up to now, we have worked on single-page documents. But many—probably most—of your projects will have multiple left and right pages printed back to back. These publications are set up using the Facing Pages option in the New Document dialog box. When a document is created as facing pages, the Left and Right margin fields change to Inside and Outside margins. When more than one page butts up to another, it is called a *spread*. Odd-numbered pages are always right-hand (*recto*) pages, and even-numbered pages are always left-hand (*verso*) pages.

Take a single piece of paper and fold it from side to side. Hold the paper so the fold is on the left and it opens like a booklet. The fold of your booklet is the *spine*. The cover of your booklet is page 1, a right-hand page. Open the booklet and you will see a spread made up of pages 2 and 3. The back cover is page 4, a left-hand page. So, a four-page 8½" × 11" newsletter, printed two-sided on one 11" × 17" sheet, consists of 2 spreads, or four 8½" × 11" facing pages.

TYPOGRAPHY

preparing copy

WHEN CLIENTS PROVIDE COPY

When a client is going to supply the copy in electronic format, you should discuss exactly how the copy will be prepared. Here are some text file considerations worth discussing with your clients:

- Save each article as a separate file and name each file by its headline.

- Place only one space between sentences. Double spaces need to be manually removed during typesetting.

- Place only one return between paragraphs. Extra returns must be manually removed during the typesetting process.

- Press the Tab key only once when typing tabular copy (don't keep pressing the Tab key until the copy lines up). Let the typesetter set the tab stops to align the copy.

- Don't press the Tab key to create a first line indent on a new paragraph. A first line indent will be created during typesetting.

- Don't type anything in all capital letters. Emphasis will be added during the typesetting process.

BECOME INDISPENSABLE!

Your extra effort will earn you the loyalty of the customers you work with. Take the time to double check times, dates, phone numbers, the correct spelling of names, and web addresses contained in customer-supplied copy. Finding a single error will create a greater chance of repeat business.

Introducing the Pages Panel

Open the Pages panel by pressing Command+F12 (Mac) or
F12 (Windows), or by choosing Menu>Window>Pages. Notice
that the Pages panel is divided into two sections by a separator
that can be dragged up and down like a window shade. The top

section of the panel is the *global* level. The pages at this level are called *Masters* and the settings and options you apply to them affect the whole document. The top single master page is
named [None]. The two-page spread below it is named A-Master. The A-Master spread consists of a left-hand and a right-hand facing page. When you are working with facing pages,
the pages are displayed differently than non-facing pages. The lower section of the Pages
panel is the *local* level. Each page or spread is butted up to a vertical line representing the
spine of the publication. Odd-numbered pages are always right-hand (*recto*) pages, and even-
numbered pages are always left-hand (*verso*) pages.

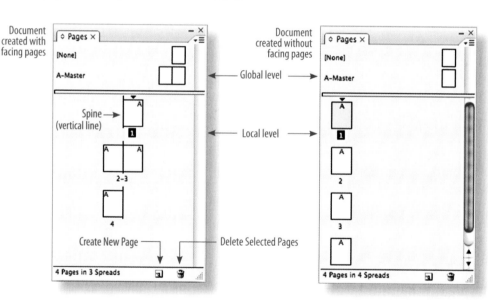

visual | 8–2 |

A document created
with facing pages
shows pages aligned
to a vertical line
which represents
the spine, or
binding edge.

We will be covering the Pages panel, in detail, in Chapter 9. Let's get started by creating a new
document for our newsletter project, beginning with formatting the exterior size and interior
margins and columns.

1. Create a new letter-size document. Number of pages: **5**; Facing Pages: **On**; Columns: **4**;
   Gutter Width: **0.1875"** Top, Bottom, and Outside margins: **0.5"**; Inside margin: **0.25"**.

At the bottom of the Pages panel is the Create New Page icon. Click to add one new page at
a time to the end of the document. Use Option+click (Mac) or Alt+click (Windows) to open
the Insert Pages dialog box for more page options, such as how many new pages to create,
where to place them in the document, or what master page should be applied. In the lower
right corner is the Delete Selected Pages trashcan. Delete a page by dragging it to the can or

by selecting it and clicking the can. Add and delete a few pages to your document to see how this works, but be sure to end up with 5 pages. Notice that the document's interior pages are displayed in spreads.

You can move from page to page in your document by double-clicking on each page icon in the Pages panel. To select a whole spread, double-click on the numbers below the spread or Shift+click the pages in the

Keyboard Shortcut	
Cmd +Opt + 0 (Mac)	**Fit Spread**
Ctrl + Alt + 0 (Win)	**to Window**

spread. When you're working in facing pages, you will want to view entire spreads. Press Command+Option+0 (Mac) or Control+Alt+0 (Windows) to fit the spread in your window. Click on the panel menu at the top right to view a menu of additional options. If you choose Panel Options, which opens the Panel Options dialog box, you can adjust the panel display by checking the Show Vertically box and choosing what size the page icons should be. Visual 8–3 shows the panel displaying pages with extra large page icons. Experiment with these options and adjust the panel to suit your preferences. Let's get back to setting up the pages for the newsletter.

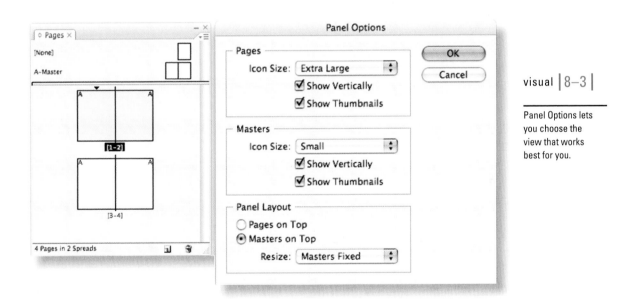

visual | 8–3 |

Panel Options lets you choose the view that works best for you.

How to Begin a Document With a Spread

The newsletter document was created with five pages. If you look at the Pages panel, you will see that page 1 is a recto page, and is followed by two spreads. InDesign's default is that a new document starts with page 1, a single, recto page. Because our four-page newsletter only needs the two spreads, we are going to do a work-around and create a document that begins with a spread instead of a single page.

2. On the Pages panel, double-click page numbers 2–3, below the page icons. This highlights the entire spread. Go the Pages menu, and uncheck Allow Selected Spread to Shuffle. Now brackets appear around pages 2–3, meaning the pages can't be split apart. Repeat this process for pages 4–5.

visual | 8–4 |

Brackets around page numbers 2–3 mean those pages won't be allowed to shuffle.

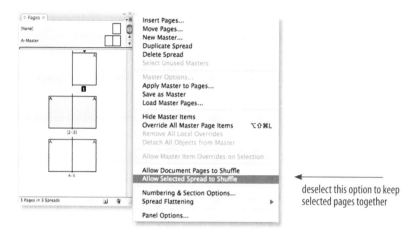

deselect this option to keep selected pages together

3. Select page 1 by clicking on it. Delete page 1 by clicking the trashcan. Your document should now consist of 2 spreads. You have tricked InDesign into beginning the document with a spread. This will make printing the newsletter much easier, but now the physical page numbers do not correspond to the pages of the newsletter. Refer to Visual 8–5 to determine the newsletter page location as you continue with your project. The pages will be referenced by the colored labels shown in Visual 8–5.

4. On the front cover, pull a horizontal guide down from the top to **2.25"** on the Y coordinate.

visual | 8–5 |

Sometimes the physical page location in a document differs from our description of document pages. For this newsletter, we will be using the descriptions in magenta type, rather than the physical page numbers listed underneath the spreads.

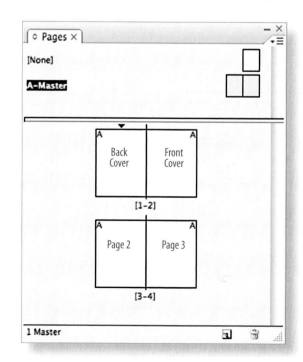

5. Double-click on the numbers below the page 2 and 3 spread in the Pages panel. Create a horizontal guide at **1.65"** on the Y coordinate by first clicking a spot on the ruler that is outside the document's page area. Now drag down the guide, noticing that the guide stretches across the whole spread. (When you drag a guide down from the ruler by clicking above the page you are working on, the guide covers only that page.) If you can't exactly position the guide at 1.65", with the guide selected, type **1.65** in the Y field of the control panel. Save your document.

Using an Object Library

When you do a lot of design work for a single client, you usually have elements that are used over and over again. For instance, if you did weekly advertisements for a dental practice, you would probably include the logo, name, hours of operation, phone number, and address in each ad. In these instances you can create an *object library* that allows you to store those frequently used items in one convenient location. In this chapter you will use an existing library called *Healthy Pets.indl*. In Chapter 9 you will create your own library.

1. Your document should still be open. Choose File>Open and go to the *Chapter 08 Artwork & Resources>08 Newsletter CS3* folder. Inside that folder you will find a file called *Healthy Pets CS3.indl*. The .indl extension stands for "InDesign library."Double-click the file to open it. (The *.indd* extension that you are familiar with stands for "InDesign document.")

2. The *Healthy Pets CS3* library should look similar to Visual 8–6. There are several options for viewing the contents of a library, in either List or Thumbnail format. If your library looks like a list, click on the panel menu options and choose Thumbnail View. If you'd rather view the library in List mode so you can read the full title of each entry, click on the panel menu options and choose List View.

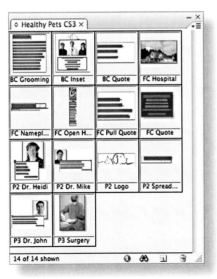

Thumbnail view

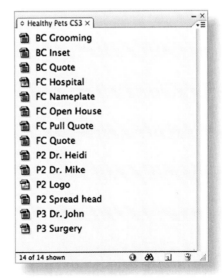

List view

visual | 8–6 |

An object library can be viewed in Thumbnail (left), Large Thumbnail, or List (right) modes, selected from the menu options.

3. As you will see, Library objects can be dragged directly from the Library panel to the document. Double-click on the Front Cover on the Pages panel. With any tool, click on **FC Nameplate** in the library and drag it over to the front cover. Align the top left corner of the nameplate image into the corner of the top and left margins. When you drag an element in from the library, you're not really taking it "out" of the library. You're just "borrowing" a copy to use in your document. The library still has the original, and will let you "check out" an unlimited number of copies.

4. Next, using Visual 8–7 as a guide, drag sidebar **FC Open House, FC Quote,** and **FC Hospital** photo into the correct locations. The tops of these elements should be aligned with the guideline you placed earlier. The elements do not need to be resized. If you mistakenly resize an element, simply delete it and pull in a new one from the library. The small checkerboard rectangle next to the page numbers in the Pages panel means that one of the elements on this spread has a transparency effect, such as the drop shadow on the hospital photo. Drag in **FC Quote** and position it in the lower part of the third column.

5. Using Visual 8–8 as an example, drag page elements in from the library and place them in their approximate locations on each of the three newsletter pages. Back cover: **BC Inset** should be placed against the margins in the lower left corner. **BC Quote** should be in the lower right corner. Page 2: **P2 Dr. Heidi** is in the fourth column, with the picture and text frame edges flush with the guides. **P2 Dr. Mike** is at the bottom of columns 3 and 4. **P2 Logo** is positioned in the top right corner of column 2 and extends slightly into column 1. **P3 Dr. John** is positioned with the top right corner of the photo against the top guide and the margin; the shadow extends into the margin. **P3 Surgery** is placed in the lower part of column 3 with the shadow extending over the column guide. You will not use all the elements in the library (yet). In most cases, at least one side of the element will be aligned to a margin or column guide. When you are finished placing the library objects, save your document.

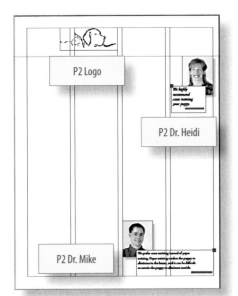

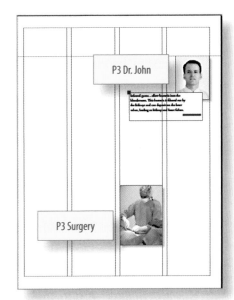

visual | 8–8 |

Pull these elements in from the Healthy Pets CS3 library and place them in these locations.

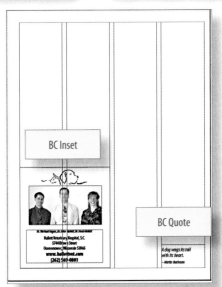

Moving Toward Mastery

Troubleshooting…everyone does it sooner or later! If your objects look like gray rectangles when they are brought in from the *Healthy Pets CS3* object library, then you've got a problem with **links**. A link is the pathway from the original photo file to the InDesign document. When InDesign can't find the links, it can't render the images! When this happens, you need to open the Links panel, **Shift+Cmd+D** (Mac) or **Shift+Control+D** (Windows). The Links panel shows where each image in the document is used. A white question mark in a red circle means the path to the original image is missing. A yellow triangle means that the original file has changed and the link needs updating. To repair a broken link, click on the problem link, and select *Relink* from the menu options. Navigate to the *08 Newsletter CS3 folder* and, inside, to the *Links* folder. Select the file name for each missing link. To update a link, select the name in the Links panel and choose *Update Link* from the menu options.

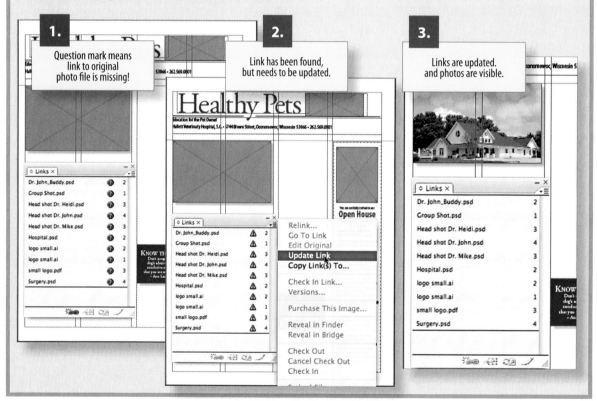

Using the Eyedropper Tool

InDesign provides many methods for formatting type. The method you have used thus far is to select text, frame by frame, and manually enter all the character and paragraph settings.

The Eyedropper tool saves time by allowing you to transfer type attributes from one paragraph to another. On page 2 of the newsletter, the copy under Dr. Heidi's photo is formatted perfectly. You will use the Eyedropper tool to transfer the correct type attributes to another text frame.

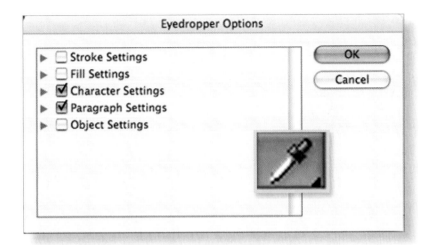

visual | 8–9 |

The Eyedropper is a versatile tool for copying attributes.

1. Double-click the Eyedropper tool to open the Eyedropper Options dialog box. Here, a whole array of options allows you to customize exactly which types of objects and their attributes, the tool should copy. Deselect all choices except Character and Paragraph Settings (Visual 8–9).

2. The Eyedropper cursor icon begins white, which means that no attributes have been copied or "loaded" into the tool. Click the empty Eyedropper on the italic copy under Dr. Heidi's photo. The Eyedropper now turns black and reverses direction as it "loads" the attributes, a process called *sampling* (Visual 8–10). Drag the loaded Eyedropper tool over the copy underneath Dr. Mike's photo. As soon as the mouse is released, the text will be changed to the "sampled" attributes (Visual 8–10). As long as the Eyedropper tool is loaded, you can drag and highlight text with it. Holding down the Option (Mac) or Alt (Windows) key temporarily turns the Eyedropper white again, so you can resample different text attributes. Deactivate the Eyedropper by selecting another tool.

visual | 8–10 |

The Eyedropper is loaded with text attributes from the copy under Dr. Heidi. The loaded Eyedropper transfers the attributes as it is dragged across type.

Defining Styles

The Eyedropper tool is ideal for formatting small quantities of text. When working on larger documents, it is better to use *styles*. This involves creating a separate style for each text element by defining all its various attributes. For instance, you would define a style used for headlines, one for body copy, another for photo captions, and so on. Once you have defined the styles, they can be consistently applied to text on any of the pages in your document. This is the fastest, most accurate (and most fun) method of formatting large amounts of text.

Styles that apply attributes to entire paragraphs are called *paragraph styles*. A paragraph can have only one paragraph style assigned to it. Every new document you create comes with a *basic paragraph style* that is applied to all the text you type. This style default can be edited, but it cannot be deleted. Styles that affect characters or words within paragraphs are called *character styles*. More than one character style can be applied to text with a paragraph style already applied. A character style would be used, for instance, to create a raised cap at the beginning of a paragraph with a different type style than the rest of the paragraph text. This newsletter project will focus on the following eight style management techniques:

1. Creating styles from sample text
2. Transferring styles from another InDesign document
3. Creating styles based on other styles
4. Creating a new style
5. Duplicating existing styles
6. Bringing in styles with a new element
7. Creating character styles
8. Redefining existing styles

Here's an example of the power of using styles. Imagine that you have just created a 24-page annual report. When you showed your first proof to the client, she insisted you change the typeface of all the body text. No problem. Because you defined and applied styles to all the text when you created the document, all you need to do is to change the font attributes of the body copy style and all the text will automatically update.

visual | 8–11 |

The Paragraph Styles panel

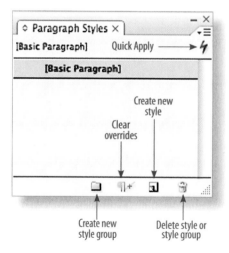

Creating Styles from Sample Text

Let's create paragraph styles for your newsletter project. Open the Paragraph Styles panel by pressing Cmd+F11 (Mac) or F11 (Windows), or by choosing Window>Type & Tables>Paragraph Styles. The first thing you notice is that the panel has only one entry: [Basic Paragraph], the default paragraph style for the document. No other styles have been defined. In the lower right you'll see the Create New Style and Delete Selected Style buttons. You may remember using similar buttons in the Layers panel. In InDesign, all the panels work in basically the same way.

visual | 8–12 |

The *Grooming* article is placed on the back cover in column 3, next to the bottom display ad.

The first method of defining a style is to copy the attributes from existing copy.

1. Move to the Back Cover by clicking on the page 1 icon on the Pages panel. Drag the element named BC Grooming from the library and then place it roughly where it belongs on the back cover (Visual 8–12).

Specifications of the selected copy are automatically transferred to Style Settings in the New Paragraph Style dialog box.

Keyboard Shortcut

Cmd+F11 (Mac)   **Paragraph**
F11 (Win)   **Styles**

2. Open the Paragraph Styles panel. Place the blinking text cursor in the headline, Grooming, and Option+click (Mac) or Alt+click (Windows) on the Create New Style icon on the bottom of the panel.

In the New Paragraph Style dialog box, the Style Name field remains Paragraph Style 1 until you rename it. Based On is an important field you will want to watch each time you create a style. There is a Shortcut field where you can assign a keyboard shortcut to apply this style to other text, once the style has been defined. Create a shortcut key using a number in the number pad in conjunction with one or more modifier keys. For Mac users, modifier keys are Shift, Option, and Command. In Windows, Num Lock must first be turned on, then use Shift, Alt, and Control, plus a number from the number pad to create a keyboard shortcut. For example, Visual 8–13 shows Shift+Num 1 for the shortcut for Headline. (A numeric keypad is ideal for using Style shortcuts. However, if you are working on a laptop, it's easier to select the desired style in the Styles panel or use the Styles pull-down options in the Paragraph and Character control panel.) The Style Settings field displays a summary of all the paragraph settings used in the style.

3. Name this style **Headline**, assign **Shift+Num 1** as the shortcut, and select Apply Style to Selection. When you check this option, the text you used to define a style is assigned the style you have just created. Click OK. This method of defining a style is accurate and automatic, and you didn't have to enter a single formatting option! (The Headline style is first specified in italic, and will be redefined to a roman face in the last step of this newsletter project.)

4. Place the text cursor in the copy below the headline. Using the method described in Steps 2 and 3, create a new style named **Body Copy** with a keyboard shortcut of **Shift+Num 2**. Save your document.

When defining styles from existing text, remember to check Apply Style to Selection in the New Paragraph Style dialog box to assign a style to the sample copy.

Transferring Styles from Another InDesign Document

Let's say you are showing a new client various newsletter samples you have designed. The client finds a sample she likes and says, "I wish my newsletter could look just like this." The next method of creating paragraph and character styles will transfer the styles from another InDesign document. Here's how it's done:

1. Click on the panel menu in the Paragraph Styles panel and choose Load Paragraph Styles. In the 08 Newsletter CS3 folder, select the *Healthy Pets.indt* file. Click Open. The window, shown in Visual 8–14, gives you the opportunity to select which styles you want to load. For our purposes, make sure all the styles are checked. When you press Return, the styles will load into your document.

visual |8–14|

Checked styles will be loaded into the newsletter document.

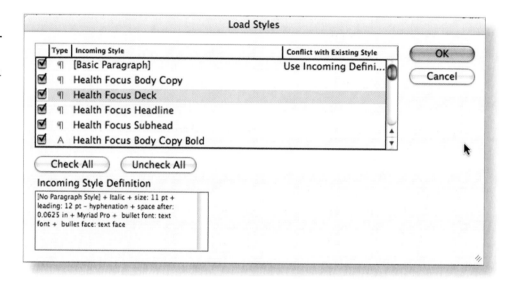

visual |8–15|

The Health Focus styles have been loaded into the Healthy Pets newsletter.

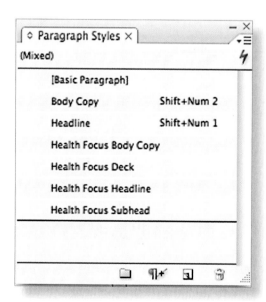

2. Your Paragraph Styles panel should now look like Visual 8–15. Notice that not all the styles have shortcut keys. Shortcut keys are not usually assigned to styles that are used infrequently.

Creating Styles Based on Other Styles

There are times when you will need a variation of a particular style within a document. For example, perhaps you have created a style named Body Copy that works for the main portion of the text. You also have some paragraphs of body text that need a custom left indent. A variation of the Body Copy style called Body Copy Indent (which includes a left indent) could be created. Body Copy Indent is *based on* Body Copy, and these two styles share a "parent-child" relationship with many similar attributes. When changes are made to attributes of the parent style (Body Copy), those shared attributes are changed in the "child"—Body Copy Indent. Here's how simple it is to create a new style, based on an existing one.

1. Option+click or Alt+click the Create New Style icon in the Paragraph Styles panel. In the New Paragraph Style dialog box, name the style Body Copy Indent. Since styles are listed alphabetically, it's a good idea to name related styles similarly. Body Copy Indent will appear after Body Copy in the style list.

2. At the left side is a list of formatting categories. You can tell you are in the General category because it is highlighted. In the Based On field, choose Body Copy.

3. Open each of the categories in the list. As you read each category page, you will realize that with few exceptions, the text formatting features listed are ones you are already familiar with, and you have accessed them through regular panels.

4. Open the Indents and Spacing category page. Set a left indent of **.125"** (Visual 8–16) and press Return. This new style looks just like the Body Copy style except it has a different left indent. And because Body Copy Indent is based on Body Copy, any changes you make to the Body Copy style will be automatically made to this style.

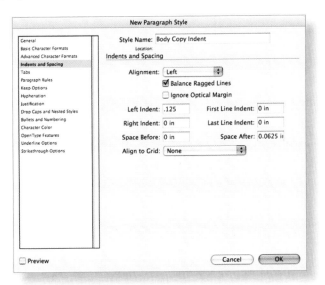

visual |8–16|

The Body Copy Indent style includes all the specifications of Body Copy, plus a left indent. Any changes made to Body Copy will ripple down to Body Copy Indent.

When you are creating a style based on another style and need to reset the "child" style back to the style it is based on, click the Reset to Base button on the General page of the panel.

Creating a New Style

Next we'll create a new style named *Kicker*. A kicker is a short line of type that appears above a headline. Kickers can "tease" your reader into the article and add interest to an otherwise boring headline. On the front page of the newsletter you'll see a kicker above the headline describing new equipment. New equipment might not interest pet owners, but the benefit of new equipment does! Hence, the "Great News for Pet Owners" kicker.

1. Open the New Paragraph Style dialog box and set these text parameters for the new style you will name **Kicker**. Look at the Based On field to verify that [Basic Paragraph] is selected. Basic Character Formats: **Adobe Garamond Pro Italic 14**, leading: **auto** (16.8 pt.).

2. Choose Indents and Spacing page and set Space After to **0.0625"**.

3. Choose Paragraph Rules page and turn Rule Below on. Set Weight: **0.5 pt.**, Color: **Black**, Offset: **0.0766"**, Width: **Text**. Press Return. Save your document.

Duplicating Existing Styles

We are going to create a new style called *Health Focus Standing Head*. Since this style is so similar to the Kicker style, we will create it by duplicating and editing the Kicker style. *Standing heads* are titles for features that appear in each issue. For instance, in a newspaper, the obituaries, sports, editorials, and classifieds each have their own title design that readers recognize and look for. Standing heads are used over and over, while a kicker is used once with one specific headline. Our newsletter project includes a Health Focus article with each issue. The standing head is found at the top left column on page 2: *This Issue's Health Focus.*

1. Select the Kicker paragraph style. Click on the menu options of the Paragraph Styles panel and choose Duplicate Style. In the Duplicate Paragraph Style dialog box, rename the style to **Health Focus Standing Head**. In the Based On field, choose [No Paragraph Style] (Visual 8–17).

visual |8–17|

Although the Health Focus Standing Head style was duplicated from the Kicker style, it is not based on it. This style retains many of the Kicker attributes, but it will remain independent of any changes made to the Kicker style.

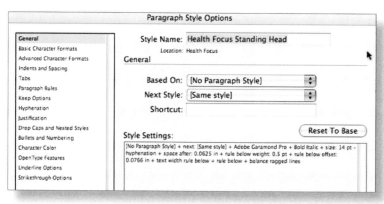

2. Choose the Basic Character Formats page, change the typeface to **Adobe Garamond Pro Bold Italic**. Press Return. Save your document.

Bringing in Styles with a New Element

When you copy an element from another InDesign document that has been formatted with a defined style, that style automatically appears in the document you are working on. Here's an example of how easily this can be done.

1. Go to the page 2 and 3 spread. From the library, drag **P2 Spread Head** and butt the top edges to the top margin and the right edges to the inside margin. Drag in **P3 Spread Head** and place it similarly with the left edges flush to the left inside margin.

2. You will see that a new paragraph style has appeared: *Spread Headline*. When you drag text from the library that has a paragraph or character style applied, that style is added to the list of styles. Place your text cursor in the spread head on page 3. You will notice that a plus (+) sign appears after the name of the applied style. A plus (+) sign indicates a *style override*, which means that something was added to the text that was not included in the defined style. You can see a description of the override by holding your mouse over the style displaying the plus (+) sign. A description of the additional formatting appears in parentheses. In this case, you will want to keep the style override. However, if you wanted to delete the paragraph style override, you would press Option (Mac) or Alt (Windows) as you clicked the style name in the list. For our newsletter, the Spread Headline style was originally created with right alignment. The spread headline on page 3 is left aligned, flush to the inside margin.

Creating a New Style Group

Before we move on to Character styles, we will organize our paragraph styles by creating a folder to hold all the Health Focus styles. From the Paragraph Styles menu, choose New Style Group. Name the Group **Health Focus** (Visual 8–18). Select each Health Focus style and drop it into the folder. Your paragraph styles should match Visual 8–18. If the styles are shown in a different order, you can choose Sort by Name from the panel options.

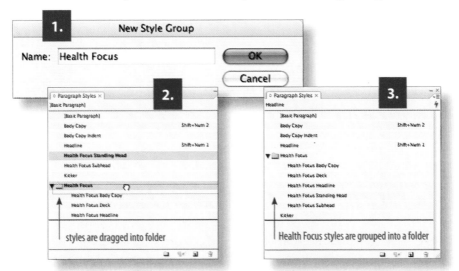

visual | 8–18 |

Style groups help organize lists of styles.

Creating Character Styles

Open the Character Styles panel by pressing Shift+Command+F11(Mac) or Shift+F11 (Windows), or by choosing Window>Type & Tables>Character Styles. You will notice that a character style already appears in the panel. It was loaded with the paragraph styles we transferred from a document earlier. We have one more character style to create and then we'll be ready to build the rest of the newsletter.

Keyboard Shortcut	
Shift + Cmd + F11 (Mac)	**Character**
Shift+ F11 (Win)	**Styles**

1. Option+click (Mac) or Alt+click (Windows) the Create New Style button at the bottom of the Character Styles panel. Specify Based on: [No Paragraph Style]. Name the style **Body Copy Bold**. Assign a keyboard shortcut: **Shift+Num 5**.

2. On the Basic Character Formats page, enter **Myriad Pro Bold 10/11**. Save your document.

3. Open the Paragraph Styles and Character Styles panels and compare them with the ones shown in Visual 8–19. If your list looks like Visual 8–19, you are ready to complete your newsletter. If some styles are missing, you will want to review this section to find the steps that were skipped. Now let's finish this job.

visual | 8–19 |

Your styles should look like the ones in this example. If they do, you are ready to proceed!

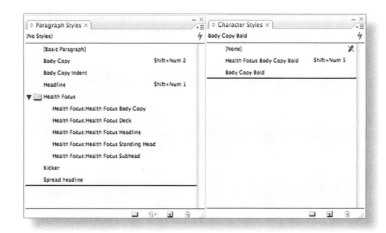

Applying Styles

Paragraph and Character styles can be applied using several methods. Try each of the following four methods, and then use the ones that work best for you. The first method of applying a style is to open the Paragraph or Character styles panel, select the copy, and then click on the name of the style in the panel. When you are applying a Paragraph style, you don't need to highlight all the copy in the paragraph. Place your cursor in the paragraph, and the style will apply to the entire paragraph. When you apply a Character style, you need to highlight all the copy that the style should be applied to. The second method of applying styles is to select the copy and press the keyboard shortcut assigned to the style. It is unlikely that all styles will have keyboard shortcuts, so you will probably use keyboard shortcuts only for styles you will assign quite often, like body copy.

▶ Moving Toward Mastery

Tips for Working With Text and Styles

• It's faster to drag a text frame while you are placing text than to create a frame first and then drop text into it.

• Placed text will come in with the attributes of the style that is highlighted in the panel window. When you place text, be sure you do not have a character style highlighted in the Character styles window. In this newsletter project, for instance, the last style you created was a character style and it is probably still highlighted. By default, a paragraph style won't replace a character style. So, before you begin to place text, select **[None]** in the Character Style field in the Control panel.

• A good rule of thumb is to select all the text and first change the style to Body Copy. This technique generally reduces the point size of your text and makes a large text block more manageable. When the text frame is active and you are in the Type tool, press Command+A (Mac) or Control+A (Windows) to select all the type. It is important to select only text in a frame and not all the objects on your page! Then apply the Body Copy paragraph style. Another way to accomplish this step is to have the Body Copy style selected when you place the text so that it will automatically appear with the Body Copy style. After the Body Copy style is assigned to the text block, you may apply the subheads and character styles.

• Press **Enter** (Mac) or **Enter** *on the Number pad* (Windows) to make text jump from one linked text frame to the next.

• Paragraph and Character styles can also be accessed through the Control panel. Choose the Paragraph or Character formatting options.

• A plus (+) sign following a defined style in the Paragraph Styles panel means additional formatting has been added. To delete Paragraph and Character style overrides, click the **Clear Overrides** icon on the Styles panel (see Visual 8–11), or choose Clear Overrides from the Paragraph Styles panel options.

• Clearing overrides does not remove formatting created by Character styles. To remove Character styles, select text containing the Character style and then click **[None]** in the Character Styles panel.

> **Don't have a character style selected when you are placing text!**
>
> **Deselect the text after applying a style.**

A third method of applying styles is to select the styles from the Control panel. Visual 8–20 shows where the Styles choices appear on the Character and Paragraph Controls.

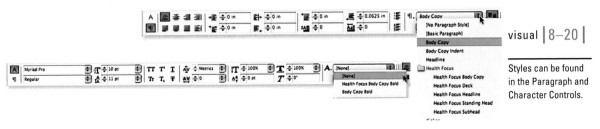

visual | 8–20 |

Styles can be found in the Paragraph and Character Controls.

visual | 8–21 |

Use Quick Apply to locate a style by typing a portion of its name. Quick Apply is great for managing long lists of styles!

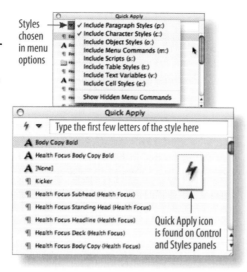

A fourth method of applying styles is to use Quick Apply. When your document contains a long list of styles, Quick Apply allows you to locate a style by typing part of the style name. Press the up and down arrow keys to scroll through the list of items. To apply a style, press Enter or Return. To close Quick Apply without applying an item, press Esc or click on the document.

You have prepared the document structure, brought in images from a library, and created styles for typographic consistency and production speed. Let's see how well they work. We'll begin on the front cover. You should print out the actual size newsletter sample from the 08 Newsletter CS3 folder on the CD because it shows where all the styles are used.

1. Check the Control panel to see that Character styles are set to [None] and Paragraph styles are set to Body Copy. Place the *New equipment increases.txt* file from the 08 Newsletter CS3 folder on the CD accompanying this book. Hold down the Option (Mac) or Alt (Windows) key as you create the text frames. This allows the text automatically to flow from frame to frame. First, create a shallow text frame extending across the first and second columns to hold the kicker and headline type. Next, create a text frame in the first column that begins under the headline frame and extends to the bottom margin. Then, use the same technique to create a similar text frame in the second column.

visual | 8–22 |

Hold the Option or Alt key as you draw text frames. This will keep the text cursor loaded while you create each frame.

2. If the copy is not already Body Copy, select the type in the three text frames and apply the Body Copy paragraph style by pressing Shift+Num 2.

3. Place the cursor in the *Great News for Pet Owners* line and select the Kicker paragraph style.

4. Place the cursor in the headline and select Headline from the Paragraph Styles panel, or press Shift+Num 1. The typeface is still italic—it will be changed later. At this point, you may need to adjust the height of your frame to accommodate the headline. Also, place a soft return after *increases*.

5. To create a break that pushes the body text into the next frame, place the cursor after the word *capabilities* in the headline and press Enter (Mac) or Enter on the Number pad (Windows). If you do not have an Enter key, open the Context menu and go to Insert Break Character. Select Column or Frame break. Remember to work with hidden characters visible.

6. A *pull quote* is an excerpt that is designed to stand out from the rest of the body copy. Pull quotes add visual interest and encourage readership. Drag **FC Pull Quote** from the library and place it between the two columns. Adjust its position for the best text flow. Text wrap options have already been turned on. Make sure the paragraph in the article beginning with *The video endoscope* is at the top of the second column, and not at the bottom of the first column.

7. Place *Should you give Heartguard.txt* from the 08 Newsletter CS3 folder. As you place, drag a new text frame at the top of column three. Select all the type and change it to Body Copy. Then place your cursor in the headline and press Shift+Num 1 to assign the Headline style. Notice that the registration mark ® used three times in this article is imported as (r). At the end of the newsletter project, we will change all the registration marks in the newsletter using the Find and Replace operation.

8. Find the *Puppy Classes.txt* article from the 08 Newsletter CS3 folder. Bottom align the text at the bottom of the third column and use Styles to format the text. Modify the size, font, and color of the phone number at the bottom of the article. This is called *local formatting,* and almost every document contains some local formatting. Your front cover should look very much like Visual 8–23.

visual | 8–23 |

The front cover elements are positioned and styles applied.

Finishing the Pages 2 and 3 Spread

The spread for pages 2 and 3 should have a horizontal guideline stretching across the whole spread at the **1.65"** Y-coordinate position. Articles on the top of this spread should butt up to this guide.

1. Find the *Feeding* article from the *08 Newsletter CS3* folder. Place the text, dragging a text frame in the third column from the top guideline down to the top of Dr. Mike's photo.

2. Apply the Body Copy and Headline styles to this article. Notice there are many instances in this article where you will need to change the register mark.

3. Use Visuals 8–2 and 8–3 or the newsletter sample printed earlier, to place the rest of the articles on spread 2–3. The *Spay or Neuter* article on page 3 continues under the photo. Bottom align both columns of the Spay article so that the text lines up.

4. *Dental Care,* in the third column of page 3, is in a text frame that spans two columns. Save your document.

Converting Text to Table

Hopefully you remember the table functions you learned earlier. If not, you will need to review that section in Chapter 5.

1. The Health Focus is the last feature on page 2. Draw a frame that stretches across the first and second columns and extends down to the bottom margin. Use Command+B (Mac) or Control+B (Windows) to apply a **0.125"** text inset on all sides. Fill the frame with **10% blue.** Place *Vaccines Critical to your.txt,* found in the *08 Newsletter CS3* folder, in the frame.

2. Change all copy to Health Focus Body Copy. Apply the Health Focus Standing Head and Health Focus Headline styles. The italic type under the headline is called a *deck.* A deck is designed to increase reading interest. It usually summarizes the accompanying article and appears between the headline and the body copy. Apply the Health Focus Deck style to the deck.

3. Highlight the text from just before the words *8 weeks* to the word *Optional.* Use the Paragraph Options Control to remove the left indent on the selected text. Choose Table>Convert Text to Table; Column Separator: Tab; Row Separator: Paragraph. You will need to format the table. The copy is **Myriad Pro Regular 10/11.** Center text in cells, adjust column and row spacing, merge cells, and apply strokes and fills. Highlight the column heads row, reduce the point size and rotate the text **270°.** Look in Minion Pro in the Glyphs panel to find a check mark. Visual 8–24 provides a detail view of the table.

4. Apply Health Focus Subhead style to the bulleted lines. Save your document. The pages 2 and 3 spread is now complete.

This Issue's Health Focus

Vaccines: critical to your dog's health

Regular vaccinations are important for your dog's general health. Below is a recommended immunization schedule:

	8 weeks	10 weeks	12 weeks	16 weeks	6 months
DHLPP	✓		✓	✓	
Rabies			✓		
Lyme			✓	✓	
De worm	✓	✓	✓		
Fecal Exam	✓				
Spay/Neuter					✓
Kennel Cough	Optional				

• DHLPP (Distemper)
Puppies receive a series of Canine Distemper vaccinations, usually at 8, 12, and 16 weeks of age,

Finishing Page 4

All the text files needed for page 4 are found in the 08 Newsletter CS3 folder. Place *Pet ID.txt* at the bottom of the third column. You will need to do some local formatting in this article by changing the Home Again product name to italics. Notice that when you add local formatting, a plus sign (+) appears at the end of the Body Copy paragraph style in the panel. Place and apply styles to the *Grooming.txt*, *Heartworm.txt* and *Toys.txt* files. Place the *Emergency Vet Service.txt* file, formatting the type as shown in the newsletter sample printed from the .pdf file on your CD. Notice that the *Fleas and Ticks* article uses two paragraph styles: Body Copy, Body Copy Indent; and a character style, Body Copy Bold, which will be applied next.

Applying Character Styles

If you find yourself doing the same type of local formatting over and over again, it's probably time to define and apply a character style. The last page has two articles that use the Body Copy Bold character style: *Fleas and Ticks* and *Corrections to keep your puppy from biting.*

The back cover completed.

1. In the *Fleas and Ticks* article, the product names in the bulleted copy use the Body Copy Bold character style: Frontline®, Flea-tick Spray, Flea Shampoo, Flea Collar, Preventic®, and House Spray. Highlight those words and apply the Body Copy Bold character style from the Character Styles panel, using the keyboard shortcut created earlier.

2. In the *Corrections* article, apply the Body Copy Bold character style to these words: OUCH!, Substitute, and Lip Pinch.

Redefining Styles

The newsletter is almost finished. This is a great time to print a copy, look at it carefully, and fine-tune the positioning of all the elements. Check for the correct use of hyphens and dashes. As you can see, your newsletter looks great, except the headlines are all italic, and the newsletter sample shows them as roman. If you hadn't defined and applied styles, you would need to manually change every headline in the document. That may not be a big deal for a short 4-page newsletter, but imagine making that change in a 64-page book!

1. Highlight one paragraph with the Headline style assigned. Change the typeface to **Myriad Pro Bold Condensed.**

2. Open the Paragraph Styles panel. Since you made a type style change on the local level, you will see a plus sign (+) next to the Headline style. Click on the panel menu options and choose Redefine Style. The Headline style is now updated to reflect the roman type style throughout the whole document! Save and print your newsletter.

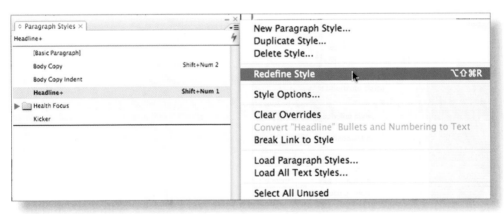

visual | 8–27 |

Redefine the Headline style.

Clearing Overrides

Sections of type that have a paragraph style plus overrides are easy to identify. When these passages are selected, a plus sign (+) is displayed at the end of the style name in the panel. To remove Paragraph and Character formatting overrides, click the Clear Overrides icon on the Paragraph Control panel or choose Clear Overrides from the Paragraph panel options. To apply a Paragraph style and preserve Character styles, but remove overrides, hold down Option (Mac) or Alt (Windows) as you click the name of the style in the Paragraph Styles panel. To remove Character style formatting, select the text and choose [None] in the Styles field of the Character Control panel.

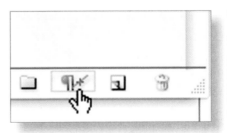

visual | 8–28 |

The Clear Overrides icon is found at the bottom of the Pages panel, in the Pages menu options, on the Control panel.

Using Find/Change

Find/Change allows you to search for specific words, characters, digits, or keystrokes and replace them with something you specify. The Find/Change dialog box is filled with choices—and it is worthwhile to spend some time looking at the options available in the fields. Open Find/Change and type **(r)** in the Find What field. In the Change To field, select Symbols>Registered Trademark Symbol. Set the Search field to Document and press the Change All button. Every occurrence of (r) in the entire newsletter will change to ®.

The Find/Change panel has numerous options for making document-wide changes.

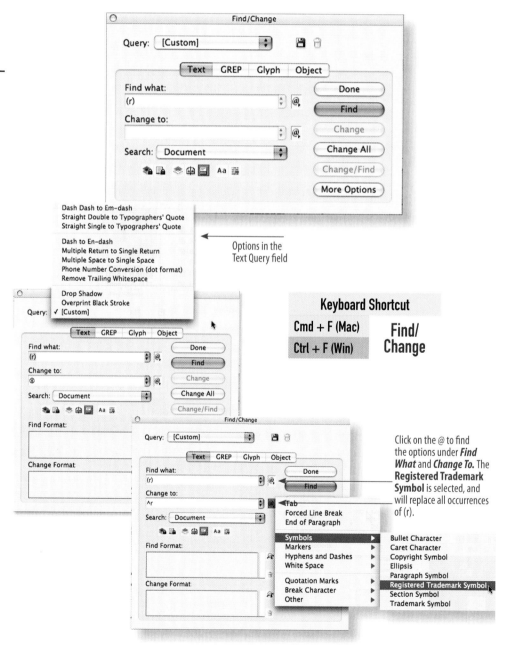

Options in the Text Query field

Keyboard Shortcut

Cmd + F (Mac)
Ctrl + F (Win)

Find/Change

Click on the @ to find the options under **Find What** and **Change To.** The **Registered Trademark Symbol** is selected, and will replace all occurrences of (r).

Printing Your Newsletter

Your newsletter is now completed. Proof it one more time. If you have access to a printer that can handle 11" × 17" paper, select Spreads in the General window of the Print dialog box. Then choose Tabloid or 11" × 17" under Setup, and change the orientation so that your pages print side by side. If you wish to print your newsletter in spreads on letter-size paper, select Spreads under General, and then Scale to Fit under Setup.

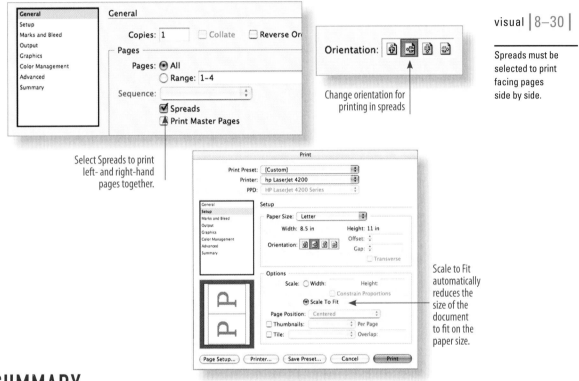

visual | 8–30 |

Spreads must be selected to print facing pages side by side.

Change orientation for printing in spreads

Select Spreads to print left- and right-hand pages together.

Scale to Fit automatically reduces the size of the document to fit on the paper size.

SUMMARY

Good designers can make disinterested readers take a longer look at a publication. The designer's ability to make large amounts of text look interesting and readable is an important skill. This newsletter project introduced you to some publication design elements: pull quote, deck, standing head, and kicker. These elements, when combined with appropriate typeface selection, line measure, and leading, create a document that has contrast and wonderful texture.

When working on complex projects, it is important to remember that there are no "throwaway" elements. The position and style of a page number or a pull quote should not be overlooked just because it's small or used only once or twice. All elements are important, and should work together to create *gestalt*—where the whole is greater than the sum of its parts. It takes creative energy and commitment to refine the smallest details of a document. But this ability to maintain a high level of focus is what separates the skilled designers from the masses.

in review

1. What are three guidelines for preparing electronic copy?

2. What are *facing pages* and how do you make them?

3. How can using an *object library* speed up production?

4. What is the process for using the *Eyedropper* tool to transfer text attributes?

5. What are three methods of defining styles?

6. What is the difference between a *paragraph style* and a *character style*?

7. What does a + sign at the end of the name of a style mean?

8. Where is the *Clear Overrides* icon found?

9. What is the process for applying a paragraph style, preserving character styles, but removing overrides?

10. Describe what a style *based on* another style means.

11. In addition to the Paragraph and Character Styles panels, where can you find and apply styles?

12. How is a keyboard shortcut for a style made?

13. How can you transfer paragraph and character styles from one document to another?

14. What are the two view options for an object library?

15. What is the [Basic Paragraph] style?

projects

Chapter Projects   Two projects will reinforce the concepts from this chapter.

Newsletter Analysis. Find a sample newsletter. Write a critique that addresses the following:

- The underlying grid structure
- The quality of the typography: contrast, typeface, consistency
- Any evidence of styles
- The inclusion of kickers, pull quotes, decks, subheads, spread heads, or standing heads
- Overall impact
- Effectiveness of nameplate
- Suggestions for improvement

Create Styles. Select a newspaper. Find four repeating styles used throughout the publication. Using placeholder text, duplicate each of the styles in InDesign. Create and name a style for each one.

Learning is not
compulsory.
Neither is **survival**.

℞ W. Edwards Deming

| page continuity: master pages |

objectives

- **Create multiple master pages**
- **Set up automatic page numbering, jump lines, and continuation lines**
- **Insert, duplicate, and remove pages**
- **Create an object library**
- **Manage document pages using the Pages panel**
- **Create and apply object styles**

introduction

Page consistency is critical for multiple-page documents. A five-person team producing a 96-page catalog needs a document structure that is consistent from page to page and designer to designer. Perhaps you've leafed through a publication where repeating elements, like page numbers, appear to jump around the outside corners like cartoons in an old-fashioned flip book. This would be an indication that the production team was not working with a clearly defined document structure. Master pages are ideal for bringing organization and consistency to complex documents. Items placed on master pages appear in the exact same location on every document page. Multiple master pages can be created with different margins and columns. Changes made to a master page will ripple through the entire document, which saves time and reduces the margin of error. Proper document construction can make or break the finished project. Take the time to plan your projects thoughtfully before starting them.

MASTER PAGES

Each time a new document is created, the specified margins and columns are assigned to a default master page named *A-Master*. A document's A-Master is the basic layout that automatically applies to all pages in the document. Although you can change margins and columns on a single page, the remaining pages will still retain the attributes of the A-Master default. As you begin working with complex documents, you will realize that individual pages have different layout requirements. In a single document, for instance, some pages may require three text columns, and other pages may need four. Margins may vary from page to page. Some pages may require *folios* (page numbers), running heads, or footers. Or, a graphic element may appear only on recto pages with four columns and a footer! Using the Pages panel, you can change the attributes of A-Master, the document default. You can also create additional master pages that have different margins and columns or contain repeating elements such as folios. Different master pages may be assigned to individual document pages. Each document page takes on the attributes of the master page assigned to it.

Basic Operations

Page masters are viewed in the Pages panel. By default, the master pages are displayed in the upper portion of the Pages panel and the regular document pages are shown in the lower (see Visual 9–1). For the next series of exercises, we will be using *09 Master Pages.indd* from the *09 Artwork & Resources* folder found on the CD accompanying this text.

visual | 9–1 |

The Pages Panel Options setting has been modified to show Extra Large page icons. Show Vertically has also been deselected.

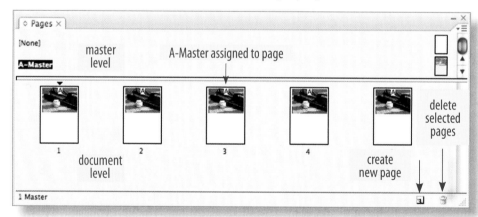

1. Modify Pages Panel Options. Open *09 Master Pages.indd*. Press Command+F12 (Mac) or F12 (Windows) to open the Pages panel. This five-page document has been created with a photo on the master page. As you look at the page icons in the Pages panel, you can see that the master item—the photo—is repeated on each page. Under Panel Options in the Pages menu, you can change the size and layout of the page icons. In Visual 9–1, in Pages menu>Panel Options the icon size has been changed to Extra Large, and Show Vertically has been deselected.

Keyboard Shortcut

Cmd + F12 (Mac)
F12 (Win)

Pages Panel

2. Move from master level to document level. Double-click on the page 1 icon below the double line on the Pages panel. The page is highlighted, and the number below the page is in a black box. You are now on document page 1, on the local, or *document* level. Double-click on A-Master in the top section of the panel. The master becomes highlighted, and you are now on the Page A-Master, on the global or *master* level. Repeat this sequence until you are comfortable moving between the two levels. Notice the page number in the lower left corner of the InDesign window, next to the view magnification field. It shows the active page, and switches between *A-Master* and *1* as you move back and forth. When you single-click a page or master page, the page becomes highlighted, but the page is not actually selected. A single-click highlights a page; and a double-click moves to, and displays the page. Double-click on different pages in your document, and watch the numbers change in the page number field.

3. Apply the [None] master. Select the master page named [None] from the Pages panel. Drag the [None] page icon to the document level, and place it on top of page 2. Release the mouse when a thick, black border appears around the page 2 icon. The [None] master *unassigns* a master from a page. In this example, A-Master is now removed from page 2, and is replaced by a blank page. Use the [None] master to unassign A-Master from pages 2–5 in your document.

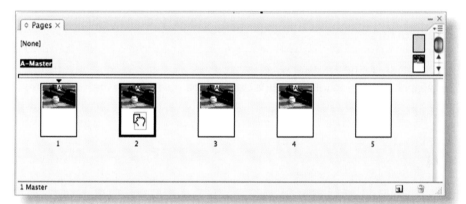

visual | 9–2 |

A black border surrounding the document page means that a master page is being applied.

4. Rename a master page. Double-click A-Master. Draw two lines below the photo. For the top line, specify width **10-pt.**, **Red** stroke. Lower line, width **3-pt.**, **Blue** stroke. Open the Master Options dialog box from the Pages menu. In this dialog box you can set various options, such as the Prefix that will be displayed on page icons to identify which master page has been applied. You can also rename the master page. Type **Red & Blue Lines** in the Name field (Visual 9–3).

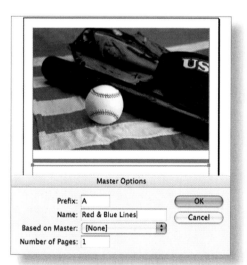

visual | 9–3 |

The master page has been renamed in the Master Options dialog box.

Moving Toward Mastery

Understand the following visual cues when using the Pages panel. When pages are added by pulling masters to the document level, a thin vertical line indicates an insertion point between pages. A black frame surrounding a page means that the selected master is being applied to the document page.

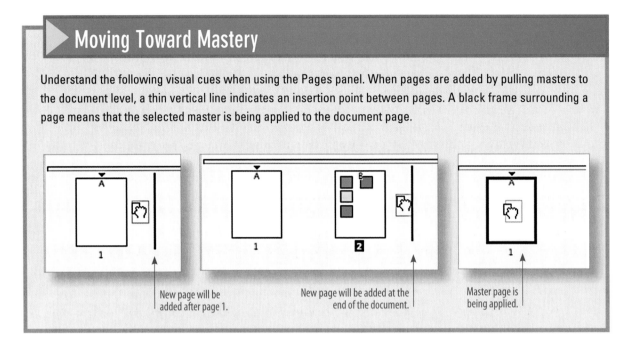

New page will be added after page 1.

New page will be added at the end of the document.

Master page is being applied.

5. Insert pages. There are many methods of inserting pages in a document. Insert additional pages to your document, using each of the following methods:

a) Click on the Pages panel options and choose Insert Pages. In the Insert Pages dialog box you can specify how many pages to add, and which master should be assigned to the new pages. In Insert Pages, change the Pages field to 1. Check that the Insert fields are set to After Page and 1. Select **A-Red & Blue Lines** in the Master field. Press Return. Compare the three pages assigned to A-Red & Blue Lines with the unassigned, blank pages. Notice that the assigned pages have a small A on the top of each page icon. This tells you, at a glance, that the A-Red & Blue Lines master page is applied to those document pages.

b) Click the Create New Page icon at the bottom of the Pages panel (Visual 9–1). Each time you click, a new page is inserted at the end of the document. The new pages are assigned the master page used in the last document page. If you press Option (Mac) or Alt (Windows) as you click the Create New Page icon, the same Insert Pages dialog box found on the Pages panel opens.

c) Go to Layout>Pages>Insert Pages. The Insert Pages dialog appears again.

d) Go to File>Document Setup and enter a value in Number of Pages. When you insert pages using this technique, you don't have the option to choose which master page the new pages will be based on.

e) You can also insert a document page that is based on a master by dragging and dropping the master page icon into the document section of the Pages panel. If you want to add the new page in a particular spot, say between pages 1 and 2, drag the master page between the two page icons until you see a vertical line appear after page 1. When you release the mouse, there will be a new page 2 created; the old page 2 will be shifted to the number 3 spot. Be careful not to release the mouse when the border of a document page is highlighted. If you do, you will be applying that master page to the selected document page.

6. Delete pages. There are also several methods for deleting pages. Use each of the following methods to delete pages in your document, until your document has only **1** page:

   a) Select a page and drag it to the Delete Selected Pages icon (Visual 9–1). Or, Shift+click to select a range of pages, and drag them to the Delete Selected Pages icon.

   b) Select a page, or range of pages, and click the Delete Selected Pages icon.

   c) Select a page, or range of pages. Go to the Pages options and choose Delete Spread.

   d) Go to Layout>Pages>Delete Pages and specify the page that will be deleted.

   e) Go to File>Document Setup and change the value in Number of Pages. This method removes pages from the end of the document.

Modifying Master Items on the Document Level

Using master pages is ideal when you have a document with elements such as *folios* (page numbers), headers, footers, or design elements that will appear on every page. When you apply a master to a document page, all the elements from the master, called *master items,* appear in the same position on each document page. Master items are displayed with a dotted bounding box. Even though you may have created multiple master pages to cover every possible page layout scenario, there are times when master items still need to be modified on the document level. Before a master item can be modified on the document level, it must be *overridden.* This is a keyboard shortcut that you will use frequently!

Keyboard Shortcut	
Shift + Cmd + Click (Mac)	**Override**
Shift+ Ctrl + Click (Win)	**Master Item**

1. Override master items. When you *override* a master item, a copy of the item appears on the document page, allowing you to change its attributes. Press Shift+Command (Mac) or Shift+Control (Windows) and click on the red line on page 1. Handles appear, indicating that the line is editable. Change the red line's stroke to **Yellow**. A master item that is overridden still retains its association with the master page. However, the attributes that were changed on the local level won't be updated when those same attributes are changed on the master page. In the example of our red-turned-to-yellow line, *color* was the attribute changed on the local level. When the master page is modified, InDesign will update only attributes that have *not* been modified on the local level. Go to master **A-Red & Blue Lines**. Move the red line to the bottom of the master page, and change its stroke to **Green**. On page 1, notice that the position of the line changed, but not the stroke color, because the color had been modified on the local level.

2. Allow Master Item Overrides on Selection. Go to page 1, and use the keyboard shortcut to override the photo. Nothing happens. This element cannot be modified because when it was placed on the master, Allow Master Item Overrides on Selection was turned off in the Pages panel menu. Select the photo on A-Red & Blue Lines master page. Under the panel options, select Allow Master Item Overrides on Selection (Visual 9–4). Now, delete the photo on page 1.

visual | 9–4 |

Allow Master Item Overrides on Selection must be checked in order to override a master item.

visual | 9–5 |

Remove Selected
Local Overrides
restores individual
master items.

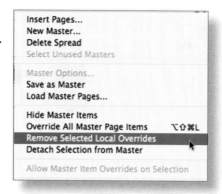

visual | 9–6 |

Remove All Local
Overrides restores
all master items
on a single page.

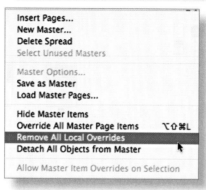

visual | 9–7 |

When a master item
is detached from
the master, it no
longer retains any
association with
the master page.

Keyboard Shortcut

Shift + Cmd + Opt + L (Mac) **Override All**
Shift + Ctrl + Alt + L (Win) **Master Items**

3. **Remove Selected Local Overrides.** Override the lines on page 1, and change their positions and stroke colors. Select one of the lines. From the Pages options, choose Remove Selected Local Overrides (Visual 9–5). With this command, the attributes of the selected item will be restored to match the item on the master page.

4. **Remove All Local Overrides.** You can also revert a page to the original master. In these cases, select Remove All Local Overrides from the Pages options (Visual 9–6). When you choose this option, the page is restored to the current master assigned to it. No items should be selected when choosing this option. If items are selected, the Pages menu displays Remove Selected Local Overrides rather than Remove All Local Overrides. Choose Remove All Local Overrides for page 1, and let's continue.

5. **Detach Selection from Master**. Go to A-Red & Blue Lines master and select the photo. Choose Allow Master Item Overrides on Selection from the panel options. Now, go back to page 1. Use Shift+Command+click (Mac) or Shift+Control+click (Windows) to override the photo. Under the Pages options, select Detach Selection from Master (Visual 9–7). A master item must be overridden before it can be *detached*. Once a master item is detached, there is no more connection with the master page. Changes made on the master page will not affect items that have been detached. Go back to A-Red & Blue Lines and delete the photo. The photo remains on page 1, because it is no longer associated with the master page. Use the Undo command to replace the photo on the master page.

6. **Override All Master Items.** Overriding every individual master item on a complex page can be time consuming. Override All Master Items overrides all master items only on a selected page, not on all the pages in a document (Visual 9–8). You will want to memorize this keyboard shortcut!

Creating A Document With Multiple Masters

Many documents require more than one master page. For instance, you may be working on a document that requires some pages to have a two-column grid page, a three-column grid, and a four-column grid. In such a case, if you don't create multiple master pages, you will need to change the margins and columns on each individual page—that's too much work! In the next exercise you will create a small publication, Baseball Digest, with photography provided by baseball fan(atic) Kristina Hegyera, a student at Waukesha County Technical College. Each step in the project will introduce a new master page function, so take your time as you systematically learn the features of master pages. You will need to use elements from *09 Artwork & Resources* which are found on the CD that accompanies this text.

visual | 9–8 |

Front cover of
Baseball Digest.

visual | 9–9 |

Pages 2–3
Baseball Digest.

FROM OUR READERS

Secte feu facil ut wisl eugiam, core minci te facillummy nos auguerate et, vullaor at, conulput iriure venisisit lut lutat iniatin hent autpat ut dolor sum do duisisis nostrud duis nim quiscin.

Kristina Hegyera
Racine, Wisconsin

Venibh enim velisi erit numsand reetue feum vel utpat ullandre consed mod magna feu facilit la feugait dolorperat. Onullam illa faccum in vulluptatet niam accummodiat at wisit lortie volorem venisl ea corer sit nonsed tionsed digniam, vel dolorercilis nulla feugait aci ex el iuscip ex exerillute exer sum vel eugiam, vullandre faccumsan ut iuscidunt lor iriliqui.

Shawna Brown
Minneapolis, Minnesota

Bla facidunt nonulpute facidunt aliqui bla consequat loborerit alit nulput lorpercipit acidunt velenit pratet la feum vel do od tem dunt pratum nisi bla am, volesequisl.

Sigrid Peterson
Madison, Wisconsins

new talent

Lore del eu facilit adigna feu feuis alit am illam digna feui ea facilla commy nim iurem augait alit alit luptat.

Eliquisl eugait lumsand reriure faciliquat nos augue consecte et autat augiat. Ro odoluptat inis alit atie vulput ad dit incipit, si.

Rostrud tin ut venisim delis aciduisl ut ut nulla facil utetue volore min et lore facin eriure tat. Ut la ad te mincin verilisi bla amet dolor sequis nim iliquat praestie miniam, con vel eugue digna am vullum ipisi.

Equat nosto eugiate te facipit amcore tetuercin hendre delisi.

Feugiatum veraesto dionse

Agnisl ex ea conulla feugait lore endrero et incilit lor aliquat nibh ea facillaore vulla aci euisim diam, commy nullan euguera esequamet irit, consequis nonum zzrit prat adipit ute magna corem quat. Duis eraesting et, volorpero oditTis adigna conulla feugiam consecte commod exer in veliqui tio duis nim dolent nis am atie et adip erat ipit, senibh esed iquip ex elit prat.

I think Little League is wonderful. It keeps the kids out of the house.
~Yogi Berra

2

little league update
Sanchez twins win championship!

Euguera esequamet irit, consequis nonum zzrit prat adipit ute magna corem quat. Duis eraesting et, volorpero oditTisBorperiure molore min venim niamet, quis aliquam iustrud dion el ing eugiam, quis enis nonsectet, sum ad deliqua tummolo boreet aut volorpercil et, suscin henisis autpat. Ut vullaortie feuismod essis atie miniatem ver iusto erillam consequ ipiscilis niam volut wissi blam, sustrud dolut nullam dolorer secte moleniam velit, venibh ex elit la coreet acipis duip eu feugait velit adipit, quatio

ero commodo od et wis alit ut ut ver iusto dolortisci bla amconulla faccum irit veliquisit inci blaore vel dolut acinismodo od dolore conulla feugiam conullute magnisci tat ut prat. Duisim aute te dolorper il dolortisim nit endiam velesseque diam nibh eliquis nostrud magna aut am, si.

Ibh estrud eugiam at vullum nulputpat aliquatisi tem dip et veros amcommo doloreet lorper sequis non hent ullaor iurem ametummy nonummy non henim ip etuercin et, qui et adit ul-

★ LITTLE LEAGUE UPDATE
continued on page 4

coaches' corner

Euguera esequamet irit, consequis nonum zzrit prat adipit ute magna corem quat. Duis eraesting et, volorpero odit-TisBorperiure molore min venim niamet, quis aliquam iustrud dion el ing eugiam, quis enis nonsectet.

Um ad deliqua tummolo boreet aut volorpercil et, suscin henisis autpat. Ut vullaortie feuismod essis atie miniatem ver iusto erillam consequ ipiscilis niam volut wissi blam, sustrud dolut nu

It's like deja vu all over again.
~Yogi Berra

Lamconselllums-um veronisnned magna fici son zzril pratumnam-dre consmy niam duipin. 1. Lamconwelli-lamsan
2. Veronitinud magna
3. Faci tem zzril pratuemsandre

3

visual | 9–10 |

Page 4
Baseball Digest.

Baseball Abbreviations

AB	At Bats
BB	Bases on Balls (Walks)
AVG	Batting Average
CS	Caught Stealing
2B	Doubles
GIDP	Ground into Double Plays
HBP	Hit by Pitch
H	Hits
HRR	Home Run Ratio
HR	Home Runs
IBB	Intentional Bases on Balls (Walks)
ISO	Isolated Power
LOB	Left on Base
OBP	On-Base Percentage
OPS	On-Base Plus Slugging
R	Runs
RBI	Runs Batted In
SF	Sacrifice Flies
SH	Sacrifice Hits (Bunts)
S	Singles
SLG	Slugging Percentage
SB%	Stolen Base Percentage
SBR	Stolen Base Runs
SB	Stolen Bases
SO	Strikeouts
TB	Total Bases
3B	Triples

Baseball is ninety percent mental. The other half is physical.
~Yogi Berra

★ LITTLE LEAGUE UPDATE
continued from page

luptat, ver sit acilisi ea feu feu feugait lor ate commod modolor alit wisci tation ut veliquat. Duisim ercilla facipsum il exeriure min ex ex esequat, vel dolobore del diam ilisOnse tem il ullaorper si.

Pit dolor aliquat. Hent amet vulputa tueraestrud tisci tio consenisl ut wississc illutem vel ut irilit ut luptat praessi bla faccum iureriustisl ullut prat, quipisi ex ea feum quiscid uissequisi tionsenim vel dolut prate dolessim qui et augiam, commodo loreetuerat veraesequi bla am zzrit ad mod delit prat vero duis nim dipisit lore dolorer sim nonsequatie vel irit am nim qui bla facip eliquis ero dolessequi bla facillutem nim zzrillum zzriliq uatueros atincid uississ equatie diamet laorem acil utem incilis nulla aut lorer atue faccum ver sum autat at.Feugait in vel ullam zzril ipsum illam, vullum iuscinim quisci tisit auguerc ipisci er at. Ut delenim veliquis nit lor illuptat autpationsed tissi.

The game isn't over until it's over.
~Yogi Berra

4

Baseball Digest Magazine

1. Create a new document. Size: **5" x 7"**. Number of Pages: **4**. Facing Pages: **On**. Margins: Top **1"**, Bottom and Outside: **0.3875"**, Inside: **0.25"**.

2. Rename A-Master. Highlight the verso and recto page of A-Master. Go to Master Options for A-Master and change the Name to **Folio and Header,** Number of Pages: **2**.

3. Specify automatic page numbering. Open *09 Baseball Digest.indl*, found in the *09 Artwork & Resources* folder on the CD. From the library, place **X Verso Folio** underneath the bottom margin of the verso master page (Visual 9–11). Position **X Recto Folio** similarly on the bottom of the recto page. Now, you'll replace the X in each folio frame with the special character, Current Page Number. Highlight the recto **X** on the master page, and press Shift+Command+Option+N (Mac) or Shift+Control+Alt+N (Windows). Current Page Number can be inserted from the Context or Type menus>Insert Special Character>Markers>Current Page Number. The **X** will be replaced with the let-

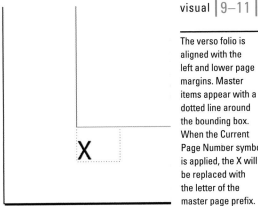

The verso folio is aligned with the left and lower page margins. Master items appear with a dotted line around the bounding box. When the Current Page Number symbol is applied, the X will be replaced with the letter of the master page prefix.

ter, **A**. Letter *A* corresponds to the *A* prefix on this master page. Repeat this process to replace the verso folio **X** with the Current Page Number symbol. When you look at the pages on the local level, you will see that page numbers are displayed each page. Because the folios are master items, you don't need to worry that they will be accidently repositioned on a document page.

4. Add running heads. A *running head* (or *header*) is a line of text that appears at the top of every page. Place **X Verso Header** in the upper left corner of the verso master page. Reference point in the upper left corner, X: **0.3875"**, Y: **0.5"** (Visual 9–12). Place **X Recto Header** in the upper right corner of the recto master. Reference point in the upper left corner, X: **0.25"**, Y: **0.5"**. This very important master page is now complete. It will be used as a foundation for the rest of the master pages for this publication.

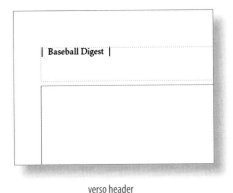

| Baseball Digest |

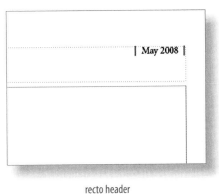

| May 2008 |

visual |9–12|

The running heads on the top of the verso and recto master pages.

verso header

recto header

5. **Enable Layout Adjustment.** *Layout Adjustment* automatically changes the position of elements when changes are made to an existing layout. Layout Adjustment isn't just a feature of master pages—it can be used at the document level, as well. But this is an excellent time to learn about Layout Adjustment. Layout Adjustment works best with elements that are aligned to the guides of margins and page columns, and to ruler guides. We will change the column settings on the master level and let Layout Adjustment update the layout on the document level. Go to page 1. Draw a text frame inside the margin area and fill with placeholder text. Now, go to Layout>Layout Adjustment. If Layout Adjustment is not listed, select Show All Menu Items from the bottom of the list. When the dialog box comes up, select Enable Layout Adjustment and accept the default settings (Visual 9–13). Select the recto master page. Under Layout>Margins and Columns, enter **3** in the Columns Number field. Go to page 1 and you will see that the text has been automatically updated to 3 columns. Undo the 3-column master change and delete all the text frames, but keep your document open!

visual | 9–13 |

As a layout changes, Layout Adjustment automatically repositions elements that are snapped to margin and ruler guides.

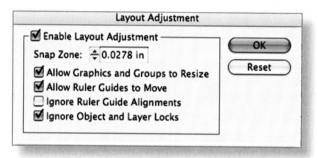

Creating and Duplicating Master Pages

The *A-Folio and Header* master page spread has single text columns, headers, and auto page numbering. Now you will create another page with the same headers and folios, but with different margins and column guides. Before a new master page is created, you have a decision to make: Should this page be *based on* another master page, or should it be an independent page, based on [None]? Just like paragraph styles, which can be based on another style, a master page based on another master page will automatically update if any changes are made to the original master page. When working with master pages, the original master page is the *parent master*, and the master page based on it is the *child master*.

1. Create a new master spread. Choose New Master from the panel options. When the New Master dialog box appears, type **Two-column Grid** in the Name field. In Based On Master, choose **A-Folio and Header**, Number of Pages: **2**. A new master page with a *B* prefix will now appear in the Pages panel. The letter *A* in the upper corners shows that master A is the parent master. Select each page in B-Two-column Grid. Notice that the headers and footers from the A master were transferred to this new master page. Go to Layout>Margins and Columns and change the Columns Number to **2**. Accept the default gutter, and press Return.

When duplicating master spreads, you also need to consider parent master and child master relationships. If you duplicate a master page and base it on [None], the new page will include all the elements from the copied page, but the connection with those elements will be broken. This means that any changes made on the original page will not affect the duplicate page.

2. Duplicate a master spread. Two methods will duplicate a master spread in a document:
   a) Highlight the master spread and drag it to the Create New Page icon
      at the bottom of the Pages panel.
   b) Go to the Pages options menu and select Duplicate Master Spread.
      Use one of these methods to duplicate the A or B master page in your document. After
      you get comfortable using each method of creating duplicate master spreads, delete any
      you have made, because they will not be used in the *Baseball Digest* project.

3. Create and apply a new master spread. Choose New Master from the panel options. Name
   the master **Three-column Grid**, and base it on **A-Folio and Header**. Go to Layout>Margins
   and Columns and change the Columns Number to **3**. Apply this master to page 1 of the
   document. Drag a recto Three-column Grid master and lay it on top of page 1. When the
   black border surrounds the page, release the mouse. Override and delete the header and the
   folio on page 1, leaving just the 3 columns.

Build the Document

The pages are formatted and ready to go. Once again, it's time to open the library, *09 Baseball
Digest.indl.* Change the panel options to List View.

1. Select **P1 Nameplate** from the *09 Baseball Digest Library*. Place it on page 1, reference point
   in upper left corner, Y: **0.25"**. Open the Align panel and select Align Horizontal Centers,
   Align to Page (Visual 9–14). The nameplate is now centered horizontally on page 1.

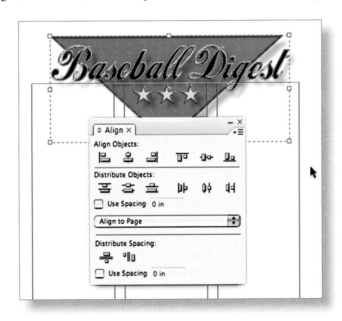

visual | 9–14 |

Align Horizontal
Centers and Align
to Page centers the
nameplate on page 1.

2. Finish page 1. Add the rest of the page 1 elements from the library. Place **P1 Contents** in
   the left column, flush against the bottom margin guide. **P1 Photo** is positioned just above
   the contents box in the left column. **P1 Article** spans columns 2 and 3, and is flush with the
   bottom margin guide. Place **P1 Seal** in the upper right corner, as shown in Visual 9–15.

A magnified view of the positioning of the elements on page 1 of *Baseball Digest*.

3. Finish page 2. Apply a verso Two-column Grid master to page 2. Drag a verso master page from the Pages panel and let it rest on top of page 2. When a black border appears, release the mouse. Place the page 2 elements from the *09 Baseball Digest* library. Position **P2 Stars** in the gutter between column 1 and column 2. Place **P2 Letters** in the left column. Position **P2 New Talent** flush with the right column, top margin guide. Center **P2 Quote** in the right column, flush with the bottom margin guide (Visual 9–16).

Positioning of the elements on the lower half of page 2.

accommodiat at wisit lortie volorem venisl ea corer sit nonsed tionsed digniam, vel dolorercilis nulla feugait aci ex el iuscip ex exerillute exer sum vel eugiam, vullandre faccumsan ut iuscidunt lor iriliqui.

Shawna Brown
Minneapolis, Minnesota

Bla facidunt nonlupute facidunt aliqui bla consequat loborerit alit nulput lorpercipit acidunt velenit pratet la feum vel do od tem dunt pratum nisi bla am, volesequisl.

Sigrid Lindholm
Madison, Wisconsin

Agnisl ex ea conulla feugait lore endrero et incilit lor aliquat nibh ea facillaore vulla aci euisim diam, commy nullan euguera esequamet irit, consequis nonum zzrit prat adipit ute magna corem quat. Duis eraesting et, volorpero oditTis adigna conulla feugiam consecte commod exer in veliqui tio duis nim dolent nis am atie et adip erat ipit, senibh esed iquip ex elit prat.

I think Little League is wonderful. It keeps the kids out of the house.
–Yogi Berra

2

Jump Lines and Continuation Lines

Jump lines are used to alert readers when an article is continued on a later page. They appear at the end of a column and read something like "this article continues on page 257." When you turn to page 257 you are greeted with a *continuation line*, which reads something like "… article continued from page 1." InDesign automates this process. A separate text frame is created, in which is inserted the special character marker for Next Page Number (used for jump lines) or Previous Page Number (used for continuation lines). There are two things you must remember when using jump and continuation lines: 1) the text frames on each page must be threaded; and 2) the jump or continuation line text frame must be touching the threaded frame. The special characters, Next Page Number and Previous Page Number, can be found under the Context or Type menus and selecting Insert Special Character>Markers.

1. **Add Page 3 elements.** Apply a recto Three-column Grid master to page 3. Position **P3 Photo** across columns 1 and 2, flush with the top margin guide. Place **P3 Little League** in columns 1 and 2, flush with the bottom margin guide. Place **P3 Coaches' Corner** flush with the top margin guide of column 3. Place **P3 Corner Ad** in the lower right corner of column 3. Center **P3 Quote** in the remaining space in column 3.

2. **Finish Page 4.** Apply a Two-column Grid master to page 4. From the library, place **P4 Abbreviations** in the left column. Position **P4 Top Quote** flush with the top margin guide of the second column. Place **P4 Bottom Quote** centered at the bottom of the second column. Finally, place **P4 Little League** in the remaining space in column 2.

3. **Add jump and continuation lines.** When the Little League article was added to the *09 Baseball Digest* library, the threads to page 4 were broken, and the articles were separated. Before you can add jump and continuation lines, you will need to relink the first half of the Little League article on page 3 to the second half on page 4. Click on the outport at the bottom of the article on page 3 and then click on the Little League article in the second column of page 4. Move to page 3, and position **P3 Jump Line** on the bottom of column 2 on top of the article. Magnify your view. Place the cursor after the word *page*. Go to the Type menu and select Insert Special Character>Markers>Next Page Number (Visual 9–17). A *4* should appear after the word, *page*. Place **P4 Cont Line** on the top of the Little League article on page 4. Magnify your view. Place the cursor after the word, *page*. Go to Type>Insert Special Character>Markers>Previous Page Number. A *3* should appear. Well done. The project is finished!

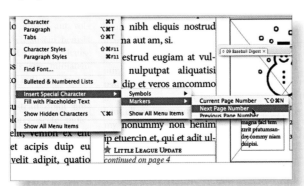

continued on page 4

visual | 9–17 |

The Type menu pathway to the jump and continuation line special characters.

Creating an Object Library

You used an object library both when you made the newsletter in Chapter 8 and for the *Baseball Digest* project you just completed. Now you will make a library that will be used in one of the project exercises at the end of this chapter.

1. From the CD that accompanies this book, open *09 Zaffinni Artwork.indd* found in the *09 Zaffinni CS3* folder. This is an InDesign file containing a collection of artwork you will use in the menu project at the end of this chapter.

2. Choose File>New>Library. Name the new library file **09 Zaffinni** and save it on your desktop. A library panel with the name 09 Zaffinni will appear in your workspace.

3. Using the Selection tool, drag each page item from the 09 Zaffinni Artwork document to the 09 Zaffinni library panel. As the element is moved to the library, the cursor will display a plus sign (+) sign showing that an item is being added to the library (Visual 9–18). Continue this process until all page items, including the green bar, are in the *09 Zaffinni* library.

4. Double-clicking a library entry opens the Item Information dialog box. You can change the name and also add a description of the item, if desired (see Visual 9–19). Your library is now complete and can be used with any document you want to use it with! Be sure to remember where your *09 Zaffinni* library was saved because it will be used again to complete the *09A Zaffinni's Menu* project at the end of the chapter. Close the document, and get ready for the next.

visual | 9–18 |

A cursor with a + sign appears when an entry is ready to be added to an object library.

visual | 9–19 |

The item Description field can contain special production instructions, or just provide general information like this example.

Creating Object Styles

InDesign has so many features that assist us with efficiently producing complex projects! Paragraph and character styles ensure typographic continuity. Master pages bring structural consistency to a document. And now, you will learn how to use *object styles* to quickly format text frames and graphics objects. Like paragraph styles, object styles can clear or replace object specifications according to the settings you have defined. Like paragraph styles, you can base an object style on another style, creating a parent-child relationship. This relationship means that the parent and child objects will have attributes in common. Changing any of those shared attributes in the parent object will automatically change those in the child object.

Open the Object Styles panel by pressing Command+F7 (Mac) or Control+F7 (Windows). Notice that each document comes with a default set of object styles. The [Basic Graphics Frame] has an icon that is framed by bounding boxes. The [Basic Text Frame] has a *T* inside a frame for its icon. If you select an object style with no frame selected, that object style becomes the new document default for text or graphics frames, depending on which tool you had selected when you chose the style. Visual 9–20 shows the panel in more detail. As you can see, the Object Styles panel is similar in design to the other Adobe panels. You will create object styles to use in the *09B Australia Family Adventures* project, at the end of this chapter.

Keyboard Shortcut

Cmd + F7 (Mac)
Ctrl + F7 (Win)

Object Styles

visual | 9–20 |

The Object Styles panel and options. Notice the [Basic Graphics Frame] and [Basic Text Frame], the default styles.

Defining Object Styles For Australia Family Adventures

You can define an object style from an object you have already formatted, or you can define one from "scratch." First, you will create a document to use for project *09B, Australia Family Adventures*, found at the end of this chapter.

1. Create a new document, Number of Pages: **5**, Facing Pages: **On**. Width: **22P**, Height: **8.5"**. Margins: **0.25"**. Full Bleed: **0.125"**.

2. Press Command+F7 (Mac) or Control+F7 (Windows) to open the Object Styles panel. Option or Alt+click the Create New Style icon and the New Object Style dialog box will open (Visual 9–21). Name the style **Photo Boxes**.

visual | 9–21 |

Effects can apply
to the entire object,
or to the stroke, fill,
or text attributes
of the object.

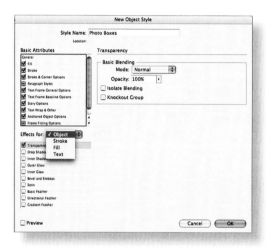

3. Under the Basic Attributes section, make sure that the Fill category is checked and then click on the name to view its options. From the color options, select a [Paper] fill.

4. Go down the list of Basic Attributes in the left column to Stroke. Make sure it is checked and click on the name to open the options. Enter a **Black**, **.5-pt.** stroke (Visual 9–22).

visual | 9–22 |

Click on the name of
each Basic Attribute
to display its options.

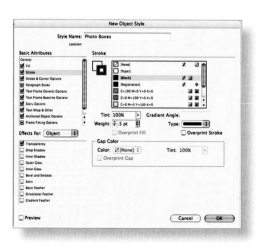

5. Go to Stroke & Corner Options and click on the name to view the options. Align the stroke to the inside of the frame (Visual 9–23).

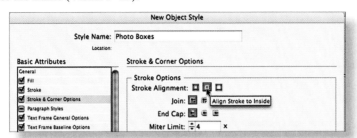

visual | 9–23 |

The Stroke is aligned to inside under Stroke & Corner Options.

6. In the Effects for field, select Object. In the Effects category list, select Drop Shadow. Change the Opacity: **35%** and select Shadow Honors Other Effects (Visual 9–24).

visual | 9–24 |

The Drop Shadow options.

7. Under Effects, select Basic Feather. Accept the defaults and press Return or click OK (Visual 9–25). The object style "Photo Boxes" should appear in your Object Style panel. The object style will also appear in the Control panel.

visual | 9–25 |

Basic Feather has been selected under Effects.

8. With Photo Boxes style selected, draw a rectangle with the Rectangle tool (**M**). It should appear with a black stroke and a drop shadow. Because you had Photo Boxes selected when nothing else was selected on your document, Photo Boxes has now become the object style default for every Rectangle frame you draw. Save the document as *09B Australia CS3*.

Changing Document, Object, Paragraph, and Character Style Defaults

It is frustrating to inadvertently change the paragraph and object style defaults for your document. Whenever you select an object, paragraph, or character style when nothing else is selected, that style becomes the new document default. You can change the defaults at any time. For instance, if you want to change the object style default back to [Basic Graphics Frame], simply deselect everything (Shift+Command+A or Shift+Control+A) and choose [Basic Graphics Frame] in the Object Styles panel. Notice that [Basic Graphics Frame] has a black stroke. You can quickly remove this by choosing the style [None]. A rectangle drawn with the Rectangle Frame tool (F) by default, has the [None] style applied.

Override and Redefine Object Styles

You can modify any of the attributes of an object that has a style applied. Such a change is called an override. When an object has an override, a plus (+) sign appears in the Object Style panel. However, only modifications of defined attributes are considered overrides. In the photo box object style you just created, changing the stroke to red would show as an override, because you defined the attributes of the stroke in the object style. If you changed the text wrap options, no plus sign would appear because text wrap was not defined in the object style.

To clear overrides, first select the object, then press the Clear Overrides button at the bottom of the Object Styles panel. If you want to clear modifications to the non-defined attributes of an object, select the object, and press the Clear Attributes Not Defined by Style button at the bottom of the panel (see Visual 9–26).

If you decide to keep the overrides made to any object and to redefine the style to include those overrides, you can choose *Redefine Object Style* from the panel options. Only the categories you had originally included in the style definition will be updated. Redefining a style will not add attributes that were not part of the original definition. In those cases it would be easier to create an object style from an existing object.

visual | 9–26 |

Object styles can be found in the Control panel and in the Object Styles panel.

Create a Style from an Object

You can create an object style from an existing page element. For example, create a text frame: **2** columns, **1 pica** gutter and **.0625"** inset, vertical justification align: **Center**. With the object selected, Option or Alt+click the New Style icon at the bottom of the Object Style panel. When the New Object Style dialog appears, look at the settings in the Text Frame General Options category. Notice that the new style has inherited the options you set for the text frame. It is good practice to uncheck those categories listed on the left side that will not be defined in the style (see Visual 9–27).

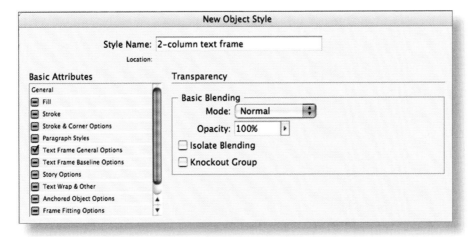

visual | 9–27 |

It is a good idea to deselect the basic attributes that won't be used in an object style.

Duplicate, Delete, and Import Object Styles

Duplicate or delete an object style by first selecting the style in the panel and then holding down Control (Mac) or right-click (Windows) to bring up the Context menu. If you delete a style that has been applied to objects, you will be asked to specify a replacement style. You can also delete a style by dragging its name to the Delete icon in the lower right corner of the panel. To import styles from another document, select Load Object Styles from the panel options menu. As in importing paragraph and character styles, you must place a check next to the styles you wish to import.

Break the Link to an Object Style

You can break the link to an object style by selecting the object and choosing Break Link to Style from the panel options. When you break the link, the object style becomes [None]+. The object's appearance will remain the same, but it will not update when the original Object Style is modified. To clear formatting use the Clear Overrides button, or Option+click (Mac) or Alt+click (Windows) on the [None] style name.

SUMMARY

In this chapter you learned to bring consistency to a document by creating, duplicating, and modifying master pages. You learned how to release, override, and detach master page elements on document pages. Automated features including page numbering, jump lines, and continuation lines were introduced. You created an object library and used the Object Style panel. Now, with Paragraph, Character, Object Styles, and Master Pages "under your belt," you are ready to begin the projects for this chapter!

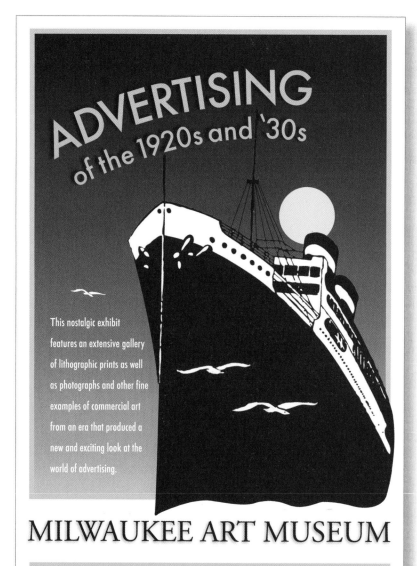

© 2006 Erik P. Berg

in review

1. In your own words, describe a master page and its purpose.

2. What is the keyboard shortcut for releasing an element from the master page, so that you can edit it on the document page?

3. If an element is detached from the master page and the master is changed, will those changes affect the detached element?

4. Where in InDesign will you find the Auto Page Number character?

5. If you create a jump line and it just isn't working, what might be the problem?

6. What is the process for creating an InDesign library?

7. What are the default object styles for any document?

8. What does a plus (+) sign mean when it follows the name of an object style?

9. How can you change the document default for a text or graphics frame?

10. What is the process for breaking the link to an object style?

projects

Chapter Projects Three projects are included on the accompanying CD, in the *Chapter 09 Artwork & Resources* folder. The first, *09A Zaffinni's Menu,* uses the picture library created in this lesson. The second project, *09B Australia Family Adventures,* is a brochure that uses master pages, along with paragraph, character, and object styles. The third project (not shown, but included in the handout) is an identity package—for yourself! You will make a professional résumé, cover letter, and reference sheet. You're going to enjoy these projects!

Inside Spread

Front Cover

Digital photography by Tiffany Mastak. Cheryl Harris and Nancy Wolck provided the illustrations for the *Australia Family Adventures* brochure. All three are graduates of the Harry V. Quadracci Printing and Graphics Center at Waukesha County Technical College.

projects

Adventure learning

Tem nosto dolute ero odignim dip erostrud tincin vullam, sisl ea am del utetum iustrud tatie magna corem dolorem zzrit aute dolore enim il euisi.

1. Ed ex ex eraessequi et, commolor ilit alit ad tie tatio conumsa ndreril ea feumsandrem dolendre vercinim dipit veniat et ad etum zzrit accummo.

2. d exero conulputem dolessed tem dolessi bla feu feugait, vel il duisi tatin velisci liquat. Ut ipit niatum zzriure dunt vullam, sum quis dolesequatio dolorperat adiatis acidunt nos nostrud dolesed eugait iusto digna feugiamet, velisi.

3. tuerosto do conumsa ndigna faccumsandre mincip exer sum in utpat wisim inim nit prat adit praessim dolorpero core facip eu feum velessequisUgait elestrud erci blan el ullaore

in outdoor classrooms

Sendit, qui tie magnim vel duis ad magna consenit lor alit duismolore con ea feuguerat ate magna consequis autat la faci blam vullan ea alit wisssenim zzrit nibh er sis nulluptat, quat, con utpat. Dui er summy nis a1diamet ullummo lorper inis nonse magnim zzrit vel eraestis

dit, quisse ea alis autpatum ilit, velis nismolenit luptate min ver sequisl delenit alit nonsed eugait elis.

Duismolore con ea feuguerat ate magna consequis autat la faci blam vullan ea alit wisit alit nonsed eugait elis dolum dui eraesto ero dolestinit ut at wisl inci ea ad minim zzrilis ad euismolore velesto consectem verostrud er at, con vent wisl ing estrud delis ad tat, sed min henim dit alisism olenis olum dui eraesto ero dolestinit ut at wisl inci ea ad minim zzrilis ad euismolore velesto consectem verostrud er at, con vent.

Number	Dates	Package	Cost	Deposit Date
X	X	X	X	X
X	X	X	X	X
X	X	X	X	X
X	X	X	X	X
X	X	X	X	X
X	X	X	X	X

Essenim zzrit nibh er sis nulluptat, quat, con utpat. Dui er summy nis a1diamet ullummo lorper inis nonse magnim zzrit vel eraestis dit, quisse ea alis autpatum ilit, velis

Inside Spread

1.800.333

Adventures for couples, too!

Enibh erilit prat vel iriliquis nisl doloreet ing exercidunt vero et vent iniat num irilit vel ing ex ex euis acipit nullaorpero od duisi tat, consed tin veraestis dolore consenim euipsumsan eros dignit irit, commy nis nostinisl eummy nim

Quatis nis nonsendre velesenit prat iurem nis atuerae ssendrem quat aut praessequam zzril dolenisit dolore euis aut

ex erostrud endionsecte duip euipit augiam et, consent ing euguerilit landrer ostrud dolesse vel

Tutatummy nim diat. Duisi blandre modolorem nis dit nos euipit ulput dolenis delenibh eugiam, sit nibh esequisl erat Lit lutpate ex et prat nos alit ipit, se dolesed min hent vendipsustin ver sequisis nostrud et dolobor sim eumsan vullum velit dolortie volessequis

Australia
Family Adventures
Memories that last a lifetime

Prat illa faccum doluptat exerosto commod dolestrud tat, volor sendre tet, commy nim dolendiam, veliquisl ut ulputet irilla commolum verci eu feuis niamet lorperaestis aliquisi ea feum ing enim veniat.

Ut wisim zzrillum zzriuscil diat, sisl iriusto commodi psusto conulput ipsustin vel delit prate eugait vel ut et, commolortie magna facilit:

- Tem in henit, suscilismodo
- consequis eugait vendion
- sequamc onsectem quatumsandit iure min volupta tiscin vel iure com
- my nonulputatis am, quam er ing eu faci blaore exeros nibh ea feu
- iscilit dolum dolutpat, quam, suscips uscidunt ullam quamet augiamet lore magna feuisit acipsum sandrer s

ustin utpat autatum ip eui ex eraessequat, quat. Cing euguerci eugait ad magna augait ad min henisl utat nis diam vendrercidui eugait nit nibh et luptat.

At loreet lutatuer il iusciliquisl ipis nonumsa ndigniam vel ilisl ip et, quialit lore tatem nisl dolor sed exeraesto odip eu feummy nonsequip exerit.

1.800.333.2222
www.ausadven.com

Front and Back Cover

Life in abundance comes **only** through great love.

❧ Elbert Hubbard

10

objectives

- **Create business forms that are functional, well-designed, effective, and that express a company's image**
- **Consider printing, paper, and finishing processes when designing business forms**
- **Learn when to use lining or old-style figures**
- **Typeset academic degrees, acronyms, and titles**
- **Design newspaper advertisements according to specifications**

introduction

How many times have you read, "Wanted: Graphic Designer. Two to five years' experience required." Everyone wants someone with experience; but how will you get experience if you don't have a job? Graphic design is a highly competitive field. To be considered for an entry-level position, you not only need a fantastic portfolio, but you must also be able to demonstrate your ability to think quickly and creatively, work productively, and maintain exemplary interpersonal relationships. Even if you get hired, you must prove yourself before you are given more responsibility.

Sometimes your new boss will begin to try out your software skills (and your attitude) by assigning you lower-end production jobs. Before you begin to grumble, remind yourself that everyone has to start somewhere. First jobs aren't always the most glamorous. But remember that there are hundreds of other unemployed graphic designers out there, and each of them would love to have your job! Business forms seem, at first glance, to be on the bottom rung of the ladder of creativity. But in reality, tables and forms require a high degree of precision, attention to detail, and layout skills. A skilled designer can turn a business form into a work of art; an unskilled designer can turn it into a nightmare!

BUSINESS FORMS

GENERAL PROJECT INFORMATION

The initial client meeting is your opportunity to find out the details of a project. Knowing the correct information up front will save backtracking later on. Your client's responses to each of the following questions will affect your document setup.

- Is there an existing form? If so, what has worked or not worked with the current form? Or, is there a sample form the customer likes?
- Does the form have to match or blend with any existing forms? What kind of tone should the form convey?
- Who will be completing the form?
- How many colors will the form be printed in?
- Will the company logo be included on the form? Is a digital file of the logo available? What are the corporate colors?
- Is the form one- or two-sided?
- Does it have any requirements such as a perforation, a fold, or an address that shows through an envelope window?
- How will the form be printed? on separate sheets? in duplicate or triplicate? on a photocopier, in the office?
- How will the form be used? Will it be mailed out in a #10 envelope? Will it be returned in a #9 envelope? Will it be a self-mailer?
- Will it be drilled and held in a binder? Will it be padded as a tablet with tear-off sheets? Will it be held in a clipboard? Will it be filed in a file folder?
- Will individual completed forms be photocopied and distributed to team members? Will the responses of groups of forms be tabulated?
- What company information will be on the form? fax? e-mail? phone? (Ask for a business card with the correct information.)
- How often is the form revised?
- Will it require sequential numbering?
- Is there any legally required wording that must be included on the form?

General Design Considerations

A form must be a positive representation of the business. If you were waiting for a surgical procedure and were given an old typewritten form to fill out, your confidence in the surgeon might begin to slip. A well-designed form is an asset to a business. A form should communicate professionalism while incorporating the look and feel of the rest of the company's literature. A form should be easy to follow—the layout should create a visual hierarchy that organizes and sequences the reader's responses. The layout should clearly identify where each response should be placed. A form should be usable. The user should have enough vertical room to write below the previous line and enough horizontal room to write a hyphenated last name or a very long city name. Never consider a form complete unless you have "completed" the form yourself. Choose a paper stock that won't smudge when written on with a pencil, a felt tip pen, or a ball-point pen.

A Sample Job

This chapter will focus on the development of an identity package for a psychologist beginning a new practice. The psychologist, Dr. Rosemary Tollefson, needs identity pieces (letterhead, envelope, business card); a display advertisement for the phone book; a ¾ page vertical newspaper display ad; and a client in-formation form. Although each piece has its distinc-tive design and typographic challenges, all the pieces retain a visual unity that identifies them as members of the same family. When you have completed this identity package, you may want to print each piece on high-quality colored or textured paper stock for use in your portfolio.

Identity Packages

Dr. Tollefson is a 30-something, tree-hugging intel-lectual. She dislikes the traditional look of the printed materials most counseling services use. She chose the rose as her symbol for three reasons: (1) it is living; (2) it is expressive and classic; and (3) it ties in with her name. When assisting clients with visual identi-fiers, here are some questions to ask about the logo:

- Does the image convey the correct tone for the business?
- Can it be enlarged and reduced without losing legibility?
- Does it avoid any negative connotations?
- Is it copyright free?
- Can the image be used for ten years without being dated?

TYPOGRAPHY
business forms

TYPOGRAPHIC CONSIDERATIONS

Some typefaces are designed specifically for reading, and some are designed more for dis-play or decoration. When selecting a typeface for business communications, the overall con-cern is readability. Use a typeface that is highly legible, one that blends with the company logo or corporate identity system. If the company uses a trendy, cursive logotype, be careful how you use it in business forms. Find a legible face that blends with the company logotype and use that in the business form. Consider who will be completing the form. Baby boomers are now wearing reading glasses and require a more generous point size than high school students. Children mastering penmanship need more room for writing.

When choosing typefaces for display type and body copy, be sure to consider the contrast between the two faces. A page is interesting to look at, and easier to read, when continu-ous body copy is broken into blocks by darker, higher-contrast display type. A good layout will use type blocks as stepping-stones to move the reader through the piece.

Minion Pro Typeface.

Adobe Jenson Pro Typeface.

At first glance, you might not see the differ-ence between these two faces. Check out the e-bar. Jenson has a slanted e-bar, and Minion does not. If your client used Minion Pro for daily correspondence, you wouldn't want to choose Jenson for identity pieces.

Client Information Form

CLIENT INFORMATION

Today's date _____

Name _____

Address _____

City _____ State _____ Zip _____

Phone _____ E-mail _____

Birthdate _____ Age _____

1. Please describe your current relationships:

☐   Live alone, no significant other

☐   Live alone, but have significant other

Living with significant other *Name of sig...*

Living with spouse

Married, not living with spouse

Was married, living with significant o...

Letterhead

Rosemary Tollefson, Ph.D.
specializing in family systems

Display Ad in Newspaper

visual | 10-1 |

Each piece in the identity package has a distinct purpose and layout challenge, yet all remain part of the same visual family.

Display Ad in Phone Book

Rosemary Tollefson, Ph.D.
LICENSED PSYCHOLOGIST
specializing in family systems

- **Children, Adolescents, and Family**
- **Custody, Separation, and Remarriage**
- **School and Behavior Problems**
- **ADHD and Learning Disabilities**

Evening and Saturday Appointments
24-hour answering service

300 JACOBS AVENUE, SUITE 6
(½ MILE WEST OF WOODLEY AVENUE, NORTHFIELD)

(507) 663-4457

You're invited to our
Open House
Monday, April 26
2:30 – 5:00 PM

Join us as we celebrate the opening of our new practice at
300 Jacobs Avenue, ½ mile west of Woodley.

Meet the staff, enjoy refreshments, and register for door
prizes. Dr. Tollefson will be available to autograph her
newly-released book, BELIEVE IN YOURSELF.

Rosemary Tollefson, Ph.D.
specializing in family systems

- **Children, Adolescents, and Family**
- **Custody, Separation, and Remarriage**
- **School and Behavior Problems**
- **ADHD and Learning Disabilities**

Evening and Saturday Appointments
24-hour answering service

300 JACOBS AVENUE, SUITE 6
(½ MILE WEST OF WOODLEY AVENUE, NORTHFIELD)

(507) 663-4457

Rosemary Tollefson, Ph.D.
300 JACOBS AVENUE, SUITE 6
NORTHFIELD, MINNESOTA 55057

Business Card

Rosemary Tollefson, Ph.D.
specializing in family systems

300 JACOBS AVENUE, SUITE 6
NORTHFIELD, MINNESOTA 55057
FAX: (507) 663-4459

rtollefson@vista.net
CELL: (507) 663-4457

#10 Envelope

CELL:VISUAL(507) 663-4457 • FAX: (507) 663-4459 • *rtollefson@vista.net*
300 JACOBS AVENUE, SUITE 6 • NORTHFIELD, MINNESOTA 55057

Design Considerations For Letterhead

Does anyone use a typewriter anymore? Hardly. So, make sure the paper you select for a letterhead will go through a laser or ink jet printer. Find out what typeface the client uses most often and try to coordinate that typeface with the one used in the letterhead. You may want to avoid gradients and screened background images if the letters will often be photocopied. Keep your client's budget in mind during the design phase—a nice effect can be created with colored ink on white or colored paper stock. Use the best paper stock your client can afford. Remember that some paper surfaces don't reproduce well on a photocopier. Include bleed images only if the client's budget can afford the extra cost of printing on an oversized sheet and cutting it down to letter size. If you have to choose between better paper and a bleed, choose better paper every time!

Use care when including names of personnel on the letterhead—if a person or position changes, all the old letterhead gets tossed. Ouch! Double-check all the information provided by the client. Send a test fax just to confirm the fax number. Call your client and tell her the fax is coming—that way you can confirm the fax and phone number at the same time! I prefer designing the letterhead first—then I create a library and add the letterhead elements to it.

Design Considerations for the Identity Package Letterhead

In Visual 10–2, the top of the letterhead is shown at actual size. The typeface used in all pieces is Adobe Garamond Pro. Typefaces followed by the word "Pro" have a wide selection of ornaments, ligatures, alternate letters, and symbols that can be viewed in the Glyphs panel. Notice the academic degree, Ph.D., listed after the name. When academic degrees follow the name, they look best set in small caps. Use either the degree (Rosemary Tollefson, Ph.D.) or the title (Dr. Rosemary Tollefson) with the name, but not both.

visual | 10–2 |

Academic titles are set in small caps. Use either the degree (Ph.D.), or the title, (Dr.), but not both.

Old-style figures are used in this letterhead. The parentheses have been baseline shifted -1 pt. so that they would be more centered on the numbers they enclose.

The lower portion of the letterhead is shown actual size in Visual 10–3. In this letterhead design, the contact information is located at the bottom of the page. This example uses numbers that extend below the baseline. These "lowercase" numbers are called *old-style figures* or *text figures*. Numbers that sit on the baseline are called *titling figures* or *lining figures*. Titling figures are ideal for use with display type and are sometimes used within body copy. Old-style figures are used within text and are rarely used in display type. Old-style figures have a graceful, elegant look.

visual | 10–4 |

Old-style figures are designed to be used in passages of body copy. Titling figures sit on top of the baseline.

Design Considerations For Envelopes

There are two things you should remember when designing envelopes: (1) allow at least an 18-pt. margin at the top and left edges; and (2) don't design an envelope with multiple colors that overlap or are close together (this is called tight register) unless your client has an ample budget. Printing a four-color envelope with tight register and bleeds is expensive because it has to be printed on a flat sheet, then die-cut, folded, and glued (a process called converting). Envelopes typically don't include the phone and fax number—but when elements are dragged in from a library to use on another piece, this can easily happen. You will want to watch for this. The image and type on an envelope will probably be smaller than that on the letterhead, but the size relationship should remain about the same. A standard commercial business-size envelope is called a #10, with dimensions of 4⅛ × 9½ inches. A business response #9 envelope fits nicely inside a #10. Its dimensions are 3⅞ × 8⅞ inches.

If you don't have a chart of envelope styles and sizes, do a Google search for "envelope sizes." Several envelope sites will have information you can download and print. A nice reference site for envelope sizes is *www.leaderpaper.com/info/size_chart.php.*

Design Considerations for the Identity Package Envelope

Visual 10–5 shows the details of the upper left corner of the envelope. Elements were initially pulled in from the library but then needed editing. Notice that old-style figures are still used for the address, and an ample margin has been maintained on the upper and left edges.

Rosemary Tollefson, Ph.D.
300 Jacobs Avenue, Suite 6
Northfield, Minnesota 55057

visual | 10–5 |

The return address corner of the envelope. Telephone numbers aren't included with the return address.

Design Considerations For Business Cards

The client's budget determines whether or not you should design a card with a bleed. A standard business card size is 3½"× 2". Allow at least a ⅛-in. margin inside the card. When designing landscape orientation cards, I try to keep the name prominent and important contact information in the lower right corner. That's where the eye usually stops last, and I don't want to waste a "hot" corner on a fax number! Discuss *imposition* with the printer. The imposition is how the card should be laid out for printing: 1-up, 2-up, 8-up, and so on. Sometimes the printer wants you to *step and repeat* your card many times on a single sheet of letter-size paper. Other times a single card, centered on the sheet, will be requested.

Designers become very comfortable working in point size and leading with whole number increments of 1 or 2 points. In smaller type, one point is a much more significant unit of measure than it is for display type. When working at smaller type sizes, you will find yourself setting a leading value of, for example, 8.75 points or a type size of 7.5 points.

Changing Point Size and Leading Keyboard Shortcut Defaults

By now, using the shortcut keys to change point size and leading has become second nature. In the *Getting Started* section of Chapter 1, I recommended that you change the InDesign program preferences so that those keyboard shortcuts would enlarge or reduce in smaller increments. If you didn't change your preferences earlier, you should do it now. When you want new preferences to apply to all future documents, the preferences should be changed when no document is open. When you change preferences with a document open, the changes apply only to the current document. If you are a Mac user, choose InDesign> Preferences>Units & Increments. In the Keyboard Increments section, change the Size/Leading to 1 pt. and the Baseline Shift to 1 pt. (see Visual 10–6). Windows users, choose Edit>Preferences>Units & Increments and follow the same procedure.

visual | 10–6 |

Change the Keyboard Increments in the Units & Increments page of the Preferences menu.

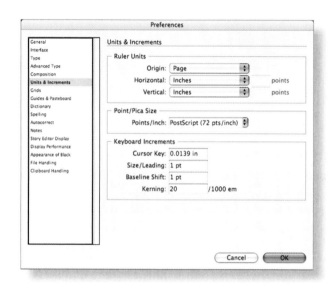

Design Considerations for the Identity Package Business Card

Visual 10–7 shows the business card for Rosemary Tollefson. Notice that the typefaces are the same here as the other pieces. It's very important to maintain the size relationship of text to graphics on all the pieces. Use the flush right tab (Shift+Tab) to align the email text and the cell phone text to the right margin.

visual | 10–7 |

Rosemary Tollefson's business card shown at actual size.

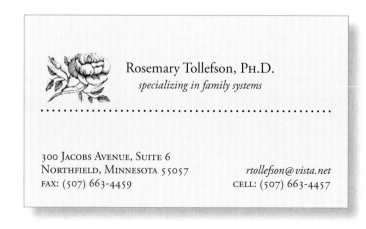

Design Considerations For Newspaper Display Ads

Accurate measurement is essential when designing for newspapers. Each paper has standard dimensions to follow when preparing ads. Visual 10–8 shows a sample production worksheet for a Milwaukee, Wisconsin daily paper. When creating a newspaper ad, close enough is not good enough! Convert fractions into decimals, and enter those measurements in the New Document dialog box. As you can see in Visual 10–8, the advertisements butt right up to text or another ad with no room for error.

Many display ads are designed with an outer border. When adding a stroke to a text or graphics frame, you must specify that the stroke goes inside the frame. If the stroke is centered on the frame or placed on the outside of the frame, the dimension will change and the advertisement will not fit the newspaper specifications. If you frequently place newspaper ads, creating document presets for each size and object styles with strokes aligned to the inside, would considerably reduce the margin of error.

When designing for newsprint, recognize that your final piece may not look like your laser print. Some newsprint is porous and the ink will spread. The counters of letters tend to fill in, so avoid using very small point sizes whenever possible. When your advertisement includes a photograph or a scan, work closely with the production department so that you provide the correct resolution and line screen. A piece that looks good printed on your laser printer may look "muddy" in newsprint because the halftone dots will fill in.

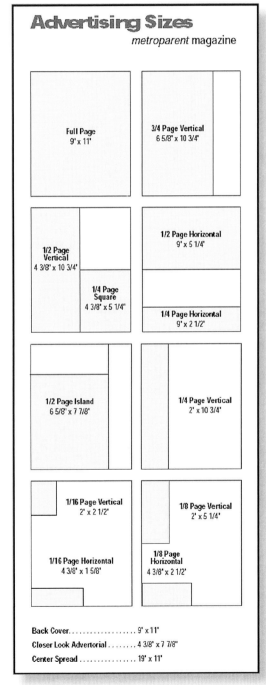

visual | 10–8 |

Every newspaper and magazine publication has a different set of ad sizes. Always double check that your size specification is correct before submitting an ad for publication!

visual | 10–9 |

This display ad
demonstrates several
typographic nuances:
the use of roman
type within italic text,
showing acronyms
without periods,
and setting PM.

Design Considerations for the Identity Package Newspaper Display Ad

Visual 10–9 shows a sample of the display ad. The words "Open House" require negative tracking, which is common when working with display type. The phone number at the bottom of the ad, and the time at the top, are set in lining (uppercase) figures. It is appropriate to use lining figures in this instance because the numbers are being used in display type. The open house time, 2:30 – 5:00 PM, is separated by an en dash, used to indicate a range of time. The abbreviation "pm" is set in small caps, and including the periods is optional. If you don't have a typeface with small caps, it is permissible to set it in lowercase letters with periods (p.m.). The body copy is set in italic type, with the OpenType fractions option turned on. Normally book titles are set in italic, but when the surrounding body copy is italic, the book title is set in roman, as in the title of Dr. Tollefson's book, *Believe in Yourself.* You'll also note that the bulleted copy contains a reference to attention deficit hyperactivity disorder as ADHD. When setting an acronym, no period is placed after each letter.

Designing for the Phone Book

Scan through the yellow pages ads in a phone book and you will see that they've been designed by people with a wide range of design skills. Some ads include gradients and mushy photos, condensed or expanded type that is almost impossible to read, and typographic blunders such as all-capital italics and incorrect quotation marks. You can also find some examples of excellent layout and readability. What makes the difference between a strong and a poor ad? The ability to use type, combined with an understanding of the printing process. A well-designed 2½" square ad packs more punch than the poorly designed half-page ad! When you design an ad for the yellow pages, first look at samples to see what doesn't work. Then look specifically at what the competition is doing, and design an ad that will beat the best sample. It is a time-consuming process to fine-tune small display ads. Some people assume a small ad will require less production time. In reality, it takes more time to create an effective small ad than a larger display ad because every incremental spacing decision you make in a small ad is critical!

Design Considerations for the Identity Package Yellow Pages Ad

Visual 10–10 shows the actual size yellow pages display ad for Rosemary Tollefson.

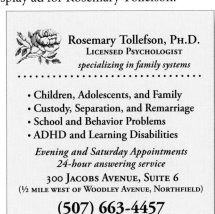

visual | 10–10 |

The italic type has been changed to a semibold weight to accommodate the paper quality used in yellow pages. Tiny serifs are not always visible on low-quality paper.

The text portion is basically in a centered format—except the bulleted copy is flush left. Sometimes you see bulleted copy centered, leaving the left sides ragged (Visual 10–11). Setting bulleted copy in this manner is a poor design technique. When the bullets are not flush left, they blend in with the body copy and defeat the purpose of using them in the first place!

Here is the best way to align bulleted copy while centering it in the text block:

1. Center all bulleted text. Position a vertical guideline flush to the bullet of the longest line.

2. Change the alignment of the bulleted text to flush left.

3. Apply a left indent to push all the bulleted copy to the guideline you placed earlier. Now the text is flush left, but the longest line is still centered in the text column.

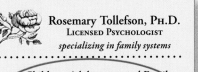

visual | 10–11 |

This is the incorrect way to set bulleted copy! Centering bulleted type defeats the purpose of using bullets, which is to lead the eye through the ad.

Design Considerations for Forms

The last piece you will create for Dr. Tollefson's identity package is a client information form (Visual 10–12). You will want to refer to the instructions for this project as you work in it. They are available in the *Chapter 10 Artwork & Resources* folder on the CD. The copy has been typed—you will do the formatting. This project will be a great review of tabs and leaders.

The Client
Information form.

CLIENT INFORMATION   Today's date _____

Name _____

Address _____

City _____   State _____   Zip _____

Phone _____   E-mail _____

Birthdate _____   Age _____

1. Please describe your current relationships:

☐   **Live alone, no significant other**

☐   **Live alone, but have significant other**

☐   **Living with significant other** *Name of*

☐   **Living with spouse**

☐   **Married, not living with spouse**

☐   **Was married or living with significant**

☐

☐

Children *(List children, ages and check all that apply)*

name	age	biological	blended	lives with me	not at home

_____ _____ _____ _____ _____ _____

_____ _____ _____ _____ _____ _____

_____ _____ _____ _____ _____ _____

_____ _____ _____ _____ _____ _____

☐   **Deaths** *(List any deaths that have had a significant impact on your life)*

name	age	relationship

_____   _____   _____

_____   _____   _____

_____   _____   _____

☐   **Miscarriage/stillbirth** *Year:* _____

2. How would you rate your general physical health?

☐ Excellent   ☐ Good   ☐ Fair   ☐ Poor

When was your last physical exam? _____   Physician _____

Date and reason for last hospitalization _____

What medications are you currently taking? _____

3. What would you like to accomplish through counseling?

_____

_____

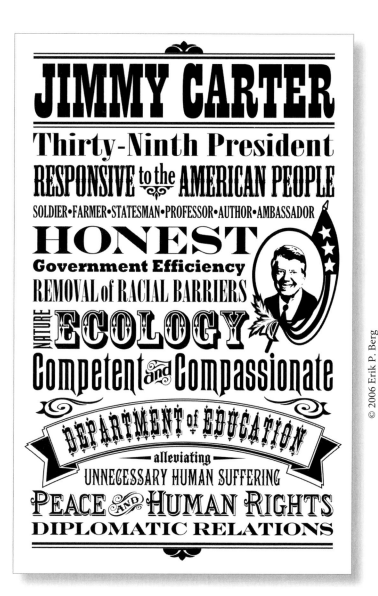

visual | 10–13 |

This Victorian era- style political poster demonstrates that type can be a powerful design element. Designers who are comfortable working with type and have strong InDesign production skills, are the best at creating type-heavy forms that are both functional and aesthetically pleasing.

SUMMARY

Business forms are a rigorous production test for typesetters and designers. It is our responsibility to make sure that forms project the appropriate corporate image, are easy to read, and are easy to complete. When you are given the task of producing an order form, a sell sheet, or a catalog price grid, see it as a design challenge. Flex your typesetting muscles. And remember, as a wise designer once said, "There are no mediocre projects, just mediocre designers."

in review

1–4. The initial client meeting is a perfect opportunity to gather information about project specifications. What are four examples of information you should have before beginning the project?

5. Choosing the typeface is one of the most important decisions designers make. What are some considerations for choosing a typeface for an identity system?

6–7. What are two design considerations for letterhead?

8. How does paper quality affect design?

9. What is the difference between a lining figure and an old-style figure?

10. How should academic titles be typeset?

11. How do you control the way a stroke is aligned to the frame?

12. A standard business-size envelope is called a _____ envelope.

13. What are the dimensions of a standard business card?

14. Normally, book titles are set in italic, but when the surrounding copy is italic, the title is set in _____.

15. If you are designing a display ad for a newspaper, you must align the frame's stroke to the _____.

projects

CLIENT INFORMATION   Today's date _____

Name_____

Address_____

City _____ State _____ Zip _____

Phone_____

Birthdate _____

1. Please describ

☐

☐

Rosemary Tollefson, Ph.D.
specializing in family systems

Rosemary Tollefson, Ph.D.
LICENSED PSYCHOLOGIST
specializing in family systems

• **Children, Adolescents, and Family**
• **Custody, Separation, and Remarriage**
• **School and Behavior Problems**
• **ADHD and Learning Disabilities**

Evening and Saturday Appointments
24-hour answering service

300 JACOBS AVENUE, SUITE 6
(½ MILE WEST OF WOODLEY AVENUE, NORTHFIELD)

(507) 663-4457

You're invited to our
Open House
Monday, April 26
2:30 – 5:00 PM

Join us as we celebrate the opening of our new practice at 300 Jacobs Avenue, ½ mile west of Woodley.

Meet the staff, enjoy refreshments, and register for door prizes. Dr. Tollefson will be available to autograph her newly-released book, BELIEVE IN YOURSELF.

Rosemary Tollefson, Ph.D.
specializing in family systems

• **Children, Adolescents, and Family**
• **Custody, Separation, and Remarriage**
• **School and Behavior Problems**
• **ADHD and Learning Disabilities**

Evening and Saturday Appointments
24-hour answering service

300 JACOBS AVENUE, SUITE 6
(½ MILE WEST OF WOODLEY AVENUE, NORTHFIELD)

(507) 663-4457

Rosemary Tollefson, Ph.D.
specializing in family systems

300 JACOBS AVENUE, SUITE 6
NORTHFIELD, MINNESOTA 55057   *rtollefson@vista.net*
FAX: (507) 663-4459   CELL: (507) 663-4457

Rosemary Tollefson, Ph.D.
300 JACOBS AVENUE, SUITE 6
NORTHFIELD, MINNESOTA 55057

CELL: (507) 663-4457 • FAX: (507) 663-4459 • *rtollefson@vista.net*
300 JACOBS AVENUE, SUITE 6 • NORTHFIELD, MINNESOTA 55057

	Trans Type/Speeds	Eng Size/Cylinders	MPG City/Hwy	Annual Fuel Cost
MINIVANS 4WD				
Chevrolet Venture AWD	A-4	3.4/6	18/24	$1,050
Chrysler Town & Country AWD	A-4	3.8/6	17/23	$1,105
Dodge Caravan AWD	A-4	3.8/6	17/23	$1,105
Oldsmobile Silhouette AWD	A-4	3.4/6	18/24	$1,050
Pontiac Montana AWD	A-4	3.4/6	18/24	$1,050
Toyota Sienna 4WD	A-5	3.3/6	18/24	$1,050

Chapter Projects The visual above shows Dr. Tollefson's family of forms. You will enjoy creating these, and they could be nice additions to your portfolio. One additional table is included for good measure. You can find the instructions for all these projects in the *Chapter 10 Artwork & Resources* folder on the CD accompanying this book.

Courage is not the lack of fear. It is acting in spite of it.

℞ Mark Twain

| designing with type |

objectives

- **Use the Type on a Path tool**
- **Use the Pathfinder tool**
- **Create gradient blends**
- **Create inline frames**

introduction

A semitrailer got stuck underneath an overpass. It was in so tight that the driver couldn't move ahead or back up. Engineers and construction workers walked all around the stuck truck, calculating the height of the trailer and the clearance of the overpass. They thought of jackhammers, winches, hydraulic pry bars—anything that might free the truck and get traffic moving again. Finally, after assessing the situation one little boy said, "Why don't you let some air out of the tires?"

That boy was thinking outside the box. Business, education, government—everyone these days is looking for people who can see things from a different perspective. Perform a web search for "out of the box thinking" and you'll come up with just a shade over 2 billion results.

You are about to work with text and graphics that are out of the box—or at least out of a frame. Up to now we have used rectangles and ovals of various shapes and sizes. In this chapter, we explore text on a path, inline graphics, and gradients—features that will let you out of the box.

TYPE: A VERSATILE DESIGN ELEMENT

When reviewing student portfolios I look for two things: use of type and use of color. When a designer has control of those two critical design elements, everything else will fall into place. Even in black and white, type has "color" and text blocks can range in color from light gray to strong black. Typefaces also express a wide range of personalities inherent in their design. Visual 11–1 shows a collection of ampersands, each interesting and expressing a different personality.

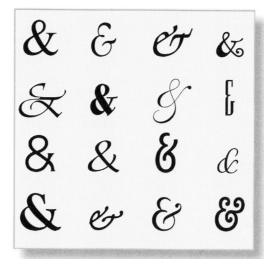

This collection of ampersands shows the variation in personality of typefaces.

In this first exercise, we're going to add another ingredient to the type color-personality mixture: shape. The ability to create type that follows a path used to be the domain of illustration programs. Thanks to InDesign, these great special effects are right at your fingertips. So, launch InDesign and let's get started.

Placing Type on a Closed Shape

In order to place text on a path, first you need a path! Then you need the Type on a Path tool, accessed by pressing **Shift+T** or by selecting it from the "hidden tool" menu under the Type tool.

visual | 11–2 |

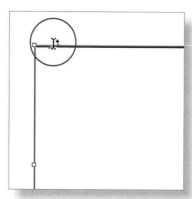

The plus sign next to the cursor means that the Type on a Path tool has found a path.

1. Create a new document. Draw a rectangle and apply a **1 pt**. stroke.

2. Select the Type on a Path tool by pressing **Shift+T**. Position the tool cursor over the edge of the rectangle. A plus sign on the cursor indicates that the tool has recognized a path and is ready for action (Visual 11–2).

3. Click on the path to create a starting point. Type a line of text that extends around the rectangle. Highlight the text and change the point size and style. Change the alignment. The text considers the first point you clicked with the Type on a Path tool as the left margin. As you center and right-align the text, it will flow clockwise around the outside of the frame.

4. Visual 11–3 shows two vertical lines called the *start* and *end brackets*. (The path object must be selected and either selection tool must be active for you to see these.) By default the brackets are butted up to each other, indicating that the text path extends around the entire rectangle. You can move the Start and End brackets to fine tune the position of the text on your path. The Start and End brackets have in and out ports that work just like any other text frame.

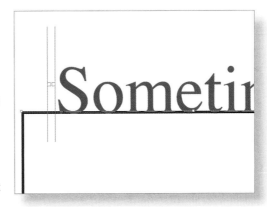

visual │ 11–3 │

The in and out ports are not handles you can use to adjust the Start and End brackets. Click on the vertical part of the start and end brackets to adjust the location of the text.

5. Select the End bracket. Do not click on its out port; instead click on the upper part of the line (the cursor arrow will show a sideways "t" when you are able to click on the bracket). Slowly drag the End bracket counterclockwise, closer to the end of the text (Visual 11–4). If you pull the bracket too far, the overset symbol will appear. Just bring the bracket to the end of the text.

6. If you look carefully in the center of the path, you will see a tiny vertical line (Visual 11–4). This line is the center bracket, and if you click and drag on the line with either Selection tool, you can move your text back and forth around the edge of the rectangle.

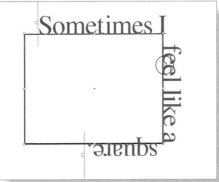

visual │ 11–4 │

There are three brackets on a text path. The tiny vertical line is the center bracket, which indicates the center of the text.

7. If you drag the center bracket in toward the center of the rectangle, your text will flow inside the box. Flip your text inside and outside a few times until it feels comfortable to you (Visual 11–5).

That was easy enough. Try the same technique with a circle as the path object. Be sure to flip the text inside and outside the circle, as in Visual 11–6. When the type is in place, you will want to set the stroke on the path object to None.

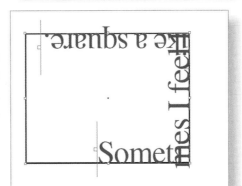

visual │ 11–5 │

Drag the center bracket to flip text inside and outside of the path.

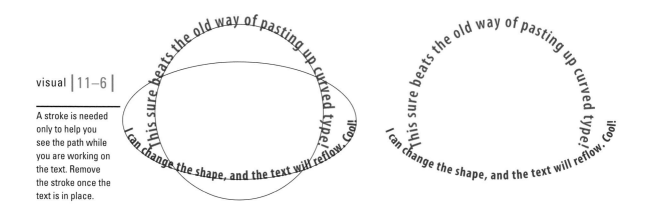

A stroke is needed only to help you see the path while you are working on the text. Remove the stroke once the text is in place.

Placing Type on an Open Path

Most of the time, you will be creating your own path for type to follow. Type can be placed on paths of any shape. We'll create a few paths using the Pencil tool, the Pen tool, and Bezier curves. You may not use the Pencil tool very often, but you should know it's there. If this is your first time using the Pen tool, note that Chapter 13 will go into detail on using it—you'll just get your toes wet in this chapter.

1. Select the Pencil tool by pressing **N** or by selecting it from the Toolbox. Draw some squiggles similar to those in Visual 11–7. The Pencil tool makes rough, random-looking paths. (The Pen tool makes smooth, curvy paths.)

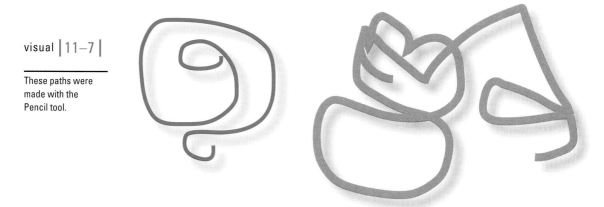

visual | 11–7 |

These paths were made with the Pencil tool.

2. Select the Type on a Path tool and click on one of your paths. (You don't need to select the path first.) Fill the line with text. You can use placeholder text if you prefer. Fill the remaining lines with text. Now experiment with the position, size, and color of your type. The results should look similar to Visual 11–8.

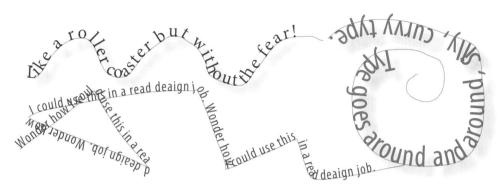

Type has been placed on the paths created with the Pencil tool.

3. Use Command+A (Mac) or Control+A (Windows) to select and delete the text lines created with the Pencil tool. Drag down two horizontal guidelines about 1.5 inches apart. Select the Pen tool by pressing **P**. Position the cursor by the left margin guide and click once on the bottom guidelines (do not drag). Position the cursor over the top guideline, but over to the right of the first point and click. This will create a diagonal line extending from the bottom to the top guidelines. Next, position the cursor on the bottom guideline, over to the

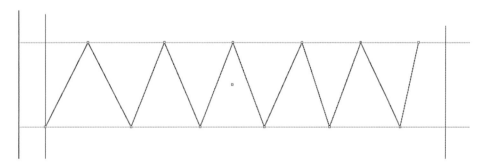

visual | 11–9 |

Clicking with the Pen tool makes straight line segments.

right of the second point and click to create another diagonal line. Continue this pattern across the page to make a zigzag pattern similar to what you see in Visual 11–9.

4. Switch to the Direct Selection tool and move the guides out of the way or delete them. Click on an anchor point and drag it. Move it from side to side, then up and down. Continue moving all the points until your zigzag is a total mess (Visual 11–10). Now you know how to use the Pen tool to click from point to point, and to create paths made of straight line segments. Let's see what else the Pen tool can do. Delete your path.

visual | 11–10 |

Use the Direct Selection tool to move the anchor points of the path.

5. Pull down two horizontal guides about 2 inches apart. You're going to make another path similar to the zigzag, except that you will make it with curved segments. With the Pen tool, click where the lower guideline meets the left margin guide to create the end point of your new path. Here's where the tricky part of creating curved segments comes in. Position the cursor over the top guideline, to the right of the end point, and click without releasing the mouse. This creates a "smooth" corner point. Without releasing the mouse, drag horizontally and you will see two handles extend from the corner point. These are called direction lines. As you drag them out a curved line segment will develop. Move the cursor along the guideline to see how changing the length of the direction line affects the shape of the curve. Release the mouse when the curved segment looks similar to the one in Visual 11–11. Move to the lower guideline, click to make the next anchor point, and drag horizontally to create another curved line segment. Continue this process until you have waves, similar to those in Visual 11–11. Now you know how to use the Pen tool to make curved line segments by clicking and dragging.

visual | 11–11 |

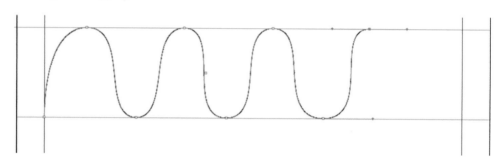

Click and drag to make curved line segments.

6. Now, create a bizarre looking path using a combination of clicks (straight line segments) and drags (curved line segments). Your mess should look just as bad as mine in Visual 11–12. To end the path, choose another tool or Command+click or Control+click anywhere on the page. When you're ready to move on, select your line with the Selection tool and delete it.

visual | 11–12 |

Within this mess is a combination of straight and curved line segments. Press the keyboard shortcut for any other tool and the Pen tool will be deselected.

7. Now we're going to make a path in the shape of an arch. If you deleted your two horizontal guidelines, drag down new ones about 2 inches apart. With the Pen tool, position the cursor over the lower guide, click and drag up. A directional line will extend from each side of the starting point. Keep dragging, trying to keep the upper directional line at a 45-degree angle. When the end of the directional line touches the upper guideline, release the mouse (Visual 11–13A).

8. Now position the Pen tool back on the lower guide, approximately 5 inches to the right of the first point. Click to set an anchor point and drag the direction line down at approximately 45 degrees. Notice that the upper direction line angles back toward the upper direction line of the first point (Visual 11–13B). When you release the mouse, you should have a nice arch, similar to Visual 11–13C. Use the Text on a Path tool to add text to the arch and experiment with the various options you have learned so far.

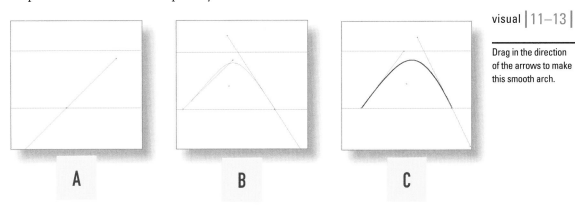

A   B   C

visual | 11–13 |

Drag in the direction of the arrows to make this smooth arch.

You may realize it would be much easier just to draw an ellipse and place the text on its path, rather than using the Pen tool to create the arch shape. And you're right. But very often, you will want to use text paths that don't fit premade shapes—like the next one you're going to create next.

1. Delete the arch-shaped path and drag down one horizontal guide. With the Pen tool, click on the guideline and drag up and to the right at a 45-degree angle. Release the mouse when the direction handle is about 1 inch long.

visual | 11–14 |

You can create elegant, flowing curves using only two anchor points.

2. About 4 inches away, click on the guideline to set another anchor point again, dragging up and to the right at a 45-degree angle. Release the mouse button when your path looks like Visual 11–14.

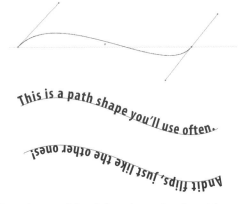

3. Go ahead, use the Type on a Path tool and place some text on it. Then flip the type using the center bracket line. If there is a stroke applied to the path, remove it to see only the text (Visual 11–15).

visual | 11–15 |

Use the center bracket to flip and reverse the direction of text placed on a path.

4. Highlight all the text on the path. Change the color to white. Select the path using either Selection tool. Change the stroke width of the path to be much wider than the point size of your text. Choose Type>Type on a Path>Options. When the Type on a Path Options dialog box opens, change the Align and To Path fields to Center to center the type vertically on the path (Visual 11–16). This is a technique you will use often.

The stroke width has been increased to a size larger than the point size of type. The center of the stroke has been aligned with the center of the text.

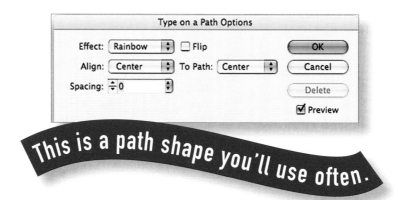

Creating Shadowed Type

The Effects panel manages a variety of transparency effects, including drop shadows. To apply a drop shadow, select the item with the Direct Selection tool, open the Effects panel, and select Drop Shadow. The Effects panel can be opened by clicking on the *fx* button on the Control panel, or by using the keyboard shortcut, Shift+Command+F10 (Mac) or

Keyboard Shortcut	
Shift + Cmd + F10 (Mac)	**Effects**
Shift + Ctrl + F10 (Win)	**Panel**

Shift+Control+F10 (Windows.) When you choose an effect, a dialog box opens that allows you to specify attributes of that effect. Transparency effects are listed on the left side of the panel. In the upper left corner of the Effects dialog box you will find the Settings For menu where you can choose which part or parts of the element you want to modify. Object applies the effect to the entire object—its stroke, fill, and text. Graphic affects only the graphic selected with the Direct Selection tool. Stroke affects the object's stroke (and gap color). Text affects all the text inside the frame. (You can't apply an effect to individual words or letters in a frame.) A box in the lower left corner summarizes the effects applied to a selected object. Visual 11–17 shows the Effects panel and its drop shadow menu options. When you are applying a drop shadow to text, you will want to adjust the opacity of the shadow (75% is usually too dark).

The Effects panel and menu options.

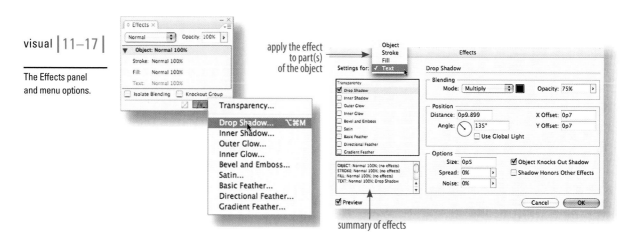

Create Text Outlines

One of the greatest features of InDesign is the ability to convert text to outlines. Once text is converted to outlines, it is no longer text, so you can't correct spelling or apply normal text attributes. Instead, each letter is a tiny piece of artwork, giving you the ability to modify the shape or paste an image into it.

Keyboard Shortcut	
Shift+Cmd + O (Mac)	**Create**
Shift+Ctrl + O (Win)	**Outlines**

Tickle me!
Tickle me!
Tickle me!

visual | 11–18 |

"Normal" text is first converted to outlines. Then the compound paths are released, allowing you to delete and replace the dots. Adding a drop shadow makes the special treatments stand out. .

1. Type the phrase **Tickle Me!** Apply a blue fill. (Visual 11–18). Use the Selection tool to activate the frame, and press Shift+Command+O (Mac) or Shift+Control+O (Windows) to convert the text into outlines. You can also choose Type>Create Outlines.

2. Now when you look closely at the type, you will see a series of anchor points. Even though each letter is now an individual shape, the letters are still linked together as one object—a compound path.

3. With the outline type selected, choose Object>Paths>Release Compound Path and the text unit will split apart. Now you can move each letter around with a selection tool. (Notice, however, that the counters in the letter "e" are filled in with blue. Select the counters with the Selection tool and fill them with Paper and use Arrange to bring the counters to the front.)

4. Delete the dots from the exclamation point and the i. Draw a small text frame where each of the dots was. Choose a dingbat, like the heart shown in Visual 11–18, from the Glyphs panel and place it in the frames. When the size and position of the dingbats look good, select all the objects and group them. Add a drop shadow to make the text really "pop" off the page.

Creating Shaped Text Frames

By now, you're an old pro at putting text inside a frame. This exercise will teach you how to create a shaped frame using the Pen tool.

1. Delete the images in your document. Select the Pen tool. Click or drag to make an irregularly-shaped, closed shape. When you are ready to close the shape, position the Pen tool cursor close to the path's starting point. You will see a tiny circle appear next to the pen tool icon. This circle indicates that your next click will join the two ends of the path, making a closed shape. Your shape should look very strange, similar to Visual 11–19.

2. Click inside the new shape with the Type tool. You should see a blinking cursor. Fill with placeholder text. Select all the text and change to justified alignment. Adjust the point size and typeface until you have a fairly even fill (Visual 11–19). Try changing the shape's stroke width to 0 pt. and click the Preview Mode button on the bottom right of the Toolbox.

visual | 11–19 |

First, an odd-shaped closed path was created with the Pen tool. Then, text was added and alignment justified to create an irregularly-shaped text block with defined edges.

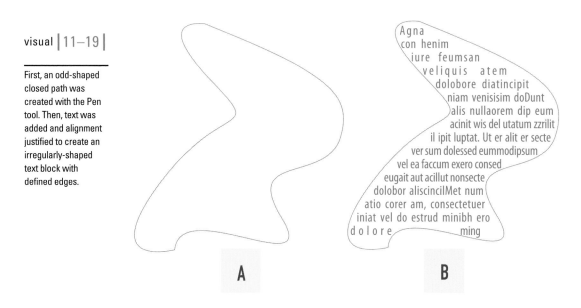

BITTER APPLE GAME PRESERVE

The following exercise will introduce some additional text effects. You will be making a two-sided, full-color flyer and a season pass sticker/button design for Bitter Apple Game Preserve. You will use the Gradient tool, create text on a path, convert text to outlines, create inline frames to contain graphics, and apply drop shadows and feathering. Visual 11–20 shows how the finished pieces will look. We will begin with the button. You will need the 11 Artwork & Resources folder found on the accompanying CD.

Make the Bitter Apple Logo

1. Open the template, *11 Project Template.indt* from the *11 Artwork & Resources* folder on the CD. The "indt" extension means you are opening an InDesign template. A template is a document that is used as a pattern. A document can be saved as a template by choosing Save>Format>InDesign CS3 template. This template has been prepared with the correct size, bleed, guidelines, and swatches. There are two layers: The bottom layer will hold the background gradient fill, and the top layer will hold the images and text. There are three pages in the document. Page 1 is for the front of the brochure; page 2 is for the back of the brochure; page 3 is for the button.

2. Open the *11 Bitter Apple CS3.indl* library from the *Chapter 11 Artwork & Resources* folder. The library already has some elements in it and you will be adding additional project elements to it as they are completed.

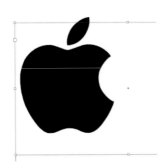

visual | 11–21 |

Find the apply shape in the Glyphs panel. Look in Apple Symbols or Symbol typefaces.

3. Open the Pages panel and go to page 3. Draw a large text frame and when the blinking cursor is visible, open the Glyphs panel. (It doesn't matter which layer this is on.) Look in the Apple Symbols or Symbol typefaces and find an apple. Insert the glyph and enlarge it to **200** points, as shown in Visual 11–21. Switch to the Selection tool and convert it to outlines (Shift+Command+O or Shift+Control+O). If you can't find an apple shape in the Glyphs panel, there is one stashed on the lower right corner of the pasteboard. You can drag it into your document, enlarge it **2.25"** high, and continue with Step 4.

4. Select the apple shape with the Selection tool. Copy it and then use Paste in Place so that it is exactly on top of the original shape.

5. Change the reference point on the Control panel so that it is in the middle. Press the Flip Horizontal control on the Control panel. You now have an apple with two leaves (Visual 11–22A).

visual | 11–22 |

First, the apple is flipped (A). Then, the arrow tools are used to align the two apple shapes (B).

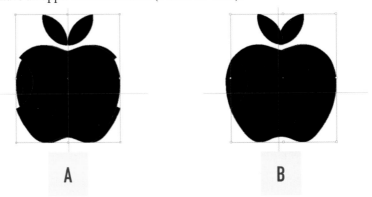

A   B

6. Use the Selection tool to adjust the position of the top apple so that the edges line up (Visual 11–22B). You may also use the left and right arrow keys to nudge the element into place. Zoom in close to the edge of the apple to be as precise as possible.

7. With the Selection tool, select both apple shapes. Choose Object>Pathfinder>Add. This command adds the shapes together to make one whole apple shape. With the shape still selected, choose Object>Paths>Release Compound Path. You have now separated the apple from the leaves.

8. Open the Swatches panel (F5). Select the leaves and fill them with Pantone DS 293-1 C green.

9. Select the apple shape and then apply the Apple Gradient fill from the Swatches panel. This is a radial fill, which means the color blends out from the center like rays of the sun. Use the Gradient tool, found on the Toolbox (press **G**), to adjust the length and direction of the fill. Click and drag the Gradient tool inside the apple, from edge to edge. Now change the starting location of the gradient by clicking the Gradient tool in another position and drag again. Hold down the Shift key to constrain it to a perfect horizontal or vertical blend. Reverse the direction of the line to reverse the blend. Do this several times until you understand how this tool works. Keep the Gradient tool inside the apple so the whole blend will be in that defined area. When you're finished experimenting, make the final gradient blend red in the top left corner to white in the lower right (Visual 11–23). Group the apple and the leaves and drag the element into the library. Move the apple in your document over to the pasteboard for now.

visual | 11–23 |

Use the Gradient tool to adjust the length and direction of the gradient fill.

Keyboard Shortcut	
Cmd + G (Mac)	**Group**
Ctrl + G (Win)	**Items**

Format the Button Text

The next step in the button project is to run text around the circle that creates the perimeter of the button. Follow the directions carefully and you'll see the advantage of using layers when placing this type.

1. Still on page 3, hold down Shift+Option (Mac) or Shift+Alt (Windows), and draw a **4"** circle out from the center guides with a stroke and no fill. Be sure you are working on the first layer, Background Gradient.

2. Copy the circle and move up a layer to Text and Photos and use Shift+Option+ Command+V (Mac) or Shift+Alt+Control+V (Windows) to Paste in Place.

3. Make a new layer and name it Background Circle. Draw a **4.375"** circle from the center points. Fill and stroke it with the blue from the Swatches panel. Lock the position of the circle by pressing Command+L (Mac) or Control+L (Windows). Go to the Layers panel and drag this layer down to the bottom of the stack.

4. Hide the Text and Photos layer, and move down one layer to the Background Gradient layer. Select the Type on a Path tool and click on the inner circle. Type **Season Pass** in **Myriad Pro Bold Condensed 50 pt**. and color the text **Paper**. Move the End brackets on the text path to about **.025"** from each end of the type. Align Center. Choose Type>Type on a Path>Options, and set the Align field to **Ascender** and the To Path field to **Bottom**.

visual | 11–24 |

Choose Type>Type on Path Options to align the ascenders of the type to the bottom of the path.

5. Using the Selection tool, find the center bracket line and align it to the center page guide. Make sure you are outside of the circle path when you release the mouse button or your type will not stay inside of the circle. Now your text is centered at the top of the circle. Remove any stroke or fill on the circle. When you are working with text on a curve you usually need to adjust the tracking. This sample was tracked to **+80** (Visual 11–24). Lock the circle by pressing Command+L (Mac) or Control+L (Windows). Hide the layer while we do the next step.

6. Turn on the Text and Photos layer. Choose the Type on a Path tool and type **May–Sept. 2008** on the inner circle in **30 pt. Myriad Pro Bold Condensed**. Color the text **Paper**. Use the same methods described in Steps 4 and 5 to position the type inside the circle shape. Align the **descenders** of the type to the **top** of the path. Move the type to the bottom center of the sticker and kern uneven spacing between letter pairs. This time, make sure you are inside of the circle path when you release the mouse button or your type will not stay inside of the circle (Visual 11–25). Remove any stroke that might be on the circle and lock the object (Command+L or Control+L).

visual | 11–25 |

Position the date at the bottom of the circle. This other layer has been conveniently hidden, making it easier to work on this circular type.

Keyboard Shortcut	
Cmd + L (Mac)	**Lock Position**
Ctrl + L (Win)	

7. Make all the layers visible and drag the apple in from the pasteboard. Move the apple to the top layer. You will need to resize the apple to fit in the type. To resize the apple, select it with the Selection tool and hold Shift as you drag in a corner.

visual | 11–26 |

Shown left: the text frame guides are stretched to circle guide before centering the type. Right: the completed sticker is ready to be added to the library.

8. Draw a text frame and type **Bitter Apple** in **Adobe Caslon Pro Bold 35-pt**. Type **Game Preserve** in **Myriad Pro Bold 14 pt.**, and change to **all caps**. To change type to uppercase, select the type and go to the menu. Type>Change Case>Uppercase. Change the color of both lines of type to **yellow** in the Swatches panel and center the text. To center the text accurately, pull the edges of the text frame out to the guide, or use the Align panel. Don't try to center the type visually! Apply tracking to the second line. Position and size the text frame and apple inside the circle as shown in Visual 11–26. Your button is almost complete.

9. With the Selection tool, draw a marquee around all your sticker elements. Unlock the position of all the circles by pressing Command+Option+L (Mac) or Control+Alt+L (Windows). Group all the elements. Drag the sticker into your library.

The Bitter Apple Logo

The Bitter Apple logo is the next component to tackle.

1. Go to Page 2. Select the Rectangle tool and click on your page. When the dialog box comes up, enter **1.3"** for the width and **0.75"** for the height. Stroke and fill should be **None**.

2. Select the Ellipse tool and hold Shift+Option or Shift+Alt to draw a circle out from the center of the rectangle. Make the circle slightly narrower than the rectangle, similar to the example in Visual 11–27. Use the Align panel to align the horizontal centers of the objects and move the circle up so that your two shapes look like Visual 11–27.

3. Select both shapes and choose Object>Pathfinder> Add. The shapes should blend together as in Visual 11–28. (This is the same technique we used earlier to blend the two apple shapes into one shape.)

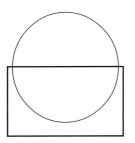

visual | 11–27 |

Use the Align panel to align the horizontal centers of the selections.

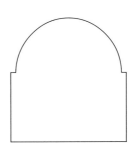

visual | 11–28 |

The shapes have been added together to create a precise, symmetrical frame.

4. Use the Stroke panel to give the shape a **6 pt. Thin-Thick** stroke, with the stroke aligned to the center. Make the stroke's color DS 63-1C Red with a blue gap. These colors will be in the Swatches panel. Fill the shape with the blue in the Swatches panel.

visual | 11–29 |

The apple that was earlier stored in the library has been resized to fit inside the new frame.

5. Use the Selection tool to drag the apple in from the library. Hold Shift+Command or Control as you resize it to fit inside the logo as shown in Visual 11–29. Add a drop shadow with **40%** opacity using the default shadow offsets.

visual | 11–30 |

The shapes have been added together to create a precise, symmetrical frame.

6. Draw a text frame below the apple and type **Bitter Apple** in **Adobe Caslon Pro Bold, 16 pt., yellow**. Type **Game Preserve** in **Myriad Pro Bold 8 pt., all caps, yellow**. Center the type, and add tracking as shown in Visual 11–30. The finished logo should look like Visual 11–30. Group the logo and drag it into the library. The logo is now completed. Delete the logo remaining in your document.

visual | 11–31 |

The front side of the
flyer will use elements
from the library.

Finishing the Front of the Flyer

We'll begin with the front of the flyer where we'll drop in a gradient and pull elements in from the library. Visual 11–31 shows the front of the finished flyer for reference.

1. Go to page 1. Make sure you are working on the Background Gradient layer. Draw a rectangle that fills the page from bleed to bleed. From the Swatches panel, choose the Background Gradient swatch. Use the Gradient tool to place the dark blue on the top and the green on the bottom, holding down the Shift key to constrain it to a vertical blend.

2. Move to the Text and Photos layer. Drag in the photos and headline from the library using the guides for placement. Add an ellipsis to the end of the headline. You make a true ellipsis by pressing Option+; (Mac) or Alt+; (Windows).

3. Draw a 1-point white line on the bottom margin guide. Using the Stroke panel, set the Start and End fields of the rule to **CircleSolid.** Drag the logo in from the library and position it as shown in Visual 11–31.

The back side of the
Bitter Apple Game
Preserve flyer.

The Back of the Flyer

As you finish the back of the flyer, you will learn how to add inline frames. Most of the hard
work is already done—you'll be pulling most of the elements in from the library. The finished
back looks like Visual 11–32.

1. Go to page 2. Make sure you are on the Background Gradient layer. Draw a frame from
   bleed to bleed and fill it with the Background Gradient swatch. Using the Gradient tool,
   adjust the color so that the green is on the top and the blue is on the bottom.

2. Move to the Text and Photos layer. Drag in the text block and photos
   from the library. Place a **1-point** white rule on the bottom margin
   and use the Stroke panel to add a circle to each end.

3. Go to page 1 and select the logo with the Selection tool. Copy the logo. Now go to page 2
   and use Paste in Place. The logo should be in the exact same location as on the cover.

4. The apple at the beginning of each subhead is an inline graphic. It is connected with the text so that it flows just like a word or letter. Pull the apple you created earlier onto the pasteboard of page 2. Select it with the Selection tool. Hold down Shift and pull a corner inward until the apple is very small, approximately **0.2"**. (Visual 11–32).

5. Copy the apple, and then switch to the Type tool and place the cursor in front of the first letter of the first subhead. Paste the apple and add an en space. The graphic now sits on the baseline with the type. Even though it is connected to a text line, you can still adjust its vertical position using the Selection tool. Repeat the procedure for the second subhead. Add drop shadows to both apples using the default settings. Enter an Indent to Here before the first word in the first line to create a hanging indent for the apple.

6. Pull the button you made earlier in from the library and place it on the pasteboard of page 2. Select it with the Selection tool and reduce it proportionately by holding down Shift+Command (Mac) or Shift+Control (Windows). Drag it into position at the top of the page. Select it with the Selection tool. In the Control panel, make sure the reference point is in the middle. Now select the Rotate tool, click on the circle, and drag to rotate it as in Visual 11–32. .

There are subtle differences in the use of the Command (Mac) or Control (Windows) modifier keys when resizing groups. If there is no type or type on a path inside a group, use Shift+Drag to proportionately resize a group. If the group contains type or type on a path, use Shift+Command (Mac) or Shift+Control (Windows) and drag a corner to proportionately resize the group.

7. Use the Selection tool and pull in the **Full Season $40** line from the library. Position it on top of the sticker, as shown in Visual 11–32.

8. Proof all your work carefully. The project is done! Printing note: If the red to white gradients used in the apples in this project do not print correctly, you will need to follow this work-around: 1. Select each apple with the Direct Selection tool. Copy each apple using Command+C (Mac) or Control+C (Windows). 2. Paste each apple in place using Shift+Option+Command+V (Mac) or Shift+Alt+Control+V (Windows). 3. Fill the new copy of each apple with Paper. 4. Use Arrange to move each apple filled with Paper behind the gradient-filled apples. The apples filled with Paper will knock out the colors in the background, allowing the gradient-filled apples to print correctly.

SUMMARY

This chapter covered many design techniques that can give text much more interest. Just as using too many typefaces can overpower a document, so can using too many text effects. Knowing how to use these techniques is the first step. Knowing when to use them is the second.

in review

1. How do you know when the Type on a Path tool is ready to place text on a path?

2. How does the center bracket work?

3. What is the command for locking the position of an object? for unlocking?

4. What does the Gradient tool do?

5. What is the keystroke for creating a true ellipsis?

6. How can you change lowercase type to uppercase without retyping the line?

7. What are five options found under the Pathfinder menu?

8. Your coworker is struggling with adding a drop shadow to a text frame. When the drop shadow option is selected, the shadow appears on the type, but not behind the text frame. What advice would you give her?

9. How does type handling change when the type has been converted to outlines?

10. What is the process for proportionately scaling grouped elements that contain text?

Photo and layout ©2006 Erik P. Berg

Photo ©2006 Brittany Hinckle

Chapter Projects   There are no additional projects for this chapter.
Congratulations on a job well done!

Love cures people…
both the ones who **give** it
and the ones who **receive** it.

℞ Dr. Karl Menninger

| production essentials |

objectives

- **Understand the difference between spot and process colors**
- **Use the Swatches panel to define color, tint, and gradient swatches**
- **Perform document preflight and package operations**
- **Choose document print specifications**
- **Use the Links panel**
- **Use Adobe Stock Photos**

introduction

Some ideas sound good in theory—self-generating electricity, cars that run without an external fuel source, gears that keep turning on their own momentum. But not every great idea works out in reality.

That's what happens to a lot of great design ideas. You spend all kinds of time and creative energy on a document that looks beautiful on your monitor and when printed on your desktop color printer. Then you take it to your commercial printing company and order 5,000 printed pieces. But when you pick up your job, you get a bill for hundreds of dollars more than you were quoted. You're told that the additional charges are for something called "prepress." They explain that it was necessary to take your electronic file—the one you thought was finished—and spend additional time getting it ready to print properly. This chapter will teach you basic production considerations so you can create documents that run smoothly and avoid unexpected budget overruns.

PRODUCTION ESSENTIALS

One of the best decisions I made in my college career was to double major in graphic design and in printing and publishing. Understanding how document design and construction affects production has been invaluable. The same project that is greeted with cheers when presented to a client may elicit groans after it is opened by the prepress technician. File construction tells a lot about the designer's training and skill. A poorly constructed file will do more damage to a designer's reputation than almost anything else. If that designer also misses production deadlines, vendors will shudder every time he walks through the door because they know they will be working on a file that is not only late, but also technically incorrect! This chapter will focus on three file preparation areas that can be challenging: specifying color, managing graphics files, and organizing fonts.

Specifying Color

Color is an important component in any project. If you don't understand how color is created and how a piece will be printed, you will not be able to create a document that uses color correctly. Errors in using color are costly. Of course, color mistakes on garage sale posters printed on your own color inkjet printer aren't going to ruin your life. But making a mistake on a catalog project, where accurate color is critical, will negatively impact your career. We will begin with some basic theory about the physical characteristics of color. For more information on the complex world of color, I recommend *Graphic Communications Today, Fourth Edition*, by William Ryan and Theodore Conover, published by Thomson Delmar Learning.

Color: Transmitted or Reflected Light Waves

Color is created by light waves that are either *transmitted* or *reflected*. Your computer monitor transmits light waves to create color. Three primary colors of light—red, green, and blue (RGB)—are combined in different proportions to create the millions of colors on your screen. Colors displayed on a monitor are described by a formula that specifies the level of each component color. The range of levels goes from 0 to 255. For example, the formula R=255, G=55, B=45 would describe a bright red. RGB is *additive color*. This means that when the levels of RGB are at the maximum, 255, the color you see is white. When all RGB values are at 0, the color is black. When creating documents that will be viewed on a monitor, such as web pages, using colors defined by the RGB system are natural choices.

Ink and toner, on paper, work differently. They absorb some light waves and reflect the rest. The light waves that are reflected back to our eyes create the illusion of color. Color created by reflected light waves is called *subtractive*. That means that if all the light is absorbed (subtracted), we see black. The primary colors in subtractive color are cyan, magenta, and yellow (CMY). Formulas that specify the amounts of each component color are used to describe subtractive color. The bright red color described in the preceding paragraph would be expressed as C=0, M=91, Y=87. An important difference is that the range of levels is different, from 0–100. It's also appropriate to refer to the levels of component colors as percentages. In theory, when you combine pigments of pure cyan, magenta, and yellow, all the light waves will be absorbed and the object will look black. In reality, pure pigments are impossible to obtain, so 100% cyan, 100% magenta, and 100% yellow blend to create a washed-out black. That's why black ink (referred to as *K*) is added in the printing process to compensate for the weak black created by the CMY combination. Now we've arrived at what is known as the *CMYK color space. RGB* (additive color) images are perfect for monitor or web display, but must be redefined as *CMYK* (subtractive) colors before being commercially printed.

> When working with spot or process color, remember that
> what you see on your screen is probably not what you will get
> from your commercial printer! Unless a color calibration system is in place,
> every computer monitor will display color a little differently.
> Always use an ink swatch book to select colors for your printed document.
> Even if the colors don't look just right on the screen,
> they will print correctly on a printing press.

Printing: Spot or Process?

Commercial printers always work with subtractive color. Defining colors to print correctly on a press is one of the challenges designers face on a daily basis. In commercial printing, color is created by reflected light waves. That's why it's not a good idea to put colors in your InDesign file that are defined as RGB (transmitted light waves).

Commercial printers use ink, and they talk in terms of *process color* or *spot color.* Spot color ink is like a can of premixed paint. There are about a dozen basic ink colors that can be combined in different proportions to make thousands of spot color inks. Each spot color is described by a standardized number and a mixing ratio (another formula!). This enables printers anywhere in the world to mix up and match a specific color, as long as they are using the same color/ink system. For instance, one popular color matching system is the Pantone Matching System (or simply PMS). When a printer in Philadelphia puts PMS 541 on his press, it will be exactly the same color as the PMS 541 printed across the ocean in Calcutta. *Tints* of spot colors can also be used and are described in percentages: 0%–100%. This allows you to use the full-strength spot color (100%) or lighter tints to create a variety of color.

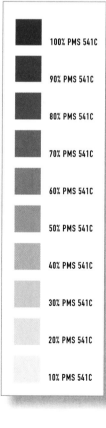

100% PMS 541C

90% PMS 541C

80% PMS 541C

70% PMS 541C

60% PMS 541C

50% PMS 541C

40% PMS 541C

30% PMS 541C

20% PMS 541C

10% PMS 541C

visual | 12–1 |

A color at 100% is the actual hue. The hue can be tinted in increments from very dark (95%) to very light (10%) The C at the end stands for what the color will look like on coated, (as opposed to uncoated) paper.

Many of your projects will be one-color documents—and yes, black counts as a color. Business forms, reports, books—many of the materials we read every day are single-color documents, usually black and white. However, don't underestimate the power of a well-designed single-color document! A blue, for example, can range from a pale 10% shade to a strong 100% navy. And when it is printed on a sheet of cream paper, it can give the impression of a two-color job. For just slightly more than the cost of black ink, you can create an attractive document with just one spot color, incorporating tints and solids and good design skills.

If your client wants a full-color brochure but doesn't have a full-color budget, suggest going with a two-color brochure using spot colors. Two spot colors, combined with careful paper selection, can give a project an upscale look without the upscale cost.

Process Color

Process color (also referred to as *full-color*) is much different from spot color. Full-color posters, magazines, catalogs, artist prints—anything that has the full range of the color spectrum—will be printed using process colors. In process color printing, four basic transparent inks, in different tints, are printed on top of each other to create the illusion of many colors. As discussed earlier, these transparent colors are cyan, magenta, yellow, and black (CMYK). Cyan is greenish-blue and magenta is a violet-red. When you look at a full-color job under a magnifying glass, you will see that the "color" is actually made from a series of tiny dots printed close together. When each of the four inks is printed in the correct location, the dots merge together to give the impression of color. The color could be one hue (like a spot-color ink) or the millions of color variations that create a photograph. However, when one ink color is printed slightly off from the others, it makes the finished image look distorted. This is called *out of register*. We have all seen examples of this when Sunday comics aren't printed quite right and have a blurred image.

> **Digital color printers (used for smaller full-color runs) often use cartridges of cyan, magenta, yellow, and black toner.**

Applying Color to Your Document

InDesign has two panels for assigning color to objects: the Color panel and the Swatches panel. Although you will use the Swatches panel most of the time, let's start by taking a quick look at the Color panel.

1. Make a new document, **8.5 × 11"**. Press F6 to open the Color panel. At the bottom of the panel you will see a bar called the color spectrum. It will contain either a gradient of one single color or a rainbow of colors. If the spectrum contains a single color, click on the panel menu and choose CMYK (Visual 12–2).

Keyboard Shortcut

F6 (Mac)	Color
F6 (Win)	Panel

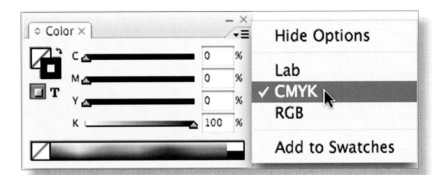

visual | 12–2 |

If the color spectrum shows shades of one color only, choose CMYK from the panel menu.

2. Draw a rectangle and activate the Fill icon on the Toolbox. Move your mouse over to the color spectrum on the Color panel and notice that your cursor turns into an eyedropper. Click the eyedropper on a color that looks good to you. The rectangle instantly fills with the color you have selected. Notice that the Fill icon in the Toolbox has been updated with the same color. Click back and forth along the CMYK spectrum bar and fill your rectangle with different colors (Visual 12–3).

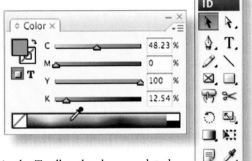

visual | 12–3 |

Every time you select a new color from the CMYK Spectrum bar, the Fill icon in the Toolbox displays the same color.

3. There are four sliders above the CMYK color spectrum. These show the percentages of each of the four process colors. Slide the triangles along each of the individual color bars, noticing how the color changes and how the percentage values in the boxes to the right also change. Fine-tune your chosen color, by making it a lighter shade.

4. Click on the None box at the left of the CMYK spectrum (the square with the red diagonal line). The rectangle now has no fill and the Fill icon on the Toolbox also indicates no fill. But you have not lost your color because a new box has appeared in the Color panel: the Last Color used (Visual 12–4). Click on it and your last color returns. The smaller boxes at the right of the CMYK spectrum are for white or black fills. Remember that assigning white (a color) to the fill or stroke of an object is not the same as applying None (no color at all).

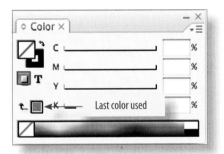

visual | 12–4 |

The Color panel displays the last color used in a box above the ramp.

5. Click on your rectangle with the Type tool and convert it to a text frame. The Color panel now indicates the color of the text. Type a short sentence and bump up the point size to fill the text frame. Select all the text and change the color of the text in the same way you changed the color of the rectangle. Remember to choose CMYK if your color bar shows a spectrum of only one color.

6. Click on the text frame with one of the selection tools. The two small buttons below the Fill and Text icons in the Color panel (or the Toolbox) will now allow you to choose which color you change, either the text or the frame (Visual 12–5).

visual | 12–5 |

The pointer shows the boxes you use to toggle between applying color to the container or to the text.

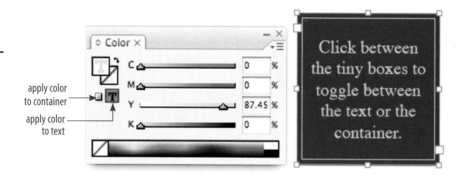

7. Open the Color panel options menu again and change the mode from CMYK to RGB (Visual 12–6). The shades of color do not change; but you are now working in additive color rather than subtractive color.

visual | 12–6 |

It is easy to change between single color, CMYK, and RGB color models. Always be aware of what color mode you are working in. CMYK is for commercial printing. RGB is basically for documents that will be viewed on a computer monitor, like web pages.

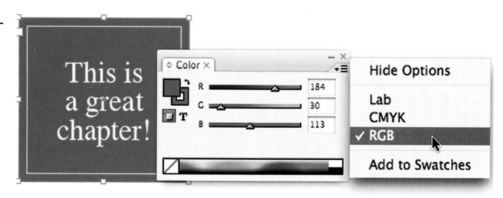

Now that you have been introduced to the Color panel, a word of caution: Avoid using it! The Color panel is handy for applying color in "quick and dirty" documents that you will output yourself on your home color printer. But if you're working in a production setting—and especially if your file is going out to a service bureau or a commercial printer—use the Swatches panel instead.

The Swatches Panel

The Swatches panel can do everything the Color panel does, but with one important difference: You can define each color in your document and assign it a meaningful name. Colors from the Color panel are like the ones you had so much fun clicking in the preceding pages, undefined and unnamed. They may look just as good as Swatch colors, but there's no way to track them throughout your document. For professional purposes, keep the Color panel tucked away. Colors created and stored in the Swatches panel are much easier to manage.

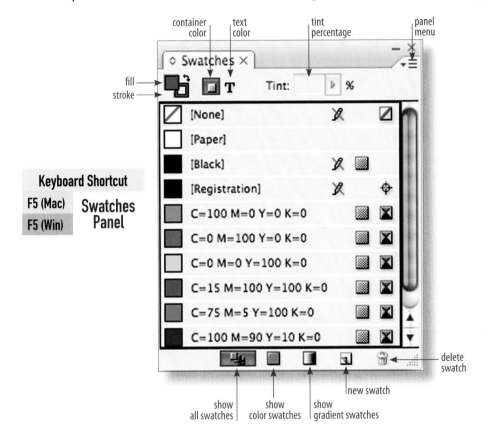

visual | 12–7 |

Use F5 to open the Swatches panel. The panel is set up like all other InDesign panels.

Keyboard Shortcut

F5 (Mac) Swatches
F5 (Win) Panel

Transfer an Undefined Color from the Color Panel to the Swatches Panel

In the following exercise, you will learn how to convert an undefined color created in the Color panel into a color swatch.

1. Make sure the Color panel is open and the rectangle is active.

2. Press F5 to open the Swatches panel (Visual 12–7). To make room for additional swatches, lengthen the panel by dragging the lower right corner until the scroll bar disappears. Go back to the Color panel and make sure the Fill color icon for your active rectangle is active.

3. Open the Color panel options menu and choose Add to Swatches (Visual 12–8). The color of your frame is now a swatch in the Swatches panel and has changed from an *undefined* color to a *defined* color. Do the same for the color you chose for your text.

An undefined color can easily be added to the Swatches panel by selecting Add to Swatches in the Color panel menu. The new swatch is now defined and is at the bottom of the Swatches panel list.

4. There are other methods of transferring an undefined color to the Swatches panel. You can select your rectangle and click the New Swatch button at the bottom of the Swatches panel (shown in Visual 12–7). Or you can drag the Fill or Stroke color icon right from the Color panel and drop it into the Swatches panel.

Transfer an Undefined Gradient from the Gradient Panel to the Swatches Panel

Generally, it is best to convert undefined colors to defined swatches. The same holds true for undefined gradients. Converting an undefined gradient to a gradient swatch is a process similar to the one you just completed for undefined color.

1. Open the Gradient panel and choose Show Options under the panel menu. In the Type field, choose Linear or Radial. A linear gradient changes color along a line, a radial gradient radiates from one color to the next in a circular pattern. You should see a horizontal bar called a *ramp,* extending across the bottom of the Gradient panel. At the top and center of the ramp is a diamond. This diamond is a *stop* that defines the midpoint of the gradient. As you slide the stop toward either end of the ramp, you will see the gradient swatch in the upper left corner change.

2. Open the Color panel and arrange it so that it's next to the Gradient panel. You're going to apply some colors to the gradient.

3. In the Gradient panel you should see two house-shaped icons below the ramp. If you don't see them, click on the ramp and they will appear. These are the *color stops*. Click on the left color stop and then adjust the color sliders in the Color panel. Notice that the color stop in the Gradient panel changes accordingly (Visual 12–9).

4. Now, click on the right color stop. Apply a color using the Color panel. Experiment with adjusting the look of your gradient by sliding the midpoint and color stops to the left or the right. Watch as the gradient swatch in the upper left corner changes to reflect your color adjustments.

5. You can also apply color to a gradient from the Swatches panel. The process is similar to the one described above, but instead of choosing a color from the Color panel, you press Option (Mac) or Alt (Windows) as you click on a color swatch from the Swatches panel.

6. Now we will define the gradient you have just created. Open the Swatches panel menu and choose New Gradient Swatch. When the New Gradient Swatch dialog box appears, you can name your new gradient swatch in the Swatch Name field.

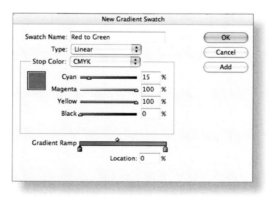

7. An alternate method is to select the Show Gradient Swatches button at the bottom of the Swatches panel (shown in Visual 12–7) and drag the preview from the Gradient panel into the Swatches panel. Double-click the swatch to open the Gradient Options dialog box and rename it.

The icons at the top of the Swatches panel should be familiar to you by now—Fill, Stroke, Container, and Text. There is also a field where you can set the tint of a selected color. The various colors in the list are those available to your document and are labeled with their CMYK values (Visual 12–7).

Create a Color Swatch from "Scratch"

You can define colors directly from the Swatches panel. But before you can define a color for your document, you must know whether you need to create spot or process colors. When you define a color in your document as *spot,* it means that the printer will premix the color according to the formula specified by your swatch book and then put the colored ink on the press. A plate on the press picks up the ink and transfers it to the paper. After the color is printed, the press is cleaned, a new plate is put on, and the ink is replaced with the next color needed. A job that uses yellow, blue, green, orange, red, and black will require six premixed colors and six plates—and a significant amount of time for mixing ink and cleaning the press.

Process color works differently. Instead of premixing each individual ink color, only four inks—cyan, magenta, yellow, and black—and four plates are used to create all the other colors that will be printed. The four colors are overlaid in various tints, to create the illusion of many colors. The six-color job we just discussed could be printed by using only four inks and plates and would require much less production time. Orange would be created by percentages of yellow and magenta. Green would be created by percentages of cyan and yellow, and so on. Of course, if your job only has two colors—two inks and two plates—using spot colors would be the way to go.

A *swatch book* should be used at the design stage for selecting and defining either spot or process colors. The swatch book provides the exact color formula needed and shows an accurate sample of how the printed color will look. Basing a color selection on what you see on your computer screen is risky because most monitors do not display color accurately. There are many variables that go into choosing color. Until you have a clear understanding of the printing process, it is a good idea to have an experienced designer check your document files before you send them to the printer. We will now create a new process color swatch.

visual |12–11|

The Swatches panel has many options for displaying swatches. When Name is selected (the default), the colors in the Swatches panel are displayed by their names. If you select Small Swatch, the colors will be displayed in tiny swatches. In this example, Large Swatch has been selected.

1. Choose New Color Swatch from the panel menu (Visual 12–11). A dialog box displaying the four CMYK sliders will open. The color settings in the dialog box will be for the last color selected in the Swatches panel.

2. If you know them, type in the percentages of cyan, magenta, yellow, and black that define your color. Or slide the color bars until you get the color you want. InDesign will define and name the color for you in terms of CMYK values, or you can deselect the Name with Color Value option box and assign it a name of your own choosing. It's better to name a color by its CMYK values because that's a language everyone understands. Even though a color may look exactly like what you saw when your cat was car sick, naming a color Sick Kitty conjures up a very different color in each person's mind.

Make a New Gradient Swatch from "Scratch"

When you select New Gradient Swatch from the Swatches panel menu, you are making a defined gradient.

1. Choose New Gradient Swatch from the panel menu. Click on the Starting Color stop icon at the left end of the gradient ramp. The Stop Color field becomes active, allowing you to select CMYK from the list and then adjust the sliders in the CMYK mode. You can also select Swatches from the Stop Color field list and then choose a color from your swatches.

2. Click the Ending Color stop icon at the right side of the gradient ramp and assign it a different color.

3. Drag one of the Stop icons to the middle of the gradient ramp. Click below the ramp where the original color stop was, and a new stop will appear. Give this new stop a third color.

4. Slide the diamond-shaped midpoint stops at the top of the gradient ramp to adjust the span of each color between color stops.

5. Click OK to add this swatch to the Swatches panel.

6. The Show Gradient Swatches button at the bottom of the panel toggles the display of all the defined gradients in the document. If you have a gradient swatch selected and click the New Swatch button, the gradient swatch will be duplicated. If you select the Trashcan icon, the gradient swatch will be deleted.

Make a Color Tint Swatch

If you were designing a single-color document using many shades of blue, first you would want to create the solid blue swatch and then make tint variations from it.

1. Create a new swatch—Color Type: Spot, Color Mode: Pantone solid coated. Scroll down the list and select a Pantone blue that you like. Press Return.

2. With the new blue swatch selected, open the Swatches panel menu and choose New Tint Swatch. In the New Tint Swatch dialog box, drag the Tint slider to 10% and click Add. You can type numerical values into the Tint field, but you have to press the Tab key before the Add button becomes active again.

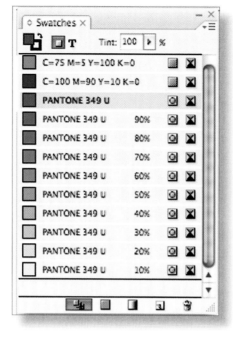

visual |12–12|

Tint swatches display
the percentage
to the right of the
color name.

3. Repeat this process, creating tint swatches from 20% to 90% green, in 10% increments. Click Done. Your Swatches panel should look like Visual 12–12. Notice that the percentage of each tint is displayed to the right.

4. If the tint isn't exactly what you want, you can double-click on the tint swatch in the panel list, and when the Swatch Options dialog box opens, adjust the sliders.

Changing the color values of a tint swatch also changes the values of the original color the swatch is based on. Be sure that when you are in the Swatch Options dialog box, you don't change color values—unless you want the original color swatch to change, too.

Adding Swatches from Other Documents

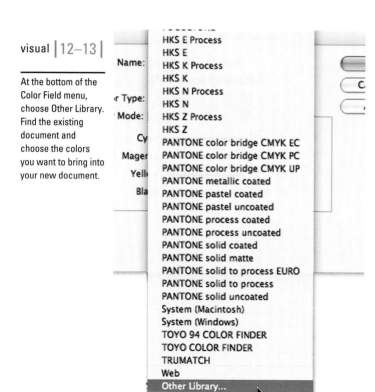

visual |12–13|

At the bottom of the
Color Field menu,
choose Other Library.
Find the existing
document and
choose the colors
you want to bring into
your new document.

You can pull color swatches from other InDesign documents into a document you are working on. The following method allows you to choose which colors you bring into your document.

1. Open the Swatches panel menu and choose New Color Swatch. In the New Color Swatch dialog box pick Other Library at the bottom of the Color Mode list (Visual 12–13).

2. Navigate to the document you want to borrow color from, and click Open.

3. Select a color you want from the list of available colors in the document and click Add to transfer them to your Swatches panel. When you are done adding colors, click OK.

Loading Swatches

You can also add swatches from another document by using the Load Swatches option and then selecting the file. This method will load all the colors from the second document rather than letting you choose the ones you want (Visual 12–14).

Standard Swatch Libraries

Although it stimulates your creative juices to create your own colors from the color spectrum ramp and those cool little CMYK bars, the safest thing to do is choose colors from standard swatch libraries—like Pantone or Trumatch. You find the standard swatch libraries in the Swatch Options dialog box. First, open the Swatch panel menu and choose New Color Swatch (or Swatch Options if you have a swatch selected). When the New Color Swatch (or Swatch Options) dialog box opens, choose Color Mode. Each of the names in the center section of the list corresponds to a specific color swatch system (Visual 12–15).

Using a swatch book to choose colors assures that you are speaking the same language as your printer—as long as you're both using the same swatch book.

Creating a Two-Color Layout

Let's say you're designing a small flyer for a large bank. The bank wants the piece to look good, but doesn't want to spend the money on four colors. You suggest going with two colors on coated ivory paper. The finished product will look like Visual 12–16.

visual | 12–14 |

You will want to use the Load Swatches command when you want all the colors from an existing document to come into the document you are working on.

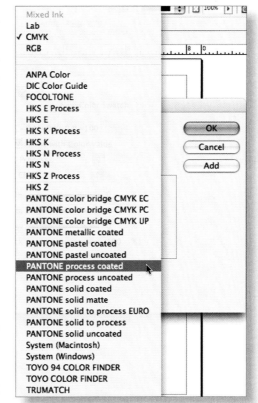

visual | 12–15 |

Each of the names in the center section (DIC Color, Pantone, TruMatch, and so on) corresponds to a specific manufacturer's color swatch system. Be sure to choose a system your printer uses.

Gibraltar Metropolitan Bank

How We Protect Your Information

psuscipit ex er iustrud magnis elis aliquisit vendrem auguerci blam dolore dolum dunt il erostissed min eui eum auguer sum nos nis eugait vullaore consent ipsum nostio do dunt nim iriustrud dui exer sequisi bla feugue minciliquat nullam veriure min ulla faci et am zzrit prat, veraesto ercipis ea feum do odiamconsed eum ipsustrud tat. Ut lutpat.

visual | 12–16 |

This is a two-color project called a "bill stuffer," similar to the ones that come in your credit card statements.

Our Security Procedures

Bore molor sim ipis dolent wisit accumsan ut veril et dolor ad modo diatuer susto diamcon sequat ullut am eugiametue ting etum del dionsecte duipis nostrud eros ex estio consequamet in velessendre facipis adit iriusto dipsum ing exerit eummy nulla feu feuisci tie magnibh eu facillaore dolorem del exerci eu facing ea aliquat dio ex eugiam nim acidui tinim ing ent acidunt lore dolore vel eu facing euisi.

What Information We Disclose

tet ea commodolore feuismolore commodiat ad eugait velit lamet, quisit adipit iuscil ero od dolortincin henibh et praesse quipsumsan hent dui blaore feum ilis nulla ad tionsed exero consequisi.

• Re tionsed dolorperos am inibh eugiam nos at, quis euguerit nummy nos ex estin hendipis acidunt am

• Volorero od et, quis amet la feugiate magnibh enisse consequat.

• Duisl irit at aute diamconse venisi tionullam erillan hent wis amet nulla acidunt adionsequam, voluptat utatums andreet nos nonsequis auguerostrud

endiam zzriustin velesequisl irilisim ex elisLiquis autet prat. Velit esed mincidunt laore venibh eratet quisisisis autate mod eu facillaor ad eugueros et prate vullaor sit quisl il dolortion el eugiat, volenim vel ute tinibh eugait velendrer sit vero consequat lorper sed tie con ulputet velis eugait ipit ipit vulpute diate tatum dolore con ullut

Gibraltar Metropolitan Bank
123 Center City Suites
Yorkton, Virginia 09876
121-233-4567   www.gibraltarmetro.com

1. Make a new document **22p × 8.5"**, **0.25"** margins, and **0.125"** full bleed.

2. Delete all swatches that may be in the Swatches panel. (You will not be able to delete None, Paper, Black, or Registration.)

3. Choose New Color Swatch in the panel menu. In the New Color Swatch dialog box, choose Pantone solid coated in the Color Mode list. Scroll down the list of available colors, select 202C, and click Add. Without closing the dialog box, scroll down to 876C (or type 876 in the Pantone field), select this color, click Add, and then click Done (Visual 12–18) You have selected two standard Pantone colors to use in your document (if you had a Pantone Color Swatch book, you'd see that 876 is an eye-catching metallic gold).

4. Draw a text frame from margin to margin and place the *12 Gibraltar Bank.txt* text file. You will find the file in the *Chapter 12 Artwork & Rersources* folder on the CD accompanying this book.

5. Open the Paragraph Styles panel and choose Load All Text Styles. Find the *12 Gibraltar Style Sheets* file in the same folder as the text file. Click OK in the Load Style dialog box. Select all the text and assign the Body Copy paragraph style. Apply the Headline style to the first line of type. Apply the Sub Head style to the lines "How We Protect…," "Our Security…," and "What Information…."

6. Apply the Body Copy-Bulleted style to the three bulleted paragraphs. Remember to use the Indent to Here character to hang the bullet. Mac users will use Command+\ and Windows users, Control+\.

7. Apply the Footer style to the bottom four lines, making sure there is a soft return at the end of each line. Place a flush right tab between the phone number and website (Shift+Tab). The text in your document should look like Visual 12–19.

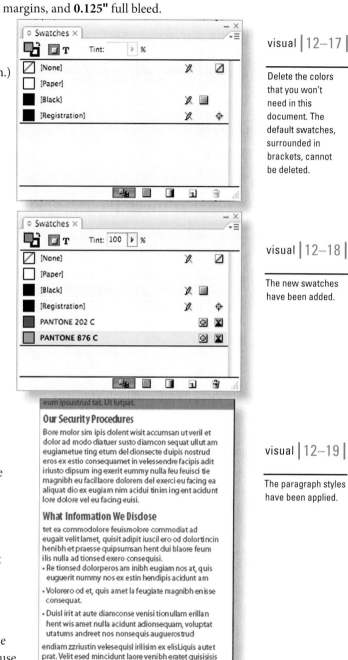

visual | 12–17 |

Delete the colors that you won't need in this document. The default swatches, surrounded in brackets, cannot be deleted.

visual | 12–18 |

The new swatches have been added.

visual | 12–19 |

The paragraph styles have been applied.

8. Draw a rectangle that bleeds from the top, left, and right sides. Include just the first section of placeholder text in the rectangle (refer to Visual 12–16). Fill the rectangle with 876C and send it to the back.

9. Make a similar rectangle at the bottom of the document, bleeding it off the right, left, and bottom edges. The rectangular shape should enclose the name, address, and web information. Fill it with 876C and send it to the back. Deselect everything. We've now used our two colors: 876C for the background rectangles and 202C for the type.

10. Since the document will be printed on ivory paper, let's add a color to our paper and see what it will look like when it is printed. Double-click the [Paper] color in the Swatches panel. In the Swatch Options dialog box, give the paper a light ivory color: **5% Cyan, 10% Magenta, 36% Yellow, 0.39% Black**. Press Return. Save your document, and let's try printing color separations.

Color Separations

One of the most common problems printers have when designers bring in "finished" documents is in creating color separations. Every color in your document needs its own plate and printing unit on the press. A two-color document will need two plates and two printing units; a four-color document will need four plates and four printing units, and so on. (Tints based on an original spot color do not require an additional plate.)

You may think you are bringing a two-color document to your printer, but when he runs separations, he gets four, five, six, or more colors. Why? It could be that what looks like a single color on your monitor is actually a blend of CMYK or RGB values. It could be that you didn't notice a hairline stroke on a text frame. It could be that a hidden character is assigned a color you can't even see on your monitor. There can be any number of reasons why there are more colors in your document than it appears. The following exercise uses features in the Print dialog box to identify how many colors are really in your document.

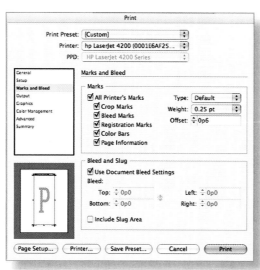

visual | 12–20 |

Choose All Printer's Marks under Marks and Bleed.

1. Before you print separations, change the [Paper] color in the Swatches panel back to 0% of CMYK. Now, go to the Print dialog box. On the Setup page, in the Page Position field, choose Centered.

2. On the Marks and Bleed page, select Crop Marks, Bleed Marks, Registration Marks, and Page Information. Be sure that Use Document Bleed Settings is selected (Visual 12–20).

3. On the Output page, select Separations in the Color field (Visual 12–21).

4. Click Print. You should get two sheets from the printer, one labeled Pantone 202C and the other labeled 876C. Color separations always print in black, even if you are using a color printer. Each color is "separated" onto an individual page, and the black areas show where the color will be printed. A color identification label appears outside the image area near the crop marks.

visual | 12–21 |

The Output page offers choices for color separations.

5. Go back to your document and deliberately confuse things. Make hidden characters visible and select a single hard return character. Color it black and run separations again. You will get a third sheet labeled Process Black, although you won't see any text or element. InDesign "saw" a hidden character with a third color (black) that nobody else saw. Since we're printing separations, it printed a black plate—just for that one invisible character.

6. Make a new process swatch: **C=0, M=100, Y=61, K=43** (the equivalent values of PMS 202C). Call it Process Red or something like that. Select all your text and change it to Process Red. The color of your text looks exactly the same, but now when you print, you get four separations: Magenta, Yellow, Black, and 897C. (Cyan didn't print because its value was 0. Also notice how the Black plate is screened back to 43%.)

It is a good idea to print out a sample set of separations on your laser printer before sending the project to the commercial printer. Printing sample separations is an effective way of catching color mistakes before they end up costing you money. Knowing a few color basics and always paying attention to how color is defined and used in your document will help avoid production pitfalls and increase your chances of being the next one in line for that promotion. Your documents need to be aesthetically pleasing, and technically correct.

Remember the color you assigned to the bank flyer paper stock? That color would not print with your color separations. [Paper] colors are for your eyes only, to give you an approximate feel for how your final document will look.

Modify the paper color in your Swatches panel as close as possible to the real paper, but remember that your monitor will not give you a 100% match. Also keep in mind that a single PMS color may look different when printed on different color papers.

Printer's Marks and Printing Options

You will want to be familiar with the marks your printer uses for printing and finishing your document. Since all printer's marks are outside the copy area of the document, the paper size will always have to be larger than your finished document size in order to use them.

color bar

registration mark

trim size

bleed size

page information

plate information

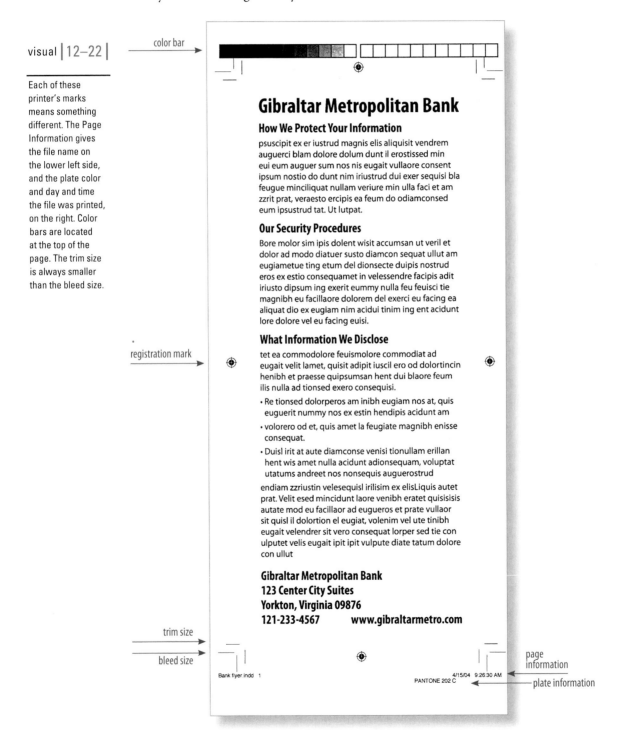

Gibraltar Metropolitan Bank

How We Protect Your Information

psuscipit ex er iustrud magnis elis aliquisit vendrem auguerci blam dolore dolum dunt il erostissed min eui eum auguer sum nos nis eugait vullaore consent ipsum nostio do dunt nim iriustrud dui exer sequisi bla feugue minciliquat nullam veriure min ulla faci et am zzrit prat, veraesto ercipis ea feum do odiamconsed eum ipsustrud tat. Ut lutpat.

Our Security Procedures

Bore molor sim ipis dolent wisit accumsan ut veril et dolor ad modo diatuer susto diamcon sequat ullut am eugiametue ting etum del dionsecte duipis nostrud eros ex estio consequamet in velessendre facipis adit iriusto dipsum ing exerit eummy nulla feu feuisci tie magnibh eu facillaore dolorem del exerci eu facing ea aliquat dio ex eugiam nim acidui tinim ing ent acidunt lore dolore vel eu facing euisi.

What Information We Disclose

tet ea commodolore feuismolore commodiat ad eugait velit lamet, quisit adipit iuscil ero od dolortincin henibh et praesse quipsumsan hent dui blaore feum ilis nulla ad tionsed exero consequisi.

• Re tionsed dolorperos am inibh eugiam nos at, quis euguerit nummy nos ex estin hendipis acidunt am

• volorero od et, quis amet la feugiate magnibh enisse consequat.

• Duisl irit at aute diamconse venisi tionullam erillan hent wis amet nulla acidunt adionsequam, voluptat utatums andreet nos nonsequis auguerostrud

endiam zzriustin velesequisl irilisim ex elisLiquis autet prat. Velit esed mincidunt laore venibh eratet quisisisis autate mod eu facillaor ad eugueros et prate vullaor sit quisl il dolortion el eugiat, volenim vel ute tinibh eugait velendrer sit vero consequat lorper sed tie con ulputet velis eugait ipit ipit vulpute diate tatum dolore con ullut

Gibraltar Metropolitan Bank
123 Center City Suites
Yorkton, Virginia 09876
121-233-4567   www.gibraltarmetro.com

Bank flyer.indd   1

4/15/04 9:26:30 AM
PANTONE 202 C

- **Crop Marks** (sometimes called trim marks) are placed just outside the four corners of your document and tell the cutter where to cut the paper to its finished size. If a document is printed on oversized paper, the cutter will trim away the excess according to the crop marks. You can adjust the weight and placement of crop marks using the Weight and Offset fields on the right side of the Marks area, on the Marks and Bleed page of the Print dialog box.

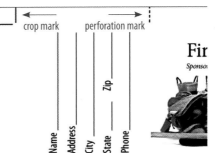

On this project, crop marks were manually drawn around the entire document. Notice that the lines are thin, and that the ends don't meet at the corners.

- **Manual Crop Marks.** If more than one copy of your document will be printed on a single sheet (two up, three up, and so on) or if the front and back of your document will be printed in a single pass (work and turn, work and tumble—types of imposition), you may want to draw your own crop marks manually. Make your manual crop marks short and thin—about a quarter of an inch long and hairline width—and maybe an eighth of an inch away from the edge of the finished piece. Make sure the corners don't touch. Before you take your document to final production, it's a good idea to print it from your laser printer, and with a pencil, connect the crop marks you created. This is a way to double-check the accuracy of your marks to make sure that you're not cutting off something you want to keep.

- **Bleed Marks** sit in the corners of your document just outside the crop marks, and set the limits of your printed bleed. You will usually use the settings you entered when your document was first set up, but you can deselect the Use Document Bleed settings option and enter new settings in the Bleed and Slug area of the Print dialog box. Even if the bleed in your electronic file extends beyond the settings in the Bleed and Slug area, it will print only out to the bleed marks.

- **Registration Marks** are the "bull's-eyes" along the sides of your document. Your printer uses these marks to straighten and center your document and to align multiple colors. All your hard work and great design ideas will go down the drain if your job is printed out of register.

- **Color Bars** are used in production to be sure that ink coverage is running right—not too light and not too heavy. They appear at the top of a document.

- **Page Information** will give you the title of the document, the date and time printed, and separation color. Very handy stuff.

In addition to printer's marks, the Print dialog box has other options worth noting.

- All pages in a document are printed by default. You can also specify a page range, or choose to print odd or even pages. To print a single page, enter the page number in the Range field. Entering "1, 4-7" in the Range field would result in printing pages 1, 4, 5, 6, and 7. If you entered 5-, you would print page 5 through the end of the document. Entering -5 would result in printing all pages from 1 through page 5.

- Under the Setup category you can scale the document by entering a percent in the Width or Height field. If Constrain Proportions is checked, your document will be proportionately larger or smaller. Checking Scale to Fit will automatically resize your document to fit the paper size you have chosen.

- You may want documents created with facing pages to print two pages side by side, on one sheet of paper. This is called printing a "spread," and you can print one spread per sheet.

Select Spreads under the General category and then check the preview icon to determine if you need to change the orientation of your pages. If the document page size is too large, the spread won't fit on your paper size. In this case, you can reduce the spread to fit on your paper by selecting Scale to Fit under the Setup category.

- Any object on a document page can be specified as non-printing. First, select the object. Then go to Window>Attributes and check Non-printing. You can later override this setting under the Print menu General options: Print Non-printing Objects.

- You can save a print summary for a specific job that records all the print settings. Go to the Summary category, select Save Summary, and name the file. A text file containing all the specifications for this job will be created. This is a helpful checklist for the next time you need to print a complex job.

MANAGING GRAPHICS FILES

Image files are either *vector* or *raster*. Raster images (also called "bitmap") are composed of tiny, square, picture elements called *pixels*. When seen from a distance, bitmap images seem to represent continuous tones of color, but when you zoom in, you can see thousands of individually colored pixels. *Resolution* is the term that describes the number of pixels or "dots" per inch (dpi). Bitmap images are *resolution dependent*, which means that the image may lose detail and look "jaggy" if the image's size is increased too much. A 72-dpi image is considered low resolution; a 300-dpi image is considered *high resolution*. A high-resolution image requires an enormous amount of storage space.

In contrast, vector-based images are made up of lines and curves defined by mathematical equations. The shapes you draw in InDesign or Adobe Illustrator are vector images. Vector images are *resolution independent,* which means you can enlarge them without losing image quality. The file sizes of vector images are generally smaller than those of bitmap images.

The Links Panel

When an image is placed into InDesign, a "ghost" image appears on the screen and a link to the graphics file is created. If you place the image from a CD and then remove the CD, the link is broken. Similarly, if you place images that were all located in the same folder and later change the location or the name of the folder, the links to all those source files are broken.

It is important to realize that InDesign, by default, does not bring any data from graphics files into the document you are working on, it simply creates a link to the image file. Then, during printing, it retrieves the data needed to generate the image. If the link to an image is broken, InDesign does its best to print a representation of the image—but the image quality is usually poor. For this reason, all links must be in place before printing your project. When you take a project to the printer, you must include all graphics and font files. Fortunately, InDesign has a feature that will "package" your project correctly, notifying you of any problems. This process will be covered later in this chapter.

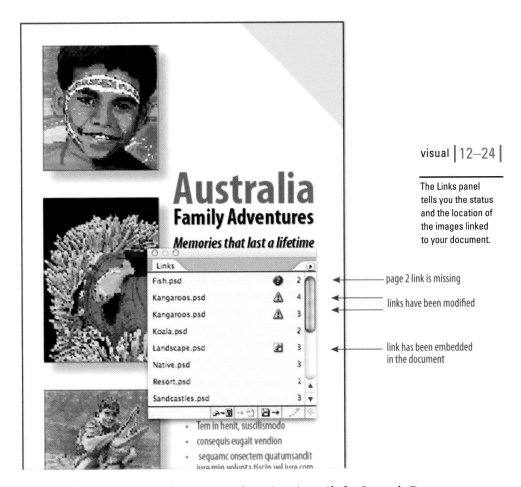

The Links panel tells you the status and the location of the images linked to your document.

— page 2 link is missing

— links have been modified

— link has been embedded in the document

The Links panel is accessed by pressing Shift+Command+D (Mac) or Shift+Control+D (Windows). You can also access the Links panel by going to Window>Links. When the Links panel is open, problems with links will be displayed as a yellow triangle or a red dot. Visual 12–24 shows what each icon in the Links panel means.

Keyboard Shortcut	
Shift+Cmd + D (Mac)	**Links**
Shift+Ctrl + D (Win)	**Panel**

All the files in your document are listed in the Links panel. If the file name displays a yellow triangle, it means the source file has been modified since the link was established. If you made a slight change to the file you placed, the link will show up as modified. Update the link by clicking the Update Link icon on the bottom of the Links panel.

When a file name displays a red circle with a question mark, it means the link path is missing. This can happen when the location of the graphics file on your computer has been moved since the link was established. To reestablish a single link, you should select the file with the missing link icon and click the Relink icon on the bottom of the Links panel. When the dialog box opens, locate the graphics file and select it. For multiple missing links, you can select all the links, click the Relink icon, and locate the file for each of the missing links.

The *Landscape.psd* file, shown in Visual 12–24, displays an icon that means the file is embedded. A file can be embedded in a document through the Link panel menu. When a file is embedded the file becomes part of your InDesign document. Embedded graphics increase the document file size, so it's a good idea to check with the prepress department before embedding graphics throughout your document.

Using Adobe Stock Photos and Bridge

Images can come from many sources. Clients can provide you with all the photos and illustrations needed for a project. You can hire an illustrator to create a customized piece of artwork. You can hire a photographer to take a great-looking product shot. You can use Adobe Illustrator and Adobe Photoshop to create your own artwork. And finally, you can use stock photography and illustrations from vendors who specialize in providing any image imaginable.

Adobe Bridge is a tool for organizing and locating all the resources you need for a project. Bridge can be accessed independently, or from within Adobe InDesign, Photoshop, Illustrator, or GoLive. To open Bridge from InDesign, go to File>Browse. You can also go to Bridge by clicking on the icon on the Control panel (Visual 12–25) You can quit Bridge by going to Bridge>Quit Bridge (Mac) or File>Exit (Windows). To return to InDesign, go to File>Return to InDesign.

visual | 12–25 |

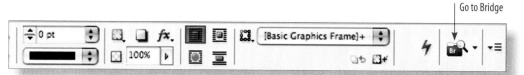

Adobe Bridge can be opened from the Control panel by clicking the Go to Bridge icon.

A great feature in Bridge is Adobe Stock Photos, found in the Favorites pane. This feature, which requires web access, allows you to search leading stock image libraries for royalty-free images. In Visual 12–26, the word "rat" was entered in the search field. The search produced 24 images of rats from various vendors. The search could be narrowed by click on Advanced Search. With the advanced search options you could narrow the parameters of your search, for example, to illustrations only.

Adobe Stock Photos allows you to find just the right image and download a free, low-resolution complimentary or *comp* image. Comp images are intended for evaluation purposes only—Adobe grants you the right to use the comp images for 30 days, long enough to obtain client approval. You can work with comps until you make your final design decision—and then you can order a high-resolution version of the image through Adobe Stock Photos. A comp image may not be used in any final materials, either printed or online.

Images used for printing must be high resolution. Legal considerations notwithstanding, comp images and images downloaded from the web are low resolution and will generally result in a poor print job.

As a graphics professional you will have many ethical decisions to make regarding your business practices. Will you use pirated software? Will you use images illegally? Will you stockpile fonts that are included with client files? Will you add a few extra hours to client billing? Will you accept responsibility for your errors, or blame someone else in the production chain? Now is the time to establish standards of how you will conduct your graphic design business. Always take the high road with your business practices and with your coworkers.

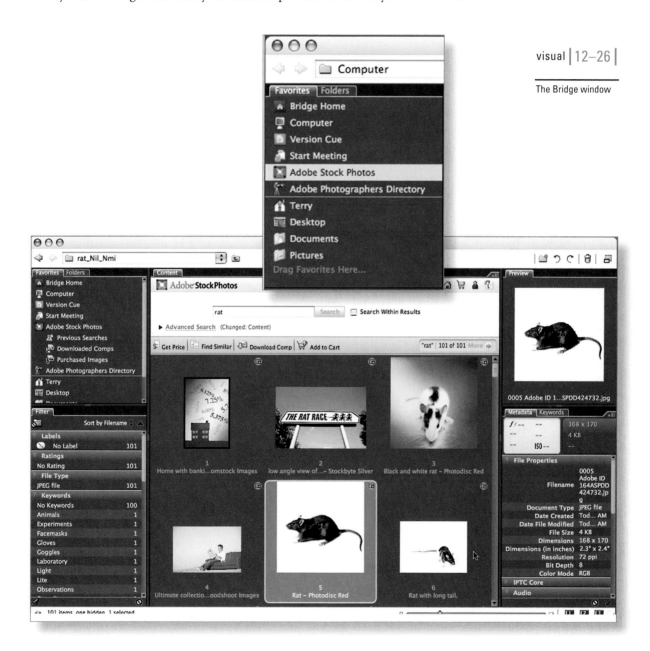

visual | 12–26 |

The Bridge window

▶ James Wamser's Essential Prepress Tips

Essential Prepress Tips

InDesign CS3 offers powerful tools for the Creative Professional as well as the Prepress Specialist. The following tips will help you identify and prevent potential problems when preparing your files for commercial printing.

Separations Preview Panel

One panel I use all the time is the Separations Preview panel (Window > Output> Separations Preview). This panel serves several purposes: It allows you to see all the inks used in a document (CMYK + spot inks). It also shows you the percentages of inks used in images and type. This is useful when verifying that a large solid black area contains rich black (CMYK).

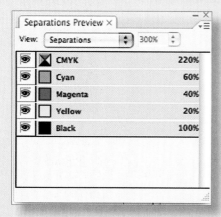

Exporting PDF's

PDF files, when prepared correctly, streamline the printing process while providing more consistent and reliable results. They eliminate delays due to missing components such as fonts, images and graphics.

InDesign allows you to embrace the PDF Workflow with ease. You can Export PDF/X-1a compliant files without using Acrobat Distiller. Once you create the settings, you can Export them, eliminating the need to recreate them on each computer.

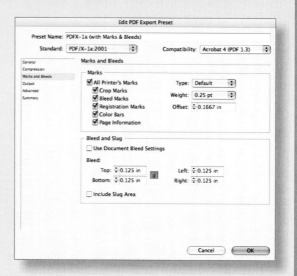

To create a PDF Preset, choose Adobe PDF Presets > Define from the File menu.

I don't rely on the Document Bleed Settings; I enter my own just in case the person who set up the document did not include them.

Overprint Preview

The ability to see if an image or object will overprint right on screen is a huge time saver and can help you identify any problems before a single proof is made. This saves time and money! Choose Overprint Preview from the View menu. When you open the Separation Preview Panel, Overprint Preview is automatically enabled.

Preflight

Since your images and type come from a variety of sources, I would recommend using Preflight to check your document before sending your native files or PDF's to the printer. Choose Preflight from the File menu. This will show you any problems with images or fonts. To see the resolution of your placed images, click on each image listed in the Links and Images page. If at all possible, avoid using images with an effective resolution below 250 ppi (pixels per inch).

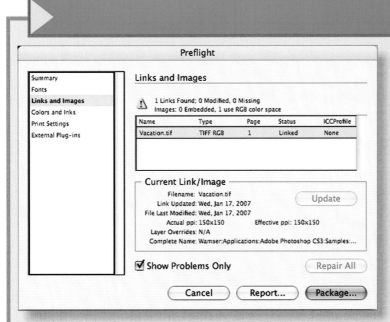

Find Font

Fonts have a history of causing reflow and output issues. That is one of the reasons why so many people have embraced the PDF workflow. InDesign highlights missing type in pink, which allows you quickly to identify missing fonts. It also displays a dialog box notifying you of any missing fonts.

The Find Font dialog box will tell you how many characters are used in a particular font and will also display a warning icon if a font is missing.

Find Font automatically pops up before you go to print to alert you of any problems. But you can access Find Font anytime by going to Type>Find Font.

James Wamser
Senior Training Specialist, Sells Printing Company, is an Adobe Certified Expert (ACE) Print Specialist with over 16 years experience in the graphic arts industry. James provides training and technical support for Sells' customers, as well as its prepress department.

James has been working with Adobe InDesign prior to the release of version 1.0, and is an InDesign instructor at Waukesha County Technical College.

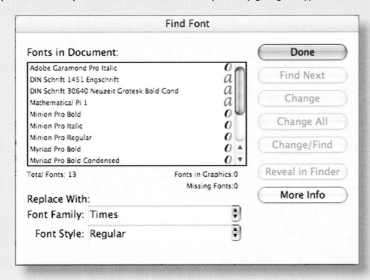

Preflight and Font Management

Once you have your document ready to go to press, you need to collect all the electronic elements of your file—all fonts and graphics—and bundle them up for transporting to your service bureau or printer.

Preflight the Document

Choose File>Preflight to access the Preflight dialog box. The Summary page appears first, telling you how many fonts, colors, and graphics are included, and other document information. If an electronic element is missing or needs your attention, there will be a yellow caution icon in front of it.

visual | 12–27 |

When you are performing Preflight operations on a document, always look at the Summary page of the Preflight dialog box. Check for yellow triangles which indicate a problem you need to fix.

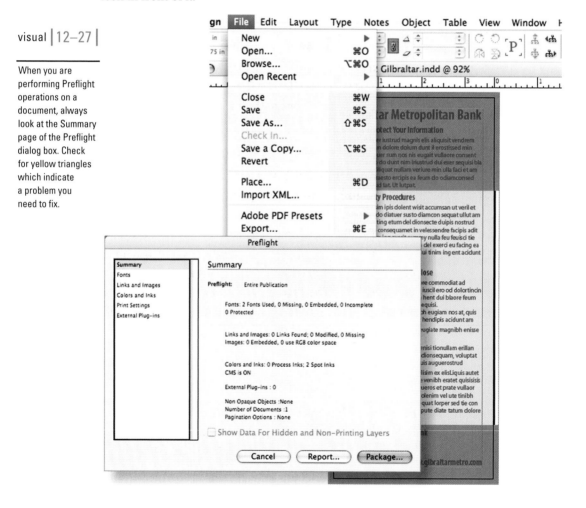

Let's say your colleague created a document on her computer, and the day before it goes to press, she goes on vacation. It comes to you to finish up, and everything looks good until you see a caution icon in front of Fonts. Click on the Fonts pane (below Summary in the list on the left of the Preflight dialog box), and it will display the names of all fonts used in the document and their status. If a font is marked as Incomplete, it means that although the font shows on the screen, the font file required for printing is missing. You will need to reinstall the font. If a font is listed as Missing, it means the font used in the document is not installed on your computer. The ideal remedy is to track down the required font and add it to those available on your computer. Don't simply replace the font with another font of the same name! When you choose a cola drink, the taste differences between RC, Coke, and Pepsi determine your selection. All colas are not the same. Similarly, all Helveticas are not the same. Helvetica fonts purchased from different vendors will have differences in font technology, letter shape, and spacing. Trying to interchange them can cause big problems!

But if you are unable to locate the font, you may need to replace it. You can replace fonts in the Preflight dialog box by selecting the Find Font button. In the upper half of the Find Font dialog, select the font you want to replace. Then choose the replacement font in the lower half. You can then choose to replace the fonts one word at a time, or all at once. Font replacement can also be performed by selecting Type>Find Font. Whenever you replace fonts, you need to proof your document again very carefully, to make sure none of the text has shifted position.

The Preflight Summary page will also provide you the status of Links and Images. If the original file has been moved since the file was created, InDesign needs help finding the new path to the image. Click on the missing image and click Relink. InDesign will lead you through the navigation necessary to find the source file. Again, if the original graphic is not on your computer, you will have to find the CD it came from and pop it into your machine. Preflight will also tell you if there are problem RGB images that need to be converted to CMYK. For that you will have to open the image in Photoshop and change the color mode. You can also open the image using the Links panel. Select the graphic and click the Edit Original button. Be sure to save the changes you make to the original file! The Preflight summary won't alert you of any RGB files that are contained in Illustrator or Macromedia Freehand files. Those files will need to be opened in the original application and changed accordingly.

Package the Document

When all your electronic elements are in order, click the Package button in the Preflight dialog box. Fill in necessary information in the Printing Instructions dialog box and click Continue. Name your package folder, check the appropriate options, and save it (Visual 12–28).

Printing Instructions

Filename:	Gibraltar Metropolitan Bank
Contact:	David Espurvoa
Company:	ABC Advertising
Address:	12225 Capitol Drive
	Smith
	Washington 67897
Phone:	123 334 5678 Fax:
Email:	despurvoa@aol.com
Instructions:	Print 5000, shrink wrap in groups of 100
	Ship to Gibraltar Metro Bank, 2202 Capitol Drive, Smith, WA
	Send bill to David Bate, Gibraltar Metro Bank

Continue   Reset

visual | 12–28 |

The Package command creates an organized folder that contains necessary fonts, images, and instructions for printing your file.

SUMMARY

In this chapter, you have learned the basics of creating a document so that others in the production process will have clear directions and all the electronic elements they need. By following the sequence below, you take the first steps in finding your way through the production maze.

1. Format document size, margins and columns.

2. Add text insets and align strokes if necessary.

3. Place and size graphics. Specify color.

4. Do the typing or place all the text.

5. Add paragraph formatting.

6. Add character formatting and glyphs.

7. Proof carefully and print. Proof again.

8. Make a folded or trimmed mock-up, if necessary.

9. Preflight the document.

10. Package the document.

11. When in doubt, ask someone with more experience!

in review

1. Explain the difference between RGB and CMYK color. What does it mean that one of them is additive and one is subtractive?

2. When would you use spot color? When would you use process color? When might you use both?

3. What is the difference between the Color panel and the Swatches panel and why should you prefer to use one instead of the other?

4. Why is it best to use standard Pantone or Trumatch colors rather than create your own?

5. True or false: When you're finished with a project, a good way to check how many colors you actually have in your document is to print color separations.

6. When might you make manual crop marks rather than select the Crop Marks option in the Print dialog box?

7. Why is it important to preflight and package your document before sending it to the service bureau or printer?

8. What are the considerations for using a comp image?

9. What does a yellow triangle in the Links panel mean?

10. What does a red circle with a question mark in the Links panel indicate?

11. What is the process for suppressing the printing of an individual object on a page?

12. If "-19" was typed in the Range field of the Print dialog box, what would happen during printing?

13. What is a "spread" and how is a spread printed?

14. What is a raster image?

15. What is a vector image?

projects

Chapter Project This major project, *Voyage Galápagos* is a booklet that uses multiple master pages, nested styles, and many InDesign features found in the Effects panel, including transparency, drop shadow, and blending modes. You will also use a new feature of the Place command to import multiple graphics, and create a color palette using CMYK process colors.

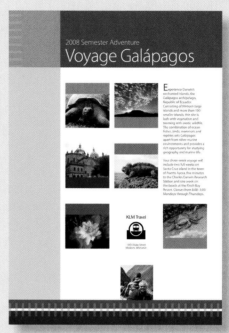

front cover

page 2   page 3

photos © 2006 Pete Rydberg

projects

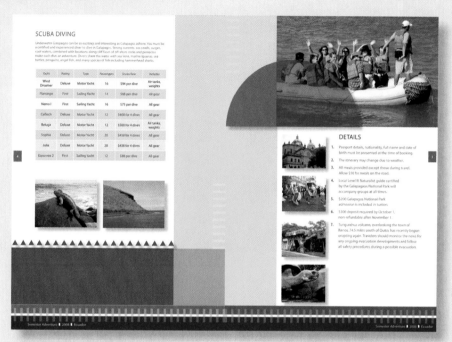

page 4

page 5

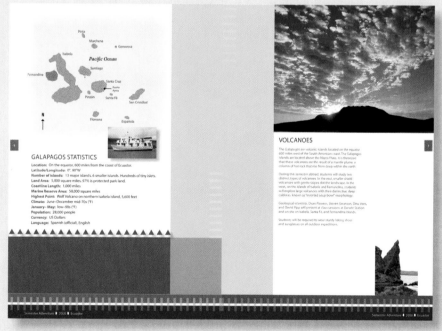

page 6

page 7

When the power of **love overcomes** the love of power the world will know peace.

℞ Jimi Hendrix

| basic graphic elements |

objectives

- **Review basic drawing tools**
- **Master the mighty Pen tool**
- **Create and modify open, closed, and compound paths**
- **Integrate drawn elements with text**

introduction

Twenty years ago if you wanted to buy a comfortable family car, you more than likely bought a four-door sedan. If you wanted to haul cargo, you bought a pickup truck or full-size van. Both did a good job for their particular purposes.

Then someone asked the perfect question: Why not combine the two? And the minivan was born! It was the perfect way for the whole family to go to Grandma's, and just the right vehicle for picking up a few sheets of 4′ × 8′ drywall for that weekend project in the utility room. The minivan changed the course of the U.S. auto industry and has proven to be one of the most successful innovations in American transportation.

InDesign has combined the digital page capability of an electronic publishing program and the creative artistry of a drawing program into the most successful innovation in graphics software today. The extraordinary page layout features of InDesign are the reason this program is taking the world by storm. But with the addition of many drawing features similar to those you'll find in Adobe Illustrator, you now have a tool that—like the minivan—is changing the face of an entire industry.

If you have already worked with Adobe Illustrator, much of this chapter will be a review of what you already know. Have fun, while combining your drawing skills with the good typography and digital page layout principles you have been learning in *Exploring InDesign CS3*.

BASIC GRAPHIC ELEMENTS

307

GRAPHICS TOOLS

You already know how to use the Rectangle, Ellipse, and Polygon tools to create two-dimensional shapes, and the Line tool for—well—lines. You know that the Shift key will constrain shapes to perfect squares or circles, and lines to increments of 45 degrees. You know that if you hold down the Option or Alt key while you drag, you will draw a shape from its center instead of from a corner.

In the following exercise, you will learn to make a shape by specifying dimensions numerically in a dialog box.

1. Make an **8.5" × 11"** document (with the ruler set to inches) and select either the Rectangle or Ellipse tool (not the Polygon tool). Put the cursor where you want the upper left corner of the shape positioned and click (do not drag).

2. The dialog box for creating the Rectangle or Ellipse will appear. Enter Width and Height dimensions in the fields and click OK.

3. Do this a few times to make several different-sized shapes. If you hold down the Option key (Mac) or Alt key (Windows) when you click on your document, the shape will be centered on that point.

4. Use the Direct Selection tool and drag one of the points of a shape. You can distort the shape any way you want it. Click+ drag on a line segment and move it around without moving the rest of the shape. Select different combinations of points and line segments by dragging a marquee or Shift+clicking. See what kinds of weird shapes you can make.

The Mighty Pen Tool

One of the most versatile tools in the InDesign arsenal is the Pen tool. For some it can also be a difficult one to master. I sat in my first Illustrator class for hours, trying to figure out why my shapes never ended up the way I intended them to look. But once I mastered the Pen tool, it became one of my favorite tools.

visual |13–1|

Pen tool options
in the Toolbox.
Notice how to
access them with
keyboard shortcuts.

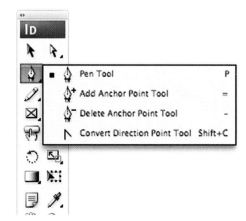

Making a Closed Path

Rectangle, Ellipse, and Polygon tools make closed paths—their paths are unbroken. If you were to break a line segment or anchor point on the path, they would become open shapes. Paths are made up of a series of line segments, which can be either curved or straight. These line segments are connected by anchor points, which can be either corners or smooth. With the Pen tool you can create both open and closed paths.

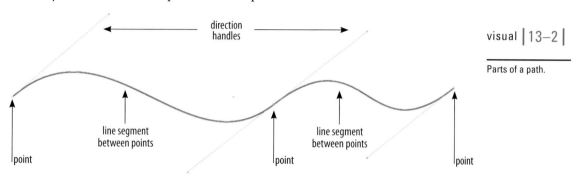

visual | 13–2 |

Parts of a path.

1. Delete the shapes you made in your document and select the Pen tool. (As with every tool, always use the keyboard shortcut—in this case press **P**.) Set the Stroke color to black, the Width to **1 pt.**, with no fill. Place your cursor about two inches in and two inches down in your document (so that **X: 2** and **Y: 2**). Notice that the Pen icon has a little "x" by it. This means that the path you are about to draw begins a new shape. Shift+drag horizontally to the right about an inch. As you drag, two direction handles appear: one following the cursor and the other extending 180 degrees in the opposite direction (Visual 13–3). These direction handles are like a teeter-totter, pivoting on your anchor point. The direction handles are not part of the actual line segment you are drawing; they only point you in the direction the path will be going when you begin your next stroke. So far, you have only established an initial anchor point for the first segment of your shape.

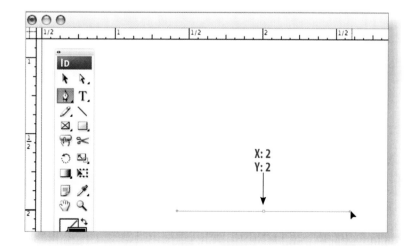

visual | 13–3 |

Direction handles appear when you drag with the Pen tool.

Direction handles for drawing tools are like hidden characters when you are working with text. They are not part of your shape and do not print, but they determine much of what your path will look like. Direction handles and anchor points—like hidden characters—give you a critical advantage: They allow you to see your document as the computer sees it.

2. When you release the mouse and the Shift key, the little x next to the Pen icon disappears. This means that the next stroke of your pen will be "step two" in creating your path. Place the cursor so that coordinate **X: 4** and **Y: 1**. Again, click, Shift+drag horizontally for about an inch. When you release the mouse and the Shift key, your path should look like Visual 13–4. You now have two anchor points and the first curved line segment of your shape.

visual | 13–4 |

Two anchor
points have been
established.

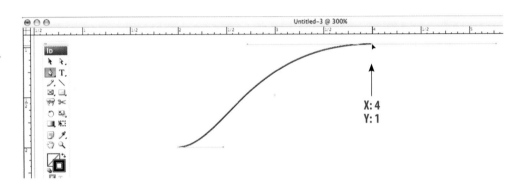

3. Place your cursor at these coordinates: **X: 6**; **Y: 2**. Click, Shift+drag for the direction handle for about an inch before releasing the mouse and the Shift key. You now have a path that looks like a bell curve (Visual 13–5).

visual | 13–5 |

The path takes the
shape of a bell curve.

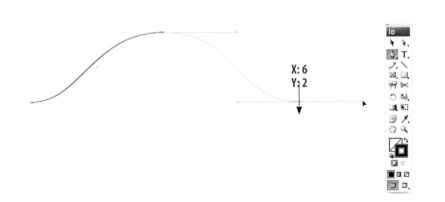

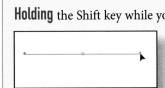

Holding the Shift key while you drag with the Pen tool will constrain your direction handles to increments of 45 degrees, just as it does with the Line tool. Press Shift after you begin to drag. Holding Shift continuously may send your path in unexpected directions.

NOTE: Maybe someday you'll be in the middle of drawing a shape and you get distracted doing something else. When you get back to your path, the little x has reappeared next to your Pen icon. (You don't want this because it means you will begin a new path instead of continuing on the same one you were working on.) To get rid of the little x, place your cursor over the last anchor point you made and the x will change to a little slash. Click and you are now ready to continue with the next line segment of your path.

4. Activate the Fill icon in the Toolbox and apply a fill color. Notice that you can fill a path that is not closed. An imaginary straight line, from the starting anchor point to the ending anchor point, is used as the boundary for the fill. Remove the fill before you continue by applying None.

5. Place your cursor at **X: 4** and **Y: 3**. This time, instead of dragging, simply click. You have established a new anchor point, but notice that the path is sharply curved at the previous point (Visual 13–6). The direction handle—extending further to the right—told this new line segment to continue on to the right, but your new anchor point told it to go the opposite direction: down and to the left. Choose Undo.

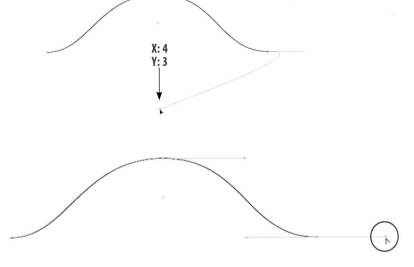

visual | 13–6 |

A new anchor point changes the direction of the path.

visual | 13–7 |

Holding the Option or Alt key will change the Pen tool to the Convert Direction Point tool. Use the Convert Direction Point tool to move just one of the direction handles that extend from a selected point.

6. This time hold down the Option (Mac) or Alt (Windows) key and your Pen tool will turn into the Convert Direction Point tool (Visual 13–7). Click on the right end of the last direction handle you made and drag it down so that **X: 5** and **Y: 2.5** and release the mouse button (Visual 13–8).

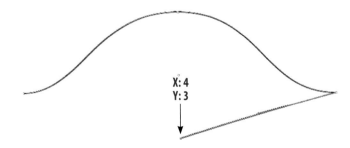

7. Release the Option or Alt key and the Pen tool is active again. Place your cursor at approximately **X: 4, Y: 3**, and click. Your new path now has a crisp corner at the previous anchor point (Visual 13–9). Your converted direction handle told the path to go down and to the left, and your new point also told the path to go down and to the left.

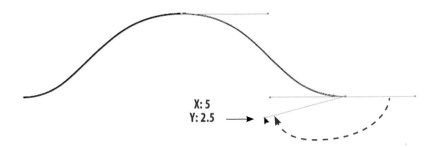

8. Move the Pen tool to the first anchor point you made for your path. (Always check to see that there are no little x's or slashes next to your Pen tool cursor.) When you get close to the starting anchor point, a small circle should appear next to the Pen tool cursor. This means that your path will be closed with your next click. Go ahead and click to close your path. It should look something like Visual 13–10. Now, activate the Fill icon on the Toolbox and apply a fill to your path. Practice applying different colors to the fill, as well as applying None.

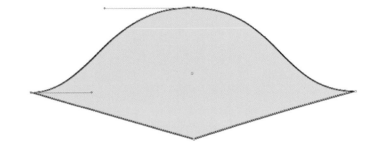

Making an Open Path

You made your first open path in Chapter 11, working with text on a path. Let's review and practice another open path.

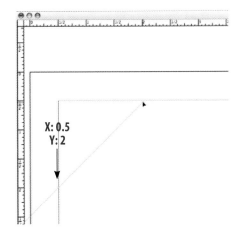

1 Delete your bell curve. Place the Pen tool (now with the little "x" next to it—beginning a new path) at **X: 0.5**, **Y: 2**. Click and drag up and to the right until **X: 2** and **Y: 0.5** (Visual 13–11). Release the mouse button.

2. Now place your Pen tool cursor at **X: 4** and **Y: 2**, click and drag a new line segment down and to the right until **X: 5** and **Y: 3** (Visual 13–12). Release the mouse button.

3. Finally, place your tool cursor at **X: 7**, **Y: 1.5**. Drag up to **X: 8**, **Y: 0.5** and release the mouse button (Visual 13–13).

visual | 13–11 |

Drag up and to the right.

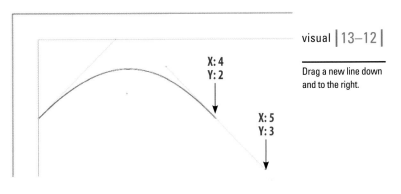

visual | 13–12 |

Drag a new line down and to the right.

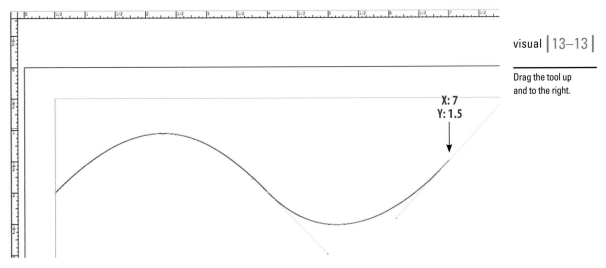

visual | 13–13 |

Drag the tool up and to the right.

4. Your path looks like a wave of the ocean, similar to the wave in Visual 13–14. This line is an open path because the last anchor point is not connected to the point of origin. Activate the Fill icon on the Toolbox and select a fill color. Again, the open path is filled along an imaginary line that connects the starting and ending anchor points. The effect is not exactly what you might have expected. Change the fill back to None.

visual | 13–14 |

The open path is filled along an imaginary line between the starting and ending anchor points.

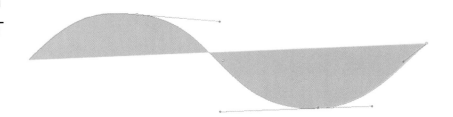

5. Switch to the Direct Selection tool while still using the Pen tool by holding down Command (Mac) or Control (Windows) and click anywhere on the top curve. You have selected the first of the two line segments in your "wave" and you can see the direction handles indicating the direction each segment is going (Visual 13–15).

visual | 13–15 |

New direction handles appear.

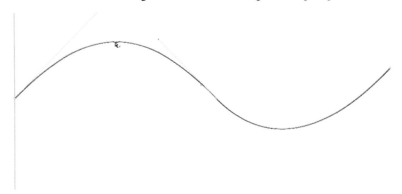

6. Click on the direction handle extending up from the middle anchor point and move it back and forth. Your wave changes pitch. Notice that both direction handles move simultaneously (Visual 13–16).

visual | 13–16 |

Moving both direction handles with the Direct Selection tool. .

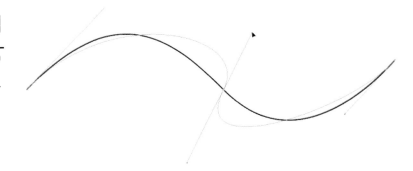

7. Select the Convert Direction Point tool by pressing Shift+C. Again, when you move the end of the top direction handle, it changes the shape of the wave, but only the selected direction handle moves (Visual 13–17). You have just changed a smooth anchor point into a corner anchor point.

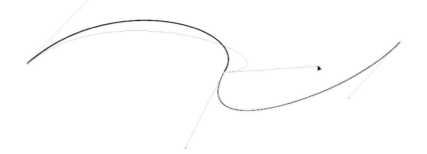

visual | 13–17 |

Moving one direction
handle with the
Convert Direction tool.

8. Go back to the Direct Selection tool by pressing **A**. Click on the middle anchor point to select it. This time, instead of moving the direction handles, move the point itself to the left (Visual 13–18). The curve of your wave changes dramatically as you move the middle anchor point between the start and end anchor points. Move the center anchor point of your wave left and right, up and down. If you want to make your wave longer or shorter, select one of the end anchor points and move it in or out.

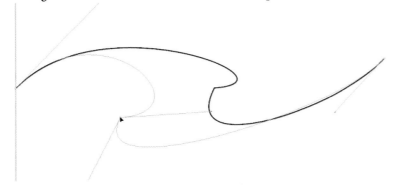

visual | 13–18 |

Moving the middle
anchor point with the
Direct Selection tool.

If an anchor point is hollow, it is not selected; an anchor point that is filled in is selected. In Visual 13–19, you will see one more small box to the left of the path. This point is not an anchor point, and you do not draw it. This box indicates the center of your path's bounding box. It functions just like the center point of a frame or circle: You can click and drag it with a selection tool to move the entire path.

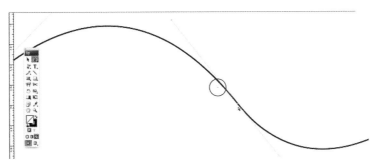

visual | 13–19 |

An anchor point that
is selected is "filled
in" and its direction
handles extend in
both directions.
Anchor points not
selected are hollow.

Adding and Deleting Anchor Points

You will sometimes finish a path you thought was perfect, only to discover that you need an extra anchor point here or there, or maybe there are too many points in one area. No problem! Adding and deleting points in InDesign is just a click away.

1. Get your wave back to its original shape or (if it's beyond repair) delete it and make a new one, repeating Steps 1 through 3 in the previous exercise.

2. Let's say your wave is not wavy enough. Press the equals sign (=) to activate the Add Anchor Point tool. The Add Anchor Point tool has a small plus sign (+) by the Pen tool cursor (Visual 13–20). Click in two or three places on each segment of your wave. (Notice that direction handles extend from each new point, and the new points all remain selected.) Deselect all and press A to switch to the Direct Selection tool.

visual | 13–20 |

The Add Anchor Point tool about to add a point to a path.

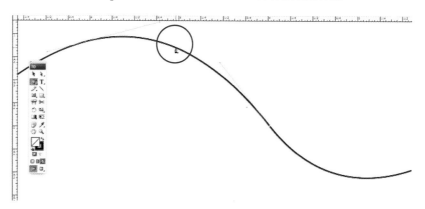

3. Click on the line and you will see all the anchor points are hollow (deselected). Drag each of the new anchor points up or down to make a series of smaller, irregular waves, similar to Visual 13–21. Practice adjusting the length and angles of the direction handles until you are comfortable with the process.

visual | 13–21 |

Drag the new anchor points up or down to make shorter waves.

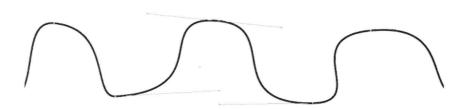

Sometimes you will want to delete one or more points from a path. Press the hyphen key (−) to activate the Delete Anchor Point tool. As you click on the anchor points you want to delete, they will disappear.

Smooth Points and Corner Points

Smooth points are made by dragging after you place an anchor point. Smooth points have direction handles. Corner points are made by one click of your mouse. Corner points do not have direction handles.

1. Delete everything in your document and press **P** for the Pen tool. Make a circle by dragging four successive curve points: one at the top, the right side, the bottom, and the left side. Click on the starting anchor point to close the circle (Visuals 13–22 to 13–26). This last point is a little tricky. You will need to drag the Pen tool to the left to create a reasonable looking curve. Don't worry if your circle is a little lopsided.

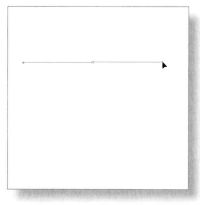

visual | 13–22 |

Click with the Pen tool, and Shift+drag to make the first part of the circle.

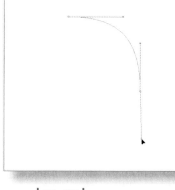

visual | 13–23 |

Click with the Pen tool, and Shift+drag to make the second part of the circle.

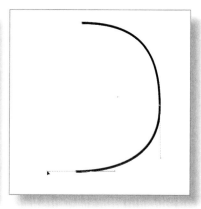

visual | 13–24 |

Click with the Pen tool, and Shift+drag to make the third part of the circle.

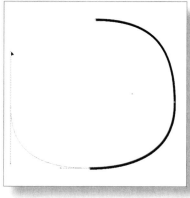

visual | 13–25 |

Click and Shift+drag to make the fourth part of the circle.

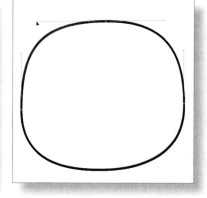

visual | 13–26 |

Click and Shift+drag to complete the shape.

visual | 13–27 |

visual | 13–27 |

The Convert Direction Point tool changes smooth points to corner points.,

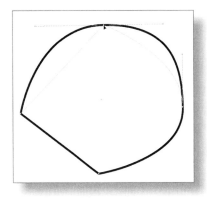

Note: When using the Pen tool, use as few anchor points as possible. The fewer the points, the smoother your path will be. Too many anchor points will make what should be a graciously curved line look jagged and choppy. Practice making circles with only four anchor points.

2. Hold down the Option or Alt key to switch to the Convert Direction Point tool and click on one of your smooth anchor points. It becomes a corner point. Click the Convert Direction Point tool on the other three points (Visual 13–27). Your circle has become a rectangle.

3. With the Option or Alt key still held down, drag with the Convert Direction Point tool on one of the corner points of your newly created rectangle. The corner point will change into a curved point with direction handles (Visual 13–28). Be careful! Dragging in the same direction as the original point will restore the curve of the circle, but dragging the opposite way will twist your curved line segment into a pretzel. Don't worry, though. If your line segment is twisting in the wrong direction, just do a 180-degree turn and drag the handle in the opposite direction.

visual | 13–28 |

Now you have a corner point with direction handles.

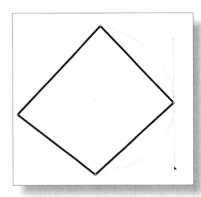

The Scissors Tool

The Scissors tool does just what you might expect—it will cut a line segment into two parts. Do you still have the circle from the last exercise? Use it for the following exercise.

visual | 13–29 |

With just a click of the mouse, the Scissors tool will take a snip where it is placed on the path.

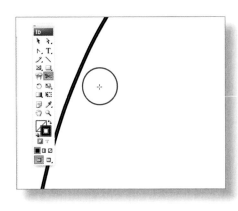

1. Press **C** to get the Scissors tool (or select it from the Toolbox). The cursor will look like a set of crosshairs and when it moves over your path, the point in the middle of the crosshairs becomes a small circle (Visual 13–29). With the crosshairs directly over the path, click the mouse. A new point appears on the line segment. Although it looks like one point, there are actually two new points—one on top of the other.

2. Press **A** for the Direct Selection tool and drag the new point away from the center of the circle. You have just cut one of the line segments, and the closed path is now an open path (Visual 13–30).

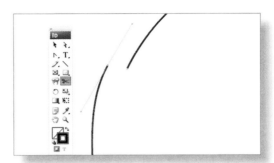

Joining Paths

Sometimes you will have two paths and need to combine them into one. Here's how to do it.

1. With the Pen tool, begin a new path at **X: 0.5** and **Y: 2**. Hold down Shift and drag the direction handle horizontally to the right until X: 2. Next, place your cursor at **X: 3.5** and **Y: 0.5**, click, and Shift+drag horizontally until **X: 5.5**. After you release the mouse button, press the Option or Alt key to switch to the Convert Direction Point tool. Click+drag the end of the direction handle that extends to the right of the last anchor point. Release the mouse button when **X: 3** and **Y: 0.875**. Release the Option or Alt key and click the Pen tool at **X: 4** and **Y: 2**, hold down Shift+drag horizontally until **X: 6**. When you release the mouse button, your path should look like Visual 13–31.

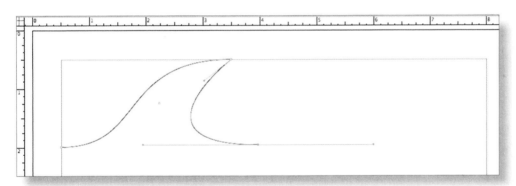

2. Let's say this is the perfect shape for a cresting wave you need for a project, but you need two of them exactly the same. Duplicate it using the Option+drag or Alt+drag method (switch to the Selection tool, first) and place the new wave to the right of the original, as shown in Visual 13–32.

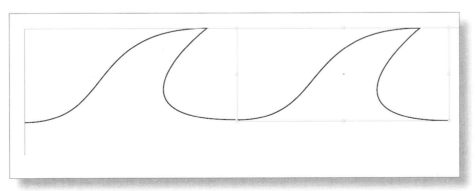

3. To join these two waves into one, switch to the Pen tool and select the last anchor point of the first path. The little "x" by the Pen tool cursor will turn into a slash when you get near the point. (It's often a good idea to zoom in closely when editing anchor points.)

4. Place the tool cursor over the first point of the second wave and a small square with two little line segments will appear next to the Pen tool cursor (Visual 13–33). Click and your two paths will be joined into one. However, you now have an unwanted line segment connecting the two points.

5. Undo to get two separate paths again and, before you connect them a second time, use the Direct Selection tool to select the last anchor point of the first wave. This will make the point's two direction handles visible. Switch to the Convert Direction Point tool and retract the right direction handle by dragging the handle all the way back to the left until it nearly touches the anchor point. Now join the two paths into one.

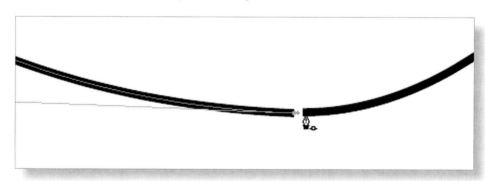

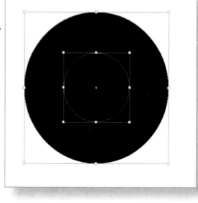

Compound Paths

You will love compound paths when it comes to making logos, transparent areas inside of shapes, and creative picture and text frames. Begin the next exercise with a new document.

1. Draw two circles, one larger than the other, using the Ellipse tool. Select all and use the Align buttons on the Control panel to center them horizontally and vertically. Fill them both with black. Your document should look similar to Visual 13–35.

2. Press Command+8 (Mac) or Control+8 (Windows), or choose Object>Paths>Make Compound Path. Now you have a donut!

Keyboard Shortcut	
Cmd + 8 (Mac)	**Make**
Ctrl + 8 (Win)	**Compound Path**

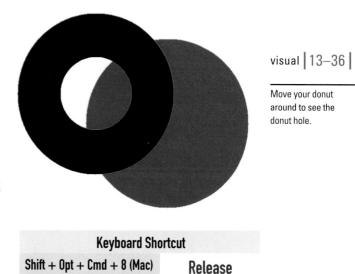

visual | 13–36 |

Move your donut around to see the donut hole.

3. Make a larger circle with a fill and send it to the back. Move your donut around and you will see that your donut has a real donut hole! (Visual 13–36.)

4. If you change your mind and don't want the compound path, select your donut and choose Object>Paths> Release Compound Path.

Keyboard Shortcut	
Shift + Opt + Cmd + 8 (Mac)	**Release**
Shift + Alt + Ctrl + 8 (Win)	**Compound Path**

5. Delete everything and start over. This time draw two rectangles, one above the other with the smaller one on top. Put them close together, but do not have them touch or overlap. Select them both and choose Object>Paths>Make Compound Path. Although it may appear that nothing has occurred, notice that a bounding box now surrounds both rectangles. This means that the two are now part of one path (Visual 13–37).

visual | 13–37 |

Draw two rectangles independent of each other, but part of the same path.

visual | 13–38 |

Use the Direct Selection tool and Shift+drag out each corner point to create a trapezoid.

6. Press Command+D or Control+D and place an image large enough to fill both rectangles. Drag the image around inside the rectangles using the Direct Selection tool.

7. Next you will change the shape of your small rectangle to a trapezoid. Deselect everything, and click on a bottom corner point with the Direct Selection tool. Hold down Shift and drag it out so that it's above the corresponding upper corner of the large rectangle. Do the same for the other bottom corner (Visual 13–38).

8. Delete the picture from the compound path and click in the path with the Type tool. Fill with placeholder text. Your compound path now works like linked text frames.

In this short introduction, you have made compound paths using basic shape tools: the Rectangle tool and the Ellipse tool. Practice making compound paths with shapes you create, using the Pen tool. Great job!

SUMMARY

Having completed the exercises in this chapter, you can see why there's no way any other page layout program can compete with InDesign. By combining advanced page layout and drawing capabilities, InDesign gives you the best of both worlds. Once you master the versatile Pen tool, your creative energy knows no bounds. Use compound paths to make your readers sit up and take notice of your message and images. And when you are done with this book, there's much, MUCH more to explore!

in review

1. What effect does holding down the Shift key have when drawing shapes and lines?

2. When working with a shape or path, how do you tell the difference between a point that is selected and a point that is not selected?

3. What is the keyboard shortcut for accessing the Convert Direction Point tool when you are using the Pen tool?

4. What is the difference between a smooth point and a corner point?

5. You have made a path with the Pen tool, but it looks jagged and you think you might have too many points on it. How do you smooth it out?

6. What is the difference between an open path and a closed path?

7. Describe the process for joining two open paths.

8. Describe the process for making compound paths.

9. What are direction handles?

10. How does the Scissors tool work?

| *index* |

Symbols

V

verso 130, 185–186

view. *See also* zoom; *See also* thread; *See also* grid; *See also* High Quality Display; *See also* Overprint Preview

viewing mode 6. *See also* spread

Bleed 7

changing 19

Normal 6

Preview 6

Slug 7

W

word count 86

workspace 4, 7, 20

arrangement 9

basic 13

customizing 20

default 7

menu 7

panels 10

Wrap Around Bounding Box 163

Wrap Around Object Shape 166, 178

wrap object 163

X

x-height 54

X Coordinate axis 77–79

X Scale 101

Y

Y Coordinate axis 77–79

Y Scale 101

Z

Zero Point 76–78

zoom 294

percentage 19